Susan Croft

Susan is a writer, historian, curator and researcher. She worked in the USA with the Omaha Magic Theatre in the early 1980s, returning to Britain to work as a dramaturg with small-scale theatre companies and founding New Playwrights Trust, of which she was Director from 1986–89.

She taught Creative Arts (Performance) at Nottingham Trent University and then was Senior Research Fellow in Performance Arts at Manchester Metropolitan University to 1996. From 1997–2005, she was Curator of Contemporary Performance at the Theatre Museum where she worked on the National Video Archive of Performance. She also curated four major exhibitions including *Let Paul Robeson Sing!* and *Architects of Fantasy* and pioneered a range of initiatives to record the history of black and Asian theatre in Britain.

She has written extensively on women playwrights, including: ... *She Also Wrote Plays: an International Guide to Women Playwrights from the 10th to the 21st Century* (Faber, 2001) and edited *Votes for Women and other plays* (Aurora Metro, 2009). She is working on *A Critical Bibliography of Plays Published by Women Playwrights in English to 1914* (working title) for Manchester University Press and a major anthology *Staging the New Woman*, with Sherry Engle.

She also runs the project *Unfinished Histories: Recording the History of Alternative Theatre*, with Jessica Higgs, a major initiative to record oral histories and preserve archives of the alternative theatre movement from the 1960s to the 1980s. See www.susan.croft.btinternet.co.uk for further details.

She lives in London with her husband and two children.

Classic Plays by Women

from 1600 to 2000

edited and introduced by

Susan Croft

Paphnutius *(extract)*
Hrotswitha

The Tragedy of Mariam *(extract)*
Elizabeth Cary

The Rover
Aphra Behn

A Bold Stroke for a Wife
Susanna Centlivre

De Monfort
Joanna Baillie

Rutherford and Son
Githa Sowerby

The Chalk Garden
Enid Bagnold

Top Girls *(extract)*
Caryl Churchill

Stones in his Pockets
Marie Jones

AURORA METRO PRESS

This volume first published in UK in 2010 by Aurora Metro Publications Ltd, 67 Grove Avenue, Twickenham, TW1 4HX www.aurorametro.com © 2010 Aurora Metro Publications: info@aurorametro.com
Cover photo: © 2010 annedehaas c/o istockphoto.com
Production editors: Gillian Wakeling, Carmel Walsh & Rebecca Gillieron
With thanks to: Neil Gregory, Lucy Ashley, Lesley Mackay, Sumedha Mane, Simon Bennett, Caroline Hennig, Stacey Crawshaw, Simon Smith, Reena Makwana.
Introduction and Bibliography © 2010 Susan Croft
Compilation and selection © 2010 Susan Croft and Cheryl Robson
Rutherford and Son by Githa Sowerby © 1912 Githa Sowerby. Reproduced by permission of Samuel French Ltd.
The Chalk Garden by Enid Bagnold © 1955 Enid Bagnold c/o Dominick Jones. First published in 1956 by Samuel French Ltd.
Top Girls by Caryl Churchill © 1982 Caryl Churchill. First published by Methuen Drama, London now an imprint of A & C Black Publishers.
Stones in his Pockets copyright © 2000 by Marie Jones is reprinted by arrangement with the publishers, Nick Hern Books: www.nickhernbooks.co.uk

Applications for performance, including professional, amateur, recitation, lecturing, public reading, broadcasting, television, and rights of translation into foreign languages should be addressed to:
Rutherford and Son by Githa Sowerby c/o theatre@samuelfrench-london.co.uk
The Chalk Garden by Enid Bagnold c/o dj@dominick-jones.com.
Top Girls by Caryl Churchill c/o Casarotto Ramsay Agency info@casarotto.co.uk
Stones In His Pockets by Marie Jones c/o info@nickhernbooks.demon.co.uk

Printed by UK
ISBN 978-1-906582-005

Contents

Introduction

This is the first anthology of British and Irish women playwrights to survey plays across four hundred years and to offer key dramatic texts in one volume. Since the first anthologies of plays by women appeared in North America in the 1970s,[i] when feminist scholars were inspired to investigate women's neglected history as playwrights, it is perhaps surprising that it has taken so long for an anthology of this kind to be produced.[i] In Britain, the first anthology of women's plays appeared in 1981, *The Female Wits: Women Playwrights of the Restoration,* edited by Fidelis Morgan (Virago). Numerous others have followed, some focused on new writing, like the Methuen *Plays by Women* volumes pioneered by Michelene Wandor in the 1980s, while others have collected plays from particular historical periods or constituencies of writers.[ii]

To examine women's playwriting within a particular cultural tradition, or to look at a particular period such as 1880-1930, which centred in many countries on the struggle for the vote and other women's rights, as Katherine Kelly does in *Modern Drama by Women*, is a relatively manageable task. In my earlier collection *Votes For Women and other plays* (2009), a new collection of suffrage drama, the material had an obvious internal coherence, creating a space to examine likeness and difference.

Perhaps the absence until now of volumes of 'women's classics' is understandable – the attempt to edit one is not an easy task – and the choice of plays is hugely difficult. One of the key projects of feminist literary criticism since its beginnings in the 1970s has been the critique of canon formation and the systematic exclusion of women's writing from the accepted list of classics. To appear to re-inscribe a new female canon with its invidious choices of what to include and what to exclude and to then call it an anthology of 'classics' is to invite criticism. In particular, the representation of recent plays, the long-term endurance of which has yet to be tested, is problematic. The choice of what to include is also constrained by ownership issues, where publishers retain exclusive publication rights.

In a context too, where some contemporary women playwrights argue that they are playwrights first and foremost and do not want to be placed within a ghetto of femaleness, resisting the very label 'woman playwright', we need to consider how useful it is to put playwrights as diverse in language, form and concerns as Elizabeth Cary and Marie Jones together in one volume, merely on the basis of their gender.

The work of the past 30 years in the English-speaking world to retrieve lost plays by women has in some ways been hugely effective. Large bodies of work have been rediscovered, republished and restaged by enterprising theatres and small-scale companies. Simultaneously, there has been an upsurge in new playwriting by women. Bodies of theatre work by women, past and present, from almost every country from Finland to South Korea, have been translated, circulated and produced. The range and diversity of work by women available in the English language to stage in theatre repertoires has never been greater. *Yet the percentage of work by women actually produced at funded theatres remains stubbornly constant.*[iii]

It is rare to find theatres like the Orange Tree Theatre in Richmond, England, which from 2007-08 staged 15 plays by women, ranging from a classic comedy by Frances Burney,[iv] through early 20th century problem plays such as Elizabeth Baker's *Chains* via a newly discovered Susan Glaspell[v] to a contemporary musical. More typical is Britain's National Theatre where the first original play commissioned from a woman to be staged in its large-scale Olivier Theatre[vi] was produced in 2008, although the theatre opened its doors in 1976. The smaller Lyttelton Theatre has a somewhat better record and the smallest, the Cottesloe, has the best record of the three, underlining the habitual confinement of women playwrights to smaller stages. The National Theatre's Artistic Director, Nicholas Hytner, has commented: 'I sometimes wonder whether ... the particular forensic gift that television requires, that the close-up requires, the ability to write in close-up, beneath the skin, is possibly, innately more suited to the way women write. And God you just fall into so many terrible clichés, but the more conflict-driven, muscular form that theatre is, is less-suited'.[vii]

Aphra Behn's muscular and most widely-recognised play *The Rover*, is not often revived in the UK despite being widely available. It is one of only two plays by women from the seventeenth and eighteenth century to have been produced by the Royal Shakespeare Company, even though the RSC's Swan Theatre was originally designed as a space to explore work from those two centuries.[viii] The detective work that led to the discovery of lost plays by women did bring about some new productions, for example at Derby Playhouse in the late 1980s, under the enlightened leadership of director Annie Castledine where notable productions of plays by Mary Pix and others[ix] were staged. Yet the knowledge of too many new, emerging directors, not to mention too many teachers, students and performers, still remains circumscribed by limited exposure to a small number of avowed classics. These plays are often, especially in the US, those studied in thick, text-book collections as 'Masterpieces of Drama' or the like, in which female playwrights often go under-recognised and under-valued. The efforts of recent editors like J. Ellen Gainor have increased the representation of women in collections like *The Norton Anthology of Drama* to 8 out of 64 plays in the 2009 volume.[x]

It is vital to continue to argue for the inclusion of women's work within such Great Traditions and indeed for the inclusion of playwrights in anthologies of women's writing, of which many early examples concentrated on stories, poems and memoirs, excluding drama as a genre entirely, though now Behn and Churchill routinely appear.

It remains important therefore to assert the classic status of plays like the handful we have included here – and numerous others – and to argue against the cultural amnesia that has relegated plays like Susannah Centlivre's *A Bold Stroke for a Wife*, once a staple of the repertoire, to the margins.

This anthology also celebrates and draws together across the centuries a female dramatic history. It is not cohesive: plays by women are as diverse as plays by men. Looking at women's plays and their history, however, certain issues and questions recur and comparisons present themselves. The exploration of performance and its potential for liberation runs through the plays of Behn, Centlivre and Jones. In *A Bold Stroke for a Wife* and *Stones in his Pockets,* the playwrights create bravura parts for male actors which demand multiple character changes, contradicting assertions that women cannot write for men, and dazzling with their confident play with theatrical convention. Both have proved hugely popular with audiences. Aphra Behn's comic analysis of the economic bargain underlying marriage in *The Rover* finds echoes in Sowerby's grim realistic appraisal in *Rutherford and Son*. Sowerby's analysis of women's exclusion from power also resonates with Caryl Churchill's exploration of the choices women make in *Top Girls*. The domineering patriarchal figure in *Rutherford and Son* invites comparison with the offstage tyrant Pinkbell, as well as the would-be matriarch Mrs St Maugham in *The Chalk Garden*.

Bringing such plays together enables the study of the development of female dramatic traditions and the examination of their similarities and differences in form, as well as an analysis of the representation of women and men, and their engagement with issues of the day. Above all, it continues to assert the presence and excellence of women's dramatic work and to argue for more productions in state-funded theatres where, despite their commitment to diversity, the repertoires remain primarily male.[xi] In every kind of context from amateur theatres, to schools and universities, from small-scale companies to large-scale buildings we need to argue that work by women is vital, moving, ambitious.

This anthology is too short. There are many more playwrights who deserve to be included: Margaret Cavendish, Mary Pix, Catherine Trotter, Hannah Cowley, Hannah More, Elizabeth Inchbald, Cicely Hamilton, Shelagh Delaney, Ann Jellicoe, Timberlake Wertenbaker, April De Angelis, Winsome Pinnock, Shelagh Stephenson, Diane Samuels, Sarah Daniels, Charlotte Keatley, Bryony Lavery, Sarah Kane and numerous others. Readers will find details of these and many, many more in my book ... *She Also Wrote Plays* or at www.susan.croft.btinternet.co.uk

The Plays

This anthology starts with an extract from *Paphnutius* (c960), one of the plays of the Bavarian medieval abbess **Hrotswitha**[xii] written in the middle of the 10th century. It was translated into English by Christopher St John (Christabel Marshall) for the Pioneer Players, who produced it in 1914. Directed by St John's partner, Edith Craig, the production benefited from Craig's mother, Dame Ellen Terry, assuming the role of the Abbess. Hrotswitha is the earliest known woman playwright and as such has assumed an iconic status, standing as an exemplary figure representing the tradition of women writing for the stage. A 1992 volume, *Women on the Canadian Stage*[xiii] is subtitled *The Legacy of Hrotsvit*, while in 2006 the feminist cultural activists, the Guerilla Girls, offered professional theatres the opportunity to win The First Annual Hrosvitha Award by taking up the challenge of choosing "to scrap their plans of producing yet another production of a Greek tragedy and instead produce a play by Hrosvitha, the first female playwright." www.guerrillagirlsontour.com

However, Hrotswitha's iconic position is a rather ironic one, given how fully her plays were embedded within her time and cultural circumstance. A writer of Latin drama, her six plays were influenced by the Senecan classical dramatist, Terence, but aimed that 'in the same genre of composition in which the shameless unchaste actions of sensual women were portrayed, the laudable chastity of holy maidens might be celebrated'.[xiv] In *Paphnutius*, subtitled *The Conversion of Thais* the prostitute, Thais, under the influence of the monk Paphnutius, rejects her former life and the values of a male worldliness that have led her astray and embraces her conversion with an ardour which gives the play a dramatic immediacy not usually associated with plays of piety. Early commentators doubted that her plays were actually performed but the vigour of her characters and the scenes she describes argue that they must have been intended for staging. For example, the comic scene in *Dulcitius* where he is persuaded by the maidens he wants to ravish, to embrace instead a sooty kitchen full of pots and pans. The plays have attracted much attention from feminist critics addressing Hrotswitha's scholarly learning, and her women characters' rejection of sexual objectification.

Hrotswitha stands alone between the Roman drama and Medieval miracle plays but emerged from a major female centre of learning. In the medieval world and beyond, abbeys offered women access to education and, in a number of instances, a space where dramas could be presented for the enjoyment of fellow nuns and sometimes girls, educated in the convent. In Britain, Katherine of Sutton adapted the litany into theatrical form while the polymath composer Hildegard of Bingen (c1098-1179) also wrote a play the *Ordo Virtutem* (*The Order Of The Virtues*)[xv]. The English nun and playwright Catherine Holland (1635-1720), converted to Catholicism, against her Protestant father's wishes, and ran away to become a member of an Augustinian house in Bruges, where she wrote 'Sacred Dramas' (now sadly lost), for feast days and other community celebrations.[xvi]

Outside the convent the attainment of learning by women remained an impossibility for most and was often a site of personal struggle, even for aristocrats. **Elizabeth Cary**, or Lady Falkland, was the first known English Renaissance woman to write an original play and have it published, though near contemporaries, Mary Sidney and Jane or Joanna Lumley made important translations and Lady Mary Wroth[xvii] wrote an original pastoral in 1621. Cary's own sufferings and internal struggle between desire and duty found dramatic expression in the character of Mariam. In her play, *The Tragedy of Mariam, the Fair Queen of Jewry* (1613), when the central character hears reports of her husband's death, she is torn between her desire for retribution to avenge the deaths of her brother and grandfather, and wifely obedience and love. The play is striking also in the prominence it gives to four other central women characters – Alexandra, Mariam's mother, who counsels submission, but rejects her daughter when things look dangerous; Doris, Herod's former wife, plotting to have her children re-inherited and finally Herod's daughter Salomé who is the most effective in her machinations and gives voice to sexual passion, claiming the right (denied to women) to divorce her husband.

Dismissed for years as a closet drama, since the 1990s it has received at least one professional production[xviii] and several others by students. According to Stephanie Wright, it emerged as 'a play peopled by ambiguous and complicated characters who, by their interactions, create a deeply psychological drama'. She goes on to say that though writing for the closet, Cary's handling of dramatic action and the complexity of her characters suggest 'she was highly influenced by, and perhaps desirous of … the drama of the public stage.'[xix]

It was with the Restoration that women first appeared unambiguously[xx] and visibly on the public stage, both as actresses and as playwrights. It was a problematic space. The desire for the public stage, a public voice and popular acknowledgement of their work clashed with the cultural demands of the time that women remain silent and invisible. This conflict remains a central concern for women playwrights, enacted in numerous Prologues and Epilogues to their plays or in Prefaces to the published scripts. Here they contest the popular assumptions about their work, some coyly, defensively or apologetically, while others like **Aphra Behn** do so outspokenly. Her third play *The Dutch Lover* (1673) opens with an Epistle addressed to the "Good, Sweet, Honey, Sugar-Candied Reader" in which she discusses the reception of her own play and how: "... that day 'twas acted first, there comes me into the pit, a long lither, phlegmatic, white, ill-favoured, wretched fop ... A thing [that] ... opening that which serves it for a mouth, out issued such a noise ... to those that sat about it, that they were to expect a woeful play, God damn him, for it was a woman's." She goes on to defend women as playwrights, commenting that theatre is a form where men's only advantage over women – a better education – is not relevant, evoking Shakespeare's superiority as a playwright over Jonson despite his inferior education. Of the men of her own age: "I dare to say I know of none that write at such a formidable rate, but that a woman may well hope to reach their greatest heights ..." she writes scathingly. Later, in the letter preceding *Sir Patient Fancy* (1677) she attributes the failure of her previous play to complaints: "That it was Bawdy, the least and most Excusable fault in the Men writers ... but from a Woman it was unnatural ..."

Her success in her own lifetime was remarkable, with over a dozen plays produced professionally. Some like *The Rover* (1677) were highly successful, and although originally staged and published anonymously, with the subtitle, *The Banish'd Cavaliers*, it was later owned as Behn's. As well as writing poetry, essays and novels such as *Oroonoko*[xxi] about the adventures of a royal slave, in later more moralistic times, her critical reputation waned.[xxii] The male writer of *Man Superior to Woman* (1740) 'by a Gentleman' mocks the idea of a Female University where the students would read Behn and Manley[xxiii] and the 'establishment teach "Impiety and Smut ... Bawdy and Blasphemy' while Pope alludes to Behn as the playwright who "fairly puts all Characters to bed."[xxiv] The 19th century had worse to add with Julia Kavanagh in *English Women of Letters: Biographical Sketches* (1863) where she states: "The inveterate coarseness of her mind sullied Aphra Behn's noblest gifts: beauty, sincerity, wit, an eloquent tongue and a ready pen, perished on that wreck of all that is delicate and refined in woman" while her plays were "so coarse as to offend even a coarse age."[xxv]

With the 1980s and 90s her work became available again[xxvi] in anthologies of women's plays, as it was celebrated and analysed by feminist critics. *The Rover's* heroine, Hellena is the match for its rakish hero, Willmore, in wit. Direct in her demand for sexual choice on her own terms Hellena refuses to allow this to be interpreted as indicating her availability on any terms: "Why must we be either guilty of Fornication or Murder, if we converse with you Men? – And is there no difference between leave to love me, and leave to lie with me?" Hellena, together with her sister and friend, initiate much of the action in the play and take advantage of the licence allowed by the carnival at Venice to disguise themselves, dressing as gypsies, boys or nymphs, experimenting with roles, as they take steps to gain the lovers and husbands they have chosen. The love of masquerade and shape-changing demonstrates not only a love of the theatrical but also a refusal of fixity that questions societal definitions. As in other plays like *The Feigned Courtesans,* Behn questions the opposition of the virtuous woman to the vicious whore, challenging the assumed differences between the sexual contracts of marriage and that of prostitution, opposing them to free choice where economic considerations are suspended.

If Behn's work disappeared from the theatre after her lifetime, **Susannah Centlivre's** continued to hold the stage, being reprinted and revived well into the nineteenth century and becoming staples of the English-speaking repertory worldwide. Her play *The Busy Body* was put on by the British military in Philadelphia and in New York; in 1777 *A Bold Stroke for a Wife* and *The Gamester* were among the opening productions at the theatre in Montego Bay, Jamaica and *The Ghost (A Man Bewitched)* was staged at Kingston in 1780. *The Busy Body* was also among the first plays staged by theatre manager and former convict Robert Sidaway at the Sydney Theatre in Australia in 1796. Between 1718 and 1800 there were 225 performances of *A Bold Stroke for a Wife* at the major London theatres alone.[xxvii] It went through numerous individual editions and appeared in anthologies and series including Elizabeth Inchbald's *The British Theatre* and Hermann Croll's *The British and American Theatre: a Choice Collection of the Most Popular Dramatic Pieces of Both Nations* (1855). Originally produced at Lincoln's Inn Fields in 1718, its relatively simple plot is brilliantly executed.

In *A Bold Stroke for a Wife*, Mrs Ann Lovely has been willed by her cantankerous old father, to the guardianship of four men "as opposite as light from darkness" – Sir Philip Modelove, a foppish old beau; Periwinkle, "a kind of silly virtuoso" obsessed with strange discoveries from foreign parts; Tradelove, a stockbroker and Obadiah Prim, a Quaker. All this because her father wanted no descendants; he "hated posterity ... and wished the world were to expire with himself. He used to swear if she had been a boy, he would have qualified him for the opera". A precondition of her inheriting £30,000 is the agreement on her choice of husband of all the four guardians, each of whom spends the three months of each year she passes with them trying to convert her to their world view. The stage is set for an exercise in bravura comic dexterity as Colonel Fainwell employs multiple disguises. Having gained Ann's consent to marry, he sets out to gain consent from each of her guardians, successively transforming himself from Dutch merchant, to grieving steward, to traveller from Egypt, to fop, to Simon Pure, a Quaking preacher. His performance as Pure is ably abetted by Ann, an equally adept actress, who undergoes a sudden spiritual conversion to find she is "the chosen vessel to raise up seed to the faithful." The neglect of Centlivre's work from the 20th and 21st century repertory is bewildering and her revival is long overdue.

While many women playwrights address the larger issues of women's writing in their prefaces and prologues, **Joanna Baillie,** writing in the late 18th and early 19th century, remains unusual in having a highly developed theory of theatre which she details in her prefaces and which she sought to demonstrate through her plays. She set out to produce a comedy and a tragedy on each passion: love, hatred, ambition, fear, hope, remorse, jealousy, pride, anger, joy, grief and religion, deliberately leaving out envy and revenge as she believed they were common motives in drama. She saw the origins of theatre in Dionysian ritual, but the influence of the Greeks as being double-edged, leading to a theatre of little action and rare passion; without them drama "would have been more irregular, more imperfect, more varied, more interesting".

De Monfort focuses on tragic hatred and was one of only a few of her plays to be produced (at Drury Lane in 1800). It forms part of the Gothic tradition which was hugely popular at the time both in the theatre and in the novel, where its many female exponents included Ann Radcliffe and Clare Reeve. Baillie displays the hallmarks of the tradition: dark atmospheric settings – castles, ruined abbeys, caverns, precipices, dark forests and moorlands; thunder and lightning; stories of mysterious ghostly figures and other supernatural activity; heroines driven mad as well as brooding passionate villains. Baillie's obsessively self-questioning protagonist, De Monfort, is both hero and villain, a good man who becomes consumed with loathing for his neighbour Rezenfelt, through a passion that is complex, contradictory and, despite having some grounds in rivalry and a sense of obligation that he resents, goes beyond any rational causes. Rezenfelt and he are at one point mistaken for each other, underlining the sense of their being doubles. When De Monfort hears rumours that Rezenfelt loves his sister, Jane, his hatred becomes murderous and he follows his enemy to a wood near an old chapel and kills him, cutting off his head. Then with his hatred spent and his double dead, he cannot endure and dies of despair. His sister Jane is presented as being an admirable figure, the voice of rationality and Christian forgiveness. The presentation of their relationship as brother and sister provides a context where his bravery and nobility, despite his obsession, can appear. The great actress, Jane Siddons, so approved of the part that she is reported as saying, "Make me some more Jane De Monforts!"[xxviii]

Baillie had a mixed reception as a woman playwright. When the true author of *De Monfort* (originally produced anonymously) was acknowledged, according to one account, "the critics announced a new era in dramatic literature"[xxix] and her eminent admirers included Walter Scott and Byron, who wrote: "Women (saving Joanna Baillie) cannot write tragedy"[xxx] but she felt the discovery that she was female won her enemies, writing to Scott in 1825: "John Any-Body would have stood higher with the critics than Joanna Baillie."

Githa Sowerby's *Rutherford and Son* (1912) must be one of the most frequently 'rediscovered' plays ever, raising questions about an apparent continued need to erase and then retrieve women's work. Its first revival in the second half of the twentieth century, by the feminist company Mrs Worthington's Daughters in 1980 was a genuine rediscovery,[xxxi] though the play had never languished unpublished in a dusty manuscript. The subsequent revival at the New End Theatre in London tried to present it as a rediscovery from the depths of the archive. It was then republished[xxxii] and received productions at the Royal Academy of Dramatic Art, the National Theatre, the Royal

Exchange, Manchester, and others, yet publicity for the Northern Stage revival in 2009, the first in Sowerby's native North East, once again emphasised the play's obscurity: "Since then [1912] Sowerby has almost vanished from history, but some theatre fans have been digging around in the archives and are attempting to get her the recognition she deserves."[xxxiii] While there clearly is much still to be discovered about Sowerby and a welcome biography has recently been published,[xxxiv] there is increasing acceptance of *Rutherford and Son* as a key 20th century play. Certainly Emma Goodman saw it as one when she included Sowerby as one of only four British playwrights (along with Shaw, Galsworthy and Stanley Houghton), to be discussed alongside Ibsen, Hauptmann, Strindberg et al in *The Social Significance of Modern Drama* (1914).

Rutherford and Son is a savage denunciation of patriarchal authority (Sowerby had originally intended to call it *The Master*) linking it intrinsically to capitalism, where all human beings, family or workers, are commodities to be used and exploited. Rutherford presides over his family and his business with dour Northern tyranny, entrapping his children in a sense of infantile powerlessness, rage and fear. John, the eldest son, pins his hopes of change on his invention of a new manu-facturing technique which he intends to sell to his father to buy escape from the family for himself, his wife and son, while his brother Richard has retreated into a feeble religious faith, scoffed at by his father. Janet is caught between the demands of respectability and the role of unpaid servant to her father. Her Aunt Ann criticises her every move, as she watches with clear-eyed bitterness any prospects of marriage and escape diminish. Even Martin, Rutherford's self-educated foreman and the only one he respects, is disposable.

Nevertheless, the women do manage to escape Rutherford's tyranny but at a price. Janet is turned out of the house, having lost both Martin and her father's financial support. She is defiant in proclaiming: "You've let me out of gaol! Whatever happens to me now I shan't go on living as I lived here." Shrewdness and desperation push Mary, Rutherford's daughter-in-law, into negotiating an agreement: "A bargain is where one person has something to sell that another wants to buy. There's no love in it – only money – money that pays for life." In return for ten years of financial support, she will give her son over to Rutherford to be trained up to take over the business. The implication is that Rutherford's power will weaken with old age and he may die first. However, she challenges his brutal reduction of all human relationships to power and money, with a mother's determination, to protect her child and herself.

Enid Bagnold's *The Chalk Garden* first appeared in 1955, a year before *Look Back in Anger* supposedly drove comedies of upper middle class drawing rooms into well-deserved oblivion. Yet Ken Tynan, renowned for hailing the arrival of John Osborne's play, also celebrated Bagnold's play calling it, "the finest artificial comedy to have flowed from an English (as opposed to an Irish pen) since the death of Congreve."[xxxv] It has divided the critics ever since and the 2008 production at London's Donmar Warehouse was no different. Critic Aleks Sierz, making the Osborne comparison again, declared that "he [Osborne] remains vital while her work is mercifully, rarely seen."[xxxvi] Whereas, the positive reviews celebrated emotional truth, subversive mockery of traditional values, subtle character drawing, tart verbal comedy and the redemptive power of the poignant ending. Margaret Drabble commented on Bagnold in 2008: "Was she old-fashioned or avant-garde? It was hard to tell. Woolf was jealous of her, frightened of her, and at times contemptuous of her. She did not know how to place her, and literary history has been equally uncertain."[xxxvii]

The Chalk Garden centres on three women: Mrs St Maugham trapped within the role of eccentric matriarch she has created for herself; her damaged, self-dramatising grand-daughter, Laurel, whose sense of rejection and neediness express themselves through pyromania, after her mother has chosen to remarry; and the outsider, Miss Madrigal, who enters this dysfunctional family as companion to Laurel but nurses her own secret past, carrying the burden of the 15 year sentence she has served for murder.

Bagnold continually disrupts and subverts traditional power relationships between classes and gender stereotypes. It is Maitland, the manservant, broken by his imprisonment as a conscientious objector, who has been the most loving and nurturing influence in Laurel's life at the play's outset. The appointment of the acerbic, clear-sighted, Miss Madrigal as a companion to Laurel sets in motion a force capable of challenging the inappropriate care given by Mrs St Maugham to both her grand-daughter and her garden, exposing its potential to cause harm and prevent proper growth.

Mother-daughter relationships are a central focus too: the real, failed relationship between Mrs St Maugham and her alienated daughter Olivia and the surrogate relationships between Laurel and both Maitland and Miss Madrigal. Olivia articulates the distinction between biological role as mother and maternal nurturing and emerges as a woman matured by her experiences: "Things come late to me. Love came late to me. Laurel was born in a strange virginity. To have a child doesn't always make a mother." Olivia has to confront her mother's desperate need to hold on to Laurel, "labelling it as compensatory exercise for her own failed mother-daughter bond."[xxxviii] All the characters have in some respect failed or been damaged in their lives and Bagnold does not evade the real harm they have done or been done, but she does offer the possibility of renewal, expressed metaphorically through the central symbolism of the chalk garden which, with proper care and knowledge, may still become fertile.

Mother and daughter relationships are also central to **Caryl Churchill's** *Top Girls* (1982), probably the most important play to emerge from The Royal Court Theatre in the 1980s. It provides a complex analysis of women's relationship to power and the costs of sharing in or being excluded from the Thatcherite dream. In the back yard scene at Joyce's house, Angie reveals to her friend Kitty that she suspects Marlene is really her mother, rather than Joyce. Joyce's treatment of Angie as a young person with no career prospects and few choices other than the dim hope of marriage, contrasts with earlier scenes in the Recruitment Agency where Marlene interviews and judges the suitability of promising young female candidates and the Restaurant Scene in Act One in which Marlene is celebrating her success as a businesswoman. Angie senses the resentment that Joyce feels towards her and has a feeling of rejection that is expressed through the underlying violence in the scene:

ANGIE   I put on this dress to kill my mother.

KIT   I suppose you thought you'd do it with a brick.

ANGIE   You can kill people with a brick.

KIT   Well, you didn't so.

Angie may well become one of society's dispossessed, the underclass. She is clearly not going to be one of the *Top Girls*, like those we have encountered in Act One in the Restaurant Scene where Churchill's daring exploration of theatrical possibilities has brought together a diverse group, celebrated by history as emblems of female success, from Pope Joan, the archetypal encroacher on male prerogative and power, to Patient Griselda, the epitome of female endurance.

Whereas the scenes in the Recruitment Agency are fast-paced, cutting slickly between settings, the extract[xxxix] we have included here from the final scene is longer and slower. Marlene is faced with a reality she can neither manipulate nor manage. She is finally confronted with what she has rejected in order to achieve her success: her working-class Fenland past; Angie, the daughter she left to be raised by her sister; and, most tellingly, the spectre of non-achievement. Joyce's socialist views challenge Marlene's Thatcherite politics, exposing Marlene's success as nothing more than individual achievement built on the exploitation of others and a kind of feminism that is lacking in care and responsibility for the needs of others.

Marie Jones's acclaimed and highly successful comedy *Stones in His Pockets* (1996), also presents a conflict between the reality of rural poverty and the slick, urban attempt to reconstruct it in a marketable package. The play sets up a confrontation between a film crew set down in the Irish countryside where the unemployed locals are hired as extras in a Hollywood fantasy of 'Oirish' history, and where the Nicole Kidman-style film star, Caroline Giovanni, flirts with the locals to help polish her accent and gain authenticity.

Like much work by contemporary women playwrights, Jones' play started out with its tiny cast and crew, touring to small community theatres in and around Belfast. The play was developed collaboratively over time before it eventually transferred to the Edinburgh Fringe, then later the West End and Broadway. As a comic *tour de force*, it has picked up several awards with productions subsequently in 20 countries and translations into 16 languages. In 2009, it was revived for a national tour.

Two actors play all the characters, initially as Charlie and Jake, local men hired to play dispossessed peasants in the bog, but who slip rapidly between all the other roles from self-absorbed female superstar to fawning assistant directors to the drug-dependent local boy, Sean. It is Sean's rejection as an extra, casting him out of the world of Hollywood escapism and precipitating his suicide by walking into a lake with stones in his pockets, that also provides the play's central confrontation.

The fast pace of the switching between roles not only offers virtuoso opportunities to the play's two actors but reflects the fast moving glossy fiction that the film world attempts to impose, through which, with Sean's death, a grimmer, darker reality starts to intrude. *Stones in His Pockets* combines a joyous theatricality, dextrous plotting and adroit deployment of actors and characters with a keen analysis of cultural exploitation, political disenfranchisement, colonisation and the collision of values. Yet it encompasses crowds, flirts with stereotypes as well as challenging them, and demolishes any remaining assumptions about how women write for theatre, their gender focus, topics of concern, structural approach, plotting ability, scale of work and use of language.

---

[i] With anthologies of new plays, edited by Honor Moore and the international collection edited by Sullivan and Hatch ranging from the 20s to the 70s.

[ii] The longest historical period covered stretches from the 10th century to the early twentieth century in Pollock's 1990 *A Sampler of Women Playwrights*, with Hrotswitha co-opted (as she also is in this collection), a Latin-writing, German abbess, as the earliest known example of a woman playwright anywhere, and a play from 1927 by Lady Gregory, included as the most recent example.

[iii] My compilation of surveys of the representation of productions of plays by women in professional theatres between 1982 and 2004 found the lowest percentage in 1982 (10%), the highest in 1987 (22%). By 2004 the percentage had dropped to16% (though the statistical basis for the surveys and numbers surveyed varied): see Croft 2007, p18A. Figures for New York in 2008 suggested a representation by women of, at best, 20%.
http://www.nytimes.com/2008/10/25/theater/25women.html

[iv] *The Woman Hater* in *The Complete Plays of Frances Burney* ed. Peter Sabor Montreal and Kinston: McGill-Queen's University Press, 1995.

[v] *Chains of Dew* at http://academic.shu.edu/glaspell/Chains%20of%20Dew.htm

[vi] *Her Naked Skin* by Rebecca Lenkiewicz, London: Faber & Faber, 2008

[vii] Hytner goes on: 'But it immediately falls apart that, as soon as you start thinking of exceptions. I mean nobody is more muscular than Caryl Churchill. But I don't

think it's wrong to say that women write differently from men. And that you can, by and large, tell whether a novelist is a woman or a man. And … [of the National Theatre's aspiration to programme more women] it's, it's just something that we are, we are, constantly worrying about, beating ourselves up about but we're not doing well enough'. *Front Row*, BBC Radio 4, 12th September 2006

[viii] The other is the 2004 production *House of Desires* by the 17th century Mexican nun Sor Juana Inez De la Cruz tr. Catherine Boyle, Oberon Books, 2004.

[ix] Pix's *The Innocent Mistress* (in Morgan ed.). Castledine also commissioned and produced translations like Gerlind Reinshagen's *Sundays Children* (translated Tinch Minter, unpublished)

[x] The plays are by Hrotsvit of Gandersheim, Aphra Behn, Sor Juana Inés De La Cruz, Susan Glaspell, Judith Thompson, Maria Irene Fornés, Suzan-Lori Parks and Caryl Churchill.

[xi] A recent study in the US by Emily Glassberg Sands showed that women directors and literary managers actually demonstrated worse bias against women playwrights than male literary managers but that generally plays featuring women, more commonly written by women, were also less likely to be produced http://www.nytimes.com/2009/06/24/theater/24play.html and http://graphics8.nytimes.com/packages/pdf/theater/Openingthecurtain.pdf Sands's study also suggested that women submitted fewer new plays than men to theatres, who therefore chose proportionately fewer plays by women to put on. Assuming a desire for parity, you would expect the existing repertory of plays by women to be produced to compensate for the lower numbers of submitted new plays by women.

[xii] One of several possible spellings of her name including Hrotsvit, Roswitha, the name used by Christopher St John in her translation. Another translation by L. Bonfante is *The Plays of Hrotswitha of Gandesheim*, NY: New York University Press, 1979.

[xiii] Ed. Rita Much. Winnipeg: Blizzard Publishing, 1992

[xiv] Preface to the Plays, quoted in Dronke (p69), his translation.

[xv] Translated by Bruce W. Hozeski in *Annuale Mediaevale* v 13 and translated by Peter Dronke in *Nine Medieval Latin Plays* ed. Dronke. Cambridge: Cambridge University Press, 1995

[xvi] In Mexico, Sor Juana Inez de la Cruz was the first playwright of the New World (1648-1695) writing dramatic poems, skits and comedies.

[xvii] Sidney's *The Tragedy of Antonie* (1592) and Wroth's *Love's Victorie* (c1620s) are in Cerasano and Wynne-Davies. Joanna Lumley's *Iphigeneia At Aulis* (c1550) London: The Malone Society Reprints, 1909

[xviii] Tinderbox Theatre Company, in Oct 1994

xix *The Tragedy of Mariam: the Fair Queen of Jewry* edited by Stephanie Wright, Keele University Press, 1996, p23. The full play is also in Cerasano and Wynne Davies and at http://www.wwnorton.com/college/english/nael/NOA/pdf/cary_e.pdf

xx Women appeared in private theatricals earlier such as those written by Queen Henrietta Maria (see Cotton) and possibly also disguised as men. The mythology of the woman performer/playwright is an enduring one from Virginia Woolf's Shakespeare's sister (in *A Room of One's Own,* 1929) to John Arden's play *Pearl,* London: Methuen, 1979.

xxi *Oroonoko: or, the Royal Slave* by Aphra Behn. First published in 1688. Now regarded as one of the earliest English novels available in Penguin Classics.

xxii Todd, p2

xxiii A reference to Delarivier Manley, the notorious author of sexually outspoken *romans à clef* and plays like *The Royal Mischief* (c1692). See *A Woman of No Character* by Fidelis Morgan, London: Faber, 1986.

xxiv In his *First Epistle of the Second Book of Horace, Imitated. To Augustus* (1737), both quoted in Todd p 31

xxv Quoted in Todd, ibid, p 49

xxvi The first and last complete edition before Janet Todd's in the 1990s, was edited by Montague Summers, an eccentric Catholic clergyman who despite anti-feminist views expressed elsewhere in his hatred of the witch: she is 'an evil liver: a social pest and parasite: the devotee of a loathly and obscene creed', celebrates Behn as 'an energetic , generous and self-reliant figure'.

xxvii According to *The London Stage*.

xxviii Carhart, p119

xxix Anonymous critic in *Dublin University Magazine* 37, quoted in Carhart.

xxx *Byron Letters and Journals* ed G.E. Prothero, vol 3, quoted in Carhart.

xxxi An interview with Mrs Worthington's Daughters company member Anne Engel forms part of the oral history project *Unfinished Histories: Recording the History of the Alternative Theatre Movement* www.unfinishedhistories.com

xxxii In Fitzsimmons & Gardner. It had previously been published in *Contemporary Plays* ed. Thomas Dickinson and Jack Crawford, New York: Houghton Mifflin, 1925.

xxxiii Publicity from BBC Woman's Hour web site 11th September 2009.

xxxiv *Looking for Githa* by Pat Riley. Newcastle: New Writing North, 2009.

xxxv Tynan, p127

xxxvi *The Tribune*, 27th June 2008.

xxxvii *The Guardian*, Saturday 31 May 2008.

xxxviii Komporaly p15

xxxix Methuen published the play in 1982 and it has been widely anthologised.

The Plays

Extract from *Paphnutius, The Conversion of Thais* by Hrotswitha, translated from Latin by Christopher St. John.

First performed in English by The Pioneer Players at The Savoy Theatre, London, on 12th January 1914.

SCENE 3

PAPHNUTIUS	Thais! Thais!
THAIS	Who is there? I do not know that voice.
PAPHNUTIUS	Thais! Your lover speaks! Thais!
THAIS	Stranger, who are you?
PAPHNUTIUS	Arise, my love, my beautiful one, and come!
THAIS	Who are you?
PAPHNUTIUS	A man who loves you!
THAIS	And what do you want with me?
PAPHNUTIUS	I will show you.
THAIS	You would be my lover?
PAPHNUTIUS	I am your lover, Thais, flame of the world!
THAIS	Whoever loves me is well paid. He receives as much as he gives.
PAPHNUTIUS	Oh, Thais, Thais! If you knew what a long and troublesome journey I have come to speak to you – to see your face!
THAIS	Well? Have I refused to speak to you, or to show you my face?
PAPHNUTIUS	I cannot speak to you here. I must be with you alone. What I have to say is secret. The room must be secret too.
THAIS	How would you like a bedchamber, fragrant with perfumes, adorned as for marriage? I have such a room. Look!
PAPHNUTIUS	Is there no room still more secret? A room that your lovers do not know? Some room where you and I might hide away from all the world?
THAIS	Yes, there is a room like that in this house. No one even knows that it exists except myself, and God.
PAPHNUTIUS	God! What God?
THAIS	The true God.
PAPHNUTIUS	You believe that He exists?
THAIS	I am a Christian.
PAPHNUTIUS	And you believe that He knows what we do?
THAIS	I believe He knows everything.

PAPHNUTIUS   What do you think, then? That He is indifferent to the actions of the sinner, or that He reserves judgement?

THAIS   I suppose that the merits of each man are weighed in the balance, and that we shall be punished or rewarded according to our deeds.

PAPHNUTIUS   O Christ! How wondrous is Thy patience! How wondrous is Thy love! Even when those who believe in Thee sin deliberately, Thou dost delay their destruction!

THAIS   Why do you tremble? Why do you turn pale? Why do you weep?

PAPHNUTIUS   I shudder at your presumption. I weep for your damnation. How, knowing what you know, can you destroy men in this manner and ruin so many souls, all precious and immortal?

THAIS   Your voice pierces my heart! Strange lover? You are cruel. Pity me!

PAPHNUTIUS   Let us pity rather those souls whom you have deprived of the sight of God – of the God Whom you confess! Oh, Thais, you have wilfully offended the divine Majesty. That condemns you.

THAIS   What do you mean? Why do you threaten me like this?

PAPHNUTIUS   Because the punishment of hell-fire awaits you if you remain in sin.

THAIS   Who are you, who rebuke me so sternly? Oh, you have shaken me to the depths of my terrified heart!

PAPHNUTIUS   I would that you could be shaken with fear to your very bowels! I would like to see your delicate body impregnated with terror in every vein, and every fibre, if that would keep you from yielding to the dangerous delights of the flesh.

THAIS   And what zest for pleasure do you think is left now in a heart suddenly awakened to a consciousness of guilt! Remorse has killed everything.

PAPHNUTIUS   I long to see the thorns of vice cut away, and the choked-up fountain of your tears flowing once more. Tears of repentance are precious in the sight of God.

THAIS   Oh, voice that promises mercy! Do you believe, can you hope that one so vile as I, soiled by thousands and thousands of impurities, can make reparation, can ever by any manner of penance obtain pardon?

PAPHNUTIUS   Thais, no sin is so great, no crime is so black, that it cannot be expiated by tears and penitence, provided they are followed up by deeds.

THAIS   Show me, I beg you ... my father, what I can do to
be reconciled with Him I have offended.

PAPHNUTIUS   Despise the world. Leave your dissolute lovers.

THAIS   And afterwards? What then?

PAPHNUTIUS   You must retire to some solitary place, where you
may learn to know yourself and realize the enormity of your sins.

THAIS   If you think this will save me, I will not delay a
moment.

PAPHNUTIUS   I have no doubt it will.

THAIS   Yet give me a little time. I must collect the wealth
that I have gained through the sins of my body – all the treasures I have
kept too long.

PAPHNUTIUS   Do not give them a moment's thought. There will
be no lack of people to find them and make use of them.

THAIS   I have another idea in my mind. I did not think of
keeping this wealth or of giving it to my friends. Nor would I distribute
it among the poor. The wages of sin are no material for good works.

PAPHNUTIUS   You are right. What then do you propose to do
with your possessions?

THAIS   Give them to the flames! Burn them to ashes!

PAPHNUTIUS   For what reason?

THAIS   That they may no longer exist in the world. Each
one was acquired at the cost of an injury to the goodness and beauty of
the Creator. Let them burn.

PAPHNUTIUS   How you are changed! Grace is on your lips! Your
eyes are calm, and impure passions no longer burn in them. Oh,
miracle! Is this Thais who was once so greedy for gold? Is this Thais,
who seeks so humbly the feet of God?

THAIS   God give me grace to change still more. My heart
is changed, but this mortal substance – how shall it be changed?

PAPHNUTIUS   It is not difficult for the unchangeable substance
to transform us.

THAIS   Now I am going to carry out my plan. Fire shall
destroy everything I have.

PAPHNUTIUS   Go in peace. Then return to me here quickly. Do
not delay! I trust your resolution, and yet –

THAIS   You need not be afraid.

PAPHNUTIUS   Thais, come back quickly! God be with you!

SCENE 4

THAIS Come, my lovers! Come, all my evil lovers! Hasten my lovers! Your Thais calls you!

LOVERS That is the voice of Thais. She calls us. Let us make haste. Let us make haste, for by delay we may offend her.

THAIS Come, lovers! Run! Hasten! What makes you so slow? Never has Thais been more impatient for your coming. Come nearer. I have something to tell you all.

LOVERS Oh Thais, what is the meaning of this pile of faggots? Why are you throwing all those beautiful and precious treasures on the pile?

THAIS You cannot guess? You do not know why I have built this fire?

LOVERS We are amazed. We wonder greatly what is the meaning of it and of your strange looks.

THAIS You would like me to tell you, evil lovers?

LOVERS We long to hear.

THAIS Look, then!

LOVERS Stop, Thais! What are you doing? Are you mad?

THAIS I am not mad. For the first time I am sane, and I rejoice!

LOVERS To waste these pounds of gold, and all the other treasure! Oh, Thais, you have lost your senses! These are beautiful things, precious things, and you burn them.

THAIS All these things I have extorted from you as the price of shameful deeds. I burn then to destroy all hope in you that I shall ever again turn to your love. And now I leave you.

LOVERS Wait, Thais. Oh wait a little, and tell us what has changed you !

THAIS I will not stay. I will not tell you anything. To talk with you has become loathsome.

LOVERS What have we done to deserve this scorn and contempt? Can you accuse us of being unfaithful? What wrong have we done? We have always sought to satisfy your desires. And now you show us this bitter hatred! Unjust woman, what have we done ?

THAIS Leave me, or let me leave you. Do not touch me. You can tear my garments, but you shall not touch me.

LOVERS Cruel Thais, speak to us! Before you go, speak to us!

THAIS I have sinned with you. But now is the end of sin, and all our wild pleasures are ended.

LOVERS   Thais, do not leave us! Thais, where are you going?

THAIS   Where none of you will ever see me again!

LOVERS   What monstrous thing is this? Thais, glory of our land, is changed! Thais, our delight, who loved riches and power and luxury – Thais, who gave herself up to pleasure day and night, has destroyed past remedy gold and gems that had no price! What monstrous thing is this? Thais, the very flower of love, insults her lovers and scorns their gifts. Thais, whose boast it was that whoever loved her should enjoy her love! What monstrous thing is this? Thais! Thais! This is a thing not to be believed.

Hrotswitha (935-c1002)

Born into German nobility and educated in the Benedictine convent at Gandersheim, famous for its piety and learning, where her special teacher was Gerberg, a niece of Otto I. She was a highly accomplished woman, and became the abbess of Gandersheim (959-1001). She later became Canonness. Her works draw on the writings of the Church fathers, the Apocrypha and show familiarity with classical texts by Plautus, Ovid, Virgil and Ovid as well as Terence. Hrotswitha's works, rediscovered in a manuscript volume in the 15th century include three books: one of legends and epic poems, one of historical writings – including a history of her religious order, and a volume of six plays: *Dulcitius, Sapienta, Abraham, Callimachus, Paphnutius and Gallicanus.* The first published translations in English appeared in 1923 when three different translators brought out versions including Christopher St John's *The Plays of Roswitha.*

Extract from *The Tragedy of Mariam, The Fair Queen of Jewry* by Elizabeth Cary

ACT ONE, SCENE 3

Mariam. Alexandra. Salomé.

SALOME   More plotting yet? Why, now you have the thing
For which so oft you spent your suppliant breath:
And Mariam hopes to have another king.
Her eyes do sparkle joy for Herod's death.

ALEXANDRA   If she desired another king to have,
She might before she came in Herod's bed
Have had her wish. More kings than one did crave
For leave to set a crown upon her head.
I think with more than reason she laments,
That she is freed from such a sad annoy:
Who is't will weep to part from discontent?
And if she joy, she did not causeless joy.

SALOME   You durst not thus have given your tongue the rein,
If noble Herod still remained in life:
Your daughter's betters far, I dare maintain,
Might have rejoiced to be my brother's wife.

MARIAM   My betters far! Base woman, 'tis untrue,
You scarce have ever my superiors seen:
For Mariam's servants were as good as you,
Before she came to be Judea's queen.

SALOME   Now stirs the tongue that is so quickly moved,
But more than once your choler have I borne:
Your furnished words are sooner said than proved,
And Salomé's reply is only scorn.

MARIAM   Scorn those that are for thy companions held!
Though I thy brother's face had never seen,
My birth thy baser birth so far excelled,
I had to both of you the princess been.
Thou parti-Jew, and parti-Edomite,
Thou mongrel: issued from rejected race! Not,
Thy ancestors against the Heavens did fight,
And thou like them wilt heavenly birth disgrace.

SALOME   Still twit you me with nothing but my birth,
   What odds betwixt your ancestors and mine?
   Both born of Adam, both were made of earth,
   And both did come from holy Abraham's line.

MARIAM   I favour thee when nothing else I say,
   With thy black acts I'll not pollute my breath:
   Else to thy charge I might full justly lay,
   A shameful life, besides a husband's death.

SALOME   'Tis true indeed, I did the plots reveal,
   That passed betwixt your favorites and you:
   I meant not, I, a traitor to conceal.
   Thus Salomé your minion Joseph slew.

MARIAM   Heaven, dost thou mean this infamy to smother?
   Let slandered Mariam ope thy closed ear:
   Self-guilt hath ever been suspicion's mother,
   And therefore I this speech with patience bear.
   No, had not Salomé's unsteadfast heart
   In Joseph's stead her Constabarus placed,
   To free herself she had not used the art
   To slander hapless Mariam for unchaste.

ALEXANDRA   Come, Mariam, let us go: it is no boot
   To let the head contend against the foot.

Mariam and Alexandra exit.

SCENE 4

Salomé alone.

SALOME   Lives Salomé to get so base a style
   As 'foot' to the proud Mariam? Herod's spirit
   In happy time for her endured exile,
   For did he live, she should not miss her merit:
   But he is dead: and though he were my brother,
   His death such store of cinders cannot cast
   My coals of love to quench: for though they smother
   The flames a while, yet will they out at last.
   Oh blest Arabia, in best climate placed,
   I by the fruit will censure of the tree:
   'Tis not in vain the happy name thou hast,

If all Arabians like Silleus be.
Had not my fate been too too contrary,
When I on Constabarus first did gaze,
Silleus had been object to mine eye:
Whose looks and personage must all eyes amaze.
But now, ill-fated Salomé, thy tongue
To Constabarus by itself is tied:
And now, except I do the Hebrew wrong,
I cannot be the fair Arabian's bride:
What childish lets are these? Why stand I now
On honourable points? 'Tis long ago
Since shame was written on my tainted brow:
And certain 'tis, that shame is honour's foe.
Had I upon my reputation stood,
Had I affected an unspotted life,
Joseph's veins had still been stuffed with blood,
And I to him had lived a sober wife.
Then had I never cast an eye of love
On Constabarus' now detested face,
Then had I kept my thoughts without remove:
And blushed at motion of the least disgrace:
But shame is gone, and honour wiped away,
And impudency on my forehead sits:
She bids me work my will without delay,
And for my will I will employ my wits.
He loves, I love; what then can be the cause
Keeps me [from] being the Arabian's wife?
It is the principles of Moses' laws,
For Constabarus still remains in life.
If he to me did bear as earnest hate,
As I to him, for him there were an ease;
A separating bill might free his fate
From such a yoke that did so much displease.
Why should such privilege to man be given?
Or given to them, why barred from women then?
Are men than we in greater grace with Heaven?
Or cannot women hate as well as men?
I'll be the custom-breaker: and begin
To show my sex the way to freedom's door,
And with an off'ring will I purge my sin;
The law was made for none but who are poor.

If Herod had lived, I might to him accuse
My present lord. But for the future's sake,
Then would I tell the king he did refuse
The sons of Baba in his power to take.
But now I must divorce him from my bed,
That my Silleus may possess his room:
Had I not begged his life, he had been dead,
I curse my tongue, the hind'rer of his doom,
But then my wand'ring heart to him was fast,
Nor did I dream of change: Silleus said,
He would be here, and see, he comes at last.
Had I not named him, longer had he stayed.

<u>Elizabeth Tanfield Cary, Viscountess Falkland</u> (1585-1639)

Elizabeth Cary was born into the Tanfield family at Burford Priory in Oxfordshire. Brought up strictly, she learnt Latin and Hebrew and modern languages. Forbidden further learning, she turned to the servants and ran up a large bill paying them to smuggle her candles for secret reading. She was married at 15 to Henry Cary, Lord Falkland and bore him 11 children, though she went through deep depression during the pregnancies. She brought up her children with a strong reverence for their father, to whom she also strove to be obedient, subordinating her own wishes and beliefs to his. However in 1626, unable to deny her convictions further, she converted to Catholicism, remaining unwavering despite Cary's removal of the children from her, his bitter recriminations and financial pressure.

Through these hardships she continued to write as she had throughout her marriage, producing many translations of Catholic works. She was gradually reunited with her seven surviving children, following Henry's death. Two of her sons became priests, four daughters became nuns and one, Anne, wrote her mother's biography.

Cary is also supposed to have written a verse tragedy of Tamberlaine now lost, but in 1627 did write *The History of Edward II,* formerly ascribed to Henry Cary, a chronicle with dramatic sections, notable for its sympathetic presentation of Queen Isabel, who was neglected by her husband for his homosexual lover Gaveston.

The Rover

Aphra Behn

First performed at The Duke's Theatre, 2nd July, 1677.

CHARACTERS
Women
Florinda, sister to Don Pedro
Valeria, a kinswoman to Florinda
Hellena, sister to Florinda, a gay young woman designed for a nun
Angellica Bianca, a famous courtesan
Moretta, her woman
Callis, governess to Florinda and Hellena
Lucetta, a jilting wench
Men
Don Antonio, the viceroy's son
Don Pedro, a noble Spaniard, his friend, and brother to Florinda
Belvile, an English Colonel
Frederick, an English gentleman, friend to Belvile and Blunt
Blunt, a country gentleman from England
Willmore, the Rover, also from England
Sebastian and **Biskey**, Angellica's bravos
Stephano, servant to Don Pedro
Diego, Page to Don Antonio
Philip, servant to Lucetta
Sancho, pimp to Lucetta
Officers and soldiers
Masquers, Servants, etc. *(men and women)*

Scene: Naples, a colony of Spain, in Carnival time

PROLOGUE

Wits, like physicians, never can agree,
When of a different society:
And Rabel's drops were never more cried down
By all the learned doctors of the town,
Than a new play whose author is unknown;
Nor can those doctors with more malice sue
(And powerful purses) the dissenting few,
Than those with an insulting pride, do rail
At all who are not of their own cabal.
If a young poet his your humour right,
You judge him then out of revenge and spite:
So amongst men there are ridiculous elves,
Who monkeys hate for being too like themselves.
So that the reason of the grand debate,
Why wit so oft is damned when good plays take,
Is that you censure as you love or hate.
Thus, like a learned conclave, poets sit,
Catholic judges both of sense and wit,
And damn or save as they themselves think fit.
Yet those who to others 'faults are so severe,
Are not so perfect by themselves may err.
Some write correct, indeed but then the whole
(Bating their own dull stuff i'th'play) is stole:
As bees do suck from flowers their honeydew,
So they rob others, striving to please you.
Some write their characters genteel and fine,
But then they do so toil for every line,
That what to you does easy seem, and plain,
Is the hard issue of their labouring brain.
And some th'effects of all their pains we see,
Is but to mimic good extempore.
Others, by long oconverse about the town,
Have wit enough to write a lewd lampoon,
But their chief skill lies in a bawdy song.
In short, the only wit that's now in fashion,
Is but the gleanings of good conversation.
As for the author of this coming play,
I asked him what he thought fit I should say
In thanks for your good company today:
He called me fool, and said it was well known,

You came not here for our sakes, but your own.
New plays are stuffed with wits, and with debauches,
That crowd and sweat like cits in May-day coaches.

ACT ONE, SCENE 1

A chamber. Enter Florinda and Hellena.

FLORINDA   What an impertinent thing is a young girl bred in a nunnery! How full of questions! Prithee no more, Hellena; I have told thee more than thou understand'st already.

HELLENA   The more's my grief. I would fain know as much as you, which makes me so inquisitive; nor is't enough I know you're a lover, unless you tell me too who 'tis you sigh for.

FLORINDA   When you're a lover I'll think you fit for a secret of that nature.

HELLENA   'Tis true, I never was a lover yet, but I begin to have a shrewd guess what 'tis to be so, and fancy it very pretty to sigh, and sing, and blush, and wish, and dream and wish, and long and wish to see the man, and when I do, look pale and tremble, just as you did when my brother brought home the fine English colonel to see you – what do you call him? Don Belvile.

FLORINDA   Fie, Hellena.

HELLENA   That blush betrays you. I am sure 'tis so; or is it Don Antonio, the viceroy's son? Or perhaps the rich old Don Vincentio, whom my father designs you for a husband? Why do you blush again?

FLORINDA   With indignation; and how near soever my father thinks I am to marrying that hated object, I shall let him see I understand better what's due to my beauty, birth, and fortune and more to my soul, than to obey those unjust commands.

HELLENA   Now hang me, if I don't love thee for that dear disobedience. I love mischief strangely, as most of our sex do, who are come to love nothing else. But tell me, dear Florinda, don't you love that fine *Inglese?* For I vow, next to loving him myself, 'twill please me most that you do so, for he is so gay and so handsome.

FLORINDA   Hellena, a maid designed for a nun ought not to be so curious in a discourse of love.

HELLENA   And dost thou think that ever I'll be a nun? Or at least till I'm so old I'm fit for nothing else: faith, no, sister; and that which makes me long to know whether you love Belville, is because I hope he has some mad companion or other that will spoil my devotion. Nay, I'm resolved to provide myself this Carnival, if there be e'er a handsome proper fellow of my humour above ground, though I ask first.

FLORINDA   Prithee be not so wild.

HELLENA   Now you have provided yourself of a man, you take no care for poor me. Prithee tell me, what dost thou see about me that is unfit for love? Have I not a world of youth? A humour gay? A beauty passable? A vigour desirable? Well-shaped? Clean-limbed? Sweet-breathed? And sense enough to know how all these ought to be employed to the best advantage? Yes, I do, and will; therefore lay aside your hopes of my fortune by my being a devotee, and tell me how you came acquainted with this Belvile; for I perceive you knew him before he came to Naples.

FLORINDA   Yes, I knew him at the siege of Pamplona; he was then a colonel of French horse, who, when the town was ran-sacked, nobly treated my brother and myself, preserving us from all insolences; and I must own, besides great obligations, I have I know not what that pleads kindly for him about my heart, and will suffer no other to enter. But see, my brother.

Enter Don Pedro, Stephano with a masking habit, and Callis.

PEDRO   Good morrow, sister. Florinda, pray when saw you your lover Don Vicentio?

FLORINDA   I know not sir – Callis when was he here? – For I consider it so little, I know not when it was.

PEDRO   I have a command from my father here to tell you you ought not to despise him, a man of so vast a fortune, and such a passion for you. – Stephano, my things. *(Don Pedro puts on his masking habit.)*

FLORINDA   A passion for me? 'Tis more than e'er I saw or he had a desire should be known. I hate Vincentio, sir, and I would not have a man so dear to me as my brother follow the ill customs of our country, and make a slave of his sister; and, sir, my father's will I'm sure you may divert.

PEDRO   I know not how dear I am to you, but I wish only to be ranked in your esteem equal with the English colonel Belvile. Why do you frown and blush? Is there any guilt belongs to the name of that cavalier?

FLORINDA   I'll not deny I value Belvile. When I was exposed to such dangers as the licensed lust of common soldiers threatened, when rage and conquest flew through the city, then Belvile, this criminal for my sake, threw himself into all dangers to save my honour: and will you not allow him my esteem?

PEDRO   Yes, pay him what you will in honour; but you must consider Don Vincentio's fortune, and the jointure he'll make you.

FLORINDA   Let him consider my youth, beauty, and fortune, which ought not to be thrown away on his age and jointure.

PEDRO   'Tis true, he's not so young and fine a gentleman as that Belvile. But what jewels will that cavalier present you with? Those of his eyes and heart?

HELLENA   And are those better than any Don Vincentio has brought from the Indies?

PEDRO   Why how now! Has your nunnery breeding taught you to understand the value of hearts and eyes?

HELLENA   Better than to believe Vincentio's deserve value from any woman: he may perhaps increase her bags, but not her family.

PEDRO   This is fine! Go, up to your devotion: you are not designed for the conversation of lovers.

HELLENA *(aside)*   Nor saints, yet awhile, I hope. Is't not enough you make a nun of me, but you must cast my sister away too, exposing her to a worse confinement than a religious life?

PEDRO   The girl's mad! It is a confinement to be carried into the country, to an ancient villa belonging to the family of the Vincentios these five hundred years, and have no other prospect than that pleasing one of seeing all her own that meets her eyes: a fine air, large fields and gardens, where she may walk and gather flowers!

HELLENA   When, by moonlight? For I am sure she dares not encounter with the heat of the sun; that were a task only for Don Vincentio and his Indian breeding, who loves it in the dog days. And if these be her daily divertisements, what are those of the night? To lie in a wide moth-eaten bedchamber, with furniture in fashion in reign of King Sancho the First; the bed, that which his forefathers lived and died in.

PEDRO   Very well.

HELLENA   This apartment, new furbished and fitted out for the young wife, he (out of freedom) makes his dressing room, and being a frugal and a jealous coxcomb, instead of a valet to uncase his feeble carcass, he desires you to do that office: signs of favour, I'll assure you, and such as you must not hope for, unless your woman be out of the way.

PEDRO   Have you done yet?

HELLENA   That honour being past, the giant stretches itself, yawns and sighs a belch or two, loud as a musket, throws himself into

bed, and expects you in his foul sheets; and ere you can get yourself
undressed, calls you with a snore or two: and are not these fine
blessings to a young lady?

PEDRO   Have you done yet?

HELLENA   And this man you must kiss: nay, you must kiss
none but him, too – and nuzzle through his beard to find his lips. And
this you must submit to for three-score years, and all for a jointure.

PEDRO   For all your character of Don Vincentio, she is as
like to marry him as she was before.

HELLENA   Marry Don Vincentio! Hang me, such a wedlock
would be worse than adultery with another man. I had rather see her in
the *Hôtel de Dieu* to waste her youth in vows, and be a handmaid to
lazars and cripples, than to lose it in such a marriage.

PEDRO *(To Florinda)*   You have considered, sister, that Belvile has no
fortune to bring you to; banished his country, despised at home, and
pitied abroad.

HELLENA   What then? The viceroy's son is better than that
old Sir Fifty. Don Vincentio! Don Indian! He thinks he's trading to
Gambo still, and would barter himself (that bell and bauble) for your
youth and fortune.

PEDRO   Callis, take her hence, and lock her up all this
Carnival, and at Lent she shall begin her everlasting penance in a
monastery.

HELLENA   I care not; I had rather be a nun than be obliged
to marry as you would have me, if I were designed for't.

PEDRO   Do not fear the blessing of that choice; you shall
be a nun.

HELLENA   Shall I so? You may chance to be mistaken in my
way of devotion. A nun! Yes, I am like to make a fine nun! I have an
excellent humour for a grate. *(aside)* No, I'll have a saint of my own to
pray to shortly, if I like any that dares venture on me.

PEDRO   Callis, make it your business to watch this
wildcat. As for you, Florinda, I've only tried you all this while and urged
my father's will; but mine is that you would love Antonio: he is brave
and young, and all that can complete the happiness of a gallant maid.
This absence of my father will give us opportunity to free you from
Vincentio by marrying here, which you must do tomorrow.

FLORINDA   Tomorrow!

PEDRO   Tomorrow, or 'twill be too late. 'Tis not only my
friendship to Antonio which makes me urge this, but love to thee, and
hatred to Vincentio; therefore resolve upon tomorrow.

FLORINDA   Sir, I shall strive to do as shall become your sister.

PEDRO   I'll both believe and trust you. Adieu.

Pedro and Stephano exit.

HELLENA   As becomes his sister! That is, to be as resolved your way as he is his. *(goes to Callis)*

FLORINDA *(aside)*   I ne'er till now perceived my ruin near;
I've no defence against Antonio's love,
For he has all the advantages of nature,
The moving arguments of youth and fortune.

HELLENA   But hark you, Callis, you will not be so cruel to lock me up indeed, will you?

CALLIS   I must obey the commands I have; besides, do you consider what a life you are going to lead?

HELLENA   Yes, Callis, that of a nun: and till then I'll be indebted a world of prayers to you, if you'll let me now see, what I never did, the divertisements of a Carnival.

CALLIS   What, go in masquerade? 'Twill be a fine farewell to the world, I take it; pray, what would you do there?

HELLENA   That which all the world does, as I am told: be as mad as the rest, and take all innocent freedoms. Sister, you'll go too, will you not? Come, prithee be not sad. We'll outwit twenty brothers, if you'll be ruled by me. Come, put off this dull humour with your clothes, and assume one as gay, and as fantastic, as the dress my cousin Valeria and I have provided, and let's ramble.

FLORINDA   Callis, will you give us leave to go?

CALLIS *(aside)*   I have a youthful itch of going myself. – Madam, if I thought your brother might not know it, and I might wait on you; for by my troth, I'll not trust young girls alone.

FLORINDA   Thou seest my brother's gone already, and thou shalt attend and watch us.

Enter Stephano.

STEPHANO   Madam, the habits are come, and your cousin Valeria is dressed and stays for you.

FLORINDA   'Tis well. I'll write a note, and if I chance to see Belvile, and want an opportunity to speak to him, that shall let him know what I've resolved in favour of him.

HELLENA   Come, let's in and dress us.

They exit.

ACT ONE, SCENE 2

A long street. Enter Belvile, melancholy, with Blunt and Frederick.

FREDERICK   Why, what the devil ails the colonel, in a time when all the world is gay, to look like mere Lent thus? Hadst thou been long enough in Naples to have been in love, I should have sworn some such judgement had befallen thee.

BELVILE   No, I have made no new amours since I came home.

FREDERICK   You have left none behind you in Paris?

BELVILE   Neither.

FREDERICK   I cannot divine the cause then, unless the old cause, the want of money.

BLUNT   And another old cause, the want of a wench; would not that revive you?

BELVILE   You are mistaken, Ned.

BLUNT   Nay, 'adsheartlikins, then thou'rt past cure.

FREDERICK   I have found it out: thou hast renewed thy acquaintance with the lady that cost thee so many sighs at the siege of Pamplona; pox on't, what d'ye call her – her brother's a noble Spaniard, nephew to the dead general – Florinda. Ay, Florinda: and will nothing serve thy turn but that damned virtuous woman? Whom on my conscience thou lovest in spite, too, because thou seest little or no possibility of gaining her?

BELVILE   Thou art mistaken, I have interest enough in that lovely virgin's heart to make me proud and vain, were it not abated by the severity of a brother, who perceiving my happiness –

FREDERICK   Has civilly forbid thee the house?

BELVILE   'Tis so, to make way for a powerful rival, the viceroy's son, who has the advantage of me in being a man of fortune, a Spaniard, and her brother's friend; which gives him liberty to make his court, whilst I have recourse only to letters, and distant looks from her window, which are as soft and as kind as those which heaven sends down on penitents.

BLUNT   Heyday! 'Adsheartlikins, simile! By this light the man is quite spoiled. – Fred, what the devil are we made of, that we cannot be thus concerned for a wench? 'Adsheartlikins, our cupids are like the cooks of the camp: they can roast or boil a woman, but they have none of the fine tricks to set 'em off, no hogoes to make the sauce pleasant and the stomach sharp.

FREDERICK   I dare swear I have had a hundred as young, kind and handsome as this Florinda; and dogs eat me if they were not as troublesome to me i'th' morning as they were welcome o'er night.

BLUNT And yet I warrant he would not touch another woman, if he might have her for nothing.

BELVILE That's thy joy, a cheap whore.

BLUNT Why, 'adsheartlikins, I love a frank soul: when did you ever hear of an honest woman that took a man's money? I warrant 'em good ones. But, gentlemen, you have been kept so poor with parliaments and protectors that the little stock you have is not worth preserving; but I thank my stars, I had more grace than to forfeit my estate by cavaliering.

BELVILE Methinks only following the court should be sufficient to entitle 'em to that.

BLUNT 'Adsheartlikins, they know I follow it to do it no good, unless they pick a hole in my coat for lending you money now and then, which is a greater crime to my conscience, gentlemen, than to the Commonwealth.

Enter Willmore.

WILLMORE Ha! Dear Belvile! Noble colonel!

BLUNT Willmore! Welcome ashore, my dear rover! What happy wind blew us this good fortune?

WILLMORE Let me salute my dear Fred, and then command me. *(To Frederick)* – How is't, honest lad?

FREDERICK Faith, sir, the old compliment, infinitely the better to see my dear mad Willmore again. Prithee, why cam'st thou ashore? And where's the prince?

WILLMORE He's well, and reigns still lord of the watery element. I must aboard again within a day or two, and my business ashore was only to enjoy myself a little this Carnival.

BELVILE Pray know our new friend, sir; he's but bashful, a raw traveller, but honest, stout, and one of us.

WILLMORE *(embraces Blunt)* That you esteem him gives him an interest here.

BLUNT Your servant, sir.

WILLMORE But well, faith. I'm glad to meet you again in a warm climate, where the kind sun has a god-like power still over the wine and women. Love and mirth are my business in Naples, and if I mistake not the place, here's an excellent market for chapmen of my humour.

BELVILE See, here be those kind merchants of love you look for.

Enter several men in masking habits, some playing on music, others dancing after, women dressed like courtesans, with papers pinned on their breasts, and baskets of flowers in their hands.

BLUNT   'Adsheartlikins, what have we here?
FREDERICK   Now the game begins.
WILLMORE   Fine pretty creatures! May a stranger have leave
to look and love? *(reads the papers)* What's here: 'Roses for every month?'
BLUNT   Roses for every month? What means that?
BELVILE   They are, or would have you think they're
courtesans, who here in Naples are to be hired by the month.
WILLMORE   Kind and obliging to inform us. *(To a woman)*
Pray, where do these roses grow? I would fain plant some of 'em in a bed of mine.
WOMAN   Beware such roses, sir.
WILLMORE   A pox of fear: I'll be baked with thee between a
pair of sheets (and that's thy proper still), so I might but strew such roses over me, and under me. Fair one, would you would give me leave to gather at your bush this idle month; I would go near to make somebody smell of it all the year after.
BELVILE   And thou has need of such a remedy, for thou
stink'st of tar and ropes' ends, like a dock or pesthouse.

The woman puts herself into the hands of a man, and both begin to leave.

WILLMORE   Nay, nay, you shall not leave me so.
BELVILE   By all means use no violence here.

Man and woman exit.

WILLMORE   Death! Just as I was going to be damnably in
love, to have her led off! I could pluck that rose out of his hand, and even kiss the bed the bush grew in.
FREDERICK   No friend to love like a long voyage at sea.
BLUNT   Except a nunnery, Fred.
WILLMORE   Death! But will they not be kind, quickly be kind?
Thou know'st I'm no tame sigher, but a rampant lion of the forest.

Advances, from the farther end of the scenes, two men dressed all over with horns of several sorts, making grimaces at one another, with papers pinned on their backs.

BELVILE Oh the fantastical rogues, how they're dressed! 'Tis a satire against the whole sex.

WILMORE Is this a fruit that grows in this warm country?

BELVILE Yes: 'tis pretty to see these Italians start, swell and stab, at the word cuckold, and yet stumble at horns on every threshold.

WILLMORE See what's on their back. *(reads)* 'Flowers of every night': ah, rogue, and more sweet than roses of every month! This is a gardener of Adam's own breeding.

The two men dressed in horns dance.

BELVILE What think you of those grave people? Is a wake in Essex half so mad or extravagant?

WILLMORE I like their sober grave way: 'tis a kind of legal authorized fornication, where the men are not chid for it, nor the women despised, as amongst our dull English; even the monsieurs want that part of good manners.

BELVILE But here in Italy, a monsieur is the humblest best-bred gentleman: duels are so baffled by bravos, that an age shows not one but between a Frenchman and a hangman, who is as much too hard for him on the Piazza, as they are for a Dutchman on the New Bridge. But see, another crew.

Enter Florinda, Hellena, and Valeria, dressed like gypsies; Callis and Stephano, Lucetta, Philippo, and Sancho in masquerade.

HELENA Sister, there's your Englishman, and with him a handsome proper fellow. I'll to him, and instead of telling him his fortune, try my own.

WILLMORE Gipsies, on my life; sure these will prattle if a man cross their hands. *(Willmore goes to Hellena.)* Dear, pretty, and I hope young, devil, will you tell an amorous stranger what luck he's like to have?

HELLENA Have a care how you venture with me, sir, lest I pick your pocket, which will more vex your English humour, than an Italian fortune will please you.

WILLMORE How the devil cam'st thou to know my country and humour?

HELLENA The first I guess by a certain forward impudence, which does not displease me at this time; and the loss of your money will vex you, because I hope you have but very little to lose.

WILLMORE Egad, child, thou'rt i'th' right; it is so little,

I dare not offer it thee for a kindness. But cannot you divine what other things of more value I have about me, that I would more willingly part with?

HELLENA   Indeed no, that's the business of a witch, and I am but a gipsy yet. Yet, without looking in your hand, I have a parlous guess 'tis some foolish heart you mean, an inconstant English heart, as little worth stealing as your purse.

WILLMORE   Nay, then thou dost deal with the devil, that's certain: thou hast guessed as right, as if thou hadst been one of that number it has languished for. I find you'll be better acquainted with it; nor can you take it in a better time, for I am come from sea, child, and Venus not being propitious to me in her own element, I have a world of love in store. Would you would be good-natured and take some on't off my hands.

HELLENA   Why, I could be inclined that way, but for a foolish vow I am going to make – to die a maid.

SANCHO   Go, or I'll beat thee. Yet, mark. You shall promise much, but pay him little.

WILLMORE   Then thou art damned without redemption, and as I am a good Christian, I ought in charity to divert so wicked a design; therefore prithee, dear creature, let me know quickly when and where I shall begin to set a helping hand to so good a work.

HELLENA   If you should prevail with my tender heart, as I begin to fear you will, for you have horrible loving eyes, there will be difficulty in't that you'll hardly undergo for my sake.

WILLMORE   Faith, child, I have been bred in dangers, and wear a sword that has been employed in a worse cause than for a handsome kind woman. Name the danger; let it be anything but a long siege, and I'll undertake it.

HELLENA   Can you storm?

WILLMORE   Oh, most furiously.

HELLENA   What think you of a nunnery wall? There's no sinner like a young saint. Nay, now there's no denying me: the old law had no curse, to a woman, like dying a maid; witness Jephtha's daughter.

HELLENA   A very good text this, if well handled; and I perceive, Father Captain, you would impose no severe penance on her who were inclined to console herself before she took orders.

WILLMORE   If she be young and handsome.

HELLENA   Aye, there's it: but if she be not –

WILLMORE   By this hand, child, I have an implicit faith, and dare venture on thee with all faults. Besides, 'tis more meritorious to leave the world when thou hast tasted and proved the pleasure on't. Then 'twill be a virtue in thee, which now will be pure ignorance.

HELLENA   I perceive, good Father Captain, you design only to make me fit for heaven. But if, on the contrary, you should quite divert me from it, and bring me back to the world again, I should have a new man to seek, I find; and what a grief that will be. For when I begin, I fancy I shall love like anything; I never tried yet.

WILLMORE   Egad, and that's kind. Prithee, dear creature, give me credit for a heart, for faith I'm a very honest fellow. Oh, I long to come first to the banquet of love, and such a swingeing appetite I bring! Oh, I'm impatient. Thy lodging, sweetheart, thy lodging, or I'm a dead man!

HELLENA   Why must we be either guilty of fornication or murder if we converse with you men? And is there no difference between leave to love me, and leave to lie with me?

WILLMORE   Faith, child, they were made to go together.

LUCETTA *(aside to Sancho, pointing to Blunt)* Are you sure this is the man?

SANCHO   When did I mistake your game?

LUCETTA   This is a stranger, I know by his gazing; if he be brisk, he'll venture to follow me, and then, if I understand my trade, he's mine. He's English, too and they say that's a sort of good-natured loving people, and have generally so kind an opinion of themselves, that a woman with any wit may flatter 'em into any sort of fool she pleases.

Lucetta often passes by Blunt, and gazes on him; he struts and cocks, and walks and gazes on her.

BLUNT *(aside)*   'Tis so, she is taken: I have beauties which my false glass at home did not discover.

FLORINDA *(aside)*   This woman watches me so, I shall get no opportunity to discover myself to him, and so miss the intent of my coming. *(To Belville, looking in his hand)* But as I was saying, sir, by this line you should be a lover.

BELVILE   I thought how right you guessed: all men are in love, or pretend to be so. Come, let me go, I'm weary of this fooling.

Belvile walks away. Florinda holds him, he strives to get from her.

FLORINDA   I will not, till you have confessed whether the passion that you have vowed Florinda, be true or false.

BELVILE *(turning quick towards her)* Florinda!

FLORINDA	Softly.
BELVILE	Thou has named one will fix me here for ever.
FLORINDA	She'll be disappointed, then, who expects you this

night at the garden gate; and if you fail not, as – *(looks on Callis, who observes them)* let me see the other hand– you will go near to do, she vows to die or make you happy.

BELVILE	What canst thou mean?
FLORINDA	That which I say; farewell. *(She offers to go.)*
BELVILE	Oh, charming sibyl, stay; complete that joy, which

as it is will turn into distraction! Where must I be? At the garden gate? I know it; at night, you say? I'll sooner forfeit heaven than disobey.

Enter Don Pedro and other maskers, and pass over the stage.

CALLIS	Madam, your brother's here.
FLORINDA	Take this to instruct you farther.

Florinda gives Belvile a letter, and goes off.

FREDERICK	Have a care, sir, what you promise; this may be a

trap laid by her brother to ruin you.

BELVILE	Do not disturb my happiness with doubts.

(He opens the letter.)

WILLMORE *(to Hellena)* My dear pretty creature, a thousand blessings on thee! Still in this habit, you say? And after dinner at this place.

HELLENA	Yes, if you will swear to keep your heart, and not

bestow it between this and that.

WILLMORE	By all the little gods of love, I swear I'll leave it with

you, and if you run away with it, those deities of justice will revenge me.

The women exit (except Lucetta).

FREDERICK	Do you know the hand?
BELVILE	'Tis Florinda's.

All blessings fall upon the virtuous maid.

FREDERICK	Nay, no idolatry: a sober sacrifice I'll allow you.
BELVILE	Oh, friends, the welcom'st news! The softest

letter! Nay, you shall all see it; and could you now be serious, I might be made the happiest man the sun shines on!

WILLMORE	The reason of this mighty joy?
BELVILE	See how kindly she invites me to deliver her from

the threatened violence of her brother: will you not assist me?

WILLMORE	I know not what thou mean'st, but I'll make one

at any mischief where a woman's concerned. But she'll be grateful to us for the favour, will she not?

BELVILE   How mean you?

WILLMORE   How should I mean? Thou know'st there's but one way for a woman to oblige me.

BELVILE   Do not profane; the maid is nicely virtuous.

WILLMORE   Ho, pox, then she's fit for nothing but a husband: let her e'en go, colonel.

FREDERICK   Peace, she's the colonel's mistress, sir.

WILLMORE   Let her be the devil, if she be thy mistress, I'll serve her. Name the way.

BELVILE   Read here this postcript. *(Belvile gives Willmore a letter.)*

WILMORE *(reads)* 'At ten at night, at the garden gate, of which, if I cannot get the key, I will contrive a way over the wall. Come attended with a friend or two.' – Kind heart, if we three cannot weave a string to let her down a garden wall, 'twere pity but the hangman wove one for us all.

FREDERICK   Let her alone for that. Your woman's wit, your fair kind woman, will out-trick a broker or a Jew, and contrive like a Jesuit in chains. But see, Ned Blunt is stolen out after the lure of a damsel.

Blunt and Lucetta exit.

BELVILLE   So, he'll scarce find his way home again, unless we get him cried by the bellman in the market-place, and 'twould sound prettily: 'a lost English boy of thirty'.

FREDERICK   I hope 'tis some common crafty sinner, one that will fit him. It may be she'll sell him for Peru; the rogue's sturdy, and would work well in a mine. At least I hope she'll dress him for our mirth: cheat him of all, then have him well-favouredly banged, and turned out naked at midnight.

WILLMORE   Prithee, what humour is he of, that you wish him so well?

BELVILE   Why, of an English elder brother's humour. Educated in a nursery, with a maid to tend him till fifteen, and lies with his grandmother till he's of age; one that knows no pleasure beyond riding to the next fair, or going up to London with his right worshipful father in parliament time, wearing his gay clothes, or making honourable love to his lady mother's laundry-maid; gets drunk at a hunting match, and ten to one then gives some proofs of his prowess. A pox upon him, he's our banker, and has all our cash about him, and if he fail, we are all broke.

FREDERICK   Oh, let him alone for that matter: he's of a
damned stingy quality, that will secure our stock. I know not in what
danger it were indeed if the jilt should pretend she's in love with him,
for 'tis a kind believing coxcomb; otherwise, if he part with more than a
piece of eight, geld him – for which offer he may chance to be eaten, if
she be a whore of the first rank.

BELVILE   Nay, the rogue will not be easily beaten, he's
stout enough. Perhaps, if they talk beyond his capacity, he may chance
to exercise his courage upon some of them; else I'm sure they'll find it
as difficult to beat as to please him.

WILLMORE   'Tis a lucky devil to light upon so kind a wench!

FREDERICK   Thou hast a great deal of talk with thy little gipsy,
couldst thou do no good upon her? For mine was hard-hearted.

WILLMORE   Hang her, she was some damned honest person
of quality, I'm sure, she was so very free and witty. If her face be but
answerable to her wit and humour, I would be bound to constancy this
month to gain her. In the meantime, have you made no kind acquaintance since you came to town? You do not use to be honest so long,
gentlemen.

FREDERICK   Faith, love has kept us honest: we have been all
fired with a beauty newly come to town, the famous Paduana, Angellica
Bianca.

WILLMORE   What, the mistress of the dead Spanish general?

BELVILE   Yes, she's now the only adored beauty of all the
youth in Naples, who put on all their charms to appear lovely in her
sight: their coaches, liveries, and themselves, all gay as on a monarch's
birthday, to attract the eyes of this fair charmer, while she has the
pleasure to behold all languish for her that see her.

FREDERICK   'Tis pretty to see with how much love the men
regard her, and how much envy the women.

WILLMORE   What gallant has she?

BELVILE   None: she's exposed to sale, and four days in the
week she's yours – for so much a month.

WILLMORE   The very thought of it quenches all manner of fire
in me; yet prithee, let's see her.

BELVILE   Let's first to dinner, and after that we'll pass the
day as you please; but at night ye must all be at my devotion.

WILLMORE   I will not fail you.

They exit.

ACT TWO, SCENE 1

The long street. Enter Belvile and Frederick in masking habits, and Willmore in his own clothes, with a vizard in his hand.

WILLMORE But why thus disguised and muzzled?

BELVILE Because whatever extravagances we commit in these faces, our own may not be obliged to answer 'em.

WILLMORE I should have changed my eternal buff too; but no matter, my little gipsy would not have found me out then; for if she should change hers, it is impossible I should know her, unless I should hear her prattle. A pox on't, I cannot get her out of my head. Pray heaven, if ever I do see her again, she prove damnable ugly, that I may fortify myself against her tongue.

BELVILE Have a care of love, for o' my conscience she was not of a quality to give thee any hopes.

WILLMORE Pox on 'em, why do they draw a man in then? She has played with my heart so, that twill never lie still, till I have met with some kind wench that will play the game out with me. Oh for my arms full of soft, white, kind – woman! Such as I fancy Angellica.

BELVILE This is her house, if you were but in stock to get admittance. They have not dined yet: I perceive the picture is not out.

Enter Blunt.

WILLMORE I long to see the shadow of the fair substance; a man may gaze on that for nothing.

BLUNT Colonel, thy hand – and thine, Fred. I have been an ass, a deluded fool, a very coxcomb from my birth till this hour, and heartily repent my little faith.

BELVILE What the devil's the matter with thee, Ned?

BLUNT Oh, such a mistress, Fred, such a girl!

WILLMORE Ha! Where?

FREDERICK Aye, where?

BLUNT So fond, so amorous, so toying and so fine; and all for sheer love, ye rogue! Oh, how she looked and kissed, and soothed my heart from my bosom; I cannot think I was awake, and yet methinks I see and feel her charms still! – Fred, try if she have not left the taste of her balmy kisses upon my lips. *(Blunt kisses Frederick.)*

BELVILE Ha, ha, ha!

WILLMORE Death, man, where is she?

BLUNT What a dog was I to stay in dull England so long! How have I laughed at the colonel when he sighed for love! But now the little archer has revenged him, and by this one dart, I can guess at all his joys, which then I took for fancies, mere dreams and fables. Well, I'm resolved to sell all in Essex, and plant here forever.

BELVILE What a blessing 'tis, thou hast a mistress thou dar'st boast of; for I know thy humour is rather to have a proclaimed clap, than a secret amour.

WILLMORE Dost know her name?

BLUNT Her name? No, 'adsheartlikins, what care I for names? She's fair, young, brisk and kind, even to ravishment; and what a pox care I for knowing her by any other title?

WILLMORE Didst give her anything?

BLUNT Give her! Ha, ha, ha! Why, she's a person of quality; that's a good one, give her! 'Adsheartlikins, dost think such creatures are to be bought? Or are we provided for such a purchase? Give her, quoth ye? Why, she presented me with this bracelet, for the toy of a diamond I used to wear. No, gentlemen, Ned Blunt is not everybody. She expects me again tonight.

WILLMORE Egad, that's well; we'll all go.

BLUNT Not a soul: no, gentlemen, you are wits; I am a dull country rogue, I.

FREDERICK Well, sir, for all your person of quality, I shall be very glad to understand your purse be secure: 'tis our whole estate at present, which we are loth to hazard in one bottom. Come, sir, unlade.

BLUNT Take necessary trifle, useless now to me, that am beloved by such a gentlewoman. 'Adsheartlikins, money! Here, take mine too.

FREDERICK Pox, 'tis some common whore, upon my life.

BLUNT A whore! Yes, with such clothes, such jewels, such a house, such furniture, and so attended. A whore!

BELVILE Why yes, sir, they are whores, though they'll neither entertain you with drinking, swearing, or bawdry; are whores in all those gay clothes, and right jewels; are whores with those great houses richly furnished with velvet beds, store of plate, handsome attendance, and fine coaches; are whores, and arrant ones.

WILLMORE Pox on't, where do these fine whores live?

BELVILE Where no rogues in office, y-clept constables, dare give 'em laws, nor the wine-inspired bullies of the town break their windows; yet they are whores, though this Essex calf believe 'em persons of quality.

BLUNT 'Adsheartlikins, y'are all fools; there are things about this Essex calf, that shall take with the ladies, beyond all your wit and parts, This shape and size, gentlemen, are not to be despised; my waist too, tolerably long, with other inviting signs that shall be nameless.

WILLMORE　　　　　　　Egad, I believe he may have met with some person of quality that may be kind to him.

BELVILE　　　　　　　Dost thou perceive any such tempting things about him, that should make a fine woman, and of quality, pick him out from all mankind, to throw away her youth and beauty upon; nay, and her dear heart too? No, no, Angellica has raised the price too high.

WILLMORE　　　　　　　May she languish for mankind till she die, and be damned for that one sin alone.

Enter two bravos (Biskey and Sebastian), and hang up a great picture of Angellica's against the balcony, and two little ones at each side of the door.

BELVILE　　　　　　　See there the fair sign to the inn where a man may lodge that's fool enough to give her price.

Willmore gazes at the picture.

BLUNT　　　　　　　'Adsheartlikins, gentlemen, what's this?

BELVILE　　　　　　　A famous courtesan, that's to be sold.

BLUNT　　　　　　　How, to be sold! Nay then, I have nothing to say to her. Sold! What impudence is practised in this country! With what order and decency whoring's established here by virtue of the Inquisition! Come, let's begone, I'm sure we're no chapmen for this commodity.

FREDERICK　　　　　　　Thou art none, I'm sure, unless thou couldst have have her in thy bed at a price of a coach in the street.

WILLMORE　　　　　　　How wondrous fair she is. A thousand crowns a month? By heaven, as many kingdoms were too little. A plague of this poverty, of which I ne'er complain but when it hinders my approach to beauty, which virtue ne'er could purchase.

Willmore turns from the picture.

BLUNT　　　　　　　What's this? *(reads)* 'A thousand crowns a month'! 'Adsheartlikins, here's a sum! Sure 'tis a mistake. *(To bravo)* Hark you, friend, does she take or give so much by the month?

FREDERICK　　　　　　　A thousand crowns! Why, 'tis a portion for the Infanta.

BLUNT　　　　　　　Hark'ee, friends, won't she trust?

BRAVO　　　　　　　This is a trade, sir, that cannot live by credit.

Enter Don Pedro in masquerade, followed by Stephano.

BELVILE   See, here's more company; let's walk off awhile.

Belvile, Willmore, Frederick, and Blunt exit; Pedro reads.

PEDRO   Fetch me a thousand crowns, I never wished to
buy this beauty at an easier rate.

*Pedro passes off (the stage). Enter Angellica and Moretta in the balcony,
and draw a silk curtain.*

ANGELICA   Prithee, what said those fellows to thee?
BRAVO   Madam, the first were admirers of beauty only,
but no purchasers; they were merry with your price and picture,
laughed at the sum, and so passed off.
ANGELICA   No matter, I'm not displeased with their rallying;
their wonder feeds my vanity, and he that wishes but to buy gives me
more pride, than he that gives my price can make my pleasure.
BRAVO   Madam, the last I knew through all his disguises
to be Don Pedro, nephew to the general, and who was with him in
Pamplona.
ANGELLICA   Don Pedro, my old gallant's nephew! When his
uncle died he left him a vast sum of money; it is he who was so in love
with me at Padua, and who used to make the general so jealous.
MORETTA   Is this he that used to prance before our window,
and take such care to show himself an amorous ass? If I am not
mistaken, he is the likeliest man to give your price.
ANGELLICA   The man is brave and generous, but of an
humour so uneasy and inconstant that the victory over his heart is as
soon lost as won: a slave that can add little to the triumph of the
conqueror; but inconstancy's the sin of all mankind, therefore I'm
resolved that nothing but gold shall charm my heart.
MORETTA   I'm glad on't: 'tis only interest that women of our
profession ought to consider, though I wonder what has kept you from
that general disease of our sex so long, I mean that of being in love.
ANGELLICA   A kind, but sullen star under which I had the
happiness to be born. Yet I have had no time for love: the bravest and
noblest of mankind have purchased my favours at so dear a rate, as if
no coin but gold were current with our trade. But here's Don Pedro
again; fetch me my lute, for 'tis for him, or Don Antonio, the viceroy's
son, that I have spread my nets.

Enter at one door Don Pedro, Stephano; Don Antonio and Diego, his page, at the other door with people following him in masquerade, anticly attired, some with music. Angellica closes the curtain. Pedro and Antonio both go up to the picture.

ANTONIO A thousand crowns! Had not the painter flattered her, I should not think it dear.

PEDRO Flattered her! By heaven, he cannot. I have seen the original, nor is there one charm here more than adorns her face and eyes; all this soft and sweet, with a certain languishing air that no artist can represent.

ANTONIO What I heard of her beauty before had fired my soul, but this confirmation of it has blown it to a flame.

PEDRO Ha!

PAGE *(to Antonio)* Sir, I have known you throw away a thousand crowns on a worse face and though you're near your marriage, you may venture a little love here; Florinda will not miss it.

PEDRO *(aside)* Ha! Florinda! Sure 'tis Antonio.

ANTONIO Florinda! Name not those distant joys, there's not one thought of her will check my passion here.

PEDRO *(aside)* Florinda scorned! And all my hopes defeated, of the possession of Angellica!

A noise of a lute above. Antonio gazes up.

PEDRO Her injuries, by heaven, he shall not boast of.
Song (performed to a lute from above)
    When Damon first began to love
    He languished in a soft desire,
    And knew not how the gods to move,
    To lessen or increase his fire:
    For Celia in her charming eyes
Wore all Love's sweets, and all his cruelties.

    But as beneath a shade he lay,
    Weaving of flowers for Celia's hair,
    She chanced to lead her flock that way,
    And saw the amorous shepherd there.
    She gazed around upon the place,
    And saw the grove (resembling night)
    To all the joys of love invite,
Whilst guilty smiles and blushes dressed her face.
At this the bashful youth all transport grew,
And with kind force he taught the virgin how
To yield what all his sighs could never do.

Angellica throws open the curtains, and bows to Antonio, who pulls off
his vizard and bows and blows up kisses. Pedro unseen, looks in his face.
The curtains closes.

ANTONIO   By heaven, she's charming fair!
PEDRO   'Tis he, the false Antonio!
ANTONIO *(to the bravo)* Friend, where must I pay my offering of love?
    My thousand crowns I mean.
PEDRO   That offering I have designed to make, and yours
    will come too late.
ANTONIO   Prithee, begone: I shall grow angry else, and then
    thou art not safe.
PEDRO   My anger may be fatal, sir, as yours, and he that
    enters here may prove this truth.
ANTONIO   I know not who thou art, but I am sure thou'rt
    worth my killing, for aiming at Angellica.

Antonio and Pedro draw and fight. Enter Willmore and Blunt.

BLUNT   'Adsheartlikins, here's fine doings.
WILLMORE   Tilting for the wench, I'm sure – Nay, gad, if that
    would win her, I have as good a sword as the best of ye.
    (Blunt and Willmore draw and part Antonio and Pedro.)
    Put up, put up, and take another time and place, for this is designed for
    lovers only.

They all put up their swords.

PEDRO   We are prevented; dare you meet me tomorrow
    morning on the Molo?
    For I've a title to a better quarrel,
    That of Florinda, in whose credulous heart
    Thou'st made an interest, and destroyed my hopes.
ANTONIO   Dare! I'll meet thee there as early as the day.
PEDRO   We will come thus disguised, that whosoever
    chance to get the better, he may escape unknown.
ANTONIO   It shall be so.

Pedro and Stephano exit.

ANTONIO   Who should this rival be? Unless the English
    colonel, of whom I've often heard Don Pedro speak: it must be he, and
    time he were removed, who lays a claim to all my happiness.

Willmore having gazed all this while on the picture, pulls down a little one.

WILLMORE   This posture's loose and negligent; the sight on't
    would beget a warm desire in souls whom impotence and age had
    chilled, this must along with me.
BRAVO   What means this rudeness, sir? Restore the
    picture.
ANTONIO   Ha! Rudeness committed to the fair Angellica!
    Restore the picture, sir.
WILLMORE   Indeed I will not, sir.
ANTONIO   By heaven, but you shall.
WILLMORE   Nay, do not show your sword: if you do, by this
    dear beauty, I will show mine too.
ANTONIO   What right can you pretend to't?
WILLMORE   That of possession, sir, which I will maintain.
    You, perhaps have a thousand crowns to give for the original.
ANTONIO   No matter, sir, you shall restore the picture –

The curtains open; Angellica and Moretta appear above.

ANGELLICA   Oh, Moretta! What's the matter?
ANTONIO   – Or leave your life behind.
WILLMORE   Death! You lie; I will do neither.

Willmore and Antonio fight; the Spaniards join with Antonio, Blunt joins with Willmore, laying on like mad.

ANGELLICA   Hold, I command you, if for me you fight.

They leave off and bow.

WILLMORE *(aside)*   How heavenly fair she is! Ah, plague of her price.
ANGELLICA   You, sir, in buff, you that appear a soldier,
    that first began this insolence –
WILLMORE   'Tis true, I did so, if you call it insolence for a
    man to preserve himself: I saw your charming picture and was
    wounded; quite through my soul each pointed beauty ran; and wanting
    a thousand crowns to procure my remedy, I laid this little picture to my
    bosom, which, if you cannot allow me, I'll resign.
ANGELLICA   No, you can keep the trifle.
ANTONIO   You shall first ask me leave, and *(flourishing his
    sword)* this.

They fight again as before. Enter Belvile and Frederick, who join the English.

ANGELLICA Hold! Will you ruin me? Biskey, Sebastian, part 'em.

The Spaniards are beaten off. The men exit.

MORETTA Oh madam, we're undone! A pox upon that rude fellow, he's set on to ruin us: we shall never see good days, till all these fighting poor rogues are sent to the galleys.

Enter Belvile, Blunt, Frederick, and Willmore with his shirt bloody.

BLUNT 'Adsheartlikins, beat me at this sport, and I'll ne'er wear sword more.

BELVILE *(to Willmore)* The devil's in thee for a mad fellow, thou art always one at an unlucky adventure. Come, let's begone whilst we're safe, and remember these are Spaniards, a sort of people that know how to revenge an affront.

FREDERICK *(to Willmore)* You bleed! I hope you are not wounded.

WILLMORE Not much: a plague on your dons, if they fight no better they'll ne'er recover Flanders. What the devil was't to them that I took down the picture?

BLUNT Took it? 'Adsheartlikins, we'll have the great one too; 'tis ours by conquest. Prithee, help me up, and I'll pull it down.

ANGELLICA *(to Willmore)* Stay, sir, and ere you affront me farther, let me know how you durst commit this outrage. To you I speak sir, for you appear to be a gentleman.

WILLMORE To me madam? *(To his companions, taking leave of them.)* Gentlemen, your servant.

Belvile stays Willmore.

BELVILE Is the devil in thee? Dost know the danger of entering the house of an incensed courtesan?

WILLMORE I thank you for your care, but there are other matters in hand, there are, though we have no great temptation. Death! Let me go.

FREDERICK Yes, to your lodging, if you will; but not in here. Damn these gay harlots; by this hand, I'll have as sound and handsome a whore for a patacoon. Death, man, she'll murder thee.

WILLMORE Oh! Fear me not. Shall I not venture where a beauty calls, a lovely charming beauty? For fear of danger! When, by heaven, there's none so great as to long for her, whilst I want money to purchase her.

FREDERICK Therefore 'tis loss of time, unless you had the thousand crowns to pay.

WILLMORE It may be she may give a favour; at least I shall have the pleasure of saluting her when I enter and when I depart.

BELVILE Pox, she'll as soon lie with thee as kiss thee, and sooner stab than do either. You shall not go.

ANGELLICA Fear not, sir, all I have to wound with is my eyes.

BLUNT Let him go: 'adsheartlikins, I believe the gentlewoman means well.

BELVILE Well, take thy fortune; we'll expect you in the next street. Farewell, fool, farewell.

WILLMORE Bye, colonel.

Willmore goes in.

FREDERICK The rogue's stark mad for a wench.

They exit.

ACT TWO, SCENE 2

A fine Chamber. Enter Willmore, Angellica and Moretta.

ANGELLICA Insolent sir, how durst you pull down my picture?

WILLMORE Rather, how durst you set it up, to tempt poor amorous mortals with so much excellence? Which I find you have but too well consulted by the unmerciful price you set upon't? Is all this heaven of beauty shown to move despair in those that cannot buy? And can you think th'effects of that despair should be less extravagant than I have shown?

ANGELLICA I sent for you to ask my pardon, sir, not to aggravate your crime. I thought I should have seen you at my feet imploring it.

WILLMORE You are deceived. I came to rail at you, and rail such truths too, as shall let you see the vanity of that pride, which taught you how to set such price on sin, for that which is love's due, is meanly bartered for.

ANGELLICA Ha, ha, ha! Alas, good captain, what pity 'tis your edifying doctrine will do no good upon me. – Moretta, fetch the gentleman a glass, and let him survey himself to see what charms he has – *(Aside, in a soft tone)* and guess my business.

MORETTA He knows himself of old: I believe those breeches and he have been acquainted ever since he was beaten at Worcester.

ANGELLICA Nay, do not abuse the poor creature.

MORETTA Good weather-beaten corporal, will you march off? We have no need of your doctrine, though you have of our charity: but at present we have no scraps, we can afford no kindness for God's sake. In fine, sirrah, the price is too high i' th' mouth for you; therefore troop, I say.

WILLMORE *(offering money to Moretta)* Here, good forewoman of the shop, serve me, and I'll be gone.

MORETTA Keep it to pay your laundress (your linen stinks of the gun room), for here's no selling by retail.

WILLMORE Thou hast sold plenty of thy stale ware at a cheap rate.

MORETTA Ay, the more silly kind heart I, but this is an age wherein beauty is at higher rates. In fine, you know the price of this.

WILLMORE I grant you 'tis here set down, a thousand crowns a month: pray, how much may come to my share for a pistole? Bawd, take your black lead and sum it up, that I may have a pistole's worth of this vain gay thing, and I'll trouble you no more.

MORETTA *(aside)* Pox on him, he'll fret me to death. – Abominable fellow, I tell thee, we only sell by the whole piece.

WILLMORE 'Tis very hard, the whole cargo or nothing. *(To Angellica)* Faith, madam, my stock will not reach it. I cannot be your chapman. Yet I have countrymen in town, merchants of love like me: I'll see if they'll put in for a share; we cannot lose much by it, and what we have no use for, we'll sell upon that Friday's mart, at 'Who gives more?' I am studying, madam, how to purchase you, though at present I am unprovided of money.

ANGELLICA *(aside)* Sure this from any other man would anger me; nor shall he know the conquest he has made. *(To Willmore)* Poor angry man, how I despise this railing.

WILLMORE Yes, I am poor but I'm a gentleman,
And one that scorns this baseness which you practise.
Poor as I am, I would not sell myself,
No, not to gain your charming high-prized person.
Though I admire you strangely for your beauty,
Yet I contemn your mind.
And yet I would at any rate enjoy you,
At your own rate, but cannot: see here
The only sum I can command on earth;

I know not where to eat when this is gone.
Yet such a slave I am to love and beauty,
This last reserve I'll sacrifice to enjoy you.
Nay, do not frown, I know you're to be bought,
And would be bought by me, by me,
For a mean trifling sum, if I could pay it down:
Which happy knowledge I will still repeat,
And lay it to my heart; it has a virtue in't,
And soon will cure those wounds your eyes have made.
And yet, there's something so divinely powerful there –
Nay, I will gaze, to let you see my strength.
(holds her, looks on her, and pauses and sighs)
By heaven, bright creature, I would not for the world
Thy fame were half so fair as is thy face.
(turns her away from him)

ANGELLICA *(aside)*   His words go through me to the very soul. *(To Willmore)* If you have nothing else to say to me –

WILLMORE   Yes, you shall hear how infamous you are,
For which I do not hate thee,
But that secures my heart, and all the flames it feels
Are but so many lusts;
I know it by their sudden bold intrusion.
The fire's impatient and betrays; 'tis false:
For had it been the purer flame of love,
I should have pined and languished at your feet,
Ere found the impudence to have discovered it.
I now dare stand your scorn, and your denial.

MORETTA *(aside)*   Sure she's bewitched, that she can stand thus tamely and hear his saucy railing. – Sirrah, will you be gone?

ANGELLICA *(to Moretta)*   How dare you take this liberty? Withdraw. – Pray tell me, sir, are not you guilty of the same mercenary crime? When a lady is proposed to you for a wife, you never ask how fair, discreet, or virtuous she is; but what's her fortune: which if but small, you cry 'she will not do my business', and basely leave her, though she languish for you. Say, is not this as poor?

WILLMORE   It is a barbarous custom, which I will scorn to defend in our sex, and do despise in yours.

ANGELLICA   Thou'rt a brave fellow! Put up thy gold, and know That were thy fortune large as is thy soul,
Thou shoulds't not buy my love, couldst thou forget
Those mean effects of vanity

Which set me out to sale,
And as a lover, prize my yielding joys.
Canst thou believe they'll be entirely thine,
Without considering they were mercenary?

WILLMORE   I cannot tell, I must bethink me first. *(Aside)*
Ha, death, I'm going to believe her.

ANGELLICA   Prithee, confirm that faith; or if thou canst not,
flatter me a little, 'twill please me from thy mouth.

WILLMORE *(aside)*   Curse on thy charming tongue! Dost thou return
My feigned contempt with so much subtlety?
(To Angellica) Thou'st found the easiest way into my heart,
Though I yet know, that all thou say'st is false.

Willmore turns from her in rage.

ANGELLICA   By all that's good, tis real;
I never loved before though oft a mistress.
Shall my first vows be slighted?

WILLMORE *(aside)*   What can she mean?

ANGELLICA *(in an angry tone)* I find you cannot credit me.

WILLMORE   I know you take me for an arrant ass,
An ass that may be soothed into belief,
And then be used at pleasure;
But, madam, I have been so often cheated
By perjured, soft, deluding hypocrites,
That I've no faith left for the cozening sex,
Especially for women of your trade.

ANGELLICA   The low esteem you have of me, perhaps
May bring my heart again:
For I have pride, that yet surmounts my love.

She turns with pride, he holds her.

WILLMORE   Throw off this pride, this enemy to bliss,
And show the power of love: 'tis with those arms
I can be only vanquished, made a slave.

ANGELLICA   Is all my mighty expectation vanished?
No, I will not hear thee talk: thou hast a charm
In every word that draws my heart away;
And all the thousand trophies I designed,
Thou hast undone. Why art thou soft?
Thy looks are bravely rough, and meant for war.
Couldst thou not storm on still?
I then perhaps had been as free as thou.

WILLMORE *(aside)*   Death, how she throws her fire about my soul!
  Take heed, fair creature, how you raise my hopes,
  Which once assumed pretends to all dominion.
  There's not a joy thou hast in store
  I shall not then command;
  For which I'll pay thee back my soul, my life!
  Come, let's begin th'account this happy minute!
ANGELLICA   And will you pay me then the price I ask?
WILLMORE   Oh, why dost thou draw me from an awful worship,
  By showing thou art no divinity?
  Conceal the fiend, and show me all the angel!
  Keep me but ignorant, and I'll be devout
  And pay my vows for ever at this shrine. *(kneels and kisses her hand)*
ANGELLICA   The pay I mean, is but thy love for mine. Can you
  give that?
WILLMORE   Entirely; come let's withdraw, where I'll renew my
  vows, and breathe 'em with such ardour thou shalt not doubt my zeal.
ANGELLICA   Thou hast a power too strong to be resisted.

Willmore and Angellica exit.

MORETTA   Now my curse go with you. Is all our project fallen
  to this: to love the only enemy to our trade? Nay, to love such a
  shameroon; a very beggar, nay, a pirate beggar, whose business is to rifle,
  and be gone; a no-purchase, no-pay tatterdemalion and English picaroon;
  a rogue that fights for daily drink, and takes a pride in being loyally lousy!
  Oh, I could curse now, if I durst. This is the fate of most whores.
  Trophies, which from believing fops we win,
  Are spoils to those who cozen us again.

She exits.

ACT THREE, SCENE 1

*A street. Enter Florinda, Valeria and Hellena, in antic, different dresses,
from what they were in before; and Callis, attending.*

FLORINDA   I wonder what should make my brother in so ill a
  humour? I hope he has not found out our ramble this morning.
HELLENA   No: if he had, we should have heard on't at both
  ears, and have been mewed up this afternoon; which I would not for the
  world should have happened. Hey ho, I'm as sad as a lover's lute.

VALERIA   Well, methinks we have learnt this trade of
gypsies as readily as if we had been bred upon the road to Loretto; and
yet I did so fumble, when I told the stranger his fortune, that I was
afraid I should have told my own and yours by mistake. But, methinks,
Hellena has been very serious ever since.

FLORINDA   I would give my garters she were in love, to be
revenged upon her for abusing me. – How is't, Hellena?

HELLENA   Ah, would I had never seen my mad monsieur!
And yet, for all your laughing, I am not in love; and yet this small
acquaintance, o' my conscience, will never out of my head.

VALERIA   Ha! Ha! Ha! I laugh to think how thou art fitted
with a lover, a fellow, that I warrant loves every new face he sees.

HELLENA   Hum, he has not kept his word with me here, and
may be taken up: that thought is not very pleasant to me. What the
deuce should this be now, that I feel?

VALERIA   What is't like?

HELLENA   Nay, the lord knows; but if I should be hanged, I
cannot choose but be angry and afraid when I think that mad fellow
should be in love with anybody but me. What to think of myself I know
not: would I could meet with some true damned gypsy, that I might
know my fortune.

VALERIA   Know it! Why there's nothing so easy; thou wilt
love this wandering inconstant, till thou find'st thyself hanged about his
neck, and then be as mad to get free again.

FLORINDA   Yes, Valeria, we shall see her bestride his baggage
horse, and follow him to the campaign.

HELLENA   So, so, now you are provided for, there's no care
taken of poor me. But since you have set my heart a-wishing, I am
resolved to know for what; I will not die of the pip, so I will not.

FLORINDA   Art thou mad to talk so? Who will like thee well
enough to have thee, that hears what a mad wench thou art?

HELLENA   Like me! I don't intend every he that likes me
shall have me, but he that I like: I should have stayed in a nunnery still,
if I had liked my lady abbess as well as she liked me. No, I came thence
not, as my wise brother imagines, to take an eternal farewell of the
world, but to love, and to be beloved; and I will be beloved, or I'll get
one of your men, so I will.

VALERIA   Am I put into the number of lovers?

HELLENA   You? Why, coz, I know thou'rt too good-natured
to leave us in any design: thou wouldst venture a cast, though thou
comest off a loser, especially with such a gamester. I observed your

man, and your willing ear incline that way; and if you are not a lover, 'tis an art soon learnt, that I find. *(sighs)*

FLORINDA I wonder how you learned to love so easily. I had a thousand charms to meet my eyes and ears, ere I could yield; and 'twas the knowledge of Belvile's merit, not the surprising person, took my soul. Thou art too rash, to give a heart at first sight.

HELLENA Hang your considering lover! I never thought beyond the fancy that 'twas a very pretty, idle, silly kind of pleasure to pass one's time with: to write little soft nonsensical billets, and with great difficulty and danger receive answers, in which I shall have my beauty praised, my wit admired (though little or none), and have the vanity and power to know I am desirable. Then I have the more inclination that way, because I am to be a nun, and so shall not be suspected to have any such earthly thoughts about me; but when I walk thus, and sigh thus, they'll think my mind's upon my monastery and cry, 'how happy 'tis she's so resolved'; but not a word of man.

FLORINDA What a mad creature's this!

HELLENA I'll warrant, if my brother hears either of you sigh, he cries gravely, 'I fear you have the indiscretion to be in love, but take heed of the honour of our house, and your own unspotted fame', and so he conjures on till he has laid the soft-winged god in your hearts, or broke the bird's nest.

Enter Belvile, Frederick, and Blunt.

HELLENA But see, here comes your lover; but where's my inconstant? Let's step aside, and we may learn something.

Hellena, Florinda, Valeria, and Callis go aside.

BELVILE What means this? The picture's taken in.

BLUNT It may be the wench is good-natured, and will be kind gratis. Your friend's a proper handsome fellow.

BELVILE I rather think she has cut his throat and is fled. I am mad he should throw himself into dangers; pox on't, I shall want him, too, at night. Let's knock and ask for him.

HELLENA My heart goes a-pit-a-pat, for fear 'tis my man they talk of.

The men knock; Moretta appears above.

MORETTA What would you have?

BELVILE Tell the stranger that entered here about two hours ago, that his friends stay here for him.

MORETTA   A curse upon him for Moretta: would he were at the devil; but he's coming to you.

Enter Willmore, from Angellica's house.

HELLENA *(aside)*   Aye, aye, 'tis he! Oh, how this vexes me!
BELVILE   And how and how, dear lad, has fortune smiled? Are we to break her windows, or raise up altars to her, ha?
WILLMORE   Does not my fortune sit triumphant on my brow? Dost not see the little wanton god there all gay and smiling? Have I not an air about my face and eyes, that distinguish me from the crowd of common lovers. By heaven, Cupid's quiver has not half so many darts as her eyes! Oh, such a bona roba! To sleep in her arms is lying in fresco, all perfumed air about me.
HELLENA *(aside)*   Here's fine encouragement for me to fool on.
WILLMORE   Hark'ee, where didst thou purchase that rich canary we drank today? Tell me, that I may adore the spigot, and sacrifice to the butt! The juice was divine, into which I must dip my rosary, and then bless all things that I would have bold or fortunate.
BELVILE   Well, sir, let's go take a bottle, and hear the story of your success.
FREDERICK   Would not French wine do better?
WILLMORE   Damn the hungry balderdash; cheerful sack has a generous virtue in't inspiring a successful confidence, gives eloquence to the tongue and vigour to the soul, and has in a few hours completed all my hopes and wishes! There's nothing left to raise a new desire in me. Come, let's be gay and wanton; and, gentlemen, study, study what you want, for here are friends that will supply gentlemen. *(jingles gold)* Hark! What a charming sound they make: 'tis he and she gold whilst here, and shall beget new pleasures every moment.
BLUNT   But hark'ee, sir, you are not married, are you?
WILLMORE   All the honey of matrimony, but none of the sting, friend.
BLUNT   'Adsheartlikins, thou'rt a fortunate rogue.
WILLMORE   I am so, sir, let these inform you! Ha, how sweetly they chime! Pox of poverty, it makes a man a slave, makes wit and honour sneak; my soul grew lean and rusty for want of credit.
BLUNT   'Adsheartlikins, this I like well, it looks like my lucky bargain! Oh, how I long for the approach of my squire, that is to conduct me to her house again. Why, here's two provided for.
FREDERICK   By this light, y'are happy men.
BLUNT   Fortune is pleased to smile on us, gentlemen, to smile on us.

Enter Sancho and pulls down Blunt by the sleeve. They go aside.

SANCHO   Sir, my lady expects you. She has removed all that might oppose your will and pleasure, and is impatient till you come.
BLUNT   Sir, I'll attend you. *(Aside)* Oh the happiest rogue! I'll take no leave, lest they either dog me or stay me.

Exit Blunt with Sancho.

BELVILE   But then the little gypsy is forgot?
WILLMORE   A mischief on thee for putting her into my thoughts, I had quite forgot her else, and this night's debauch had drunk her quite down.
HELLENA   Had it so, good captain!
(Hellena claps Willmore on the back.)
WILLMORE *(aside)*   Ha! I hope she did not hear me.
HELLENA   What, afraid of such a champion?
WILLMORE   Oh, you're a fine lady of your word, are you not? To make a man languish a whole day –
HELLENA   In tedious search of me.
WILLMORE   Egad, child, thou'rt in the right: hadst thou seen what a melancholy dog I have been since was a lover, how I have walked the streets like a capuchin, with my hands in my sleeves, faith sweetheart, thou wouldst pity me.
HELLENA *(aside)*   Now, if I should be hanged, I can't be angry with him, he dissembles so heartily. *(To Willmore)* Alas, good captain, what pains you have taken: now were I ungrateful not to reward so true a servant.
WILLMORE   Poor soul, that's kindly said, I see thou bearest a conscience. Come then, for a beginning show me thy dear face.
HELLENA   I'm afraid, my small acquaintance, you have been staying that swingeing stomach you boasted of this morning: I then remember my little collation would have gone down with you, without the sauce of a handsome face; is your stomach so queasy now?
WILLMORE   Faith, long fasting, child, spoils a man's appetite. Yet, if you durst treat, I could so lay about me still –
VALERIA   And would you fall to, before a priest says grace?
WILLMORE   Oh fie, fie, what an old out-of-fashioned thing hast thou named? Thou couldst not dash me more out of countenance shouldst thou show me an ugly face.

Whilst he is seemingly courting Hellena, enter Angellica, Moretta, Biskey, and Sebastian, all in masquerade. Angellica sees Willmore and stares.

ANGELLICA   Heavens, 'tis he! And passionately fond to see
another woman!

MORETTA   What could you less expect from such a
swaggerer?

ANGELLICA   Expect? As much as I paid him: a heart entire,
Which I had pride enough to think whene'er I gave,
It would have raised the man above the vulgar,
Made him all soul! And that all soft and constant.

HELLENA   You see, captain, how willing I am to be friends
with you (till time and ill luck make us lovers), and ask you the question
first, rather than put your modesty to the blush, by asking me; for alas,
I know you captains are such strict men, and such severe observers of
your vows to chastity, that 'twill be hard to prevail with your tender
conscience to marry a young willing maid.

WILLMORE   Do not abuse me, for fear I should take thee at
thy word and marry thee indeed, which I'm sure will be revenge
sufficient.

HELLENA   O' my conscience, that will be our destiny,
because we are both of one humour: I am as inconstant as you, for I
have considered, captain, that a handsome woman has a great deal to
do whilst her face is good, for then is our harvest-time to gather friends;
and should I in these days of my youth, catch a fit of foolish constancy, I
were undone; 'tis loitering by daylight in our great journey. Therefore, I
declare, I'll allow but one year for love, one year for indifference, and
one year for hate; and then, go hang yourself: for I profess myself the
gay, the kind, and the inconstant. The devil's in't if this won't please
you.

WILLMORE   Oh, most damnably. I have a heart with a hole
quite through it too, no prison mine to keep a mistress in.

ANGELLICA *(aside)*   Perjured man! How I believe thee now!

HELLENA   Well, I see our business as well as humours are
alike: yours to cozen as many maids as will trust you, and I as many
men as have faith. See if I have not as desperate a lying look, as you can
have for the heart of you. *(Hellena pulls off her vizard: Willmore
starts.)* How do you like it, captain?

WILLMORE   Like it! By heaven, I never saw so much beauty!
Oh, the charms of those sprightly black eyes, that strangely fair face, full
of smiles and dimples, those soft round melting cherry lips and small
even white teeth! Not to be expressed, but silently adored! *(Hellena
replaces her vizard)* Oh, one look more, and strike me dumb, or I shall
repeat nothing else till I'm mad.

He seems to court her to pull off her vizard: she refuses.

ANGELLICA I can endure no more; nor is it fit to interrupt him, for if I do, my jealousy has so destroyed my reason, I shall undo him; therefore I'll retire – *(To one of her bravos)* and you, Sebastian, follow that woman and learn who 'tis – *(To the other bravo)* while you tell the fugitive I would speak to him instantly.

Exit Angellica. During this time Florinda is talking to Belvile, who stands sullenly. Frederick is courting Valeria.

VALERIA Prithee, dear stranger, be not so sullen, for though you have lost your love, you see my friend frankly offers you hers to play with in the meantime.

BELVILE Faith, madam, I am sorry I can't play at her game.

FREDERICK *(to Valeria)* Pray leave your intercession and mind your own affair, they'll better agree apart: he's a modest sigher in company, but alone no woman 'scapes him.

FLORINDA *(aside)* Sure, he does but rally; yet, if it should be true – I'll tempt him farther. *(To Belvile)* Believe me, noble stranger, I'm no common mistress, and for a little proof on't, wear this jewel. Nay, take it, sir, 'tis right, and bills of exchange may sometimes miscarry.

BELVILE Madam, why am I chose out of all mankind to be the object of your bounty?

VALERIA There's another civil question asked.

FREDERICK *(aside)* Pox of's modesty; it spoils his own markets and hinders mine.

FLORINDA Sir, from my window I have often seen you, and women of my quality have so few opportunities for love, that we ought to lose none.

FREDERICK Aye, this is something! Here's a woman! *(To Valeria)* When shall I be blessed with so much kindness from your fair mouth? *(Aside to Belvile)* Take the jewel, fool.

BELVILE You tempt me strangely, madam, every way –

FLORINDA *(aside)* So, if I find him false, my whole repose is gone.

BELVILE And but for a vow I've made to a very fair lady, this goodness had subdued me.

FREDERICK *(aside to Belvile)* Pox on't, be kind, in pity to me be kind. For I am to thrive here but as you treat her friend.

HELLENA Tell me what you did in yonder house, and I'll unmask.

WILLMORE Yonder house? Oh – I went to – a –to –why, there's a friend of mine lives there.

HELLENA   What, a she or a he friend?
WILLMORE   A man, upon honour! A man. A she friend? No,
no, madam, you have done my business, I thank you.
HELLENA   And was't your man friend, that had more darts
in's eyes, than Cupid carries in's whole budget of arrows?
WILLMORE   So –
HELLENA   'Ah, such a bona roba! To be in her arms is lying
in fresco, all perfumed air about me.' Was this your man friend too?
WILLMORE   So –
HELLENA   That gave you 'the he and the she gold, that
begets young pleasures'?
WILLMORE   Well, well, madam, then you see there are ladies
in the world that will not be cruel; there are, madam, there are.
HELLENA   And there be men too, as fine, wild, inconstant
fellows as yourself; there be, captain, there be, if you go to that now:
therefore I'm resolved.
WILLMORE   Oh!
HELLENA   – To see your face no more –
WILLMORE   Oh!
HELLENA   – Till tomorrow.
WILLMORE   Egad, you frighted me.
HELLENA   Nor then neither, unless you'll swear never to see
that lady more.
WILLMORE   See her! Why, never to think of womankind
again.
HELLENA   Kneel, and swear.

Willmore kneels; Hellena gives him her hand.

WILLMORE   I do, never to think, to see, to love, nor lie – with
any but thyself.
HELLENA   Kiss the book.
WILLMORE *(kisses her hand)* Oh, most religiously.
HELLENA *(aside)*   Now, what a wicked creature am I, to damn a
proper fellow.
CALLIS *(to Florinda)* Madam, I'll stay no longer. 'Tis e'en dark.
FLORINDA *(to Belvile)* However, I'll leave this with you, that when I'm
gone, you may repent the opportunity you have lost by your modesty .

*Florinda gives Belvile the jewel, which is her picture, and exits. He gazes
after her.*

WILLMORE   'Twill be an age till tomorrow, and till then I will most impatiently expect you. Adieu, my dear pretty angel.

All the women exit.

BELVILE   Ha! Florinda's picture: 'twas she herself. What a dull dog was I! I would have given the world for one minute's discourse with her.

FREDERICK   This comes of your modesty! Ah, pox o' your vow, 'twas ten to one but we had lost the jewel by't.

BELVILE   Willmore, the blessed'st opportunity lost! Florinda, friends, Florinda!

WILLMORE   Ah, rogue! Such black eyes, such a face, such a mouth, such teeth – and so much wit!

BELVILE   All, all, and a thousand charms besides.

WILLMORE   Why, dost thou know her?

BELVILLE   Know her! Ay, ay, and a pox take me with all my heart for being modest.

WILLMORE   But hark'ee, friend of mine, are you my rival? And have I been only beating the bush all this while?

BELVILE   I understand thee not. I'm mad, see here –

He shows the picture.

WILLMORE   Ha! Whose picture's this? 'Tis a fine wench!

FREDERICK   The colonel's mistress, sir.

WILLMORE   Oh, oh – here. *(gives the picture back)* I thought it had been another prize. Come, come, a bottle will set thee right again.

BELVILE   I am confident to try, and by that time 'twill be late enough for our design.

WILLMORE   Agreed.
    Love does all day the soul's great empire keep,
    But wine at night lulls the soft god asleep.

They exit.

ACT THREE, SCENE 2

Lucetta's house. Enter Blunt and Lucetta with a light.

LUCETTA   Now we are safe and free: no fears of the coming home of my old jealous husband, which made me a little thoughtful when you came in first, but now love is all the business of my soul.

BLUNT   I am transported! *(Aside)* Pox on't, that I had but
some fine things to say to her, such as lovers use. I was a fool not to
learn of Fred a little by heart before I came. Something I must say. *(To
Lucetta)* 'Adsheartlikins, sweet soul! I am not used to compliment, but
I'm an honest gentleman, and thy humble servant.

LUCETTA   I have nothing to pay for so great a favour, but
such a love as cannot but be great, since at first sight of that sweet face
and shape, it made me your absolute captive.

BLUNT *(aside)*   Kind heart, how prettily she talks! Egad, I'll show
her husband a Spanish trick: send him out of the world, and marry her;
she's damnably in love with me, and will ne'er mind settlements, and so
there's that saved.

LUCETTA   Well, sir, I'll go and undress me, and be with you
instantly.

BLUNT   Make haste then, for 'adsheartlikins, dear soul,
thou canst not guess at the pain of a longing lover, when his joys are
drawn within the compass of a few minutes.

LUCETTA   You speak my sense, and I'll make haste to prove
it. *(She exits.)*

BLUNT   'Tis a rare girl, and this one night's enjoyment
with her, will be worth all the days I ever passed in Essex. Would she
would go with me into England; though to say truth, there's plenty of
whores already. But a pox on 'em, they are such mercenary prodigal
whores, that they want such a one as this, that's free and generous, to
give 'em good examples. Why, what a house she has, how rich and fine!

Enter Sancho.

SANCHO   Sir, my lady has sent me to conduct you to her
chamber.

BLUNT   Sir, I shall be proud to follow. *(Exit Sancho.)*
Here's one of her servants too! 'Adsheartlikins, by this garb and gravity,
he might be a justice of peace in Essex, and is but a pimp here.

He exits.

ACT THREE, SCENE 3

The scene changes to a chamber with an alcove bed in it, a table, etc.
Lucetta in bed. Enter Sancho and Blunt, who takes the candle of Sancho
at the door.

SANCHO   Sir, my commission reaches no farther.
BLUNT   Sir, I'll excuse your compliment. *(Exit Sancho.)*
  – What, in bed, my sweet mistress?
LUCETTA   You see, I still out-do you in kindness.
BLUNT   And thou shall see what haste I'll make to quit
  scores. *(Aside)* Oh, the luckiest rogue! *(undresses himself)*
LUCETTA   Should you be false or cruel now?
BLUNT   False! 'Adsheartlikins, what dost thou take me
  for? A Jew? An insensible heathen? A pox of thy old jealous husband;
  an he were dead, egad, sweet soul, it should be none of my fault, if I did
  not marry thee.
LUCETTA   It never should be mine.
BLUNT   Good soul! I'm the fortunatest dog!
LUCETTA   Are you not undressed yet?
BLUNT   As much as my patience will permit.
  (goes towards the bed in his shirt, drawers, etc.)
LUCETTA   Hold, sir, put out the light, it may betray us else.
BLUNT   Anything; I need no other light, but that of thine
  eyes! *(Aside)* 'Adsheartlikins, there I think I had it.
  (puts out the candle; the bed descends by means of a trap; he gropes
  about to find it) Why – why – where am I got? What, not yet? Where are
  you, sweetest? – Ah, the rogue's silent now, a pretty love-trick this: how
  she'll laugh at me anon! – You need not, my dear rogue, you need not!
  I'm all on fire already. Come, come, now call me in pity. – Sure I'm
  enchanted! I have been round the chamber, and can find neither woman,
  nor bed. I locked the door, I'm sure she cannot go that way; or if she
  could, the bed could not. – Enough, enough, my pretty wanton, do not
  carry the jest too far. – Ha, betrayed! Dogs! Rogues! Pimps! Help! help!

Blunt lights on a trap, and is let down. Enter Lucetta, Philippo, and
Sancho with a light.

PHILIPPO   Ha, ha, ha, he's dispatched finely.
LUCETTA   Now, sir, had I been coy, we had missed of this
  booty.
PHILIPPO   Nay, when I saw 'twas a substantial fool, I was
  mollified; but when you dote upon a serenading coxcomb, upon a face,
  fine clothes, and a lute, it makes me rage.

LUCETTA   You know I was never guilty of that folly, my dear
Philippo, but with yourself. But come, let's see what we have got by this.
PHILIPPO   A rich coat! Sword and hat; these breeches, too,
are well-lined! See here, a gold watch! A purse-ha! Gold! At least two
hundred pistoles! A bunch of diamond rings, and one with the family
arms! A gold box, with a medal of his king, and his lady mother's
picture! These are sacred relics, believe me! See, the waistband of his
breeches have a mine of gold: old Queen Bess's; we have a quarrel to
her ever since eighty-eight, and may therefore justify the theft, the
Inquisition might have committed it.
LUCETTA   See, a bracelet of bowed gold! These his sisters
tide about his arm at parting. But well, for all this, I fear his being a
stranger may make a noise and hinder our trade with them hereafter.
PHILLIPO   That's our security; he is not only a stranger to
us, but to the country too. The common shore into which he is
descended, thou know'st, conducts him into another street, which this
light will hinder him from ever finding again. He knows neither your
name, nor that of the street where your house is; nay, nor the way to his
own lodgings.
LUCETTA   And art thou not an unmerciful rogue, not to
afford him one night for all this? I should not have been such a Jew.
PHILLIPO   Blame me not, Lucetta, to keep as much of thee
as I can to myself. Come, that thought makes me wanton: let's to bed! –
Sancho, lock up these.
This is the fleece which fools do bear,
Designed for witty men to shear.

They exit.

ACT THREE, SCENE 4

*The scene changes, and discovers Blunt, creeping out of a common-shore,
his face, etc., all dirty.*

BLUNT *(climbing up)* Oh, Lord, I am got out at last, and which is a
miracle, without a clue; and now to damning and cursing! But if that
would ease me, where shall I begin? With my fortune, myself, or the
quean that cozened me? What a dog was I to believe in woman! Oh
coxcomb! Ignorant conceited coxcomb! To fancy she could be enamoured with my person, at first sight enamoured! Oh, I'm a cursed
puppy! 'Tis plain, fool was writ upon my forehead! She perceived it;
saw the Essex calf there; for what allurements could there be in this
countenance, which I can endure because I'm acquainted with it?

Oh, dull silly dog, to be thus soothed into a cozening! Had I been drunk,
I might fondly have credited the young quean, but as I was in my right
wits, to be thus cheated confirms it: I am a dull believing English
country fop. But my comrades! Death and the devil, there's the worst of
all; then a ballad will be sung tomorrow on the Prado, to a lousy tune, of
the enchanted 'squire, and the annihilated damsel; but Fred, that rogue,
and the colonel, will abuse me beyond all Christian patience. Had she
left me my clothes, I have a bill of exchange at home, would have saved
my credit, but now all hope is taken from me. Well, I'll home, if I can
find the way, with this consolation, that I am not the first kind believing
coxcomb; but there are, gallants, many such good natures amongst ye.
And though you've better arts to hide your follies,
'Adsheartlikins, y'are all as arrant cullies.

He exits.

ACT THREE, SCENE 5

*The garden in the night. Enter Florinda in an undress, with a key and a
little box.*

FLORINDA   Well, thus far I'm in my way to happiness: I have
got myself free from Callis; my brother too, I find by yonder light, is got
into his cabinet, and thinks not of me; I have by good fortune got the
key of the garden back-door. I'll open it to prevent Belvile's knocking; a
little noise will now alarm my brother. Now am I as fearful as a young
thief. *(unlocks the door)* Hark, what noise is that? Oh, 'twas the wind
that played amongst the boughs. Belvile stays long, methinks; it's time.
Stay, for fear of a surprise I'll hide these jewels in yonder jessamine.

Florinda goes to lay down the box. Enter Willmore, drunk.

WILLMORE   What the devil is become of these fellows Belvile,
and Frederick? They promised to stay at the next corner for me, but
who the devil knows the corner of a full moon? Now, whereabouts am
I? Ha, what have we here, a garden! A very convenient place to sleep in.
Ha, what has God sent us here? A female! By this light, a woman! I'm a
dog if it be not a very wench!

FLORINDA *(aside)*   He's come! – Ha! Who's there?

WILLMORE   Sweet soul, let me salute thy shoe-string.

FLORINDA *(aside)*   'Tis not my Belvile. Good heavens! I know him
not.– Who are you, and from whence come you?

WILLMORE   Prithee, prithee, child, not so many hard
questions! Let it suffice I am here, child. Come, come kiss me.
FLORINDA   Good gods! What luck is mine!
WILLMORE   Only good luck child, parlous good luck. Come
hither. *(Aside)* 'Tis a delicate shining wench; by this hand, she's
perfumed, and smells like any nosegay. – Prithee, dear soul, let's not
play the fool and lose time, precious time; for as Gad shall save me, I'm
as honest a fellow as breathes, though I'm a little disguised at present.
Come, I say; why, thou mayst be free with me, I'll be very secret. I'll not
boast who 'twas obliged me, not I: for hang me if I know thy name.
FLORINDA   Heavens! What a filthy beast is this!
WILLMORE   I am so, and thou ought'st the sooner to lie with
me for that reason: for look you, child, there will be no sin in't, because
'twas neither designed not premeditated; 'tis pure accident on both
sides, that's a certain thing now. Indeed, should I make love to you, and
vow you fidelity, and swear and lie till you believed and yielded, that
were to make it wilful fornication, the crying sin of the nation. Thou art
therefore, as thou art a good Christian, obliged in conscience to deny
me nothing. Now, come, be kind without any more idle prating.
FLORINDA   Oh, I am ruined! – Wicked man, unhand me!
WILLMORE   Wicked? Egad, child, a judge, were he young and
vigorous, and saw those eyes of thine, would know i'twas they gave the
first blow, the first provocation. Come, prithee let's lose no time, I say;
this is a fine convenient place.
FLORINDA   Sir, let me go, I'll conjure you, or I'll call out.
WILMORE   Aye, aye, you were best to call witness to see how
finely you treat me, do.
FLORINDA   I'll cry murder, rape, or anything, if you do not
instantly let me go.
WILLMORE   A rape! Come, come, you lie, you baggage, you
lie: what I'll warrant you would fain have the world believe now that
you are so forward as I. No, not you! Why, at this time of night, was
your cobweb door set open, dear spider, but to catch flies? Ha, come, or
I shall be damnably angry. Why, what a coil is here!
FLORINDA   Sir, can you think –
WILLMORE   That you would do't for nothing? Oh, oh, I find
what you would be at. Look here, here's a pistole for you. Here's a work
indeed! Here, take it I say.
FLORINDA   For heaven's sake, sir, as you're a gentleman –
WILLMORE   So – now, now – she would be wheedling me for
more. What, you will not take it then, you are resolved you will not?

Come, come, take it or I'll put it up again, for look ye, I never give more. Why how now mistress, are you so high i'th mouth a pistole won't down with you? Ha, why, what a work's here! In good time! Come, no struggling to be gone; but an y'are good at a dumb wrestle, I'm for ye, look ye, I'm for ye.

Florinda struggles with Willmore. Enter Belvile and Frederick.

BELVILE The door is open. A pox of this mad fellow, I'm angry that we've lost him; I durst have sworn he had followed us.

FREDERICK But you were so hasty, colonel, to be gone.

FLORINDA Help, help! Murder! Help! Oh, I am ruined!

BELVILE Ha! Sure that's Florinda's voice!
(Belvile comes up to Florinda and Wilmore.)
A man! – Villain, let go that lady!

A noise (offstage). Willmore turns and draws, Frederick interposes.

FLORINDA *(aside)* Belvile! Heavens! My brother too is coming, and 'twill be impossible to escape. – Belvile, I conjure you to walk under my chamber window, from whence I'll give you some instructions what to do. This rude man has undone us.

Exit Florinda.

WILLMORE Belvile!

Enter Pedro, Stephano and other servants, with lights.

PEDRO I'm betrayed! Run, Stephano, and see if Florinda be safe.

Exit Stephano. The two groups of men fight, and Pedro's party beats Willmore's party out.

PEDRO So, whoe'er they be, all is not well. I'll to Florinda's chamber. *(going out, he meets Stephano re-entering)*

STEPHANO You need not, sir; the poor lady's fast asleep, and thinks no harm. I would not awake her, sir, for fear of frighting her with your danger.

PEDRO I'm glad she's here. – Rascals, how came the garden door open?

STEPHANO That question comes too late, sir. Some of my fellow servants masquerading, I'll warrant.

PEDRO Masquerading! A lewd custom to debauch our youth! *(Aside)* There's something more in this than I imagine.

They exit.

ACT THREE, SCENE 6

The street. Enter Belvile in rage, Frederick holding him, and Willmore melancholy.

WILLMORE   Why, how the devil should I know Florinda?
BELVILE   Ah, plague of your ignorance! If it had not been
Florinda, must you be a beast, a brute, a senseless swine?
WILLMORE   Well, sir, you see I am endued with patience; I
can bear; though egad, y'are very free with me, methinks. I was in good
hopes the quarrel would have been on my side, for so uncivilly
interrupting me.
BELVILE   Peace, brute, whilst thou'rt safe. Oh, I'm
distracted.
WILLMORE   Nay, nay, I'm an unlucky dog, that's certain.
BELVILE   Ah, curse upon the star that ruled my birth, or
whatsoever other influence that makes me still so wretched!
WILLMORE   Thou break'st my heart with these complaints;
there is no star in fault, no influence but sack, the cursed sack I drunk.
FREDERICK   Why, how the devil came you so drunk?
WILLMORE   Why, how the devil came you so sober?
FREDERICK   Prithee, dear colonel, forgive him, he's sorry for
his fault.
BELVILE   He's always so after he has done a mischief. A
plague on all such brutes!
WILLMORE   By this light, I took her for an arrant harlot.
BELVILE   Damn your debauched opinion! Tell me, sot,
hadst thou so much sense and light about thee to distinguish her
woman, and couldst not see something about her face and person, to
strike an awful reverence into thy soul?
WILLMORE   Faith no, I considered her as mere a woman as I
could wish.
BELVILE   'Sdeath, I have no patience. – Draw, or I'll kill
you.
WILLMORE   Let that alone till tomorrow, and if I set not all
right again, use your pleasure.
BELVILE   Tomorrow! Damn it,
The spiteful light will lead me to no happiness.
Tomorrow is Antonio's, and perhaps
Guides him to my undoing: oh, that I could meet
This rival, this powerful fortunate!
WILLMORE   What then?

BELVILE	Let thy own reason, or my rage, instruct thee.
WILLMORE	I shall be finely informed then, no doubt. Hear me, colonel, hear me: show me the man and I'll do his business.
BELVILE	I know him no more than thou, or if I did I should not need thy aid.
WILLMORE	This you say is Angellica's house; I promised the kind baggage to lie with her tonight.

Willmore offers to go in. Enter Antonio and his page. Antonio knocks on Angellica's door with the hilt of his sword.

ANTONIO	You paid the thousand crowns I directed?
PAGE	To the lady's old woman, sir, I did.
WILLMORE	Who the devil have we here?
BELVILE	I'll now plant myself under Florinda's window, and if I find no comfort there, I'll die.

Belvile and Frederick exit. Enter Moretta.

MORETTA	Page!
PAGE	Here's my lord.
WILLMORE	How is this? A picaroon going to board my frigate? – Here's one chase gun for you!

Drawing his sword, Willmore jostles Antonio who turns and draws. Willmore and Antonio fight. Antonio falls.

MORETTA	Oh bless us, we're all undone!

She runs in and shuts the door.

PAGE	Help! Murder!

Belvile returns at the noise of fighting.

FREDERICK	Ha, the mad rogue's engaged in some unlucky adventure again.

Enter two or three masqueraders.

MASQUERADER	Ha, a man killed!
WILLMORE	How, a man killed? Then I'll go home to sleep.

Willmore puts up his sword and reels out. The masqueraders exit another way.

BELVILE	Who should it be? Pray heaven the rogue is safe, for all my quarrel to him.

As Belvile is groping about, enter an officer and six soldiers.

SOLDIER	Who's there?
OFFICER	So, here's one dispatched. Secure the murderer.
BELVILE	Do not mistake my charity for murder! I came to his assistance.

Soldiers seize on Belvile.

OFFICER	That shall be tried, sir. St Jago, swords drawn in the carnival time!

Officer goes to Antonio.

ANTONIO	Thy hand, prithee.
OFFFICER	Ha, Don Antonio! *(To soldiers)* Look well to the villain there. *(To Antonio)* How is it, sir?
ANTONIO	I'm hurt.
BELVILE	Has my humanity made me a criminal?
OFFICER	Away with him.
BELVILE	What a cursed chance is this!

The soldiers exit with Belvile.

ANTONIO *(aside)*   This is the man that has set upon me twice. *(To the officer)* Carry him to my apartment, till you have farther orders from me.

Antonio exits, following.

ACT FOUR, SCENE 1

A fine room. Belvile in the dark, alone.

BELVILE   When shall I be weary of railing on fortune, who is resolved never to turn with smiles upon me? Two such defeats in one night none but the devil, and that mad rogue, could have contrived to have plague me with. I am here a prisoner, but where, heaven knows; and if there be murder done, I can soon decide the fate of a stranger in a nation without mercy; yet this is nothing to the torture my soul bows with, when I think of losing my fair, my dear Florinda. Hark, my door opens: a light; a man, and seems of quality; armed, too! Now shall I die like a dog, without defence.

Enter Antonio in a night-gown, with a light; his arm in a scarf, and a sword under his arm. He sets the candle on the table.

ANTONIO Sir, I come to know what injuries I have done you, that could provoke you to so mean an action as to attack me basely, without allowing time for my defence?

BELVILE Sir, for a man in my circumstances to plead innocence, would look like fear: but view me well, and you will find no marks of coward on me, nor anything that betrays that brutality you accuse me with.

ANTONIO In vain, sir, you impose upon my sense. You are not only he who drew on me last night, but yesterday before the same house, that of Angellica.
Yet there is something in your face and mien
That makes me wish I were mistaken.

BELVILE I own I fought today, in the defence of a friend of mine, with whom you (if you're the same) and your party were first engaged. Perhaps you think this crime enough to kill me,
But if you do, I cannot fear you'll do it basely.

ANTONIO No sir, I'll make you fit for a defence with this.

Antonio gives Belvile the sword.

BELVILE This gallantry surprises me; nor know I how to use this present, sir, against a man so brave.

ANTONIO You shall not need; for know, I come to snatch you from a danger that is decreed against you: perhaps your life, or long imprisonment; and 'twas with so much courage you offended, I cannot see you punished.

BELVILE How shall I pay this generosity?

ANTONIO It had been safer to have killed another, than have attempted me. To show your danger, sir, I'll let you know my quality: and 'tis the viceroy's son, whom you have wounded.

BELVILE The viceroy's son!
(Aside) Death and confusion! Was this plague reserved
To complete all the rest? Obliged by him!
The man of all the world I would destroy.

ANTONIO You seem disordered, sir.

BELVILE Yes, trust me, sir, I am, and 'tis with pain
That man receives such bounties,
Who wants the power to pay 'em back again.

ANTONIO To gallant spirits 'tis indeed uneasy;
But you may quickly overpay me, sir.

BELVILE Then I am well. *(Aside)* Kind heaven! But set us even,
That I may fight with him and keep my honour safe.

– Oh, I'm impatient, sir, to be discounting
The mighty debt I owe you. Command me quickly.
ANTONIO   I have a quarrel with a rival, sir,
About the maid we love.
BELVILE *(aside)*   Death, 'tis Florinda he means.
That thought destroys my reason,
And I shall kill him.
ANTONIO   My rival, sir,
Is one has all the virtues man can boast of –
BELVILE *(aside)*   Death, who should this be?
ANTONIO   He challenged me to meet him on the Molo
As soon as day appeared, but last night's quarrel
Has made my arm unfit to guide a sword.
BELVILE   I apprehend you, sir; you'd have me kill the man
that lays a claim to the maid you speak of. I'll do't. I'll fly to do't!
ANTONIO   Sir, do you know her?
BELVILE   No, sir, but 'tis enough she is admired by you.
ANTONIO   Sir, I shall rob you of the glory on't,
For you must fight under my name and dress.
BELVILE   That opinion must be strangely obliging that
makes you think I can personate the brave Antonio, whom I can but
strive to imitate.
ANTONIO   You say too much to my advantage. Come, sir,
the day appears that calls you forth. Within, sir, is the habit.

Exit Antonio.

BELVILE   Fantastic fortune, thou deceitful light,
That cheats the wearied traveller by night,
Though on a precipice each step you tread,
I am resolved to follow where you lead. *(He exits.)*

ACT FOUR, SCENE 2

The Molo. Enter Florinda and Callis in masks, with Stephano.

FLORINDA *(aside)*   I'm dying with my fears; Belvile's not coming as I
expected under my window, makes me believe that all those fears are
true. *(To Stephano)* Canst thou not tell with whom my brother fights?
STEPHANO   No, madam, they were both in masquerade. I was
by when they challenged one another, and they had decided the quarrel
then, but were prevented by some cavaliers, which made 'em put it off
till now; but I am sure 'tis about you they fight.

FLORINDA *(aside)*   Nay, then, 'tis with Belvile, for what other lover
have I that dares fight for me? (Except Antonio, and he is too much in
favour with my brother.) If it be he, for whom shall I direct my prayers
to heaven?

STEPHANO   Madam, I must leave you, for if my master sees
me, I shall be hanged for being your conductor. I escaped narrowly for
the excuse I made for you last night i' th'garden.

FLORINDA   And I'll reward thee for it; prithee, no more.

Exit Stephano. Enter Don Pedro in his masking habit.

PEDRO   Antonio's late today; the place will fill, and we
may be prevented.

Pedro walks about.

FLORINDA *(aside)*   Antonio? Sure, I heard amiss.

PEDRO   But who will not excuse a happy lover,
When soft fair arms confine the yielding neck
And the kind whisper languishingly breathes,
'Must you be gone so soon?'
Sure I had dwelt forever on her bosom.

Enter Belvile dressed in Antonio's clothes.

FLORINDA *(aside)*   'Tis not Belvile; half my fears are vanished.

PEDRO   Antonio!

BELVILE *(aside)*   This must be he. *(To Pedro)* You're early, sir; I do
not use to be outdone this way.

PEDRO   The wretched, sir, are watchful, and 'tis enough
you've the advantage of me in Angellica.

BELVILE *(aside)*   Angellica! Or I've mistook my man, or else
Antonio. Can he forget his interest in Florinda, and fight for a common
prize?

PEDRO   Come, sir, you know our terms.

BELVILE *(aside)*   By heaven, not I. – No talking. I am ready, sir.

Belvile offers to fight. Florinda runs in between the two men.

FLORINDA *(to Belvile)* Oh, hold! Whoe'er you be. I do conjure you to
hold! If you strike here, I die.

PEDRO   Florinda!

BELVILE   Florinda imploring for my rival!

PEDRO   Away, this kindness is unseasonable.

Pedro puts Florinda by. Belvile and Pedro fight; Florinda runs in just as Belvile disarms Pedro.

FLORINDA   Who are you, sir, that dares deny my prayers?
BELVILE   Thy prayers destroy him: if thou wouldst
preserve him.
Do that thou'rt unacquainted with, and curse him.

Florinda holds Belvile.

FLORINDA   By all you hold most dear, by her you love, I do
conjure you, touch him not.
BELVILE   By her I love?
See, I obey, and at your feet resign
The useless trophy of my victory.

Belvile lays his sword at Florinda's feet.

PEDRO   Antonio, you've done enough to prove you love
Florinda.
BELVILE   Love Forinda! Does heaven love adoration,
prayer, or penitence? Love her? Here, sir, your sword again.
(Belvile snatches up the sword and gives it to Pedro.)
Upon this truth I'll fight my life away.
PEDRO   No, you've redeemed my sister and my
friendship.

Pedro gives Florinda to Belvile. Pedro pulls off his vizard to show his face, and puts it on again.

BELVILE   Don Pedro!
PEDRO   Can you resign your claims to other women,
And give your heart enitirely to Florinda?
BELVILE   Entire! As dying saints confessions are!
I can delay my happiness no longer:
This minute let me make Florinda mine!
PEDRO   This minute let it be: no time so proper;
This night my father will arrive from Rome,
And possibly may hinder what we purpose.
FLORINDA   Oh heavens! This minute!

Enter masqueraders, and pass over.

BELVILE *(to Florinda)* Oh, do not ruin me!
PEDRO   The place begins to fill, and that we may not be
observed, do you walk off to St. Peter's church, where I will meet you
and conclude your happiness.

BELVILE   I'll meet you there. *(Aside)* If there be no more
saints' churches in Naples.
FLORINDA   Oh stay, sir, and recall your hasty doom!
Alas, I have not yet prepared my heart
To entertain so strange a guest.
PEDRO   Away; this silly modesty is assumed too late.
BELVILE   Heaven, madam! What do you do?
FLORINDA   Do? Despise the man that lays a tyrant's claim
To what he ought to conquer by submission.
BELVILE   You do not know me; move a little this way.

Belvile draws Florinda aside.

FLORINDA   Yes, you may force me even to the altar,
But not the holy man that offers there
Shall force me to be thine.

Pedro talks to Callis this while.

BELVILE   Oh, do not lose so blest an opportunity!
See, 'tis your Belvile, not Antonio,
Whom your mistaken scorn and anger ruins.

Belvile pulls off his vizard.

FLORINDA   Belvile!
Where was my soul it could not meet thy voice,
And take this knowledge in?

As they are talking, enter Willmore, finely dressed, and Frederick.

WILLMORE   No intelligence! No news of Belvile yet. Well, I
am the most unlucky rascal in nature. Ha, am I deceived, or is it he?
Look, Fred, 'tis he, my dear Belvile!

Willmore runs and embraces Belvile. Belvile's vizard falls out of his hand.

BELVILE   Hell and confusion seize thee!
PEDRO   Ha! Belvile! I beg your pardon, sir.

Pedro takes Florinda from Belvile.

BELVILE   Nay, touch her not. She's mine by conquest, sir,
I won her by my sword.
WILLMORE   Didst thou so? And egad, child, we'll keep her by
the sword.

Willmore draws on Pedro. Belvile goes between Willmore and Pedro.

BELVILE   Stand off!
Thou'rt so profanely lewd, so cursed by heaven,
All quarrels thou espousest must be fatal.
WILLMORE   Nay, an you be so hot, my valour's coy, and shall
be courted when you want it next. *(puts up his sword)*
BELVILE *(to Pedro)*   You know I ought to claim a victor's right,
But you're the brother to divine Florinda,
To whom I'm such a slave: to purchase her
I durst not hurt the man she holds so dear.
PEDRO   'Twas by Antonio's, not by Belvile's sword
This question should have been decided, sir.
I must confess much to your bravery's due,
Both now, and when I met you last in arms:
But I am nicely punctual in my word,
As men of honour ought, and beg your pardon.
For this mistake another time shall clear.
(Aside to Florinda as they are going out)
This was some plot between you and Belvile,
But I'll prevent you.

*Pedro and Florinda exit. Belvile looks after Florinda and begins to walk
up and down in rage.*

WILLMORE   Do not be modest now and lose the woman, but if
we shall fetch her back, so.
BELVILE   Do not speak to me.
WILLMORE   Not speak to you? Egad, I'll speak to you, and will
be answered too.
BELVILE   Will you, sir?
WILLMORE   I know I've done some mischief, but I'm so dull a
puppy, that I'm the son of a whore if I know how or where. Prithee
inform my understanding.
BELVILE   Leave me, I say, and leave me instantly.
WILLMORE   I will not leave you in this humour, not till I know
my crime.
BELVILE   Death, I'll tell you, sir!

*Belvile draws and runs at Willmore. Frederick interposes. Willmore
begins to run out, Belvile after him. Enter Angellica, Moretta, and
Sebastian.*

ANGELLICA   Ha! Sebastian, is not that Willmore? Haste, haste
and bring him back.

Willmore and Belvile exit.

FREDERICK   The colonel's mad, I never saw him thus before.
I'll after 'em lest he do some mischief, for I am sure Willmore will not
draw on him.

Exit Frederick.

ANGELLICA   I am all rage! My first desires defeated!
For one, for aught he knows, that has
No other merit than her quality,
Her being Don Pedro's sister: he loves her!
I know 'tis so. Dull, dull, insensible;
He will not see me now, though oft invited,
And broke his word last night: false perjured man!
He that but yesterday fought for my favours,
And would have made his life a sacrifice
To've gained one night with me,
Must now be hired and courted to my arms.

MORETTA   I told you what would come on't, but Moretta's
an old doting fool. Why did you give him five hundred crowns, but to
set himself out for other lovers? You should have kept him poor, if you
had meant to have had any good from him.

ANGELLICA   Oh, name not such mean trifles; had I given
Him all my youth has earned from sin,
I had not lost a thought, nor sigh upon't.
But I have given him my eternal rest,
My whole repose, my future joys, my heart!
My virgin heart, Moretta! Oh, 'tis gone!

Enter Willmore and Sebastian.

MORETTA   Curse on him, here he comes. How fine she has
made him, too. *(Angellica turns and walks away.)*
WILLMORE   How now, turned shadow?
Fly when I pursue, and follow when I fly?
(sings) 'Stay, gentle shadow of my dove,
And tell me ere I go,
Whether the substance may not prove
A fleeting thing like you.'

As Angellica turns she looks on Willmore.

WILLMORE   There's a soft kind look remaining yet.

ANGELLICA   Well, sir, you may be gay: all happiness, all joys
pursue you still; fortune's your slave, and gives you every hour choice of
new hearts and beauties, till you are cloyed with the repeated bliss,
which others vainly languish for.
But know, false man, that I shall be revenged.

Angellica turns away in rage.

WILLMORE   So, gad, there are of those faint-hearted lovers,
whom such a sharp lesson next their hearts, would make as impotent as
fourscore. Pox o' this whining! My business is to laugh and love; a pox
on't, I hate your sullen lover; a man shall lose as much time to put you
in humour now, as would serve to gain a new woman.

ANGELLICA   I scorn to cool that fire I cannot raise,
Or do the drudgery of your virtuous mistress.

WILLMORE   A virtuous mistress! Death, what a thing thou
hast found out for me! Why, what the devil should I do with a virtuous
woman? A sort of ill-natured creatures, that take a pride to torment a
lover. Virtue is but an infirmity in woman; a disease that renders even
the handsome ungrateful; whilst the ill-favoured, for want of
solicitations and address, only fancy themselves so. I have lain with a
woman of quality, who has all the while been railing at whores.

ANGELLICA   I will not answer for your mistress's virtue,
Though she be young enough to know no guilt;
And I could wish you would persuade my heart
'Twas the two hundred thousand crowns you courted.

WILLMORE   Two hundred thousand crowns! What story's
this, what trick? What woman? Ha!

ANGELLICA   How strange you make it. Have you forgot the
creature you entertained on the Piazza last night?

WILLMORE *(aside)*   Ha! My gipsy worth two hundred thousand
crowns? Oh, how I long to be with her. Pox, I knew she was of quality.

ANGELLICA   False man! I see my ruin in thy face.
How many vows you breathed upon my bosom
Never to be unjust: have you forgot so soon?

WILLMORE   Faith, no. I was just coming to repeat 'em. But
here's a humour, indeed, would make a man a saint. *(Aside)* Would she
would be angry enough to leave me, and command me not to wait on
her.

Enter Hellena, dressed in man's clothes.

HELLENA *(aside)* This must be Angellica, I know it by her
   mumping matron here; aye, aye, 'tis she! My mad captain's with her
   too, for all his swearing. How this unconstant humour makes me love
   him! *(To Moretta)* Pray, good grave gentlewoman, is not this Angellica?
MORETTA   My too young sir, it is. *(Aside)* I hope 'tis one
   from Don Antonio.

Moretta goes to Angellica.

HELLENA   Well something I'll do to vex him for this.
ANGELLICA *(to Moretta)* I will not speak with him; am I in humour to
   receive a lover?
WILLMORE   Not speak with him! Why, I'll begone, and wait
   your idler minutes. Can I show less obedience to the thing I love so
   fondly? *(Willmore offers to go.)*
ANGELLICA   A fine excuse this! Stay.
WILLMORE   And hinder your advantage? Should I repay your
   bounties so ungratefully?
ANGELLICA *(to Hellena)* Come hither, boy – *(To Willmore)* that I may
   let you see
   How much above the advantages you name
   I prize one minute's joy with you.
WILLMORE   Oh, you destroy me with this endearment,
   (Aside, impatient to be gone) Death! How shall I get away? – Madam,
   'twill not be fit I should be seen with you; besides, it will not be
   convenient; and I've a friend – that's dangerously sick.
ANGELLICA   I see you're impatient; yet you shall stay.
WILLMORE *(aside)*   And miss my assignation with my gypsy.

*Willmore walks about impatiently. Moretta brings Hellena, who
addresses herself to Angellica.*

HELLENA   Madam,
   You'll hardly pardon my intrusion
   When you shall know my business,
   And I'm too young to tell my tale with art;
   But there must be a wondrous store of goodness,
   Where so much beauty dwells.
ANGELLICA   A pretty advocate, whoever sent thee. Prithee
   proceed. *(To Willmore, who is stealing off.)* Nay, sir, you shall not go.
WILLMORE *(aside)*   Then I shall lose my dear gipsy forever. Pox on't,
   she stays me out of spite.

HELLENA   I am related to a lady, madam,
   Young, rich, and nobly born, but has the fate
   To be in love with a young English gentleman.
   Strangely she loves him, at first sight she loved him,
   But did adore him when she heard him speak;
   For he, she said, had charms in every word,
   That failed not to surprise, to wound and conquer.
WILLMORE *(aside)*   Ha! Egad, I hope this concerns me.
ANGELLICA   'Tis my false man he means: would he were gone.
   This praise will raise his pride, and ruin me. *(To Willmore)* Well,
   Since you are so impatient to be gone,
   I will release you, sir.
WILLMORE *(aside)*   Nay, then I'm sure 'twas me he spoke of – this
   cannot be the effects of kindness in her.
   – No, madam, I've considered better on't,
   And will not give you cause of jealousy.
ANGELLICA   But sir, I've – business, that –
WILLMORE   This shall not do; I know 'tis but to try me.
ANGELLICA   Well, to your story, boy. *(Aside)* – though 'twill
   undo me.
HELLENA   With this addition to his other beauties,
   He won her unresisting tender heart:
   He vowed, and sighed, and swore he loved her dearly;
   And she believed the cunning flatterer,
   And thought herself the happiest maid alive.
   Today was the appointed time by both
   To consummate their bliss;
   The virgin, altar, and the priest were dressed;
   And whilst she languished for th'expected bridegroom,
   She heard, he paid his broken vows to you.
WILLMORE *(aside)*   So, this is some dear rogue that's in love with me,
   and this way lets me know it; or if it be not me, she means someone
   whose place I may supply.
ANGELLICA   Now I perceive
   The cause of thy impatience to be gone,
   And all the business of this glorious dress.
WILLMORE   Damn the young prater, I know not what he
   means.
HELLENA   Madam,
   In your fair eyes I read too much concern,
   To tell my farther business.

ANGELLICA   Prithee, sweet youth, talk on: thou mayst perhaps
  Raise here a storm that may undo my passion,
  And then I'll grant thee anything.
HELLENA   Madam, 'tis to entreat you (oh unreasonable)
  You would not see this stranger;
  For if you do, she vows you are undone,
  Though nature never made a man so excellent,
  And sure he's been a god, but for inconstancy.
WILLMORE *(aside)*   Ah, rogue, how finely he's instructed!
  'Tis plain: some woman that has seen me *en passant*.
ANGELLICA   Oh, I shall burst with jealousy! Do you know the
  man you speak of?
HELLENA   Yes, madam, he used to be in buff and scarlet.
ANGELLICA *(to Willmore)* Thou, false as hell, what canst thou say to
  this?
WILLMORE   By heaven –
ANGELLICA   Hold, do not damn thyself –
HELLENA   Nor hope to be believed.

Willmore walks about, Angellica and Hellena follow.

ANGELLICA   Oh, perjured man!
  Is't thus you pay my generous passion back?
HELLENA   Why would you, sir, abuse my lady's faith?
ANGELLICA   And use me so inhumanely?
HELLENA   A maid so young, so innocent –
WILLMORE   Ah, young devil.
ANGELLICA   Dost thou know thy life is in my power?
HELLENA   Or think my lady cannot be revenged?
WILLMORE *(aside)*   So, so, the storm comes finely on.
ANGELLICA   Now thou art silent: guilt has struck thee dumb.
  Oh, hadst thou still been so, I'd lived in safety.

Angellica turns away and weeps.

WILLMORE *(aside to Hellena)* Sweetheart, the lady's name and house,
  quickly! I'm impatient to be with her.

*Willmore looks toward Angellica to watch her turning, and as she comes
towards them, he meets her.*

HELLENA *(aside)*   So, now is he for another woman.
WILLMORE   The impudent'st young thing in nature; I cannot
  persuade him out of his error, madam.

ANGELLICA　　　　　I know he's in the right; yet thou'st a tongue
That would persuade him to deny his faith.

In rage, Angellica walks away.

WILLMORE *(said softly to Hellena)* Her name, her name, dear boy.
HELLENA　　　　　Have you forgot it, sir?
WILLMORE *(aside)*　　Oh, I perceive he's not to know I am a stranger to
his lady. *(To Hellena)* Yes, yes, I do know, but – I have forgot the –
(Angellica turns. Willmore addresses her.)
By heaven, such early confidence I never saw.
ANGELLICA　　　　　Did I not charge you with this mistress, sir?
Which you denied, though I beheld your perjury.
This little generosity of thine has rendered back my heart. *(She walks
away.)*
WILLMORE *(aside to Hellena)* So, you have made sweet work here, my
little mischief; look your lady be kind and good-natured now, or I shall
have but a cursed bargain on't.
(Angellica turns toward them. He addresses her.)
The rogue's bred up to mischief; art thou so great a fool to credit him?
ANGELLICA　　　　　Yes, I do, and you in vain impose upon me. –
Come hither, boy, is not this he you spake of?
HELLENA　　　　　I think it is. I cannot swear, but I vow he has just
such another lying lover's look. *(looks in Willmore's face; he gazes on her.)*
WILLMORE *(aside)*　　Ha! Do not I know that face? By heaven, my little
gypsy! What a dull dog was I! Had I but looked that way I'd known her.
Are all my hopes of a new woman banished? *(To Hellena)* Egad, if I do not
fit thee for this, hang me. *(To Angellica)* Madam, I have found out the plot.
HELLENA *(aside)*　　Oh lord, what does he say? Am I discovered now?
WILLMORE　　　　　Do you see this young spark here?
HELLENA *(aside)*　　He'll tell her who I am.
WILLMORE　　　　　Who do you think this is?
HELLENA *(aside)*　　Aye, aye, he does know me.
(To Willmore) Nay, dear captain! I am undone if you discover me.
WILLMORE *(aside to Hellena)* Nay, nay, no cogging; she shall know
what a precious mistress I have.
HELLENA *(aside to Willmore)* Will you be such a devil?
WILLMORE *(aside to Hellena)* Nay, nay, I'll teach you to spoil sport you
will not make. *(To Angellica)* This small ambassador comes not from a
person of quality, as you imagine, and he says; but from a very arrant
gipsy, the talking'st, prating'st, canting'st little animal thou ever saw'st.
ANGELLICA　　　　　What news you tell me: that's the thing I mean.

HELLENA *(aside)*   Would I were well off the place! If ever I go a-captain-hunting again.

WILLMORE   Mean that thing, that gypsy thing? Thou mayst as well be jealous of thy monkey or parrot as of her: a German motion were worth a dozen of her, and a dream were a better enjoyment; a creature of a constitution fitter for heaven than man.

HELLENA *(aside)*   Though I'm sure he lies, yet this vexes me.

ANGELLICA   You are mistaken: she's a Spanish woman Made up of no such dull materials.

WILLMORE   Materials! Egad, an she be made of any that will either dispense or admit of love, I'll be bound to continence.

HELLENA *(aside to Willmore)* Unreasonable man, do you think so?

WILLMORE   You may return, my little brazen head, and tell your lady, that till she be handsome enough to be beloved, or I dull enough to be religious, there will be small hopes of me.

ANGELLICA   Did you not promise, then, to marry her?

WILLMORE   Not I, by heaven.

ANGELLICA   You cannot undeceive my fears and torments, Till you have vowed you will not marry her.

HELLENA *(aside)*   If he swears that, he'll be revenged on me indeed for all my rogueries.

ANGELLICA   I know what arguments you'll bring against me, fortune, and honour.

WILLMORE   Honour? I tell you, I hate it in your sex; and those that fancy themselves possessed of that foppery, are the most impertinently troublesome of all womankind, and will transgress nine commandments to keep one: and to satisfy your jealousy, I swear –

HELLENA *(aside to him)* Oh, no swearing, dear captain.

WILLMORE   If it were possible I should ever be inclined to marry, it should be some kind young sinner; one that has generosity enough to give a favour handsomely to one that can ask it discreetly; one that has wit enough to manage an intrigue of love. Oh, how civil such a wench is, to a man that does her the honour to marry her!

ANGELLICA   By heaven, there's no faith in anything he says.

Enter Sebastian.

SEBASTIAN   Madam, Don Antonio –

ANGELLICA   Come hither.

HELLENA *(aside)*   Ha! Antonio! He may be coming hither, and he'll certainly discover me. I'll therefore retire without a ceremony.

Exit Hellena.

ANGELLICA   I'll see him; get my coach ready.

SEBASTIAN   It waits you, madam.

WILLMORE *(aside)*   This is lucky. *(To Angellica)* What, madam, now I
may be gone, and leave you to the enjoyment of my rival?

ANGELLICA   Dull man, that canst not see how ill, how poor,
That false dissimulation looks: begone,
And never let me see thy cozening face again,
Lest I relapse and kill thee.

WILLMORE   Yes you can spare me now. Farewell, till you're in
better humour. *(Aside)* I'm glad of this release; now for my gipsy?
For though to worse we change, yet still we find
New joys, new charms, in a new miss that's kind.

Exit Willmore.

ANGELLICA   He's gone, and in this ague of my soul
The shivering fit returns:
Oh, with what willing haste he took his leave,
As if the longed-for minute were arrived
Of some blessed assignation.
In vain I have consulted all my charms,
In vain this beauty prized, in vain believed
My eyes could kindle any lasting fires;
I had forgot my name, my infamy,
And the reproach that honour lays on those
That dare pretend a sober passion here.
Nice reputation, though it leave behind
More virtues than inhabit where that dwells,
Yet that once gone, those virtues shine no more.
Then since I am not fit to be beloved,
I am resolved to think on a revenge
On him that soothed me thus to my undoing.

They exit.

ACT FOUR, SCENE 3

*A street. Enter Florinda and Valeria, in habits different from what they
have been seen in.*

FLORINDA   We're happily escaped, and yet I tremble still.

VALERIA   A lover and fear! Why, I am but half an one, and yet
I have courage for any attempt. Would Hellena were here; I would fain
have had her as deep in this mischief as we: she'll fare but ill else, I doubt.

FLORINDA   She pretended a visit to the Augustine nuns, but I believe some other design carried her out; pray heaven we light on her. Prithee, what didst do with Callis?

VALERIA   When I saw no reason would do good on her, I followed her into the wardrobe, and as she was looking for something in a great chest, I toppled her in by the heels, snatched the key of the apartment where you were confined, locked her in, and left her bawling for help.

FLORINDA   'Tis well you resolve to follow my fortunes, for thou darest never appear at home again after such an action.

VALERIA   That's according as the young stranger and I shall agree. But to our business: I delivered your note to Belvile, when I got out under pretence of going to mass. I found him at his lodging, and believe me it came seasonably; for never was man in so desperate a condition. I told him of your resolution of making your escape today, if your brother would be absent long enough to permit you; if not, to die rather than be Antonio's.

FLORINDA   Thou shouldst have told him I was confined to my chamber, upon my brother's suspicion that the business on the Molo was a plot laid between him and I.

VALERIA   I said all this, and told him your brother was now gone to his devotion; and he resolves to visit every church till he find him, and not only undeceive him in that, but caress him so as shall delay his return home.

FLORINDA   O heavens, he's here, and Belvile with him too.

Florinda and Valeria put on their vizards. Enter Don Pedro, Belvile, and Willmore; Belvile and Don Pedro seeming in serious discourse.

VALERIA   Walk boldly by them, and I'll come at distance, lest he suspect us.

Florinda walks by Don Pedro, Belvile and Willmore, and looks back on them.

WILLMORE   Ha! A woman, and of excellent mien!

PEDRO   She throws a kind look back on you.

WILLMORE   Death, 'tis a likely wench, and that kind look shall not be cast away. I'll follow her.

BELVILE   Prithee do not.

WILLMORE   Do not? By heavens, to the antipodes, with such an invitation. *(Florinda goes out, and Willmore follows her.)*

BELVILE   'Tis a mad fellow for a wench.

Exit Valeria, following Willmore and Florinda. Enter Frederick.

FREDERICK	Oh, colonel such news!
BELVILE	Prithee what?
FREDERICK	News that will make you laugh in spite of fortune.
BELVILE	What, Blunt has had some damned trick put

upon him: cheated, banged, or clapped?

FREDERICK   Cheated, sir; rarely cheated of all but his shirt and drawers. The unconsionable whore, too, turned him out before consummation, so that, traversing the streets at midnight, the watch found him in this fresco, and conducted him home. By heaven, 'tis such a sight, and yet I durst as well been hanged as laughed at him, or pity him; he beats all that do but ask him a question, and is in such an humour!

PEDRO   Who is't has met with this ill usage, sir?

BELVILE   A friend of ours, whom you must see for mirth's sake. *(Aside)* I'll employ him to give Florinda time for an escape.

PEDRO   What is he?

BELVILE   A young countryman of ours, one that has been educated at so plentiful a rate, he yet ne'er knew the want of money, and 'twill be a great jest to see how simply he'll look without it; for my part I'll lend him none, an the rogue know not how to put on a borrowing face, and ask first; I'll let him see how good 'tis to play our parts whilst I play his. – Prithee, Fred, do you go home and keep him in that posture till we come.

Exit Frederick, Don Pedro, and Belvile. Enter Florinda from the farther end of the scene, looking behind her.

FLORINDA   I am followed still. Ha, my brother, too, advancing this way: good heavens defend me from being seen by him.

Florinda goes off. Enter Willmore, and after him Valeria, at a little distance.

WILLMORE   Ah! There she sails. She looks back as she were willing to be boarded; I'll warrant her prize.

Willmore goes out, Valeria following. Enter Hellena, just as he goes out, with a page.

HELLENA   Ha, is not that my captain that has a woman in chase? 'Tis not Angellica. – Boy, follow those people at a distance, and bring me an account where they go in.

Exit Page.

HELLENA   I'll find his haunts, and plague him everywhere.
Ha, my brother.

Belvile, Willmore, and Pedro cross the stage. Hellena runs off.

ACT FOUR, SCENE 4

Another street. Enter Florinda.

FLORINDA   What shall I do? I fear my brother now pursues
me; will no kind power protect me from his tyranny? Ha, here's a door
open; I'll venture in, since nothing can be worse than to fall into his
hands; my life and honour are at stake, and my necessity has no choice.

*Florinda goes in. Enter Valeria, and Hellena's page peeping after
Florinda.*

PAGE   Here she went in; I shall remember this house.

Exit Page.

VALERIA   This is Belvile's lodging; she's gone in as readily
as if she knew it. Ha, here's that mad fellow again. I dare not venture in;
I'll watch my opportunity.

Exit Valeria. Enter Willmore, gazing about him.

WILLMORE   I have lost her hereabouts. Pox on't, she must not
'scape me so.

He goes out.

ACT FOUR, SCENE 5

*Scene changes to Blunt's chamber; discovers him sitting on a couch in his
shirt and drawers, reading.*

BLUNT   So, now my mind's a little at peace, since I have
resolved revenge. A pox on this tailor, though, for not bringing home the
clothes I bespoke; and a pox of all poor cavaliers: a man can never keep a
spare suit for 'em, and I shall have these rogues come in and find me
naked, and then I'm undone; but I'm resolved to arm myself; the rascals
shall not insult over me too much. *(puts on an old rusty sword, and buff
belt)* Now, how like a morris dancer I am equipped! A fine ladylike whore
to cheat me thus, without affording me a kindness for my money!

A pox light on her, I shall never be reconciled to the sex more: she has made me as faithless as a physician, as uncharitable as a churchman, and as ill-natured as a poet. Oh, how I'll use all womankind hereafter! What would I give to have one of 'em within my reach now! Any mortal thing in petticoats, kind fortune, send me and I'll forgive thy last night's malice! Here's a cursed book, too, *A Warning to All Young Travellers*, that can instruct me how to prevent such mischiefs now 'tis too late. Well, 'tis a rare convenient thing to read a little now and then, as well as hawk and hunt.

Blunt sits down again and reads. Enter to him Florinda.

FLORINDA   This house is haunted, sure; 'tis well furnished, and no living thing inhabits it. Ha! A man; heavens, how he's attired! Sure 'tis some rope-dancer, or fencing master. I tremble now for fear, and yet I must venture now to speak to him. – Sir, if I may not interrupt your meditations –

BLUNT *(starts up and gazes)* Ha, what's here? Are my wishes granted? And is not that a she creature? 'Adsheartlikins, 'tis – What wretched thing art thou, ha?

FLORINDA   Charitable sir, you've told yourself already what I am: a very wretched maid, forced by a strange unlucky accident, to seek safety here, and must be ruined, if you do not grant it.

BLUNT   Ruined! Is there any ruin so inevitable as that which now threatens thee? Dost thou know, miserable woman, into what den of mischiefs thou art fallen, what abyss of confusion, ha? Dost not see something in my looks that frights thy guilty soul, and makes thee wish to change that shape of woman for any humble animal, or devil? For those were safer for thee, and less mischievous.

FLORINDA   Alas, what mean you, sir? I must confess, your looks have something in 'em makes me fear, but I beseech you, as you seem a gentleman, pity a harmless virgin that takes your house for sanctuary.

BLUNT   Talk on, talk on; and weep, too till my faith return. Do, flatter me out of my senses again. A harmless virgin with a pox! As much one as t'other, 'adsheartlikins. Why, what the devil, can I not be safe in my house for you; not in my chamber? Nay, even being naked, too, cannot secure me: this is an impudence greater than has invaded me yet. Come, no resistance. *(He pulls Florinda rudely.)*

FLORINDA   Dare you be so cruel?

BLUNT   Cruel? 'Adsheartlikins, as a galley-slave, or a Spanish whore. Cruel, yes: I will kiss and beat thee all over; kiss, and see thee all over; thou shalt lie with me too, not that I care for the enjoyment, but to let thee see I have ta'en deliberated malice to thee, and will be revenged on one whore for the sins of another. I will smile and deceive thee, flatter thee, and beat thee, kiss and swear, and lie to thee, embrace thee and rob thee, as she did me; fawn on thee, and strip thee stark naked, then hang thee out at my window by the heels, with a paper of scurvy verses fastened to thy breast, in praise of damnable women. Come, come, along.

FLORINDA   Alas, sir, must I be sacrificed for the crimes of the most infamous of my sex? I never understood the sins you name.

BLUNT   Do, persuade the fool you love him, or that one of you can be just or honest; tell me I was not an easy coxcomb, or any strange impossible tale: it will be believed sooner than thy false showers or protestations. A generation of damned hypocrites! To flatter my very clothes from my back! Dissembling witches! Are these the returns you make an honest gentleman, that trusts, believes, and loves you: But if I be not even with you – come along, or I shall –

Enter Frederick.

FREDERICK   Ha, what's here to do?

BLUNT   'Adsheartlikins, Fred, I am glad thou art come, to be a witness of my dire revenge.

FREDERICK   What's this? A person of quality too, who is upon the ramble to supply the defects of some grave impotent husband?

BLUNT   No, this has another pretence: some very unfortunate accident brought her hither, to save a life pursued by I know not who or why, and be forced to take sanctuary here at fool's haven. 'Adsheartlikins, to me of all mankind , for protection? Is the ass to be cajoled again, think ye? – No, young one, no prayers or tears shall mitigate my rage; therefore prepare for both my pleasures of enjoyment and revenge, for I am resolved to make up my loss here on thy body: I'll take it out in kindness and in beating.

FREDERICK   Now, mistress of mine, what do you think of this?

FLORINDA   I think he will not, dares not be so barbarous.

FREDERICK   Have a care, Blunt, she fetched a deep sigh; she is enamoured with thy shirt and drawers; she'll strip thee even of that. There are of her calling such unconscionable baggages and such dextrous thieves, they'll flay a man and he shall ne'er miss his skin, till he feels the cold. There was a countryman of ours robbed of a row of teeth whilst he was a-sleeping, which the jilt made him buy again when he waked. – You see, lady, how little reason we have to trust you.

BLUNT   'Adsheartlikins, why this is most abominable.

FLORINDA   Some such devils there may be, but by all that's
holy, I am none such; I entered here to save a life in danger.

BLUNT   For no goodness, I'll warrant her.

FREDERICK   Faith, damsel, you had e'en confessed the plain
truth, for we are fellows not to be caught twice in the same trap: look on
that wreck, a tight vessel when he set out of haven, well trimmed and
laden; and see how a female picaroon of this island of rogues has
shattered him; and canst thou hope for any mercy?

BLUNT   No, no, gentlewoman, come along;
'adsheartlikins, we must be better acquainted. – We'll both lie with her,
and then let me alone to bang her.

FREDERICK   I'm ready to serve you in matters of revenge that
has a double pleasure in't.

BLUNT   Well said – You hear, little one, how you are
condemned by public vote to the bed within; there's no resisting your
destiny, sweetheart. *(pulls Florinda)*

FLORINDA   Stay, sir; I have seen you with Belvile, an English
cavalier: for his sake use me kindly; you know him, sir.

BLUNT   Belvile, why yes, sweeting, we do know Belvile,
and wish he were with us now; he's a cormorant at whore and bacon,
he'd have a limb or two of thee, my virgin pullet; but 'tis no matter, we'll
leave him the bones to pick.

FLORINDA   Sir, if you have any esteem for that Belvile, I conjure
you to treat me with more gentleness; he'll thank you for the justice.

FREDERICK   Hark'ee, Blunt, I doubt we are mistaken in this
matter.

FLORINDA   Sir, if you find me not worth Belvile's care, use
me as you please; and that you may think I merit better treatment than
you threaten, pray take this present.

Florinda gives Blunt a ring. He looks on it.

BLUNT   Hum, a diamond! Why 'tis a wonderul virtue now
that lies in this ring, a mollifying virtue; 'adsheartlikins, there's more
persuasive rhetoric in't, than all her sex can utter.

FREDERICK   I begin to suspect something, and 'twould anger
us vilely to be trussed up for a rape upon a maid of quality, when we
only believe we ruffle a harlot.

BLUNT   Thou art a credulous fellow, but 'adsheartlikins, I
have no faith yet: why, my saint prattled as parlously as this does; she
gave me a bracelet too, a devil on her, but I sent my man to sell it today
for necessaries, and it proved as counterfeit as her vows of love.

FREDERICK　　　　However, let it reprieve her till we see Belvile.
BLUNT　　　　　　That's hard, yet I will grant it.

Enter a servant.

PHILIP　　　　　Oh, sir, the colonel is just come in with his new
friend and a Spaniard of quality, and talks of having you to dinner with
'em.
BLUNT　　　　　'Adsheartlikins, I'm undone; I would not see 'em
for the world. Hark'ee Fred, lock up the wench in your chamber.
FREDERICK　　　　Fear nothing, madam; whate'er he threatens, you
are safe whilst in my hands.

Exit Frederick and Florinda.

BLUNT　　　　　And, sirrah, upon your life, say I am not at home,
or that I am asleep, or – or anything: away, I'll prevent their coming
this way.

Blunt locks the door and goes.

ACT FIVE, SCENE 1

Blunt's chamber. After a great knocking as at his chamber door, enter
Blunt, softly crossing the stage, in his shirt and drawers as before.

VOICES *(offstage, call within)* Ned, Ned Blunt, Ned Blunt!
BLUNT　　　　　The rogues are up in arms: 'adsheartlikins, this
villainous Frederick has betrayed me; they have heard of my blessed
fortune.
VOICES *(calling and knocking within)* Ned Blunt, Ned, Ned!
BELVILE *(within)*　Why, he's dead sir, without dispute dead, he has
not been seen today: let's break open the door. – Here, boy –
BLUNT　　　　　Ha, break open the door? 'Adsheartlikins, that
mad fellow will be as good as his word.
BELVILE *(within)*　Boy, bring something to force the door.

A great noise within, at the door again.

BLUNT　　　　　So, now must I speak in my own defence; I'll try
what rhetoric will do. – Hold, hold, what do you mean, gentlemen, what
do you mean?
BELVILE *(within)*　Oh, rogue, art alive? Prithee open the door and
convince us.

BLUNT   Yes, I am alive, gentlemen; but at present a little busy.

BELVILE *(within)*   How, Blunt grown a man of business? Come, come, open and let's see this miracle.

BLUNT   No, no, no, no, gentlemen, 'tis no great business, but – I am – at – my devotion; 'adsheartlikins, will you not allow a man time to pray?

BELVILE *(within)*   Turned religious! A greater wonder than the first; therefore open quickly, or we shall unhinge, we shall.

BLUNT   This won't do. – Why, hark'ee, colonel, to tell you the plain truth, I am about a necessary affair of life: I have a wench with me; you apprehend me? – The devil's in't if they be so uncivil as to disturb me now.

WILLMORE *(within)*   How, a wench! Nay then, we must enter and partake, no resistance; unless it be your lady of quality, and then we'll keep our distance.

BLUNT   So, the business is out.

WILLMORE *(within)*   Come, come, lend's more hands to the door; now heave altogether; so, well done my boys.

Willmore breaks open the door. Enter Belvile, Willmore, Frederick, and Pedro. Blunt looks simply; they all laugh at him; he lays his hand on his sword, and comes up to Willmore

BLUNT   Hark'ee, sir, laugh out your laugh quickly, D'ye hear, and begone. I shall spoil your sport else, 'adsheartlikins, sir, I shall; the jest has been carried on too long. *(Aside)* A plague upon my tailor.

WILLMORE   'Sdeath, how the whore has dressed him! Faith sir, I'm sorry.

BLUNT   Are you so, sir? Keep't to yourself then, sir, I advise you, d'ye hear; for I can as little endure your pity as his mirth. *(lays his hand on his sword)*

BELVILE   Indeed, Willmore, thou wert a little too rough with Ned Blunt's mistress: call a person of quality whore? And one so young, so handsome, and so eloquent! Ha, ha, he.

BLUNT   Hark'ee, sir, you know me, and know I can be angry; have a care, for 'adsheartlikins, I can fight too, I can, sir, do you mark me; no more.

BELVILE   Why so peevish, good Ned? Some disappointments, I'll warrant. What, did the jealous count her husband return just in the nick?

BLUNT   Or the devil, sir. *(They laugh.)* D'ye laugh? Look ye settle me a good sober countenance, and that quickly too, or you shall know Ned Blunt is not –

BELVILE   – Not everybody, we know that.

BLUNT   Not an ass to be laughed at, sir.

WILLMORE   Unconscionable sinner, to bring a lover so near his happiness, a vigorous passionate lover, and then not only cheat him of his moveables, but his very desires too.

BELVILE   Ah, sir, a mistress is a trifle with Blunt; he'll have a dozen the next time he looks abroad: his eyes have charms, not to be resisted; there needs no more than to expose that taking person to the view of the fair, and he leads 'em all in triumph.

PEDRO   Sir, though I'm a stranger to you, I am ashamed at the rudeness of my nation; and could you learn who did it, would assist you to make an example of 'em.

BLUNT   Why aye, there's one speaks sense now, and handsomely; and let me tell you, gentlemen, I should not have showed myself like a jack pudding thus to have made you mirth, but that I have revenge within my power: for know, I have got into my possession a female, who had better have fallen under any curse, than the ruin I design her. 'Adsheartlikins, she assaulted me here in my own lodgings, and had doubtless committed a rape upon me, had not this sword defended me.

FREDERICK   I know not that, but o' my conscience thou hadst ravished her, had she not redeemed herself with a ring; let's see it, Blunt.

Blunt shows the ring.

BELVILE *(aside)*   Ha, the ring I gave Florinda, when we exchanged our vows. – Hark'ee, Blunt –

Belvile goes to whisper to Blunt.

WILLMORE   No whispering, good colonel, there's a woman in the case; no whispering.

BELVILE *(aside to Blunt)* Hark'ee, fool, be advised, and conceal both the ring and the story for your reputation's sake; do not let people know what despised cullies we English are: to be cheated and abused by one whore, and another rather bribe thee than be kind to thee, is an infamy to our nation.

WILLMORE   Come, come, where's the wench? We'll see her; let her be what she will, we'll see her.

PEDRO Aye, aye, let us see her; I can soon discover whether she be of quality, or for your diversion.

BLUNT She's in Fred's custody.

WILLMORE *(to Frederick)* Come, come, the key.

Frederick gives Willmore the key; Willmore, Frederick, Blunt, and Don Pedro are going.

BELVILE *(aside)* Death, what shall I do? – Stay, gentlemen. *(Aside)* Yet if I hinder'em I shall discover all. Hold, let s go one at once; give me the key.

WILLMORE Nay, hold there, colonel; I'll go first.

FREDERICK Nay, no dispute; Ned and I have the propriety of her.

WILLMORE Damn propriety; then we'll draw cuts. *(Belvile goes to whisper to Willmore.)* Nay, no corruption, good colonel. Come, the longest sword carries her.

They all draw, forgetting Don Pedro, being a Spaniard, had the longest.

BLUNT I yield up my interest to you, gentlemen, and that will be revenge sufficient.

WILLMORE *(to Pedro)* The wench is yours. *(Aside)* Pox of his toledo, I had forgot that.

FREDERICK Come, sir, I'll conduct you to the lady.

Frederick and Pedro exit.

BELVILE *(aside)* To hinder him will certainly discover her. *(To Willmore, who is walking up and down out of humour)* Dost know, dull beast, what mischief thou hast done?

WILLMORE Aye, aye; to trust our fortune to lots! A devil on't, 'twas madness, that's the truth on't.

BELVILE Oh, intolerable sot!

Enter Florinda, running, masked, Pedro after her. Willmore gazing round her.

FLORINDA *(aside)* Good heaven, defend me from discovery.

PEDRO 'Tis but in vain to fly me; you're fallen to my lot.

BELVILE *(aside)* Sure she's undiscovered yet, but now I fear there is no way to bring her off.

WILLMORE Why, what a pox, is not this my woman, the same I followed but now?

PEDRO *(talking to Florinda, who walks up and down)* As if I did not know ye, and your business here.

FLORINDA *(aside)*   Good heaven, I fear he does indeed.

PEDRO   Come, pray be kind; I know you meant to be so when you entered here, for these are proper gentlemen.

WILLMORE   But, sir, perhaps the lady will not be imposed upon; she'll choose her man.

PEDRO   I am better bred, than not to leave her choice free.

Enter Valeria, surprised at the sight of Don Pedro.

VALERIA *(aside)*   Don Pedro here! There's no avoiding him.

FLORINDA *(aside)*   Valeria! Then I'm undone.

VALERIA *(to Pedro, running to him)* Oh, have I found you, sir? The strangest accident – if I had breath – to tell it.

PEDRO   Speak! Is Florinda safe? Hellena well?

VALERIA   Aye, aye, sir. Florinda – is safe – *(Aside)* from any fears of you.

PEDRO   Why, where's Florinda? Speak!

VALERIA   Aye, where indeed sir, I wish I could inform you; but to hold you no longer in doubt –

FLORINDA *(aside)*   Oh, what will she say?

VALERIA   She's fled away in the habit – of one of her pages, sir but Callis thinks you may retrieve her yet, if you make haste away. She'll tell you, sir, the rest – *(Aside)* if you can find her out.

PEDRO   Dishonourable girl, she has undone my aim. *(To Belvile)* Sir, you see my necessity of leaving you, and hope you'll pardon it. My sister, I know, will make her flight to you; and if she do, I shall expect she should be rendered back.

BELVILE   I shall consult my love and honour, sir.

Exit Pedro.

FLORINDA *(to Valeria)* My dear preserver, let me embrace thee.

WILLMORE   What the devil's all this?

BLUNT   Mystery, by this light.

VALERIA   Come, come, make haste and get yourselves married quickly, for your brother will return again.

BELVILE   I'm so surprised with fears and joys, so amazed to find you here in safety, I can scarce persuade my heart into a faith of what I see.

WILLMORE   Hark'ee, colonel, is this that mistress who has cost you so many sighs, and me so many quarrels with you?

BELVILE   It is. *(To Florinda)* Pray give him the honour of your hand.

WILLMORE *(kneels and kisses her hand)* Thus it must be received then; and with it give your pardon too.

FLORINDA   The friend to Belvile may command me anything.

WILLMORE *(aside)*   Death, would I might; 'tis a surprising beauty.

BELVILE   Boy, run and fetch a Father instantly.

Exit Page.

FREDERICK   So, now do I stand like a dog, and have not a syllable to plead my own cause with. By this hand, madam, I was never thoroughly confounded before, nor shall I ever more dare look up with confidence, till you are pleased to pardon me.

FLORINDA   Sir, I'll be reconciled to you on one condition: that you'll follow the example of your friend, in marrying a maid that does not hate you, and whose fortune, I believe, will not be unwelcome to you.

FREDERICK   Madam, had I no inclinations that way, I should obey your kind commands.

BELVILE   Who, Fred marry? He has so few inclinations for womankind, that had he been possessed of paradise, he might have continued there to this day, if no crime but love could have disinherited him.

FREDERICK   Oh, I do not use to boast of my intrigues.

BELVILE   Boast? Why, thou dost nothing but boast; and I dare swear wert thou as innocent from the sin of the grape, as thou art from the apple, thou might'st yet claim that right in Eden which our first parents lost by too much loving.

FREDERICK   I wish this lady would think me so modest a man.

VALERIA   She would be sorry then, and not like you half so well; and I should be loath to break my word with you, which was that if your friend and mine agreed, it should be a match between you and I. *(gives him her hand)*

FREDERICK *(kisses her hand)* Bear witness colonel, 'tis a bargain.

BLUNT *(to Florinda)*   I have a pardon to beg, too, but 'adsheartlikins, I am so out of countenance that I'm a dog if I can say anything to purpose.

FLORINDA   Sir, I heartily forgive you all.

BLUNT   That's nobly said, sweet lady. – Belvile prithee present her her ring again; for I find I have not courage to approach her myself.

Blunt gives Belvile the ring. Belvile gives it to Florinda. Enter Page.

PAGE　　　　　　　　Sir, I have brought the father that you sent for.
BELVILE　　　　　　'Tis well. And now, my dear Florinda, let's fly to complete that mighty joy we have so long wished and sighed for. – Come, Fred, you'll follow?
FREDERICK　　　　　Your example, sir, 'twas ever my ambition in war, and must be so in love.
WILLMORE　　　　　And must not I see this juggling knot tied?
BELVILE　　　　　　No, thou shalt do us better service, and be our guard, lest Don Pedro's sudden return interrupt the ceremony.
WILLMORE　　　　　Content; I'll secure this pass.

Belvile, Florinda, Frederick, and Valeria exit. Enter Page.

PAGE *(to Willmore)*　Sir, there's a lady without would speak to you.
WILLMORE　　　　　Conduct her in; I dare not quit my post.
PAGE *(to Blunt)*　　And sir, your tailor waits you in your chamber.
BLUNT　　　　　　　Some comfort yet; I shall not dance naked at the wedding.

Blunt and Page exit. Enter again the Page, conducting in Angellica in a masking habit and a vizard. Willmore runs to her.

WILLMORE *(aside)*　This can be none but my pretty gipsy. *(To Angellica)* Oh, I see you can follow as well as fly. Come, confess thyself the most malicious devil in nature; you think you have done my business with Angellica.
ANGELLICA　　　　　Stand off, base villain.

Angellica draws a pistol, and holds it to Willmore's breast.

WILLMORE *(aside)*　Ha, 'tis not she. – Who art thou? And what's thy business?
ANGELLICA　　　　　One thou hast injured, and who comes to kill thee for't.
WILLMORE　　　　　What the devil canst thou mean?
ANGELLICA　　　　　By all my hopes, to kill thee.–

Angellica holds still the pistol to Willmore's breast, he going back, she following still.

WILLMORE　　　　　Prithee, on what acquaintance? For I know thee not.

ANGELLICA *(pulls off her vizard)* Behold this face, so lost to thy
    remembrance,
    And then call all thy sins about thy soul,
    And let 'em die with thee.
WILLMORE   Angellica!
ANGELLICA   Yes, traitor!
    Does not thy guilty blood run shivering through thy veins?
    Hast thou no horror at this sight, that tells thee, thou hast not long to
    boast thy shameful conquest?
WILLMORE   Faith, no, child. My blood keeps its old ebbs and
    flows still, and that usual heat too, that could oblige thee with a
    kindness, had I but opportunity.
ANGELLICA   Devil! Dost wanton with my pain? Have at thy
    heart.
WILLMORE   Hold, dear virago! Hold thy hand a little; I am
    not now at leisure to be killed; hold and hear me. *(Aside)* Death, I think
    she's in earnest.
ANGELLICA *(aside, turning from him)* Oh, if I take not heed,
    My coward heart will leave me to his mercy.
    – What have you, sir, to say? But should I hear thee
    Thoud'st talk away all that is brave about me,
    (follows him with the pistol to his breast)
    And I have vowed thy death, by all that's sacred.
WILLMORE   Why then, there's an end of a proper handsome
    fellow, that might'a lived to have done good service yet; that's all I can
    say to't.
ANGELLICA *(pausingly)* Yet, I would give thee – time for – penitence.
WILLMORE   Faith, child, I thank God, I have ever took care to
    lead a good sober, hopeful life, and am of a religion that teaches me to
    believe, I shall depart in peace.
ANGELLICA   So will the devil! Tell me,
    How many poor believing fools thou hast undone?
    How many hearts thou hast betrayed to ruin?
    Yet these are little mischiefs to the ills
    Thou'st taught mine to commit: thou'st taught it love.
WILLMORE   Egad, 'twas shrewdly hurt the while.
ANGELLICA   Love, that has robbed it of its unconcern
    Of all that pride that taught me how to value it.
    And in its room
    A mean submissive passion was conveyed,
    That made me humbly bow, which I ne'er did

To anything but heaven.
Thou, perjured man, didst this, and with thy oaths,
Which on thy knees thou didst devoutly make,
Softened my yielding heart, and then, I was a slave;
Yet still had been content to've worn my chains,
Worn'em with vanity and joy forever,
Hadst thou not broke those vows that put them on.
'Twas then I was undone.

All this while she follows him with the pistol to his breast.

WILLMORE   Broke my vows! Why, where hast thou lived?
Amongst the gods? For I never heard of mortal man,
That has not broke a thousand vows.

ANGELLICA   Oh, impudence!

WILLMORE   Angellica, that beauty has been too long
tempting, not to have made a thousand lovers languish, who, in the
amorous fever, no doubt have sworn like me: did they all die in that
faith, still adoring? I do not think they did.

ANGELLICA   No, faithless man: had I repaid their vows, as I
did thine, I would have killed the ingrateful that had abandoned me.

WILLMORE   This old general has quite spoiled thee: nothing
makes a woman so vain as being flattered; your old lover ever
supplies the defects of age with intolerable dotage, vast charge, and
that which you call constancy; and attributing all this to your own
merits, you domineer, and throw your favours in's teeth, upbraiding
him still with the defects of age, and cuckold him as often as he
deceives your expectations. But the gay, young, brisk lover, that
brings his equal fires, and can give you dart for dart, you'll find will be
as nice as you sometimes.

ANGELLICA   All this thou'st made me know, for which I hate thee.
Had I remained in innocent security,
I should have thought all men were born my slaves,
And worn my power like lightning in my eyes,
To have destroyed at pleasure when offended:
But when love held the mirror, the undeceiving glass
Reflected all the weakness of my soul, and made me know
My richest treasure being lost, my honour,
All the remaining spoil could not be worth
The conqueror's care or value.
Oh, how I fell, like a long worshipped idol

Discovering all the cheat.
Would not the incense and rich sacrifice
Which blind devotion offered at my altars,
Have fallen to thee?
Why wouldst thou then destroy my fancied power?

WILLMORE   By heaven thou'rt brave, and I admire thee strangely.
I wish I were that dull, that constant thing
Which thou wouldst have, and nature never meant me:
I must, like cheerful birds, sing in all groves,
And perch on every bough,
Billing the next kind she that flies to meet me;
Yet, after all, could build my nest with thee,
Thither repairing when I'd loved my round,
And still reserve a tributary flame.
To gain your credit, I'll pay you back your charity,
And be obliged for nothing but for love.

He offers her a purse of gold.

ANGELLICA   Oh, that thou wert in earnest!
So mean a thought of me
Would turn my rage to scorn, and I should pity thee,
And give thee leave to live;
Which for the public safety of our sex,
And my own private injuries, I dare not do.
Prepare: *(follows still, as before)*
I will no more be tempted with replies.

WILLMORE   Sure –

ANGELLICA   Another word will damn thee! I've heard thee
talk too long.

She follows him with the pistol ready to shoot; he retires still amazed.
Enter Don Antonio, his arm in a scarf, and lays hold on the pistol.

ANTONIO   Ha, Angellica!

ANGELLICA   Antonio! What devil brought thee hither?

ANTONIO   Love and curiosity, seeing your coach at door.
Let me disarm you of this unbecoming instrument of death. *(takes away the pistol)* Amongst the number of your slaves, was there not one worthy the honour to have fought your quarrel? *(To Willmore)* Who are you, sir, that are so very wretched to merit death from her?

WILLMORE   One, sir, that could have made a better end of an amorous quarrel without you, than with you.

ANTONIO Sure 'tis some rival. Ha! The very man took down
her picture yesterday; the very same that set on me last night; blest
opportunity!

Antonio offers to shoot Willmore.

ANGELLICA Hold, you're mistaken, sir.
ANTONIO By heaven, the very same! – Sir, what
pretensions have you to this lady?
WILLMORE Sir, I do not use to be examined, and am ill at all
disputes but this.

Willmore draws; Antonio offers to shoot.

ANGELLICA *(to Willmore)* Oh, hold! You see he's armed with certain death;
And you, Antonio, I command you hold,
By all the passion you've so lately vowed me.

Enter Don Pedro, sees Antonio, and stays.

PEDRO *(aside)* Ha, Antonio! And Angellica!
ANTONIO When I refuse obedience to your will,
May you destroy me with your mortal hate.
By all that's holy, I adore you so,
That even my rival, who has charms enough
To make him fall a victim to my jealousy,
Shall live, nay and have leave to love on still.
PEDRO *(aside)* What's this I hear?
ANGELLICA *(pointing to Willmore)* Ah thus, 'twas thus, he talked,
and I believed.
Antonio, yesterday,
I'd not have sold my interest in his heart,
For all the sword has won and lost in battle. *(To Willmore)*
But now to show my utmost of contempt,
I give thee life, which if thou wouldst preserve,
Live where my eyes may never see thee more,
Live to undo someone whose soul may prove
So bravely constant to revenge my love.

Angellica goes out. Antonio follows, but Pedro pulls him back.

PEDRO Antonio, stay.
ANTONIO Don Pedro!
PEDRO What coward fear was that prevented thee
From meeting me this morning on the Molo?

ANTONIO   Meet thee?
PEDRO   Yes, me; I was the man that dared thee to 't.
ANTONIO   Hast thou so often seen me fight in war
    To find no better cause to excuse my absence?
    I sent my sword and one to do thee right
    Finding myself uncapable to use a sword.
PEDRO   But 'twas Florinda's quarrel that we fought,
    And you, to show how little you esteemed her
    Sent me your rival, giving him your interest.
    But I have found the cause of this affront
    And when I meet you fit for the dispute
    I'll tell you my resentment.
ANTONIO   I shall be ready, sir, ere long to do you reason.

Exit Antonio.

PEDRO   If I could find Florinda, now whilst my anger's
    high, I think I should be kind, and give her to Belvile in revenge.
WILLMORE   Faith, sir, I know not what you would do, but I
    believe the priest within has been so kind.
PEDRO   How! My sister married?
WILLMORE   I hope by this time he is, and bedded too or he
    has not my longings about him.
PEDRO   Dares he do this? Does he not fear my power?
WILLMORE   Faith, not at all: if you will go in and thank him
    for the favour he has done your sister, so; if not, sir, my power's greater
    in this house than yours: I have a damned surly crew here, that will
    keep you till the next tide and then clap you on board for prize. My ship
    lies but a league off the Molo, and we shall show your donship a
    damned Tramontana rover's trick.

Enter Belvile.

BELVILE *(aside)*   This rogue's in some new mischief. Ha, Pedro
    returned!
PEDRO   Colonel Belvile, I hear you have married my
    sister?
BELVILE   You have heard truth then, sir.
PEDRO   Have I so; then, sir, I wish you joy.
BELVILE   How?
PEDRO   By this embrace I do, and I am glad on't.
BELVILE   Are you in earnest?
PEDRO   By our long friendship and my obligations to
    thee, I am. The sudden change I'll give you reasons for, anon. Come,
    lead me to my sister, that she may know I now approve her choice.

Exit Belvile with Pedro. Willmore goes to follow them. Enter Hellena, as before in boy's clothes, and pulls him back.

WILLMORE   Ha, my gipsy! Now a thousand blessings on thee for this kindness. Egad, child, I was e'en in despair of ever seeing thee again; my friends are all provided for within, each man his kind woman.

HELLENA   Ha! I thought they had served me some such trick!

WILLMORE   And I was e'en resolved to go aboard, and condemn myself to my lone cabin, and the thoughts of thee.

HELLENA   And could you have left me behind? Would you have been so ill-natured?

WILLMORE   Why, 'twould have broke my heart, child; but since we are met again, I defy foul weather to part us.

HELLENA   And would you be a faithful friend, now, if a maid should trust you?

WILLMORE   For a friend I cannot promise; thou art of a form so excellent, a face and humour too good for cold dull friendship; I am parlously afraid of being in love, child, and you have not forgot how severely you have used me?

HELLENA   That's all one; such usage you must still look for: to find out all your haunts, to rail at you to all that love you, till I have made you love only me in your own defence, because nobody else will love you.

WILLMORE   But hast thou no better quality, to recommend thyself by?

HELLENA   Faith, none, captain: why, 'twill be the greater charity to take me for thy mistress. I am a lone child, a kind of orphan lover; and why I should die a maid, and in a captain's hands too, I do not understand.

WILLMORE   Egad, I was never clawed away with broadsides from any female before. Thou hast one virtue I adore, good nature. I hate a coy demure mistress, she's as troublesome as a colt; I'll break none: no, give me a mad mistress when mewed, and in flying, one I dare trust upon the wing, that whilst she's kind will come to the lure.

HELLENA   Nay, as kind as you will, good captain, whilst it lasts but let's lose no time.

WILLMORE   My time's as precious to me as thine can be: therefore, dear creature, since we are so well agreed, let's retire to my chamber, and if ever thou wert treated with such savoury love! Come, my bed's prepared for such a guest, all clean and sweet as thy fair self. I love to steal a dish and a bottle with a friend, and hate long graces: come, let's retire and fall to.

HELLENA   'Tis but getting my consent, and the business is
soon done. Let but old gaffer Hymen and his priest say amen to't and I
dare lay my mother's daughter by as proper a fellow as your father's
son, without fear or blushing.

WILLMORE   Hold, hold, no bug words, child. Priest and
Hymen? Prithee add a hangman to 'em to make up the consort. No, no,
we'll have no vows but love, child, nor witness but the lover: the kind
deity enjoins naught but love and enjoy! Hymen and priest wait still
upon portion, and jointure; love and beauty have their own ceremonies.
Marriage is as certain a bane to love, as lending money is to friendship:
I'll neither ask nor give a vow; though I could be content to turn gipsy,
and become a left-handed bridegroom, to have the pleasure of working
that great miracle of making a maid a mother, if you durst venture. 'Tis
upse gipsy that, and if I miss, I'll lose my labour.

HELLENA   And if you do not lose, what shall I get? A cradle
full of noise and mischief, with a pack of repentance at my back? Can you
teach me to weave incle to pass my time with? 'Tis upse gipsy that too.

WILLMORE   I can teach thee to weave a true love's knot
better.

HELLENA   So can my dog.

WILLMORE   Well, I see we are both upon our guards and I
see, there's no way to conquer good nature, but by yielding. Here, give
me thy hand; one kiss and I am thine.

HELLENA   One kiss! How like my page he speaks! I am
resolved you shall have none, for asking such a sneaking sum. He that
will be satisfied with one kiss will never die of that longing. Good friend
single-kiss, is all your talking come to this? A kiss, a caudle! Farewell,
captain single-kiss.

Hellena is going out; Willmore stays her.

WILLMORE   Nay, if we part so, let me die like a bird upon a
bough, at the sheriff's charge. By heaven both the Indies shall not buy
thee from me. I adore thy humour and will marry thee, and we are so of
one humour it must be a bargain. Give me thy hand. *(kisses her hand)*
And now let the blind ones, love and fortune, do their worst.

HELLENA   Why, God-a-mercy, captain!

WILLMORE   But hark'ee: the bargain is now made; but is it
not fit we should know each other's names? That when we have reason
to curse one another hereafter and people ask me who 'tis I give to the
devil, I may at least be able to tell what family you came of?

HELLENA   Good reason, captain; and where I have cause (as I doubt not but I shall have plentiful), that I may know at whom to throw my – blessings, I beseech ye your name.

WILLMORE   I am called Robert the Constant.

HELLENA   A very fine name; pray was it your faulkner or butler who christened you? Do they not use to whistle when they call you?

WILLMORE   I hope you have a better, that a man may name without crossing himself – you are so merry with mine.

HELLENA   I am called Hellena the Inconstant.

Enter Pedro, Belvile, Florinda, Frederick, and Valeria.

PEDRO   Ha, Hellena!

FLORINDA   Hellena!

HELLENA   The very same. Ha, my brother! Now, captain, show your love and courage; stand to your arms, and defend me bravely, or I am lost forever.

PEDRO   What's this I hear? False girl, how came you hither, and what's your business? Speak!

Pedro goes roughly to Hellena. Willmore puts himself between them.

WILLMORE   Hold off, sir, you have leave to parley only.

HELLENA   I had e'en as good tell it, as you guess it. Faith, brother, my business is the same with all living creatures of my age: to love, and be beloved; and here's the man.

PEDRO   Perfidious maid, hast thou deceived me too, deceived thyself and heaven?

HELLENA   'Tis time enough to make my peace with that; Be you but kind, let me alone with heaven.

PEDRO   Belvile, I did not expect this false play from you. Wasn't not enough you'd gain Florinda (which I pardoned) but your lewd friends too must be enriched with the spoils of a noble family?

BELVILE   Faith, sir, I am as much surprised at this as you can be. Yet, sir, my friends are gentlemen, and ought to be esteemed for their misfortunes, since they have the glory to suffer with the best of men and kings: 'tis true, he's a rover of fortune, Yet a prince, aboard his little wooden world.

PEDRO   What's this to the maintenance of a woman of her birth and quality?

WILLMORE   Faith, sir, I can boast of nothing but a sword which does me right where'er I come, and has defended a worse cause than a woman's; and since I loved her before I either knew her birth or name, I must pursue my resolution, and marry her.

PEDRO   And is all your holy intent of becoming a nun
debauched into a desire of man?

HELLENA   Why, I have considered the matter, brother, and
find, the three hundred thousand crowns my uncle left me, and you
cannot keep from me, will be better laid out in love than in religion, and
turn to as good an account. *(To the others)* Let most voices carry it: for
heaven or the captain?

ALL *(cry)*   A captain! A captain!

HELLENA   Look ye sir, 'tis a clear case.

PEDRO   Oh, I am mad! *(Aside)* If I refuse, my life's in
danger. *(To Willmore)* Come, there's one motive induces me.
(Don Pedro gives Hellena to Willmore.) Take her: I shall now be free
from fears of her honour. Guard it you now, if you can; I have been a
slave to't long enough.

WILLMORE   Faith, sir, I am of a nation that are of opinion a
woman's honour is not worth guarding when she has a mind to part with it.

HELLENA   Well said, captain.

PEDRO *(to Valeria)*   This was your plot, mistress, but I hope you have
married one that will revenge my quarrel to you.

VALERIA   There's no altering destiny, sir.

PEDRO   Sooner than a woman's will: therefore I forgive
you all, and wish you may get my father's pardon as easily, which I fear.

*Enter Blunt dressed in a Spanish habit, looking very ridiculously; his
Man adjusting his band.*

MAN   'Tis very well, sir.

BLUNT   Well, sir? 'Adsheartlikins, I tell you 'tis damnable
ill, sir. A Spanish habit, good lord! Could the devil and my tailor devise
no other punishment for me, but the mode of a nation I abominate?

BELVILE   What's the matter, Ned?

BLUNT *(turns round)*   Pray view me round, and judge.

BELVILE   I must confess thou art a kind of an odd figure.

BLUNT   In a Spanish habit with a vengeance! I had rather
be in the Inquisition for Judaism, than in this doublet and breeches; a
pillory were an easy collar to this, three handfuls high; and these shoes
too, are worse than the stocks, with the sole an inch shorter than my
foot. In fine, gentlemen, methinks I look altogether like a bag of bays
stuffed full of fool's flesh.

BELVILE   Methinks 'tis well, and makes thee look *en
cavalier*. Come, sir, settle your face, and salute our friends. *(turns to
Hellena)* Lady –

BLUNT   Ha! *(To Hellena)* Say'st thou so, my little rover?
Lady, if you be one, give me leave to kiss your hand, and tell you,
'adsheartlikins, for all I look so, I am your humble servant. *(Aside)*
A pox of my Spanish habit.

Music is heard to play.

WILLMORE   Hark, what's this?

Enter Page.

PAGE   Sir, as the custom is, the gay people in
masquerade, who make every man's house their own, are coming up.

*Enter several men and women in masking habits, with music; they put
themselves in order and dance.*

BLUNT'   'Adsheartlikins, would 'twere lawful to pull off
their false faces, that I might see if my doxy were not amongst 'em.

BELVILE *(to the maskers)* Ladies and gentlemen, since you are come so *a
propos*, you must take a small collation with us.

WILLMORE *(to Hellena)* Whilst we'll to the good man within, who stays
to give us a cast of his office. Have you no trembling at the near
approach?

HELLENA   No more than you have in an engagement or a
tempest.

WILLMORE   Egad, thou'rt a brave girl, and I admire thy love
and courage.
Lead on, no other dangers they can dread
Who venture in the storms o'th' marriage bed.

They exit.

EPILOGUE

The banished cavaliers! A roving blade!
A popish carnival! A masquerade!
The devil's in't if this will please the nation,
In these our blessèd times of reformation,
When conventicling is so much in fashion.
And yet –
That mutinous tribe less factions do beget,

Than your continual differing in wit;
Your judgement's (as your passion's) a disease:
Nor muse nor miss your appetite can please;
You're grown as nice as queasy consciences,
Whose each convulsion, when the spirit moves,
Damns everything that maggot disapproves.
With canting rule you would the stage refine,
And to dull method all our sense confine.
With th'insolence of commonwealths you rule,
Where each gay fop, and politic grave fool
On monarch wit impose, without control.
As for the last, who seldom sees a play,
Unless it be the old Blackfriars way,
Shaking his empty noddle o'er bamboo,
He cries, 'Good faith, these plays will never do.
Ah, sir, in my young days, what lofty wit,
What high strained scenes of fighting there were writ:
These are slight airy toys. But tell me, pray,
What has the House of Commons done today?'
Then shows his politics, to let you see,
Of state affairs he'll judge as notably,
As he can do of wit and poetry.
The younger sparks, who hither do resort,
Cry, 'Pox o' your genteel things. Give us more sport!
Damn me, I'm sure 'twill never please the court.'
Such fops are never pleased unless the play
Be stuffed with fools, as brisk and dull as they.
Such might the half-crown spare, and in a glass
At home behold a more accomplished ass,
Where they may set their cravats, wigs and faces,
And practise all their buffoonry grimaces:
See how this huff becomes, this damme, stare,
Which they at home may act, because they dare,
But must with prudent caution do elsewhere.
Oh that our Nokes, or Tony Leigh, could show
A fop but half so much to th' life as you.

The Curtain falls.

The End.

Aphra Behn (1640-1689)

She was born Aphra Johnson in Canterbury, probably daughter to Bartholomew Johnson and Elizabeth Denham (though accounts differ, and much of her early history has been reconstructed on the basis of conflicting versions that have come down of her) and the foster sister of Thomas Culpeper in whose house she may have been educated. There seems to have been a close relation between her family and that of Lord Willoughby, Governor of Surinam. Her father travelled to the colony in 1663, taking his family with him. Behn claimed to have witnessed the slave rebellion there and its barbarous crushing, which she wrote about many years later in the novel *Oroonoko* (1688), (dramatized by Thomas Southerne in 1695).

She returned to England in 1664 where she apparently married the Dutch merchant, whose name she kept and who probably died in the Great Plague of 1666. Aphra Behn lived out the rest of her life as a widow. That same year, she went to Holland to spy for Charles II, a job she undertook to support herself, sending back useful information about a planned Dutch invasion, under the code name, Astrea, later her pseudonym.

She went unpaid for her activities and, on her return to England, was thrown in jail for debt. Her career as the first woman to make a living from writing came from being "Forced to write for Bread and not ashamed to owne it". She also produced novels such as *Love Letters between a Nobleman and His Sister* (1684-7), a romance in verse and prose *A Voyage to the Island of Love* (1684); *Poems on Several Occasions* (1684) and translations of authors including Ovid and Sappho. Her plays include: *Abdelazar* (1677); *The Rover* (Part 1, 1677); *The False Count* (1682); *The Lucky Chance* (1686); *The Widow Ranter* (1690); *The Forced Marriage* (1671); *The Dutch Lover* (1673); *The Debauchee* (1677); *Sir Patient Fancy* (1678); *The Feigned Courtesans* (1679); *The Rover* (Part 2, 1681); *The Roundheads* (1682); and *The City Heiress* (1682).

A Bold Stroke for a Wife

Susanna Centlivre

First performed at Lincoln's Inn Fields on 3rd February, 1718.

CHARACTERS

Men

Sir Philip Modelove, an old beau, Guardian to Ann
Periwinkle, a kind of a silly virtuoso, Guardian to Ann
Tradelove, a change-broker Guardian to Ann
Obadiah Prim, a Quaker [hosier], Guardian to Ann
Colonel Fainwell, in love with Ann
Freeman, his friend, a merchant
Simon Pure, a Quaking preacher
Sackbut, a tavern-keeper

Women

Mistress Ann Lovely, a maiden with a fortune of thirty thousand pound
Sarah Prim, wife to Obadiah Prim
Betty, servant to Ann

Footmen, Drawers, Servants, Stockjobbers etc.

Scene: London

PROLOGUE

Spoken by Mrs Ann Lovely.

Tonight we come upon a bold design,
To try to please without one borrowed line.
Our plot is new, and regularly clear,
And not one single tittle from Moliere.
O'er buried poets we with caution tread,
And parish sextons leave to rob the dead.
For you, bright British fair, in hopes to charm ye,
We bring tonight a lover from the army.
You know the soldiers have the strangest arts,
Such a proportion of prevailing parts,
You'd think that they rid post to women's hearts.
I wonder whence they draw their bold pretense;
We do not choose them sure for our defence:
That plea is both impolitic and wrong,
And only suits such dames as want a tongue.
Is it their eloquence and fine address?
The softness of their language? – Nothing less.
Is it their courage, that they bravely dare
To storm the sex at once? – Egad, 'tis there.
They act by us as in the rough campaign,
Unmindful of repulses, charge again;
They mine and countermine, resolved to win,
And, if a breach is made – they will come in.
You'll think, by what we have of soldiers said,
Our female wit was in the service bred;
But she is to the hardy toil a stranger,
She loves the cloth, indeed, but hates the danger;
Yet to this circle of the brave and gay,
She bid me for her good intentions say,
She hopes you'll not reduce her to half pay.
As for our play, 'tis English humour all;
Then will you let our manufacture fall?
Would you the honour of our nation raise,
Keep English credit up, and English plays.

ACT ONE, SCENE 1

A tavern. Colonel Fainwell and Freeman over a bottle.

FREEMAN　　　　Come, Colonel, his Majesty's health! You are as melancholy as if you were in love; I wish some of the beauties at Bath ha'n't snapped your heart.

COLONEL　　　　Why faith, Freeman, there is something in't; I have seen a lady at Bath who has kindled such a flame in me that all the waters there can't quench.

FREEMAN　　　　Women, like some poisonous animals, carry their antidote about 'em. Is she not to be had, Colonel?

COLONEL　　　　That's a difficult question to answer; however, I resolve to try. Perhaps you may be able to serve me; you merchants know one another. – The lady told me herself she was under the charge of four persons.

FREEMAN　　　　Odso! 'Tis Mrs Ann Lovely.

COLONEL　　　　The same; do you know her?

FREEMAN　　　　Know her! Ay-faith, Colonel, your condition is more desperate than you imagine; why she is the talk and pity of the whole town; and it is the opinion of the learned that she must die a maid.

COLONEL　　　　Say you so? That's somewhat odd in this charitable city. She's a woman, I hope.

FREEMAN　　　　For aught I know; but it had been as well for her had nature made her any other part of the creation. The man which keeps this house served her father; he is a very honest fellow and may be of use to you; we'll send for him to take a glass with us. He'll give you the whole history, and 'tis worth your hearing.

COLONEL　　　　But may one trust him?

FREEMAN　　　　With your life; I have obligations enough upon him to make him do anything; I serve him with wine. (*knocks*)

COLONEL　　　　Nay, I know him pretty well myself; I once used to frequent a club that was kept here.

Enter Drawer.

DRAWER　　　　Gentlemen, d'you call?

FREEMAN　　　　Ay, send up your master.

DRAWER　　　　Yes, sir.

Exit.

COLONEL　　　　Do you know any of this lady's guardians, Freeman?

FREEMAN   Yes, I know two of them very well.

COLONEL   What are they?

Enter Sackbut.

FREEMAN   Here comes one will give you an account of them all. Mr. Sackbut, we sent for you to take a glass with us. 'Tis a maxim among the friends of the bottle that as long as the master is in company one may be sure of good wine.

SACKBUT   Sir, you shall be sure to have as good wine as you send in. Colonel, your most humble servant; you are welcome to town.

COLONEL   I thank you, Mr Sackbut.

SACKBUT   I am as glad to see you as I should a hundred tun of French claret custom free. My service to you, sir. *(drinks)* You don't look so merry as you used to do; are you not well, Colonel?

FREEMAN   He has got a woman in his head, landlord; can you help him?

SACKBUT   If 'tis in my power, I shan't scruple to serve my friend.

COLONEL   'Tis one perquisite of your calling.

SACKBUT   Aye, at t'other end of the town, where you officers use, women are good forcers of trade; a well-customed house, a handsome barkeeper, with clean, obliging drawers, soon get the master an estate; but our citizens seldom do anything but cheat within the walls. But as to the lady, Colonel; point you at particulars, or have you a good champagne stomach? Are you in full pay, or reduced, Colonel?

COLONEL   Reduced, reduced, landlord.

FREEMAN   To the miserable condition of a lover!

SACKBUT   Pish! That's preferable to half pay; a woman's resolution may break before the peace; push her home, Colonel; there's no parleying with that sex.

COLONEL   Were the lady her own mistress I have some reasons to believe I should soon command in chief.

FREEMAN   You know Mrs Lovely, Mr Sackbut?

SACKBUT   Know her! Ay, poor Nancy; I have carried her to school many a frosty morning. Alas, if she's the woman, I pity you, Colonel. Her father, my old master, was the most whimsical, out-of-the-way tempered man I ever heard of, as you will guess by his last will and testament. This was his only child. I have heard him wish her dead a thousand times.

COLONEL   Why so?

SACKBUT   He hated posterity, you must know, and wished the world were to expire with himself. He used to swear if she had been a boy, he would have qualified him for the opera.

FREEMAN   'Tis a very unnatural resolution in a father.

SACKBUT   He died worth thirty thousand pounds, which he left to this daughter provided she married with the consent of her guardians. But that she might be sure never to do so, he left her in the care of four men, as opposite to each other as light and darkness. Each has his quarterly rule, and three months in a year she is obliged to be subject to each of their humors, and they are pretty different, I assure you. She is just come from Bath.

COLONEL   'Twas there I saw her.

SACKBUT   Aye, sir, the last quarter was her beau guardian's. She appears in all public places during his reign.

COLONEL   She visited a lady who boarded in the same house with me. I liked her person and found an opportunity to tell her so. She replied she had no objection to mine, but If I could not reconcile contradictions, I must not think of her, for that she was condemned to the caprice of four persons who never yet agreed in any one thing, and she was obliged to please them all.

SACKBUT   'Tis most true, sir; I'll give you a short description of the men and leave you to judge of the poor lady's condition. One is a kind of a virtuoso, a silly, half-witted fellow but positive and surly; fond of nothing but what is antique and foreign, and wears his clothes of the fashion of the last century; dotes upon travelers and believes Sir John Mandeville more than the Bible.

COLONEL   That must be a rare old fellow!

SACKBUT   Another is a changebroker, a fellow that will outlie the devil for the advantage of stock and cheat his father that got him in a bargain. He is a great stickler for trade and hates everything that wears a sword.

FREEMAN   He is a great admirer of the Dutch management and swears they understand trade better than any nation under the sun.

SACKBUT   The third is an old beau that has May in his fancy and dress but December in his face and his heels; he admires nothing but new fashions, and those must be French; loves operas, balls, masquerades, and is always the most tawdry of the whole company on a birthday.

COLONEL   These are pretty opposite to one another truly. And the fourth, what is he, landlord?

SACKBUT   A very rigid Quaker, whose quarter begun this day. I saw Mrs Lovely go in not above two hours ago. Sir Philip set her down. What think you now, Colonel; is not the poor lady to be pitied?

COLONEL   Aye, and rescued too, landlord.

FREEMAN   In my opinion, that's impossible.

COLONEL   There is nothing impossible to a lover. What would not a man attempt for a fine woman and thirty thousand pounds? Besides, my honor is at stake; I promised to deliver her and she bade me win her and take her.

SACKBUT   That's fair, faith.

FREEMAN   If it depended upon knight-errantry, I should not doubt your setting free the damsel; but to have avarice, impertinence, hypocrisy, and pride at once to deal with requires more cunning than generally attends a man of honour.

COLONEL   My fancy tells me I shall come off with glory; I resolve to try, however. – Do you know all the guardians, Mr Sackbut?

SACKBUT   Very well, sir; they all use my house.

COLONEL   And will you assist me, if occasion be?

SACKBUT   In everything I can, Colonel.

FREEMAN   I'll answer for him; and whatever I can serve you in, you may depend on. I know Mr Periwinkle and Mr Tradelove; the latter has a very great opinion of my interest abroad. I happened to have a letter from a correspondent two hours before the news arrived of the French king's death; I communicated it to him; upon which he bought up all the stock he could, and what with that and some wagers he laid, he told me he had got to the tune of five hundred pounds; so that I am much in his good graces.

COLONEL   I don't know but you may be of service to me, Freeman.

FREEMAN   If I can, command me, Colonel.

COLONEL   Is it not possible to find a suit of clothes ready-made at some of these sale shops, fit to rig out a beau, think you, Mr Sackbut?

SACKBUT   O hang 'em, no, Colonel; they keep nothing ready-made that a gentleman would be seen in. But I can fit you with a suit of clothes, if you'd make a figure-velvet and gold brocade – they were pawned to me by a French count who had been stripped at play and wanted money to carry him home; he promised to send for them, but I have heard nothing from him.

FREEMAN   He has not fed upon frogs long enough yet to recover his loss, ha, ha!

COLONEL   Ha, ha! Well, those clothes will do, Mr Sackbut, though we must have three or four fellows in tawdry liveries. Those can be procured, I hope.

FREEMAN   Egad, I have a brother come from the West Indies that can match you; and, for expedition sake, you shall have his servants. There's a black, a tawny-moor, and a Frenchman. They don't speak one word of English, so can make no mistake.

COLONEL   Excellent. Egad, I shall look like an Indian prince. First I'll attack my beau guardian. Where lives he?

SACKBUT   Faith, somewhere about St James's; though to say in what street, I cannot. But any chairman will tell you where Sir Philip Modelove lives.

FREEMAN   O, you'll find him in the Park at eleven every day; at least I never passed through at that hour without seeing him there. But what do you intend?

COLONEL   To address him in his own way and find what he designs to do with the lady.

FREEMAN   And what then?

COLONEL   Nay, that I can't tell, but I shall take my measures accordingly.

SACKBUT   Well, 'tis a mad undertaking, your success, Colonel. *(drinks)*

COLONEL   'Tis something out of the way, I confess; but fortune may chance to smile, and I succeed. Come, landlord, let me see those clothes. – Freeman, I shall expect you'll leave word with Mr Sackbut where one may find you upon occasion and send my equipage of India immediately, do you hear?

FREEMAN   Immediately. *(exits)*

COLONEL   Bold was the man who ventured first to sea,
But the first vent'ring lovers bolder were.
The path of love's a dark and dangerous way,
Without a landmark, or one friendly star,
And he that runs the risk, deserves the fair.

Exit with Sackbut.

ACT ONE, SCENE 2

Prim's house. Enter Mrs Lovely and her maid Betty.

BETTY   Bless me, madam! Why do you fret and tease yourself so? This is giving them the advantage with a witness.

MRS LOVELY   Must I be condemned all my life to the preposterous humours of other people; and pointed at by every boy in town? – O! I could tear my flesh, and curse the hour I was born. Is it not monstrously ridiculous that they should desire to impose their Quaking dress upon me at these years? When I was a child, no matter what they made me wear; but now –

BETTY   I would resolve against it, madam; I'd see 'em hanged before I'd put on the pinched cap again.

MRS LOVELY   Then I must never expect one moment's ease; she has rung such a peal in my ears already that I shan't have the right use of them this month – what can I do?

BETTY   What can you not do, if you will but give your mind to it? Marry, madam.

MRS LOVELY   What! And have my fortune go to build churches and hospitals?

BETTY   Why, let it go. If the Colonel loves you, as he pretends, he'll marry you without a fortune, madam; and I assure you, in my mind; a Colonel's lady is no despicable thing; a Colonel's post will maintain you like a gentlewoman, madam.

MRS LOVELY   So you would advise me to give up my own fortune and throw myself upon the Colonel's.

BETTY   I would advise you to make yourself easy, madam.

MRS LOVELY   That's not the way, I am sure. No, no, girl, there are certain ingredients to be mingled with matrimony, without which I may as well change for the worse as for the better. When the woman has fortune enough to make the man happy, if he has either honor or good manners, he'll make her easy. Love makes but a slovenly figure in that house where poverty keeps the door.

BETTY   And so you resolve to die a maid, do you, madam?

MRS LOVELY   Or have it in my power to make the man I love master of my fortune.

BETTY   Then you don't like the Colonel so well as I thought you did, madam, or you would not take such a resolution.

MRS LOVELY   It is because I do like him, Betty, that I take such a resolution.

BETTY   Why, do you expect, madam, the Colonel can work miracles? Is it possible for him to marry you with the consent of all your guardians?

MRS LOVELY   Or he must not marry me at all, and so I told him; and he did not seem displeased with the news. He promised to set me free, and I, on that condition, promised to make him master of that freedom.

BETTY   Well! I have read of enchanted castles, ladies
delivered from the chains of magic, giants killed, and monsters
overcome; so that I shall be the less surprised if the Colonel should
conjure you out of the power of your guardians. If he does, I am sure he
deserves your fortune.

MRS LOVELY   And shall have it, girl, if it were ten times as
much; for I'll ingenuously confess to thee that I do like the Colonel
above all men I ever saw. There's something so *jantée* in a soldier, a
kind of a *je ne sais quoi* air that makes 'em more agreeable than the rest
of mankind. They command regard, as who should say, "We are your
defenders; we preserve your beauties from the insults of rude
unpolished foes and ought to be preferred before those lazy indolent
mortals who, by dropping into their father's estate, set up their coaches
and think to rattle themselves into our affections."

BETTY   Nay, madam, I confess that the army has
engrossed all the prettiest fellows. A laced coat and feather have
irresistible charms.

MRS LOVELY   But the Colonel has all the beauties of the mind,
as well as person. – O all ye powers that favor happy lovers, grant he
may be mine! Thou god of love, if thou be'st aught but name, assist my
Fainwell.
Point all thy darts to aid my love's design,
And make his plots as prevalent as thine.

ACT TWO, SCENE 1

The Park. Enter Colonel, finely dressed, three Footmen after him.

COLONEL   So, now if I can but meet this beau – egad,
methinks I cut a smart figure and have as much of the tawdry air as any
Italian count or French marquis of 'em all. Sure I shall know this knight
again – ha, yonder he sits, making love to a mask, i' faith. I'll walk up
the Mall and come down by him.

*Exit. Scene draws and discovers Sir Philip upon a bench with a Woman,
masked.*

SIR PHILIP   Well, but, my dear, are you really constant to
your keeper?

WOMAN   Yes, really sir. Hey day, who comes yonder? He
cuts a mighty figure.

SIR PHILIP   Ha! A stranger by his equipage keeping so close at his heels – he has the appearance of a man of quality – positively French by his dancing air.

WOMAN   He crosses as if he meant to sit down here.

SIR PHILIP   He has a mind to make love to thee, child.

Enter Colonel and seats himself upon the bench by Sir Philip.

WOMAN   It will be to no purpose if he does.

SIR PHILIP   Are you resolved to be cruel then?

COLONEL   You must be very cruel, indeed, if you can deny anything to so fine a gentleman, madam. *(takes out his watch.)*

WOMAN   I never mind the outside of a man.

COLONEL   And I'm afraid thou art no judge of the inside.

SIR PHILIP   I am positively of your mind, sir, for creatures of her function seldom penetrate beyond the pocket.

WOMAN *(aside)*   Creatures of your composition have, indeed, generally more in their pockets than in their heads.

SIR PHILIP *(pulling out his watch)* Pray, what says your watch? Mine is down.

COLONEL   I want thirty-six minutes of twelve, sir.

Puts up his watch and takes out his snuffbox.

SIR PHILIP   May I presume, sir?

COLONEL   Sir, you honour me. *(presenting the box.)*

SIR PHILIP *(aside)*   He speaks good English, though he must be a foreigner. *(aloud)* This snuff is extremely good and the box prodigious fine; the work is French, I presume, sir.

COLONEL   I bought it in Paris, sir; I do think the workmanship pretty neat.

SIR PHILIP   Neat, 'tis exquisitely fine, sir. Pray, sir, if I may take the liberty of inquiring, what country is so happy to claim the birth of the finest gentleman in the universe? France, I presume.

COLONEL   Then you don't think me an Englishman?

SIR PHILIP   No, upon my soul don't I.

COLONEL   I am sorry for't.

SIR PHILIP   Impossible you should wish to be an Englishman! Pardon me, sir, this island could not produce a person of such alertness.

COLONEL   As this mirror shows you, sir –

Puts up a pocket glass to Sir Philip's face.

WOMAN *(aside)*   Coxcombs; I'm sick to hear 'em praise one another. One seldom gets anything by such animals, not even a dinner, unless one can dine upon soup and celery.

Exit.

SIR PHILIP   O Ged, sir! – *(calls after her)* Will you leave us, madam? Ha, ha.

COLONEL   She fears 'twill be only losing time to stay here, ha, ha. – I know not how to distinguish you, sir, but your mien and address speak you *Right Honorable.*

SIR PHILIP   Thus great souls judge of others by themselves. I am only adorned with knighthood, that's all, I assure you, sir; my name is Sir Philip Modelove.

COLONEL   Of French extraction?

SIR PHILIP   My father was French.

COLONEL   One may plainly perceive it. There is a certain gaiety peculiar to my nation (for I will own myself a Frenchman), which distinguishes us everywhere. A person of your figure would be a vast addition to a coronet.

SIR PHILIP   I must own I had the offer of a barony about five years ago, but I abhorred the fatigue which must have attended it. I could never yet bring myself to join with either party.

COLONEL   You are perfectly in the right, Sir Philip; a fine person should not embark himself in the slovenly concern of politics. Dress and pleasure are objects proper for the soul of a fine gentleman.

SIR PHILIP   And love –

COLONEL   O, that's included under the article of pleasure.

SIR PHILIP   *Parbleu, il est un homme d'esprit*; I must embrace you. *(rises and embraces)* Your sentiments are so agreeable to mine that we appear to have but one soul, for our ideas and conceptions are the same.

COLONEL *(aside)*   I should be sorry for that. – You do me too much honour, Sir Philip.

SIR PHILIP   Your vivacity and *jantée* mien assured me at first sight there was nothing of this foggy island in your composition. May I crave your name, sir?

COLONEL   My name is La Fainwell, sir, at your service.

SIR PHILIP   The La Fainwells are French, I know; though the name is become very numerous in Great Britain of late years. I was sure you was French the moment I laid my eyes upon you; I could not come into the supposition of your being an Englishman. This island produces few such ornaments.

COLONEL   Pardon me, Sir Philip, this island has two things superior to all nations under the sun.

SIR PHILIP   Aye? What are they?

COLONEL   The ladies and the laws.

SIR PHILIP   The laws indeed do claim a preference of other nations, but by my soul, there are fine women everywhere. I must own I have felt their power in all countries.

COLONEL   There are some finished beauties, I confess, in France, Italy, Germany, nay, even in Holland; *mais sont bien rares*. But *les belles Anglaises*! O, Sir Philip, where find we such women? Such symmetry of shape! Such elegancy of dress! Such regularity of features! Such sweetness of temper! Such commanding eyes! And such bewitching smiles.

SIR PHILIP   Ah! *Parbleu, vous êtes attrapé*.

COLONEL   *Non, je vous assure, chevalier* but I declare there is no amusement so agreeable to my *goût* as the conversation of a fine woman. I could never be prevailed upon to enter into what the vulgar calls the pleasure of the bottle.

SIR PHILIP   My own taste, *positivement*. A ball or masquerade is certainly preferable to all the productions of the vineyard.

COLONEL   Infinitely. I hope the people of quality in Europe will support that branch of pleasure which was imported with their peace and since naturalized by the ingenious Mr Heidegger.

SIR PHILIP.   The ladies assure me it will become part of the constitution upon which I subscribed an hundred guineas; it will be of great service to the public, at least to the company of surgeons and the City in general.

COLONEL   Ha, ha, it may help to ennoble the blood of the City. Are you married, Sir Philip?

SIR PHILIP   No, nor do I believe I ever shall enter into that honorable state; I have an absolute tender for the whole sex.

COLONEL *(aside)*   That's more than they have for you, I dare swear.

SIR PHILIP   And I have the honor to be very well with the ladies, I can assure you, sir, and I won't affront a million of fine women to make one happy.

COLONEL   Nay, marriage is really reducing a man's taste to a kind of half pleasure, but then it carries the blessing of peace along with it; one goes to sleep without fear and wakes without pain.

SIR PHILIP   There is something of that in't; a wife is a very good dish for an English stomach – but gross feeding for nicer palates, ha, ha, ha!

COLONEL   I find I was very much mistaken. I imagined you had been married to that young lady which I saw in the chariot with you this morning in Gracechurch Street.

SIR PHILIP   Who, Nancy Lovely? I am a piece of a guardian to that lady, you must know; her father, I thank him, joined me with three of the most preposterous old fellows, that, upon my soul, I'm in pain for the poor girl. She must certainly lead apes, as the saying is. Ha, ha.

COLONEL   That's pity, Sir Philip; if the lady would give me leave, I would endeavour to avert that curse.

SIR PHILIP   As to the lady, she'd gladly be rid of us at any rate, I believe; but here's the mischief: he who marries Miss Lovely must have the consent of us all four, or not a penny of her portion. For my part, I shall never approve of any but a man of figure, and the rest are not only averse to cleanliness but have each a peculiar taste to gratify. For my part, I declare, I would prefer you to all men I ever saw.

COLONEL   And I her to all women.

SIR PHILIP   I assure you, Mr Fainwell, I am for marrying her, for I hate the trouble of a guardian, especially among such wretches, but resolve never to agree to the choice of any one of them, and I fancy they'll be even with me, for they never came into any proposal of mine yet.

COLONEL   I wish I had your leave to try them, Sir Philip.

SIR PHILIP   With all my soul, sir, I can refuse a person of your appearance nothing.

COLONEL   Sir, I am infinitely obliged to you.

SIR PHILIP   But do you really like matrimony?

COLONEL   I believe I could with that lady, sir.

SIR PHILIP   The only point in which we differ; but you are master of so many qualifications that I can excuse one fault, for I must think it a fault in a fine gentleman, and that you are such, I'll give it under my hand.

COLONEL   I wish you'd give me your consent to marry Mrs Lovely under your hand, Sir Philip.

SIR PHILIP   I'll do't if you'll step into St. James's Coffee House, where we may have pen and ink; though I can't foresee what advantage my consent will be to you without you could find a way to get the rest of the guardians', but I'll introduce you; however, she is now at a Quaker's where I carried her this morning, when you saw us in Gracechurch Street. I assure you she has an odd *ragoût* of guardians, as you will find when you hear the characters, which I'll endeavour to give you as we go along. *(calls the Servants)* Hey, Pierre, Jacques, Renno, where are you all, scoundrels? Order the chariot to St. James's Coffee House.

COLONEL   *Le noir, le brun, le blanc-mortbleu, où sont ces coquins-là? Allons, monsieur le chevalier.*
SIR PHILIP   Ah, *pardonnez-moi, monsieur.*
COLONEL (*refusing to go first*) Not one step, upon my soul, Sir Philip.
SIR PHILIP   The best bred man in Europe, positively.

ACT TWO, SCENE 2

Obadiah Prim's house. Enter Mrs Lovely, followed by Mrs Prim.

MRS PRIM   Then thou wilt not obey me; and thou dost really think those fallals becometh thee?
MRS LOVELY   I do, indeed.
MRS PRIM   Now will I be judged by all sober people, if I don't look more like a modest woman than thou dost, Ann.
MRS LOVELY   More like a hypocrite, you mean, Mrs Prim.
MRS PRIM   Ah, Ann, Ann, that wicked Philip Modelove will undo thee, Satan so fills thy heart with pride during the three months of his guardianship that thou becomest a stumbling block to the upright.
MRS LOVELY   Pray, who are they? Are the pinched cap and formal hood the emblems of sanctity? Does your virtue consist in your dress, Mrs Prim?
MRS PRIM   It doth not consist in cut hair, spotted face, and bare necks. O, the wickedness of this generation! The primitive women knew not the abomination of hooped petticoats.
MRS LOVELY   No, nor the abomination of cant neither. Don't tell me, Mrs Prim, don't. I know you have as much pride, vanity, self-conceit, and ambition among you, couched under that formal habit and sanctified countenance, as the proudest of us all; but the world begins to see your prudery.
MRS PRIM   Prudery! What, do they invent new words as well as new fashions? Ah, poor fantastic age, I pity thee – poor deluded Ann. Which dost thou think most resemblest the saint and which the sinner, thy dress or mine? Thy naked bosom allureth the eye of the bystander, encourageth the frailty of human nature, and corrupteth the soul with evil longings.
MRS LOVELY   And pray, who corrupted your son Tobias with evil longings? Your maid Tabitha wore a handkerchief, and yet he made the saint a sinner.
MRS PRIM   Well, well, spit thy malice. I confess Satan did buffet my son Tobias and my servant Tabitha; the evil spirit was at that too strong, and they both became subject to its workings, not from any

outward provocation but from an inward call. He was not tainted with rottenness of the fashions, nor did his eyes take in the drunkenness of beauty.

MRS LOVELY No! That's plainly to be seen.

MRS PRIM Tabitha is one of the faithful; he fell not with a stranger.

MRS LOVELY So! Then you hold wenching no crime, provided it be within the pale of your own tribe? You are an excellent casuist, truly.

Enter Obadiah Prim.

PRIM Not stripped of thy vanity yet, Ann! – Why dost not thou make her put it off, Sarah?

MRS PRIM She will not do it.

PRIM Verily, thy naked breasts troubleth my outward man; I pray thee hide 'em, Ann. Put on a handkerchief, Ann Lovely.

MRS LOVELY I hate handkerchiefs when 'tis not cold weather, Mr Prim.

MRS PRIM I have seen thee wear a handkerchief – nay, and a mask to boot – in the middle of July.

MRS LOVELY Aye, to keep the sun from scorching me.

PRIM If thou couldst not bear the sunbeams, how dost thou think man should bear thy beams? Those breasts inflame desire; let them be hid, I say.

MRS LOVELY Let me be quiet, I say. Must I be tormented thus forever? Sure no woman's condition ever equaled mine; foppery, folly, avarice, and hypocrisy are by turns my constant companions, and I must vary shapes as often as a player. I cannot think my father meant this tyranny. No, you usurp an authority which he never intended you should take.

PRIM Hark thee, dost thou call good counsel tyranny? Do I or my wife tyrannize when we desire thee in all love to put off thy tempting attire and veil thy provokers to sin?

MRS LOVELY Deliver me, good Heaven! Or I shall go distracted. (*walks about)*

MRS PRIM So! Now thy pinners are tossed and thy breasts pulled up. Verily, they were seen enough before; fie upon the filthy tailor who made them stays.

MRS LOVELY I wish I were in my grave! Kill me rather than treat me thus.

PRIM Kill thee! Ha, ha, thou think'st thou are acting

some lewd play, sure-kill thee! Art thou prepared for death, Ann Lovely? No, no, thou wouldst rather have a husband, Ann. Thou wantest a gilt coach with six lazy fellows behind to flaunt it in the ring of vanity, among the princes and rulers of the land who pamper themselves with the fatness thereof. But I will take care that none shall squander away thy father's estate; thou shalt marry none such, Ann.

MRS LOVELY   Would you marry me to one of your own canting sex?

PRIM   Yea, verily, none else shall ever get my consent, I assure thee, Ann.

MRS LOVELY   And I do assure thee, Obadiah, that I will as soon turn papist and die in a convent.

MRS PRIM   O wickedness!

MRS LOVELY   O stupidity!

PRIM   O blindness of heart!

MRS LOVELY *(aside to Prim)* Thou blinder of the world, don't provoke me, lest I betray your sanctity and leave your wife to judge of your purity. What were the emotions of your spirit when you squeezed Mary by the hand last night in the pantry, when she told you you bussed so filthily? Ah, you had no aversion to naked bosoms when you begged her to show you a little, little, little bit of her delicious bubby. Don't you remember those words, Mr Prim?

MRS PRIM   What does she say, Obadiah?

PRIM   She talketh unintelligibly, Sarah. *(Aside)* Which way did she hear this? This should not have reached the ears of the wicked ones; verily, it troubleth me.

Enter Servant.

SERVANT   Philip Modelove, whom they call Sir Philip, is below and such another with him; shall I send them up?

PRIM   Yea.

SIR PHILIP   How dost thou do, Friend Prim? *(To Mrs Prim)* Odso, my she-friend here too! What, you are documenting Miss Nancy, reading her a lecture upon the pinched coif, I warrant ye.

MRS PRIM   I am sure thou never readest her any lecture that was good. *(Aside)* My flesh riseth so at these wicked ones that prudence adviseth me to withdraw from their sight.

Exit.

COLONEL *(aside)*   O, that I could find means to speak to her. How charming she appears. I wish I could get this letter into her hand.

SIR PHILIP   Well, Miss Cocky, I hope thou has got the better of them.

MRS LOVELY   The difficulties of my life are not to be surmount-
ed, Sir Philip. *(Aside)* I hate the impertinence of him as much as the
stupidity of the other.

PRIM   Verily, Philip, thou wilt spoil this maiden.

SIR PHILIP   I find we still differ in opinion; but that we may
none of us spoil her, prithee, Prim, let us consent to marry her. I have
sent for our brother guardians to meet me here about that very thing. –
Madam, will you give me leave to recommend a husband to you? Here's
a gentleman which, in my mind, you can have no objection to.

Presents the Colonel to her; she looks another way.

MRS LOVELY *(aside)*   Heaven deliver me from the formal and the
fantastic fool.

COLONEL   A fine woman, a fine horse, and fine equipage are
the finest things in the universe. And if I am so happy to possess you,
madam, I shall become the envy of mankind, as much as you outshine
your whole sex.

*As he takes her hand to kiss it, he endeavours to put the letter into it; she
lets it drop; Prim takes it up.*

MRS LOVELY   I have no ambition to appear conspicuously
ridiculous. *(turning from him)*

COLONEL   So falls the hopes of Fainwell.

MRS LOVELY *(aside)*   Ha! Fainwell! 'Tis he. What have I done? Prim
has the letter, and all will be discovered.

PRIM   Friend, I know not thy name, so cannot call thee
by it; but thou seest thy letter is unwelcome to the maiden; she will not
read it.

MRS LOVELY   Nor shall you. *(snatches the letter)* I'll tear it in a
thousand pieces and scatter it, as I will the hopes of all those that any of
you shall recommend to me.

Tears the letter.

SIR PHILIP   Ha! Right woman, faith.

COLONEL *(aside)*   Excellent woman.

PRIM   Friend thy garb savoreth too much of the vanity
of the age for my approbation; nothing that resembleth Philip
Modelove shall I love, mark that. Therefore Friend Philip, bring no
more of thy own apes under my roof.

SIR PHILIP   I am so entirely a stranger to the monsters of thy
breed that I shall bring none of them, I am sure.

COLONEL *(aside)*　　　I am likely to have a pretty task by that time I have through them all; but she's a city worth taking, and egad, I'll carry on the siege. If I can blow up the outworks, fancy I am pretty secure of the town.

SERVANT *(to Sir Philip)* Toby Periwinkle and Thomas Tradelove demandeth to see thee.

SIR PHILIP　　　　　　Bid them come up.

Exit Servant.

MRS LOVELY *(aside)* Deliver me from such an inundation of noise and nonsense. O, Fainwell! Whatever thy contrivance is, prosper it Heaven – but O, I fear thou never canst redeem me. *(exits)*

SIR PHILIP　　　　　　*Sic transit gloria mundi!*

Enter Mr Periwinkle and Tradelove.

SIR PHILIP *(aside to the Colonel)* These are my brother guardians, Mr Fainwell; prithee observe the creatures.

TRADELOVE　　　　　　Well, Sir Philip, I obey your summons.

PERIWINKLE　　　　　Pray, what have you to offer for the good of Mrs Lovely, Sir Philip?

SIR PHILIP　　　　　　First, I desire to know what you intend to do with that lady. Must she be sent to the Indies for a venture, or live to be an old maid and then entered amongst your curiosities and shown for a monster, Mr Periwinkle?

COLONEL *(aside)*　　Humph, curiosities. That must be the virtuoso.

PERIWINKLE　　　　　Why, what would you do with her?

SIR PHILIP　　　　　　I would recommend this gentleman to her for a husband, sir, a person whom I have picked out from the whole race of mankind.

PRIM　　　　　　　　I would advise thee to shuffle him again with the rest of mankind, for I like him not.

COLONEL　　　　　　Pray, sir, without offense to your formality, what may be your objections?

PRIM　　　　　　　　Thy person; thy manners; thy dress; thy acquaintance – thy everything, friend.

SIR PHILIP　　　　　　You are most particularly obliging, friend, ha ha.

TRADELOVE.　　　　　What business do you follow, pray sir?

COLONEL *(aside)*　　Humph, by that question he must be the broker. *(Aloud)* Business, sir! The business of a gentleman.

TRADELOVE　　　　　　That is as much as to say you dress fine, feed high, lie with every woman you like, and pay your surgeon's bills better than your tailor's or your butcher s.

COLONEL   The court is much obliged to you, sir, for your
character of a gentleman.

TRADELOVE   The court, sir! What would the court do without
us citizens?

SIR PHILIP   Without your wives and daughters, you mean, Mr
Tradelove?

PERIWINKLE   Have you ever traveled, sir?

COLONEL *(aside)*   That question must not be answered now.
(aloud) In books I have, sir.

PERIWINKLE   In books? That's fine traveling indeed! – Sir
Philip, when you present a person I like, he shall have my consent to
marry Mrs Lovely; till when, your servant. *(exits)*

COLONEL *(aside)*   I'll make you like me before I have done with you
or I am mistaken.

TRADELOVE   And when you can convince me that a beau is
more useful to my country than a merchant, then you shall have mine;
till then, you must excuse me.

COLONEL *(aside)*   So much for trade. I'll fit you too. *(exits)*

SIR PHILIP   In my opinion this, this is a very inhumane
treatment as to the lady, Mr Prim.

PRIM   Thy opinion and mine happens to differ as much
as our occupations, friend. Business requireth my presence and folly
thine, and so I must bid thee farewell. *(exits)*

SIR PHILIP   Here's breeding for you, Mr Fainwell. Gad take
me I'd give half my estate to see these rascals bit.

COLONEL *(aside)*   I hope to bite you all, if my plots hit.

They exit.

ACT THREE, SCENE 1

The tavern. Sackbut and the Colonel in an Egyptian dress.

SACKBUT   A lucky beginning, Colonel. You have got the old
beau's consent.

COLONEL   Aye, he's a reasonable creature; but the other
three will require some pains. Shall I pass upon him, think you? Egad,
in my mind I look as antique as if I had been preserved in the ark.

SACKBUT   Pass upon him! Aye, aye, as roundly as white
wine dashed with sack does for mountain and sherry, if you have but
assurance enough.

COLONEL   I have no apprehension from that quarter; assurance is the cockade of a soldier.

SACKBUT   Aye, but the assurance of a soldier differs much from that of a traveler. Can you lie with a good grace?

COLONEL   As heartily, when my mistress is the prize, as I would meet the foe when my country called and king commanded; so don't you fear that part; if he don't know me again, I'm safe. I hope he'll come.

SACKBUT   I wish all my debts would come as sure. I told him you had been a great traveler, had many valuable curiosities, and was a person of a most singular taste; he seemed transported and begged me to keep you till he came.

COLONEL   Aye, ay, he need not fear my running away. Let's have a bottle of sack, landlord; our ancestors drank sack.

SACKBUT   You shall have it.

COLONEL   And whereabouts is the trap door you mentioned?

SACKBUT   There's the conveyance, sir.

Exit.

COLONEL   Now, if I should cheat all these roguish guardians and carry off my mistress in triumph, it would be what the French call a *grand coup d'éclat* – odso! Here comes Periwinkle. Ah, deuce take this beard; pray Jupiter it does not give me the slip and spoil all.

Enter Sackbut with wine, and Periwinkle following.

SACKBUT   Sir, this gentleman, hearing you have been a great traveler and a person of fine speculation, begs leave to take a glass with you; he is a man of a curious taste himself.

COLONEL   The gentleman has it in his face and garb. – Sir, you are welcome.

PERIWINKLE   Sir, I honour a traveler and men of your inquiring disposition. The oddness of your habit pleases me extremely; 'tis very antique, and for that I like it.

COLONEL   It is very antique, sir. This habit once belonged to the famous Claudius Ptolemeus, who lived in the year a hundred and thirty-five.

SACKBUT *(aside)*   If he keeps up to the sample, he shall lie with the devil for a bean-stack, and win it every straw.

PERIWINKLE   A hundred and thirty-five! Why, that's prodigious now well, certainly 'tis the finest thing in the world to be a traveler.

COLONEL For my part, I value none of the modern fashions of a fig leaf.

PERIWINKLE No more do I, sir; I had rather be the jest of a fool than his favorite. I am laughed at here for my singularity. This coat, you must know, sir, was formerly worn by that ingenious and very learned person John Tradescant.

COLONEL John Tradescant! Let me embrace you, sir. John Tradescant was my uncle, by mother side; and I thank you for the honour you do his memory; he was a very curious man indeed.

PERIWINKLE Your uncle, sir! Nay then, 'tis no wonder that your taste is so refined; why, you have it in your blood – my humble service to you, sir. To the immortal memory of John Tradescant, your never-to-be-forgotten uncle. *(drinks)*

COLONEL Give me a glass, landlord.

PERIWINKLE I find you are primitive even in your wine. Canary was the drink of our wise forefathers; 'tis balsamic and saves the charge of apothecaries' cordials. – O, that I had lived in your uncle's days! Or rather, that he were now alive. O, how proud he'd be of such a nephew.

SACKBUT *(aside)* O pox! That would have spoiled the jest.

PERIWINKLE A person of your curiosity must have collected many rarities.

COLONEL I have some, sir, which are not yet come ashore, as an Egyptian's idol.

PERIWINKLE Pray, what might that be?

COLONEL It is, sir, a kind of an ape which they formerly worshipped in that country. I took it from the breast of a female mummy.

PERIWINKLE Ha, ha, our women retain part of their idolatry to this day, for many an ape lies on a lady's breast, ha, ha.

SACKBUT *(aside)* A smart old thief.

COLONEL Two tusks of an hippopotamus, two pair of Chinese nutcrackers, and one Egyptian mummy.

PERIWINKLE Pray, sir, have you never a crocodile?

COLONEL Humph, the boatswain brought one with design to show it, but touching at Rotterdam and hearing it was no rarity in England, he sold it to a Dutch poet.

SACKBUT The devil's in that nation; it rivals us in everything.

PERIWINKLE. I should have been very glad to have seen a living crocodile.

COLONEL My genius led me to things more worth my regard. Sir, I have seen the utmost limits of this globular world;

I have seen the sun rise and set; know in what degree of heat he is at noon to the breadth of a hair, and what quanity of combustibles he burns in a day, how much of it turns to ashes how much to cinders.

PERIWINKLE.   To cinders? You amaze me, sir; I never heard that the sun consumed anything. Descartes tells us –

COLONEL.   Descartes, with the rest of his brethren, both ancient and modern, knew nothing of the matter. I tell you, sir, that nature admits an annual decay, though imperceptible to vulgar eyes. Sometimes his rays destroy below, sometimes above. You have heard of blazing comets, I suppose?

PERIWINKLE   Yes, yes I remember to have seen one; and our astrologers tell us of another which shall happen very quickly.

COLONEL   Those comets are little islands bordering on the sun, which at certain times are set on fire by that luminous body's moving over them perpendicular, which will one day occasion a general conflagration.

SACKBUT (aside)   One need not scruple the Colonel's capacity, faith.

PERIWINKLE   This is marvelous strange. These cinders are what I never read of in any of our learned dissertations.

COLONEL (aside)   I don't know how the devil you should.

SACKBUT (aside)   He has it at his fingers' ends; one would swear he had learned to lie at school, he does it so cleverly.

PERIWINKLE   Well, you travelers see strange things. Pray, sir, have you any of those cinders?

COLONEL   I have, among my other curiosities.

PERIWINKLE   O, what have I lost for want of traveling! Pray, what have you else?

COLONEL   Several things worth your attention. I have a muff made of the feathers of those geese that saved the Roman Capitol.

PERIWINKLE   Is't possible?

SACKBUT (aside)   Yes, if you are such a goose to believe him.

COLONEL   I have an Indian leaf which, open, will cover an acre of land, yet folds up into so little a compass you may put it into your snuffbox.

SACKBUT (aside)   Humph! That's a thunderer.

PERIWINKLE   Amazing!

COLONEL   Ah, mine is but a little one; I have seen some of them tht would cover one of the Caribbean Islands.

PERIWINKLE   Well, if I don't travel before I die, I shan't rest in my grave. Pray, what do the Indians with them?

COLONEL   Sir, they use them in their wars for tents, the old women for riding hoods, the young for fans and umbrellas.

SACKBUT *(aside)*   He has a fruitful invention.

PERIWINKLE   I admire our East India Company imports none of them; they would certainly find their account in them.

COLONEL *(aside)*   Right if they could find the leaves. *(Aloud)* Look ye, sir, do you see this little vial?

PERIWINKLE   Pray you, what is it?

COLONEL   This is called *poluflosboio*.

PERIWINKLE   *Poluflosboio!* It has a rumbling sound.

COLONEL   Right, sir, it proceeds from a rumbling nature. This water was part of those waves which bore Cleopatra's vessel when she sailed to meet Anthony.

PERIWINKLE   Well, of all that ever traveled, none had a taste like you.

COLONEL   But here's the wonder of the world: this, sir, is called *zona*, or *moros musphonon*; the virtues of this is inestimable.

PERIWINKLE   *Moros musphonon!* What in the name of wisdom can that be? To me it seems a plain belt.

COLONEL   This girdle has carried me all the world over.

PERIWINKLE   You have carried it, you mean.

COLONEL   I mean as I say, sir. Whenever I am girded with this, I am invisible; and, by turning this little screw, can be in the court of the Great Mogul, the Grand Signior, and King George in as little time as your cook can poach an egg.

PERIWINKLE   You must pardon me, sir; I can't believe it.

COLONEL   If my landlord pleases, he shall try the experiment immediately.

SACKBUT   I thank you kindly, sir, but I have no inclination to ride post to the devil.

COLONEL   No, no, you shan't stir a foot; I'll only make you invisible.

SACKBUT   But if you could not make me visible again –

PERIWINKLE   Come try it upon me, sir; I'm not afraid of the devil nor all his tricks. 'Sbud, I'll stand 'em all.

COLONEL   There, sir, put it on. – Come, landlord, you and I must face the east. *(They tum about)* – Is it on, sir?

PERIWINKLE   'Tis on.

They turn about again.

SACKBUT   Heaven protect me! Where is he?

PERIWINKLE   Why here, just where I was.

SACKBUT   Where, where, in the name of virtue? Ah, poor Mr Periwinkle! – Egad, look to't, you had best, sir, and and let him be seen again, or I shall have you burnt for a wizard.

COLONEL   Have patience, good landlord.

PERIWINKLE.   But really, don't you see me now?

SACKBUT   No more than I see my grandmother that died forty years ago.

PERIWINKLE.   Are you sure you don't lie? Methinks I stand just where I did, and see you as plain as I did before.

SACKBUT   Ah, I wish I could see you once again!

COLONEL   Take off the girdle, sir.

He takes it off.

SACKBUT   Ah, sir, I am glad to see you with all my heart. *(embraces him)*

PERIWINKLE   This is very odd; certainly there must be some trick in't – pray, sir, will you do me the favor to put it on yourself?

COLONEL   With all my heart.

PERIWINKLE   But first I'll secure the door.

COLONEL   You know how to turn the screw Mr Sackbut.

SACKBUT   Yes, yes – come, Mr Periwinkle, we must turn full east

They turn. The Colonel sinks down a trap door.

COLONEL   'Tis done; now turn.

They turn.

PERIWINKLE.   Ha! Mercy upon me! My flesh creeps upon my bones – this must be a conjurer, Mr Sackbut

SACKBUT   He is the devil, I think.

PERIWINKLE   O! Mr Sackbut, why do you name the devil, when perhaps he may be at your elbow.

SACKBUT   At my elbow! Marry, Heaven forbid.

COLONEL *(below)*   Are you satisfied, sir?

PERIWINKLE   Yes, sir, yes – how hollow his voice sounds!

SACKBUT   Yours seemed just the same. Faith I wish this girdle were mine; I'd sell wine no more. Hark ye, Mr Periwinkle, *(takes him aside till the Colonel rises again)* if he would sell this girdle you might travel with great expedition.

COLONEL   But it is not to be parted with for money.

PERIWINKLE.   I am sorry for't, sir, because I think it the greatest curiosity ever heard of.

COLONEL   By the advice of a learned physiognomist in Grand Cairo, who consulted the lines in my face, I returned to England, where, he told me, I should find a rarity in the keeping of four men which I was born to possess for the benefit of mankind, and the first of the four that gave me his consent, I should present him with this girdle. Till I have found this jewel, I shall not part with the girdle.

PERIWINKLE   What can that rarity be? Did he not name it to you?

COLONEL   Yes, sir; he called it a chaste, beautiful, unaffected woman.

PERIWINKLE   Pish! Women are no rarities. I never had any great taste that way. I married, indeed, to please a father, and I got a girl to please my wife; but she and the child (thank Heaven) died together. Women are the very gewgaws of the creation, playthings for boys which, when they write man, they ought to throw aside.

SACKBUT *(aside)*   A fine lecture to be read to a circle of ladies.

PERIWINKLE   What woman is there, dressed in all the pride and foppery of the times, can boast of such a foretop as the cockatoo?

COLONEL *(aside)*   I must humour him. *(Aloud)* Such a skin as the lizard?

PERIWINKLE   Such a shining breast as the hummingbird?

COLONEL   Such a shape as the antelope?

PERIWINKLE   Or, in all the artful mixture of their various dresses, have they half the beauty of one box of butterflies?

COLONEL   No, that must be allowed – for my part, if it were not for the benefit of mankind, I'd have nothing to do with them, for they are as indifferent to me as a sparrow or a flesh fly.

PERIWINKLE   Pray, sir, what benefit is the world to reap from this lady?

COLONEL   Why, sir, she is to bear me a son, who shall restore the art of embalming and the old Roman manner of burying their dead; and, for the benefit of posterity, he is to discover the longitude, so long sought for in vain.

PERIWINKLE   Od! These are very valuable things, Mr Sackbut

SACKBUT *(aside)*   He hits it off admirably and t'other swallows it like sack and sugar. – *(To Periwinkle)* Certainly this lady must be your ward, Mr Periwinkle, by her being under the care of four persons.

PERIWINKLE   By the description it should. *(Aside)* Egad, if I could get that girdle, I'd ride with the sun, and make the tour of the whole world in four and twenty hours. – *(To the Colonel)* And are you to give that girdle to the first of the four guardians that shall give his consent to marry that lady, say you, sir?

COLONEL   I am so ordered, when I can find him.

PERIWINKLE   I fancy I know the very woman. Her name is Ann Lovely.

COLONEL   Excellent! He said, indeed, that the first letter of her name was L.

PERIWINKLE   Did he really? Well, that's prodigiously amazing, that a person in Grand Cairo should know anything of my ward.

COLONEL   Your ward?

PERIWINKLE   To be plain with you, sir, I am one of those four guardians.

COLONEL   Are you indeed, sir? I am transported to find the man who is to possess this *moros musphonon* is a person of so curious a taste. Here is a writing drawn up by that famous Egyptian, which, if you will please to sign, you must turn your face full north, and the girdle is yours.

PERIWINKLE   If I live till this boy is born, I'll be embalmed and sent to the Royal Society when I die.

COLONEL   That you shall most certainly.

Enter Drawer.

DRAWER   Here's Mr Staytape, the tailor, inquires for you, Colonel.

SACKBUT   Who do you speak to, you son of a whore?

PERIWINKLE *(aside)* Ha! Colonel!

COLONEL *(aside)*   Confound the blundering dog.

DRAWER   Why, to Colonel –

SACKBUT   Get you out, you rascal. *(kicks him out, and exits after him)*

DRAWER *(leaving)*   What the devil is the matter?

COLONEL *(aside)*   This dog has ruined all my scheme, I see by Periwinkle's looks.

PERIWINKLE   How finely I should have been choused. Colonel, you'll pardon me that I did not give you your title before; it was pure ignorance, faith it was. Pray – hem, hem pray, Colonel, what post had this learned Egyptian in your regiment?

COLONEL *(aside)*   A pox of your sneer. *(Aloud)* I don't understand you, sir.

PERIWINKLE   No? That's strange. I understand you, Colonel –

an Egyptian of Grand Cairo! Ha, ha, ha. I am sorry such a well-invented tale should do you no more service. We old fellows can see as far into a millstone as him that picks it. I am not to be tricked out of my trust; mark that.

COLONEL *(aside)* The devil! I must carry it off; I wish I were fairly out. *(Aloud)* Look ye, sir, you may make what jest you please, but the stars will be obeyed, sir, and, depend upon it, I shall have the lady, and you none of the girdle. *(Aside)* Now for Freeman's part of the plot.

Exit (unseen by Periwinkle).

PERIWINKLE The stars! Ha, ha, no star has favored you, it seems. The girdle! Ha, ha, ha, none of your legerdemain tricks can pass upon me. Why, what a pack of trumpery has this rogue picked up. His *pagod, poluflosboios,* his *zonas, moros musphonons,* and the devil knows what. But I'll take care – ha gone? Aye, 'twas time to sneak off. – *(calls out)* Soho! The house!

Enter Sackbut.

PERIWINKLE Where is this trickster? Send for a constable; I'll have this rascal before the Lord Mayor. I'll Grand Cairo him, with a pox to him. I believe you had a hand in putting this imposture upon me, Sackbut.

SACKBUT Who, I, Mr Periwinkle? I scorn it; I perceived he was a cheat and left the room on purpose to send for a constable to apprehend him, and endeavored to stop him when he went out; but the rogue made but one step from the stairs to the door, called a coach, leapt into it, and drove away like the devil, as Mr Freeman can witness, who is at the bar and desires to speak with you. He is this minute come to town.

PERIWINKLE Send him in.

Exit Sackbut.

PERIWINKLE What a scheme this rogue had laid. How I should have been laughed at, had it succeeded.

Enter Freeman, booted and spurred.

PERIWINKLE Mr Freeman, your dress commands your welcome to town; what will you drink? I had like to have been imposed upon here by the veriest rascal.

FREEMAN I am sorry to hear it. The dog flew for't; he had not 'scaped me, if I had been aware of him; Sackbut struck at him but missed his blow, or he had done his business for him.

PERIWINKLE   I believe you never heard of such a contrivance, Mr Freeman, as this fellow had found out.

FREEMAN   Mr Sackbut has told me the whole story, Mr Periwinkle. But now I have something to tell you of much more importance to yourself. I happened to lie one night at Coventry, and knowing your uncle, Sir Toby Periwinkle, I paid him a visit and to my great surprise found him dying.

PERIWINKLE   Dying!

FREEMAN   Dying, in all appearance; the servants weeping, the room in darkness. The apothecary, shaking his head, told me the doctors had given him over, and then there is small hopes, you know.

PERIWINKLE   I hope he has made his will. He always told me he would make me his heir.

FREEMAN   I have heard you say as much and therefore resolved to give you notice. I should think it would not be amiss if you went down tomorrow morning.

PERIWINKLE   It is a long journey, and the roads very bad.

FREEMAN   But he has a great estate, and the land very good. Think upon that.

PERIWINKLE   Why, that's true, as you say. I'll think upon it. In the meantime, I give you many thanks for your civility, Mr Freeman, and should be glad of your company to dine with me.

FREEMAN   I am obliged to be at Jonathan's Coffee House at two and it is now half an hour after one; if I dispatch my business I'll wait on you. I know your hour.

PERIWINKLE   You shall be very welcome, Mr Freeman; and so, your humble servant.

Exit.

FREEMAN   Ha, ha, ha, I have done your business, Colonel; he has swallowed the bait.

COLONEL   I overheard all, though I am a little in the dark. I am to personate a highwayman, I suppose. That's a project I am not fond of; for though I may fright him out of his consent he may fright me out of my life when he discovers me as he certainly must in the end.

FREEMAN   No, no, I have a plot for you without danger; but first we must manage Tradelove. Has the tailor brought your clothes?

SACKBUT   Yes, pox take the thief.

COLONEL   Pox take your drawer for a jolt-headed rogue.

FREEMAN   Well, well, no matter; I warrant we have him yet, but now you must put on the Dutch merchant.

COLONEL The deuce of this trading plot. I wish he had been an old soldier that I might have attacked him in my own way: heard him fight over all the battles of the Civil War – but for trade, by Jupiter, I shall never do it.

SACKBUT Never fear, Colonel, Mr Freeman will instruct you.

FREEMAN You'll see what others do; the coffee house will instruct you.

COLONEL I must venture, however. But I have a farther plot in my head upon Tradelove which you must assist me in, Freeman; you are in credit with him I heard you say.

FREEMAN I am, and will scruple nothing to serve you, Colonel.

COLONEL Come along then. Now for the Dutchman –
honest Ptolemy, by your leave,
Now must bob wig and business come in play,
And a fair thirty thousand pounder leads the way.

ACT FOUR, SCENE 1

Jonathan's Coffee House in Exchange Alley. Crowd of people with rolls of paper and parchment in their hands; a bar and Coffee Boys waiting. Enter Tradelove and Stockjobbers, with rolls of paper and parchment.

1st STOCKJOBBER South Sea at seven-eighths! Who buys?

2nd STOCKJOBBER South Sea bonds due at Michaelmas, 1718! Class Lottery tickets!

3rd STOCKJOBBER East India bonds?

4th STOCKJOBBER What, all sellers and no buyers? Gentlemen, I'll buy a thousand pound for Tuesday next at three-fourths.

COFFEE BOY Fresh coffee, gentlemen, fresh coffee?

TRADELOVE Hark ye, Gabriel, you'll pay the difference of that stock we transacted for t'other day.

GABRIEL Aye, Mr Tradelove, here's a note for the money, upon the Sword Blade Company. *(gives him a note)*

COFFEE BOY Bohea tea, gentlemen?

Enter a Man.

MAN Is Mr Smuggle here?

COFFEE BOY Mr Smuggle's not here, sir; you'll find him at the books.

2nd STOCKJOBBER   Ho! Here comes two sparks from the other end of the town; what news bring they?

Enter two Gentlemen.

TRADELOVE   I would fain bite that spark in the brown coat; he comes very often into the Alley but never employs a broker.

Enter Colonel and Freeman.

2nd STOCKJOBBER   Who does anything in the Civil List Lottery? Or Caco? – Zounds, where are all the Jews this afternoon? – *(To Third Stockjobber)* Are you a bull or a bear today, Abraham?

3rd STOCKJOBBER   A bull, faith – but I have a good put for next week.

TRADELOVE   Mr Freeman, your servant. *(points to the Colonel)* Who is that gentleman?

FREEMAN   A Dutch merchant, just come to England; but hark ye, Mr Tradelove – I have a piece of news will get you as much as the French king's death did, if you are expeditious.

TRADELOVE   Say you so, sir! Pray, what is it?

FREEMAN *(showing him a letter)* Read there; I received it just now from one that belongs to the Emperor's minister.

TRADELOVE *(reads aloud)* "Sir, As I have many obligations to you, I cannot miss any opportunity to show my gratitude; this moment, my lord has received a private express that the Spaniards have raised their siege from before Cagliari; if this prove any advantage to you, it will answer both the ends and wishes of, sir, your most obliged humble servant, Henricus Dusseldorp." "Postscript. In two or three hours the news will be public." *(Aside to Freeman)* May one depend upon this, Mr Freeman?

FREEMAN   You may – I never knew this person send me a false piece of news in my life.

TRADELOVE *(aside to Freeman)* Sir, I am much obliged to you; egad, 'tis rare news. *(Aloud)* Who sells South Sea for next week?

STOCKJOBBERS *(all together)* I sell; I, I, I, I, I sell.

1st STOCKJOBBER   I'll sell five thousand pounds for next week at five-eighths.

2nd STOCKJOBBER   I'll sell ten thousand at five-eighths for the same time.

TRADELOVE   Nay, nay, hold, hold, not all together, gentlemen; I'll be no bull; I'll buy no more than I can take. Will you sell ten thousand pound at a half, any day next week except Saturday?

1st STOCKJOBBER   I'll sell it to you, Mr Tradelove.

Freeman whispers to one of the Gentlemen.

GENTLEMAN *(aloud)* The Spaniards raise the siege of Cagliari! I don't believe one word of it.

2nd GENTLEMAN   Raised the siege! As much as you have raised the Monument.

FREEMAN   'Tis raised, I assure you, sir.

2nd GENTLEMAN   What will you lay on't?

FREEMAN   What you please.

1st GENTLEMAN   Why I have a brother upon the spot in the Emperor's service; I am certain if there were any such thing, I should have had a letter.

A STOCKJOBBER   How's this? The siege of Cagliari raised – I wish it may be true; 'twill make business stir and stocks rise.

1st STOCKJOBBER   Tradelove's a cunning fat bear if this news proves true, I shall repent I sold him the five thousand pounds. *(To Freeman)* Pray sir, what assurance have you that the siege is raised?

FREEMAN   There is come an express to the Emperor's minister.

2nd STOCKJOBBER   I'll know that presently.

Exit.

1st GENTLEMAN   Let it come where it will. I'll hold you fifty pounds 'tis false.

FREEMAN   'Tis done.

2nd GENTLEMAN   I'll lay you a brace of hundreds upon the same.

FREEMAN   I'll take you.

4th STOCKJOBBER   Egad, I'll hold twenty pieces 'tis not raised, sir.

FREEMAN   Done with you, too.

TRADELOVE   I'll lay any man a brace of thousands the siege is raised.

FREEMAN *(aside to Tradelove)* The Dutch merchant is your man to take in.

TRADELOVE   Does not he know the news?

FREEMAN *(to Tradelove)* Not a syllable; if he did he would bet a hundred thousand pound as soon as one penny. He's plaguy rich and a mighty man at wagers.

TRADELOVE   Say you so – egad, I'll bite him if possible. *(To the Colonel)* Are you from Holland, sir?

COLONEL   Ya, mynheer.

TRADELOVE   Had you the news before you came away?

COLONEL   Wat believe you, mynheer?

TRADELOVE   What do I believe? Why, I believe that the Spaniards have actually raised the siege of Cagliari.

COLONEL   What duyvel's niews is dat? 'Tis niet waer, mynheer – 'tis no true, sir.

TRADELOVE   'Tis so true, mynheer that I'll lay you two thousand pounds upon it. *(Aside to Freeman)* You are sure the letter may be depended upon, Mr Freeman?

FREEMAN *(aside to Tradelove)* Do you think I would venture my money if I were not sure of the truth of it?

COLONEL   Two duysend pond, mynheer; 'tis gedhaen. Dis gentleman sal hold de gelt. *(gives Freeman money)*

FREEMAN   With all my heart. This binds the wager.

TRADELOVE   You have certainly lost, mynheer; the siege is raised indeed.

COLONEL   Ik gelove't niet, Mynheer Freeman; ik sal ye dubbled houden, if you please.

FREEMAN   I am let into the secret, therefore won't win your money.

TRADELOVE *(aside)*   Ha, ha, ha! I have snapped the Dutchman, faith, ha, ha! This is no ill day's work. *(Aloud)* Pray, may I crave your name, mynheer?

COLONEL   Myn naem, mynheer? Myn naem is Jan van Timtamtirelereletta Heer van Fainwell.

TRADELOVE   Zounds, 'tis a damned long name; I shall never remember it. Mynheer van Tim-Tim-Tim-what the devil is it?

FREEMAN   O, never heed; I know the gentleman and will pass my word for twice the sum.

TRADELOVE   That's enough.

COLONEL *(aside)*   You'll hear of me sooner than you wish, old gentleman, I fancy. You'll come to Sackbut's, Freeman?

FREEMAN *(aside to the Colonel)* Immediately.

Exit Colonel.

1st MAN   Humphrey Hump here?

COFFEE BOY   Mr Humphrey Hump is not here you'll find him upon the Dutch Walk.

TRADELOVE   Mr Freeman, I give you many thanks for your kindness.

FREEMAN *(aside)*   I fear you'll repent when you know all.

TRADELOVE   Will you dine with me?
FREEMAN   I am engaged at Sackbut's; adieu.

Exit.

TRADELOVE   Sir, your humble servant. Now I'll see what I can do upon Change with my news.

Exit.

ACT FOUR, SCENE 2

The tavern. Enter Freeman and Colonel.

FREEMAN   Ha, ha, ha! The old fellow swallowed that bait as greedily as a gudgeon.

COLONEL   I have him, faith ha, ha, ha. His two thousand pound's secure; if he would keep his money, he must part with the lady, ha, ha. – What came of your two friends? They performed their part very well; you should have brought 'em to take a glass with us.

FREEMAN   No matter; we'll drink a bottle together another time. I did not care to bring them hither; there's no necessity to trust them with the main secret, you know, Colonel.

COLONEL   Nay, that's right, Freeman.

Enter Sackbut.

SACKBUT   Joy, joy, Colonel; the luckiest accident in the world!

COLONEL   What say'st thou?

SACKBUT   This letter does your business.

COLONEL *(reads aloud)* "To Obadiah Prim, hosier, near the building called the Monument, in London."

FREEMAN   A letter to Prim. – *(To Sackbut)* How came you by it?

SACKBUT   Looking over the letters our postwoman brought, as I always do to see what letters are directed to my house (for she can't read, you must know), I spied this, to Prim, so paid for't among the rest; I have given the old jade a pint of wine on purpose to delay time, till you see if the letter will be of any service; then I'll seal it up again and tell her I took it by mistake. I have read it and fancy you'll like the project – read, read, Colonel.

COLONEL *(reads aloud)* "Friend Prim, There is arrived from Pennsylvania one Simon Pure, a leader of the faithful, who hath sojourned with us eleven days and hath been of great comfort to the Brethren. He intendeth for the quarterly meeting in London; I have recommended him to thy house; I pray thee entreat him kindly, and let thy wife cherish him, for he's of weakly constitution. He will depart from us the third day; which is all from thy friend in the faith, Aminadab Holdfast." Ha, ha, excellent. I understand you, landlord, I am to personate this Simon Pure, am I not?

SACKBUT   Don't you like the hint?

COLONEL   Admirably well.

FREEMAN   'Tis the best contrivance in the world, if the right Simon gets not there before you.

COLONEL   No, no, the Quakers never ride post; he can't be here before tomorrow at soonest. Do you send and buy me a Quaker's dress, Mr Sackbut; and suppose, Freeman, you should wait at the Bristol coach, that if you see any such person, you might contrive to give me notice.

FREEMAN   I will. – The country dress and boots, are they ready?

SACKBUT   Yes, yes, everything, sir.

FREEMAN   Bring 'em in then. *(Sackbut exits.)* Thou must dispatch Periwinkle first. Remember, his uncle, Sir Toby Periwinkle, is an old bachelor of seventy-five, that he has seven hundred a year, most in abbey land; that he was once in love with your mother, and shrewdly suspected by some to be your father – that you have been thirty years his steward and ten years his gentleman; remember to improve these hints.

COLONEL   Never fear; let me alone for that. But what's the steward's name?

FREEMAN   His name is Pillage.

COLONEL   Enough. *(Sackbut enters with the clothes.)* Now for the country put.

FREEMAN   Egad, landlord, thou deservest to have the first night's lodging with the lady for thy fidelity. – What say you, Colonel, shall we settle a club here, you'll make one?

COLONEL   Make one? I'll bring a set of honest officers that will spend their money as freely to the king's health, as they would his blood in their service.

SACKBUT   I thank you Colonel. *(Bell rings)* – Here, here.

Exit Sackbut.

COLONEL   So now for my boots. *(puts on boots)* Shall I find you here, Freeman, when I come back?

FREEMAN Yes, or I'll leave word with Sackbut where he may send for me. Have you the writings? The will and everything?

COLONEL All, all.

Enter Sackbut.

SACKBUT Zounds, Mr Freeman, yonder is Tradelove in the damned'st passion in the world. He swears you are in the house; he says you told him you was to dine here.

FREEMAN I did so, ha, ha, ha. He has found himself bit already.

COLONEL The devil! He must not see me in this dress.

SACKBUT *(to Freeman)* I told him I expected you here but you were not come yet.

FREEMAN Very well. Make you haste out, Colonel, and let me alone to deal with him. Where is he?

SACKBUT In the King's Head.

COLONEL You remember what I told you?

FREEMAN Aye, ay, very well, landlord; let him know I am come in – and now Pillage, success attend you.

Exit Sackbut.

COLONEL Mr Proteus, rather. –
From changing shape and imitating Jove
I draw the happy omens of my love.
I'm not the first young brother of the blade
Who made his fortune in a masquerade.

Exit Colonel.

FREEMAN Zounds Mr Tradelove, we're bit, it seems.

TRADELOVE Bit, do you call it, Mr Freeman, I am ruined – pox on your news.

FREEMAN Pox on the rascal that sent it me.

TRADELOVE Sent it you! Why Gabriel Skinflint has been at the minister's and spoke with him, and he has assured him 'tis every syllable false; he received no such express.

FREEMAN I know it. I this minute parted with my friend, who protested he never sent me any such letter. Some roguish stockjobber has done it on purpose to make me lose my money; that's certain; I wish I knew who he was; I'd make him repent it. I have lost three hundred pounds by it.

TRADELOVE   What signifies your three hundred pounds to what I have lost? There's two thousand pounds to that Dutchman with the cursed long name, besides the stock I bought; the devil! I could tear my flesh. I must never show my face upon Change more, for, by my soul, I can't pay it.

FREEMAN   I am heartily sorry for't. What can I serve you in? Shall I speak to the Dutch merchant and try to get you time for the payment?

TRADELOVE   Time! Adsheart, I shall never be able to look up again.

FREEMAN   I am very much concerned that I was the occasion and wish I could be an instrument of retrieving your misfortune; for my own, I value it not. Adso! A thought comes into my head that, well improved, may be of service.

TRADELOVE   Ah, there's no thought can be of any service to me without paying the money, or running away.

FREEMAN   How do you know? What do you think of my proposing Mrs Lovely to him? He is a single man, and I heard him say he had a mind to marry an English woman; nay, more than that, he said somebody told him you had a pretty ward. He wished you had betted her instead of your money.

TRADELOVE   Aye, but he'd be hanged before he'd take her instead of the money; the Dutch are too covetous for that; besides, he did not know that there were three more of us, I suppose.

FREEMAN   So much the better; you may venture to give him your consent, if he'll forgive you the wager. It is not your business to tell him that your consent will signify nothing.

TRADELOVE   That's right as you say; but will he do it, think you?

FREEMAN   I can't tell that; but I'll try what I can do with him. He has promised me to meet me here an hour hence; I'll feel his pulse and let you know. If I find it feasible, I'll send for you; if not, you are at liberty to take what measures you please.

TRADELOVE   You must extol her beauty, double her portion, and tell him I have the entire disposal of her, and that she can't marry without my consent – and that I am a covetous rogue and will never part with her without a valuable consideration.

FREEMAN   Aye, aye, let me alone for a lie at a pinch.

TRADELOVE   Egad, if you can bring this to bear Mr Freeman, I'll make you whole again. I'll pay the three hundred pounds you lost, with all my soul.

FREEMAN   Well, I'll use my best endeavours. Where will you be?

TRADELOVE   At home; pray Heaven you prosper. If I were but the sole trustee now, I should not fear it. Who the devil would be a guardian,
If when cash runs low, our coffers t'enlarge,
We can't, like other stocks, transfer our charge?

Exit.

FREEMAN   Ha, ha, ha, he has it!

Exit.

ACT FOUR, SCENE 3

Periwinkle's house. Enter Periwinkle on one side and a Footman on the other.

FOOTMAN   A gentleman from Coventry inquires for you, sir.

PERIWINKLE   From my uncle, I warrant you bring him up. *(Footman exits.)* This will save me the trouble as well as the expenses of a journey.

COLONEL   Is your name Periwinkle, sir?

PERIWINKLE   It is, sir.

COLONEL   I am sorry for the message I bring. My old master, whom I served these forty years, claims the sorrow due from a faithful servant to an indulgent master. *(weeps)*

PERIWINKLE   By this I understand, sir, my uncle, Sir Toby Periwinkle, is dead.

COLONEL   He is, sir, and he has left you heir to seven hundred a year, in as good abbey land as ever paid Peter's pence to Rome. I wish you long to enjoy it, but my tears will flow when I think of my benefactor. *(weeps)* Ah, he was a good man; he has not left many of his fellows. The poor laments him sorely.

PERIWINKLE   I pray, sir, what office bore you?

COLONEL   I was his steward, sir.

PERIWINKLE   I have heard him mention you with much respect; your name is –

COLONEL   Pillage, sir.

PERIWINKLE   Aye, Pillage. I do remember he called you Pillage. Pray, Mr Pillage, when did my uncle die?

COLONEL   Monday last at four in the morning. About two, he signed this will and gave it into my hands and strictly charged me to leave Coventry the moment he expired, and deliver it to you with what speed I could. I have obeyed him, sir, and there is the will. *(gives it to Periwinkle)*

PERIWINKLE   'Tis very well; I'll lodge it in the Commons.

COLONEL   There are two things which he forgot to insert but charged me to tell you that he desired you'd perform them as readily as if you had found them written in the will, which is to remove his corpse and bury him by his father in St. Paul-Covent-Garden, and to give all his servants mourning.

PERIWINKLE *(aside)* That will be a considerable charge; a pox of all modern fashions. – *(Aloud)* Well, it shall be done, Mr Pillage; I will agree with one of death's fashion mongers, called an undertaker, to go down and bring up the body.

COLONEL   I hope, sir, I shall have the honour to serve you in the same station I did your worthy uncle; I have not many years to stay behind him and would gladly spend them in the family where I was brought up. *(weeps)* He was a kind and tender master to me.

PERIWINKLE   Pray, don't grieve, Mr Pillage; you shall hold your place and everything else which you held under my uncle. You make me weep to see you so concerned. *(weeps)* He lived to a good old age, and we are all mortal.

COLONEL   We are so, sir, and therefore I must beg you to sign this lease. You'll find Sir Toby has ta'en particular notice of it in his will. I could not get it time enough from the lawyer, or he had signed it before he died. *(gives him a paper)*

PERIWINKLE   A lease for what?

COLONEL   I rented a hundred a year of Sir Toby upon lease, which lease expires at Lady Day next and I desire to renew it for twenty years; that's all, sir.

PERIWINKLE   Let me see. *(looks over the lease)*

COLONEL *(aside)*   Matters go swimmingly, if nothing intervene.

PERIWINKLE   Very well, let's see what he says in his will about it. *(lays the lease upon the table and looks on the will)*

COLONEL *(aside)*   He's very wary, yet I fancy I shall be too cunning for him.

PERIWINKLE   Ho, here it is – "the farm lying ... now in possession of Samuel Pillage ... suffer him to renew his lease ... at the same rent ..." Very well, Mr Pillage, I see my uncle does mention it, and I'll perform his will. Give me the lease.

Colonel gives it him; he looks upon it and lays it upon the table.

PERIWINKLE   Pray you, step to the door and call for a pen and ink, Mr Pillage.

COLONEL   I have pen and ink in my pocket, sir. *(pulls out an inkhorn)* I never go without that.

PERIWINKLE   I think it belongs to your profession. *(He looks upon the pen while the Colonel changes the lease and lays down the contract.)* I doubt this is but a sorry pen, though it may serve to write my name. *(writes)*

COLONEL *(aside)*   Little does he think what he signs.

PERIWINKLE   There is your lease, Mr Pillage. *(gives him the paper)* Now I must desire you to make what haste you can down to Coventry and take care of everything, and I'll send down the undertaker for the body; do you attend it up, and whatever charge you are at, I will repay you.

COLONEL *(aside)*   You have paid me already, I thank you, sir.

PERIWINKLE   Will you dine with me?

COLONEL   I would rather not; there are some of my neighbors which I met as I came along, who leave the town this afternoon they told me, and I should be glad of their company down.

PERIWINKLE   Well, well, I won't detain you.

COLONEL *(aside)*   I don't care how soon I am out.

PERIWINKLE   I will give orders about mourning.

COLONEL *(aside)*   You will have cause to mourn, when you know your estate imaginary only.
You'll find your hopes and cares alike are vain.
In spite of all the caution you have ta'en.
Fortune rewards the faithful lover's pain.

He exits.

PERIWINKLE   Seven hundred a year! I wish he had died seventeen years ago. What a valuable collection of rarities might I have had by this time! I might have traveled over all the known parts of the globe and made my own closet rival the Vatican at Rome. – Odso, I have a good mind to begin my travels now. Let me see – I am but sixty. My father, grandfather, and great-grandfather reached ninety odd. I have almost forty years good. – Let me consider – what will seven hundred a year amount to – in – aye, in thirty years; I'll say but thirty. Thirty times seven is seven times thirty – that is – just twenty-one thousand pound. 'Tis a great deal of money. I may very well reserve sixteen hundred of it for a collection of such rarities as will make my name famous to posterity.

I would not die like other mortals,
forgotten in a year or two as my uncle will be – no.
With nature's curious works I'll raise my fame
That men, till doomsday, may repeat my name.

Exit.

ACT FOUR, SCENE 4

A tavern. Freeman and Tradelove over a bottle.

TRADELOVE   Come, Mr Freeman, here's Mynheer Jan van Tim
– Tam – Tam – I shall never think of that Dutchman's name.

FREEMAN   Mynheer Jan van Timtamtirelireletta Heer van
Fainwell.

TRADELOVE   Aye, Heer van Fainwell; I never heard such a
confounded name in my life. Here's his health, I say. *(drinks)*

FREEMAN   With all my heart.

TRADELOVE   Faith, I never expected to have found so generous
a thing in a Dutchman.

FREEMAN   O, he has nothing of the Hollander in his temper,
except an antipathy to monarchy. As soon as I told him your circumstances, he replied he would not be the ruin of any man for the world
and immediately made this proposal himself: "Let him take what time
he will for the payment," said he, "or if he'll give me his ward, I'll
forgive him the debt."

TRADELOVE   Well, Mr Freeman, I can but thank you. Egad,
you have made a man of me again; and if ever I lay a wager more, may I
rot in a jail.

FREEMAN   I assure you, Mr Tradelove, I was very much
concerned because I was the occasion – though very innocently, I
protest.

TRADELOVE   I dare swear you was, Mr Freeman

Enter a Fiddler with his Wife.

FIDDLER   Please to have a lesson of music or a song,
gentlemen?

FREEMAN   A song, aye, with all our hearts; have you ever a
merry one?

FIDDLER   Yes, sir, my wife and I can give you a merry
dialogue.

They sing a song.

TRADELOVE	'Tis very pretty, faith.
FREEMAN	There's something for you to drink, friend; go, lose no time.
FIDDLER	I thank you, sir.

They exit.
Enter Drawer and Colonel, dressed for the Dutch Merchant.

COLONEL   Ha, Mynheer Tradelove, ik ben sorry voor your troubles – maer ik sal you easy maeken; ik wil de gelt niet hebben.

TRADELOVE   I shall forever acknowledge the obligation, sir.

FREEMAN   But you understand upon what condition, Mr Tradelove: Mrs Lovely.

COLONEL   Ya, de juffrow sal al te regt setten, mynheer.

TRADELOVE   With all my heart, mynheer, you shall have my consent to marry her freely.

FREEMAN   Well then, as I am a party concerned between you, Mynheer Jan van Timtamtirelireletta Heer van Fainwell shall give you a discharge of your wager under his own hand and you shall give him your consent to marry Mrs Lovely under yours. That is the way to avoid all manner of disputes hereafter.

COLONEL   Ya, waeragtig.

TRADELOVE   Aye, ay, so it is, Mr Freeman; I'll give it under mine this minute. *(sits down to write)*

COLONEL   And so sal ik.

FREEMAN   Soho, the house! *(Drawer enters.)* Bid your master come up. *(Aside)* I'll see there be witnesses enough to the bargain.

Exit Drawer. Enter Sackbut.

SACKBUT   Do you call, gentlemen?

FREEMAN   Aye, Mr Sackbut, we shall want your hand here.

TRADELOVE   There, mynheer, there's my consent as amply as you can desire; but you must insert your own name, for I know not how to spell it; I have left a blank for it. *(gives the Colonel a paper)*

COLONEL   Ya, ik sal dat well doen.

FREEMAN   Now, Mr Sackbut, you and I will witness it.

COLONEL   Daer, Mynheer Tradelove, is your discharge.
       (gives him a paper)

TRADELOVE   Be pleased to witness this receipt too, gentlemen.

Freeman and Sackbut put their hands.

FREEMAN   Aye, aye, that we will.

COLONEL   Well, mynheer, ye most meer doen; ye most myn voorspraek to de juffrow syn.

FREEMAN   He means you must recommend him to the lady.

TRADELOVE   That I will, and to the rest of my brother guardians.

COLONEL   Wat voor den duyvel heb you meer guardians?

TRADELOVE   Only three, mynheer.

COLONEL   Wat, donder heb ye myn betrocken, mynheer? Had ik that gewoeten, soude eaven met yon geweest syn.

SACKBUT   But Mr Tradelove is the principal, and he can do a great deal with the rest, sir.

FREEMAN   And he shall use his interest, I promise you, mynheer.

TRADELOVE   I will say all that ever I can think on to recommend you, mynheer and if you please, I'll introduce you to the lady.

COLONEL   Well, dat is waer. Maer ye must first spreken of myn to de juffrow, and to de oudere, gentlemen.

FREEMAN   Aye, that's the best way, and then I and the Heer van Fainwell will meet you there.

TRADELOVE   I will go this moment, upon honour. Your most obedient humble servant. *(Aside)* My speaking will do you little good, mynheer, ha, ha; we have Ait you, faith, ha, ha; my debt's discharged, and for the man,
He's my consent to get her if he can. *(He exits.)*

COLONEL   Ha, ha, ha, this was a masterpiece of contrivance, Freeman.

FREEMAN   He hugs himself with his supposed good fortune and little thinks the luck's of our side. But come, pursue the fickle goddess while she's in the mood. Now for the Quaker.

COLONEL   That's the hardest task.
Of all the counterfeits performed by man,
A soldier makes the simplest Puritan.

Exit.

ACT FIVE, SCENE 1

Prim's house. Enter Mrs Prim and Mrs Lovely in Quaker's dress, meeting.

MRS PRIM   So now I like thee, Ann. Art thou not better without thy monstrous hoop coat and patches? If Heaven should make thee so many black spots upon thy face, would it not fright thee, Ann?

MRS LOVELY   If it should turn your inside outward and show all the spots of your hypocrisy, 'twould fright me worse.

MRS PRIM   My hypocrisy! I scorn thy words, Ann; I lay no baits.

MRS LOVELY   If you did, you'd catch no fish.

MRS PRIM   Well, well, make thy jests, but I'd have thee to know, Ann, that I could have catched as many fish (as thou call'st them) in my time as ever thou didst with all thy fool traps about thee. If admirers be thy aim, thou wilt have more of them in this dress than thy other. The men, take my word for't, are most desirous to see what we are most careful to conceal.

MRS LOVELY   Is that the reason of your formality, Mrs Prim? Truth will out. I ever thought, indeed, there was more design than godliness in the pinched cap.

MRS PRIM   Go, thou art corrupted with reading lewd plays and filthy romances, good for nothing but to lead youth into the high road of fornication. Ah! I wish thou art not already too familiar with the wicked ones.

MRS LOVELY   Too familiar with the wicked ones! Pray, no more of those freedoms, madam; I am familiar with none so wicked as yourself. How dare you talk thus to me. You, you, you unworthy woman, you –! *(bursts into tears)*

Enter Tradelove.

TRADELOVE   What, in tears, Nancy?– What have you done to her, Mrs Prim, to make her weep?

MRS LOVELY   Done to me! I admire I keep my senses among you. But I will rid myself of your tyranny if there be either law or justice to be had. I'll force you to give me up my liberty.

MRS PRIM   Thou hast more need to weep for thy sins, Ann– yea, for thy manifold sins.

MRS LOVELY   Don't think that I'll be still the fool which you have made me. No, I'll wear what I please, go when and where I please, and keep what company I think fit, and not what you shall direct I will.

TRADELOVE   For my part, I do think all this very reasonable,
Mrs Lovely. 'Tis fit you should have your liberty, and for that very
purpose I am come.

Enter Mr Periwinkle and Obadiah Prim with a letter in his hand.

PERIWINKLE   I have bought some black stockings of your
husband, Mrs Prim, but he tells me the glover's trade belongs to you;
therefore, I pray you look me out five or six dozen of mourning gloves,
such as are given at funerals, and send them to my house.

PRIM   My friend Periwinkle has got a good windfall
today – seven hundred a year.

MRS PRIM   I wish thee joy of it, neighbour.

TRADELOVE   What, is Sir Toby dead then?

PERIWINKLE   He is. – You'll take care, Mrs Prim?

MRS PRIM   Yea, I will, neighbour.

PRIM *(to Mrs Prim)*   This letter recommendeth a speaker; 'tis from
Aminadab Holdfast of Bristol; peradventure he will be here this night;
therefore, Sarah, do thou take care for his reception. *(gives her the
letter)*

MRS PRIM   I will obey thee. *(exits)*

PRIM   What art thou in the dumps for, Ann?

TRADELOVE   We must marry her, Mr Prim.

PRIM   Why truly, if we could find a husband worth
having, I should be as glad to see her married as thou wouldst,
neighbour.

PERIWINKLE   Well said; there are but few worth having.

TRADELOVE   I can recommend you a man now that I think you
can none of you have an objection to!

Enter Sir Philip Modelove.

PERIWINKLE   You recommend! Nay, whenever she marries, I'll
recommend the husband.

SIR PHILIP   What must it be, a whale or a rhinoceros, Mr
Periwinkle, ha, ha, ha? – Mr Tradelove, I have a bill upon you *(gives
him a paper)*, and have been seeking for you all over the town.

TRADELOVE   I'll accept it, Sir Philip, and pay it when due.

PERIWINKLE   He shall be none of the fops at your end of the
town with full perukes and empty skulls, nor yet none of your trading
gentry, who puzzle the heralds to find arms for their coaches. No, he
shall be a man famous for travels, solidity, and curiosity – one who has
searched into the profundity of nature. When Heaven shall direct

such a one, he shall have my consent, because it may turn to the benefit of mankind.

MRS LOVELY   The benefit of mankind! What, would you anatomize me?

SIR PHILIP   Aye, ay, madam, he would dissect you.

TRADELOVE   Or pore over you through a microscope to see how your blood circulates from the crown of your head to the sole of your foot, ha, ha! But I have a husband for you, a man that knows how to improve your fortune; one that trades to the four corners of the globe.

MRS LOVELY   And would send me for a venture, perhaps.

TRADELOVE   One that will dress you in all the pride of Europe, Asia, Africa, and America – a Dutch merchant, my girl.

SIR PHILIP   A Dutchman! Ha, ha, there's a husband for a fine lady – ya juffrow, will you met myn slapen-ha, ha. He'll learn you to talk the language of the hogs, madam, ha, ha.

TRADELOVE   He'll learn you that one merchant is of more service to a nation than fifty coxcombs. The Dutch know the trading interest to be of more benefit to the state than the landed.

SIR PHILIP   But what is either interest to a lady?

TRADELOVE   'Tis the merchant makes the belle. How would the ladies sparkle in the box without the merchant? The Indian diamonds! The French brocade! The Italian fan! The Flanders lace! The fine Dutch holland! How would they vent their scandal over their tea tables? And where would you beaus have champagne to toast your mistresses, were it not for the merchant?

PRIM   Verily, neighbor Tradelove, thou dost waste thy breath about nothing. All that thou hast said tendeth only to debauch youth and fill their heads with the price and luxury of this world. The merchant is a very great friend to Satan and sendeth as many to his dominions as the pope.

PERIWINKLE   Right, I say knowledge makes the man.

PRIM   Yea, but not thy kind of knowledge. It is the knowledge of truth. Search thou for the light within and not for baubles, friend.

MRS LOVELY   Ah, study your country's good, Mr. Periwinkle, and not her insects; rid you of your home-bred monsters before you fetch any from abroad. I dare swear you have maggots enough in your own brain to stock all the virtuosos in Europe with butterflies.

SIR PHILIP   By my soul, Miss Nancy's a wit.

PRIM   That is more than she can say by thee, friend.

Look ye, it is in vain to talk; when I meet a man worthy of her, she shall have my leave to marry him.

MRS LOVELY   Provided he be one of the faithful. *(Aside)* Was there ever such a swarm of caterpillars to blast the hopes of a woman? *(Aloud)* Know this: that you contend in vain. I'll have no husband of your choosing, nor shall you lord it over me long. I'll try the power of an English senate – orphans have been redressed and wills set aside, and none did ever deserve their pity more.

(Aside) O Fainwell! Where are thy promises to free me from these vermin?

Alas, the task was more difficult than he imagined!

A harder task than what the poets tell
Of yore, the fair Andromeda befell;
She but one monster feared, I've four to fear,
And see no Perseus, no deliv'rer near.

She exits. Enter Servant who whispers to Prim.

SERVANT   One Simon Pure inquireth for thee.
PERIWINKLE   The woman is mad.
SIR PHILIP   So are you all, in my opinion. *(exits)*
PRIM   Friend Tradelove, business requireth my presence.
TRADELOVE   O, I shan't trouble you. – *(Aside)* Pox take him for an unmannerly dog – however, I have kept my word with my Dutchman and will introduce him too for all you.

He exits. Enter Colonel in a Quaker's habit.

PRIM   Friend Pure, thou art welcome; how is it with Friend Holdfast and all Friends in Bristol? Timothy Littlewit, John Slenderbrain, and Christopher Keepfaith?
COLONEL *(aside)*   A goodly company! *(Aloud)* They are all in health, I thank thee for them.
PRIM   Friend Holdfast writes me word that thou camest lately from Pennsylvania; how do all Friends there?
COLONEL *(aside)*   What the devil shall I say? I know just as much of Pennsylvania as I do of Bristol.
PRIM   Do they thrive?
COLONEL   Yea, Friend, the blessing of their good works fall upon them.
PRIM   Sarah, know our Friend Pure.
MRS PRIM   Thou art welcome. *(He salutes her.)*

COLONEL *(aside)*   Here comes the sum of all my wishes. How charming she appears, even in that disguise.

PRIM   Why dost thou consider the maiden so intentively, friend?

COLONEL   I will tell thee. About four days ago, I saw a vision – this very maiden, but in vain attire, standing on a precipice; and heard a voice, which called me by my name and bade me put forth my hand and save her from the pit. I did so, and methought the damsel grew to my side.

MRS PRIM   What can that portend?

PRIM   The damsel's conversion, I am persuaded.

MRS LOVELY *(aside)*   That's false, I'm sure.

PRIM   Wilt thou use the means, Friend Pure?

COLONEL   Means! What means? Is she not thy daughter and already one of the faithful?

MRS PRIM   No, alas. She's one of the ungodly.

PRIM *(to Mrs Lovely)*   Pray thee, mind what this good man will say unto thee; he will teach thee the way that thou shouldest walk, Ann.

MRS LOVELY   I know my way without his instructions. I hoped to have been quiet when once I had put on your odious formality here.

COLONEL   Then thou wearest it out of compulsion, not choice, friend?

MRS LOVELY   Thou art in the right of it, Friend.

MRS PRIM   Art not thou ashamed to mimic the good man? Ah, thou art a stubborn girl.

COLONEL   Mind her not; she hurteth not me. If thou wilt leave her alone with me, I will discuss some few points with her that may, perchance, soften her stubbornness and melt her into compliance.

PRIM   Content; I pray thee put it home to her. Come, Sarah, let us leave the good man with her.

Mrs Lovely catching hold of Prim; he breaks loose and exits with Mrs Prim.

MRS LOVELY *(calls after them)* What do you mean – to leave me with this old enthusiastical canter? Don't think, because I complied with your formality, to impose your ridiculous doctrine upon me.

COLONEL   I pray thee, young woman, moderate thy passion.

MRS LOVELY   I pray thee, walk after thy leader; you will but lose your labour upon me. – These wretches will certainly make me mad.

COLONEL   I am of another opinion; the spirit telleth me that I shall convert thee, Ann.

A Bold Stroke for a Wife

MRS LOVELY	'Tis a lying spirit; don't believe it.
COLONEL	Say'st thou so? Why, then thou shalt convert me,

my angel. *(catching her in his arms)*

MRS LOVELY *(shrieks)* Ah! Monster, hold off, or I'll tear thy eyes out.

COLONEL *(whispers)* Hush! For Heaven's sake – dost thou know me? I am Fainwell.

MRS. LOVELY Fainwell!

Enter Old Prim.

MRS LOVELY *(aside)* O, I'm undone; Prim here –I wish with all my soul I had been dumb.

PRIM What is the matter? Why didst thou shriek out, Ann?

MRS LOVELY Shriek out! I'll shriek and shriek again, cry murder, thieves, or anything to drown the noise of that eternal babbler, if you leave me with him any longer.

PRIM Was that all? Fie, fie, Ann.

COLONEL No matter; I'll bring down her stomach, I'll warrant thee. Leave us, I pray thee.

PRIM Fare thee well.

Exit.

COLONEL My charming lovely woman. *(embraces her)*

MRS LOVELY What means thou by this disguise, Fainwell?

COLONEL To set thee free, if thou wilt perform thy promise.

MRS LOVELY Make me mistress of my fortune, and make thy own conditions.

COLONEL This night shall answer all thy wishes. See here, I have the consent of three of thy guardians already, and doubt not but Prim shall make the fourth.

Door opens slightly, unobserved, Prim listening.

PRIM *(aside)* I would gladly hear what argument the good man useth to bend her.

MRS LOVELY *(unaware of Prim)* Thy words give me new life, methinks.

PRIM *(aside)* What do I hear?

MRS LOVELY *(still unaware of Prim)* Thou best of men! Heaven meant to bless me sure, when first I saw thee.

PRIM *(aside)* He hath mollified her. O wonderful conversion!

COLONEL *(sees Prim; aside to Mrs Lovely)* Ha! Prim listening– no more, my love; we are observed; seem to be edified, and give 'em hopes that thou wilt turn Quaker, and leave the rest to me.

COLONEL *(aloud)*   I am glad to find that thou art touched with what I said unto thee, Ann; another time I will explain the other article to thee. In the meanwhile be thou dutiful to our Friend Prim.

MRS LOVELY   I shall obey thee in everything.

Enter old Prim.

PRIM   O, what a prodigious change is here! Thou hast wrought a miracle, Friend! Ann, how dost thou like the doctrine he hath preached?

MRS LOVELY   So well that I could talk to him forever, methinks. I am ashamed of my former folly and ask your pardon, Mr Prim.

COLONEL   Enough, enough that thou art sorry; he is no pope, Ann.

PRIM   Verily, thou dost rejoice me exceedingly, friend; will it please thee to walk into the next room and refresh thyself? Come, take the maiden by the hand.

COLONEL   We will follow thee.

SERVANT   There is another Simon Pure inquireth for thee, master.

COLONEL *(aside)*   The devil there is.

PRIM   Another Simon Pure? I do not know him; is he any relation of thine?

COLONEL   No, friend, I know him not. *(Aside)* Pox take him; I wish he were in Pennsylvania again, with all my blood.

MRS LOVELY *(aside)* What shall I do?

PRIM *(to Servant)*   Bring him up. *(Servant exits.)*

COLONEL *(aside)*   Humph, then one of us must go down; that's certain. Now impudence assist me.

Enter Simon Pure.

PRIM   What is thy will with me, Friend?

PURE   Didst thou not receive a letter from Aminadab Holdfast of Bristol, concerning one Simon Pure?

PRIM   Yea, and Simon Pure is already here, Friend.

COLONEL *(aside)*   And Simon Pure will stay here, Friend, if possible, if possible.

PURE   That's an untruth, for I am he.

COLONEL   Take thou heed, Friend, what thou dost say; I do affirm that I am Simon Pure.

PURE   Thy name may be Pure, Friend, but not that Pure.

COLONEL   Yea, that Pure which my good friend Aminadab
Holdfast wrote to my Friend Prim about, the same Simon Pure that
came from Pennsylvania and sojourned in Bristol eleven days; thou
wouldst not take my name from me, wouldst thou? – *(Aside)* Till I have
done with it.

PURE   Thy name! I am astounded.

COLONEL   At what? At thy own assurance? *(going up to
him; Simon Pure starts back.)*

PURE   Avaunt, Satan; approach me not! I defy thee and
all thy works.

MRS LOVELY *(aside)* O, he'll outcant him – undone, undone forever.

COLONEL   Hark thee, friend, thy sham will not take. Don't
exert thy voice; thou art too well acquainted with Satan to start at him,
thou wicked reprobate. What can thy design be here?

Enter Servant and gives Prim a letter.

PRIM   One of these must be a counterfeit, but which I
cannot say.

Exit Servant.

COLONEL *(aside)*   What can that letter be?

PURE   Thou must be the devil, friend; that's certain, for
no human power can stock so great a falsehood.

PRIM *(to Pure)*   This letter sayeth that thou art better acquainted
with that Prince of Darkness than any here. Read that, I pray thee,
Simon. *(gives it the Colonel)*

COLONEL *(aside)*   'Tis Freeman's hand. *(reads aloud)* "There is a
design formed to rob your house this night and cut your throat, and for
that purpose there is a man disguised like a Quaker who is to pass for
one Simon Pure; the gang whereof I am one, though now resolved to
rob no more, has been at Bristol; one of them came up in the coach with
the Quaker, whose name he hath taken, and from what he gathered
from him, formed that design and did not doubt but he should impose
so far upon you as to make you turn out the real Simon Pure and keep
him with you. Make the right use of this. Adieu." *(Aside)* Excellent well!

PRIM *(to Pure)*   Dost thou hear this?

PURE   Yea, but it moveth me not; that, doubtless, is the
impostor. *(pointing at the Colonel)*

COLONEL   Ah, thou wicked one! Now I consider thy face, I
remember thou didst come up in the leathern convenience with me; thou
hadst a black bob wig on and a brown camblet coat with brass buttons.

COLONEL	Canst thou deny it, ha?
PURE	Yea, I can and with a safe conscience too, Friend.
PRIM	Verily, friend, thou art the most impudent villain

I ever saw.

MRS LOVELY *(aside)*   Nay then, I'll have a fling at him too. *(Aloud)* I remember the face of this fellow at Bath – ay, this is he that picked my Lady Raffle's pocket upon the grove; don't you remember that the mob pumped you, friend? This is the most notorious rogue –

PURE   What doth provoke thee to seek my life? Thou wilt not hang me, wilt thou, wrongfully?

PRIM   She will do thee no hurt, nor thou shalt do me none; therefore, get thee about thy business, Friend, and leave thy wicked course of life, or thou mayst not come off so favorably everywhere.

COLONEL   Go, Friend, I would advise thee, and tempt thy fate no more.

PURE   Yea, I will go, but it shall be to thy confusion; for I shall clear myself. I will return with some proofs that shall convince thee, Obadiah, that thou art highly imposed upon.

Exit.

COLONEL *(aside)*   Then here will be no staying for me, that's certain. What the devil shall I do?

PRIM   What monstrous works of iniquity are there in this world, Simon!

COLONEL   Yea, the age is full of vice. *(Aside)* 'Sdeath, I am so confounded I know not what to say.

PRIM   Thou art disordered, Friend; art thou not well?

COLONEL   My spirit is greatly troubled, and something telleth me that though I have wrought a good work in converting this maiden, this tender maiden, yet my labour will be in vain; for the evil spirit fighteth against her; and I see, yea, I see with the eyes of my inward man that Satan will rebuffet her again whenever I withdraw myself from her; and she will, yea, this very damsel will return again to that abomination from whence I have retrieved her, as if it were, yea, as if it were out of the jaws of the fiend – hum –

PRIM   Good lack! Thinkest thou so?

MRS LOVELY *(aside)*   I must second him. *(Aloud)* What meaneth this struggling within me? I feel the spirit resisting the vanities of this world, but the flesh is rebellious, yea, the flesh – I greatly fear the flesh, and the weakness thereof – hum –

PRIM   The maid is inspired.
COLONEL   Behold, her light begins to shine forth. *(Aside)*
Excellent woman.
MRS LOVELY   This good man hath spoken comfort unto me,
yea, comfort, I say; because the words which he hath breathed into my
outward ears are gone through and fixed in mine heart, yea, verily in
mine heart, I say – and I feel the spirit doth love him exceedingly,
hum–
COLONEL *(aside)*   She acts it to the life.

Enter Mrs Prim.

PRIM   Prodigious! The damsel is filled with the spirit,
Sarah.
MRS PRIM   I am greatly rejoiced to see such a change in our
beloved Ann. – I came to tell thee that supper stayeth for thee.
COLONEL   I am not disposed for thy food; my spirit longeth
for more delicious meat. Fain would I redeem this maiden from the tribe of
sinners and break those cords asunder wherewith she is bound – hum –
MRS LOVELY   Something whispers in my ears, methinks, that I
must be subject to the will of this good man and from him only must
hope for consolation – hum – it also telleth me that I am a chosen
vessel to raise up seed to the faithful and that thou must consent that
we two be one flesh according to the Word – hum –
PRIM   What a revelation is here! This is certainly part of
thy vision, friend; this is the maiden's growing to thy side. Ah, with
what willingness should I give thee my consent, could I give thee her
fortune too; but thou will never get the consent of the wicked ones.
COLONEL *(aside)*   I wish I was as sure of yours.
PRIM *(to Mrs Lovely)*   My soul rejoiceth, yea, it rejoiceth, I say, to find
the spirit within thee; for lo, it moveth thee with natural agitation – yea,
with natural agitation, I say again, and stirreth up the seeds of thy
virgin inclination towards this good man – yea, it stirreth, as one may
say, yea, verily, I say, it stirreth up thy inclination – yea, as one would
stir a pudding.
MRS LOVELY   I see, I see – the spirit guiding of thy hand, good
Obadiah Prim, and now behold thou art signing thy consent. – And now
I see myself within thy arms, my friend and brother, yea, I am become
bone of thy bone and flesh of thy flesh *(embraces him)* – hum –
COLONEL *(aside)*   Admirably performed. *(Aloud)* And I will take
thee in all spiritual love for an helpmeet, yea, for the wife of my bosom.
– And now, methinks, I feel a longing – yea, a longing, I say,

for the consummation of thy love, hum – yea, I do long exceedingly.

MRS LOVELY   And verily, verily, my spirit feeleth the same longing.

MRS PRIM   The spirit hath greatly moved them both. Friend Prim, thou must consent; there is no resisting of the spirit.

PRIM   Yea, the light within showeth me that I shall fight a good fight, and wrestle through those reprobate fiends, thy other guardians – yea, I perceive the spirit will hedge thee into the flock of the righteous – thou art a chosen lamb – yea, a chosen lamb, and I will not push thee back – no, I will not, I say, no, thou shalt leap-a and frisk-a and skip-a and bound, and bound, I say – yea, bound within the fold of the righteous –yea, even within thy fold, my brother. Fetch me the pen and ink, Sarah, and my hand shall confess its obedience to the spirit.

Exit Mrs Prim.

COLONEL *(aside)*   I wish it were over.

Enter Mrs Prim with pen and ink.

MRS LOVELY *(aside)*   I tremble lest this Quaking rogue should return and spoil all.

PRIM   Here, friend, do thou write what the spirit prompteth, and I will sign it.

Colonel sits down.

MRS PRIM   Verily, Ann, it greatly rejoiceth me to see thee reformed from that original wickedness wherein I found thee.

MRS LOVELY   I do believe thou art, and I thank thee.

COLONEL *(reads aloud)* "This is to certify all whom it may concern that I do freely give up all my right and title in Ann Lovely to Simon Pure and my full consent that she shall become his wife, according to the form of marriage. Witness my hand."

PRIM   That is enough. Give me the pen. *(signs it)*

Enter Betty, running to Mrs Lovely.

BETTY   O, madam, madam, here's the Quaking man again; he has brought a coachman and two or three more.

MRS LOVELY *(aside to Colonel)* Ruined past redemption.

COLONEL *(aside to Mrs Lovely)* No, no, one minute sooner had spoiled all, but now – *(Aloud)* here is company coming, Friend; give me the paper. *(going up to Prim hastily)*

PRIM   Here it is, Simon, and I wish thee happy with the
maiden.

MRS LOVELY   'Tis done, and now, devil do thy worst.

Enter Simon Pure and coachman etc.

PURE   Look thee, Friend, I have brought these people to
satisfy thee that I am not that impostor which thou didst take me for;
this is the man which did drive the leathern conveniency that brought
me from Bristol, and this is –

COLONEL   Look ye, friend, to save the court the trouble of
examining witnesses, I plead guilty, ha, ha!

PRIM   How's this? Is not thy name Pure, then?

COLONEL   No, really, sir, I only made bold with this
gentleman's name. But I here give it up safe and sound; it has done the
business which I had occasion for, and now I intend to wear my own,
which shall be at his service upon the same occasion at any time,
ha, ha, ha!

PURE   O, the wickedness of this age.

COACHMAN *(to Pure)* Then you have no farther need of us, sir.

They exit.

COLONEL   No, honest man, you may go about your business.

PRIM   I am struck dumb with thy impudence, Ann; thou
hast deceived me and perchance undone thyself.

MRS PRIM   Thou art a dissembling baggage, and shame will
overtake thee. *(exits)*

PURE   I am grieved to see thy wife so much troubled; I
will follow and console her.

Exit. Enter Servant.

SERVANT   Thy brother guardians inquireth for thee; there is
another man with them.

Exit.

MRS LOVELY *(to the Colonel)* Who can that other man be?

COLONEL *(aside to Mrs Lovely)* 'Tis one Freeman, a friend of mine,
whom I ordered to bring the rest of thy guardians here.

Enter Sir Philip, Tradelove, Periwinkle and Freeman.

FREEMAN *(to the Colonel)* Is all safe? Did my letter do you service?

COLONEL *(aside to Freeman)* All, all's safe; ample service.

SIR PHILIP   Miss Nancy, how dost do, child?

MRS LOVELY   Don't call me Miss, Friend Philip; my name is Ann, thou knowest.

SIR PHILIP   What, is the girl metamorphosed?

MRS LOVELY   I wish thou wert so metamorphosed. Ah, Philip, throw off that gaudy attire and wear the clothes becoming of thy age.

PRIM *(aside)*   I am ashamed to see these men.

SIR PHILIP   My age! The woman is possessed.

COLONEL   No, thou art possessed rather, Friend.

TRADELOVE   Hark ye, Mrs Lovely, one word with you. *(takes hold of her hand)*

COLONEL   This maiden is my wife, thanks to Friend Prim, and thou hast no business with her. *(takes her from him)*

TRADELOVE   His wife! Hark ye, Mr Freeman.

PERIWINKLE   Why, you have made a very fine piece of work of it, Mr Prim.

SIR PHILIP   Married to a Quaker! Thou art a fine fellow to be left guardian to an orphan, truly. There's a husband for a young lady.

COLONEL   When I have put on my beau clothes, Sir Philip, you'll like me better.

SIR PHILIP   Thou wilt make a very scurvy beau, friend.

COLONEL   I believe I can prove it under your hand that you thought me a very fine gentleman in the Park today, about thirty-six minutes after eleven. Will you take a pinch, Sir Philip, out of the finest snuffbox you ever saw? *(offers him snuff)*

SIR PHILIP   Ha, ha, ha, I am overjoyed, faith I am, if thou be'st that gentleman. I own I did give my consent to the gentleman I brought here today, but if this is he, I can't be positive.

PRIM   Canst thou not? Now, I think thou art a fine fellow to be left guardian to an orphan – thou shallow-brained shuttle-cock; he may be a pickpocket for aught thou dost know.

PERIWINKLE   You would have been two rare fellows to have been trusted with the sole management of her fortune, would ye not, think ye? But Mr Tradelove and myself shall take care of her portion.

TRADELOVE   Aye, ay, so we will. Did not you tell me the Dutch merchant desired me to meet him here, Mr Freeman?

FREEMAN   I did so, and I am sure he will be here, if you'll have a little patience.

COLONEL   What, is Mr Tradelove impatient; nay then, ik ben gereet voor you; heb ye Jan van Timtamtirelireletta Heer van Fainwell vergeeten?

TRADELOVE   O, pox of the name! What, have you tricked me too, Mr Freeman?

COLONEL   Tricked, Mr Tradelove! Did I not give you two thousand pound for your consent fairly? And now do you tell a gentleman that he has tricked you?

PERIWINKLE   So, so, you are a pretty guardian, faith; sell your charge! What did you look upon her as, part of your stock?

PRIM   Ha, ha, ha! I am glad thy knavery is found out, however. I confess the maiden overreached me and no sinister end at all.

PERIWINKLE   Aye, ay, one thing or another overreached you all; but I'll take care he shall never finger a penny of her money, I warrant you – overreached, quoth'a? Why, I might have been overreached too, if I had had no more wit. I don't know but this very fellow may be him that was directed to me from Grand Cairo today. Ha, ha, ha.

COLONEL   The very same, sir.

PERIWINKLE   Are you so, sir? But your trick would not pass upon me.

COLONEL   No, as you say, at that time it did not; that was not my lucky hour. But hark ye, sir, I must let you into one secret. You may keep honest John Tradescant's coat on, for your uncle, Sir Toby Periwinkle, is not dead; so the charge of mourning will be saved, ha, ha. Don't you remember Mr Pillage, your uncle's steward, ha, ha, ha?

PERIWINKLE   Not dead! I begin to fear I am tricked too.

COLONEL   Don't you remember the signing of a lease, Mr Periwinkle?

PERIWINKLE   Well, and what signifies that lease, if my uncle is not dead? Ha! I am sure it was a lease I signed –

COLONEL   Aye, but it was a lease for life, sir, and of this beautiful tenement, I thank you. *(taking hold of Mrs Lovely)*

ALL   Ha, ha, ha, neighbour's fare!

FREEMAN   So, then, I find you are all tricked, ha, ha.

PERIWINKLE   I am certain I read as plain a lease as ever I read in my life.

COLONEL   You read a lease, I grant you, but you signed this contract. *(showing a paper)*

PERIWINKLE   How durst you put this trick upon me, Mr Freeman; did not you tell me my uncle was dying?

FREEMAN   And would tell you twice as much to serve my friend, ha, ha.

SIR PHILIP   What, the learned, famous Mr Periwinkle choused, too? Ha, ha, ha! I shall die with laughing, ha, ha, ha.

PRIM   It had been well if her father had left her to wiser heads than thine and mine, friend, ha, ha.

TRADELOVE   Well, since you have outwitted us all, pray you, what and who are you, sir?

SIR PHILIP   Sir, the gentleman is a fine gentleman. – I am glad you have got a person, madam, who understands dress and good breeding. – I was resolved she should have a husband of my choosing.

PRIM   I am sorry the maiden is fallen into such hands.

TRADELOVE   A beau! Nay, then she is finely helped up.

MRS LOVELY   Why, beaus are great encouragers of trade, sir, ha, ha.

COLONEL   Look ye, gentlemen, I am the person who can give the best account of myself, and I must beg Sir Philip's pardon when I tell him that I have as much aversion to what he calls dress and breeding as I have to the enemies of my religion. I have had the honour to serve his Majesty and headed a regiment of the bravest fellows that ever pushed bayonet in the throat of a Frenchman; and notwithstanding the fortune this lady brings me, whenever my country wants my aid, this sword and arm are at her service.

And now, my fair, if you'll but deign to smile,
I meet a recompense for all my toil.
Love and religion ne'er admit restraint,
Force makes many a sinner, not one saint;
Still free as air the active mind does rove,
And searches proper objects for its love;
But that once fixed, 'tis past the power of art,
To chase the dear ideas from the heart.
'Tis liberty of choice that sweetens life,
Makes the glad husband, and the happy wife.

EPILOGUE

Spoken by Mrs Ann Lovely.

What new strange ways our modern beaus devise!
What trials of love skill to gain the prize!
The heathen gods, who never mattered rapes,
Scarce wore such strange variety of shapes.
The devil take their odious barren skulls,
To court in form of snakes and filthy bulls.
Old Jove once nicked it, I am told,
In a whole lapful of true standard gold;
How must his godship then fair Danaë warm?
In trucking ware for ware there is no harm.
Well, after all – that money has a charm.
But now indeed that stale invention's past;
Besides, you know that guineas fall so fast,
Poor nymph must come to pocket piece at last.
Old Harry's face, or good Queen Bess's ruff –
Not that I'd take 'em – may do well enough;
No – my ambitious spirit's far above
Those little tricks of mercenary love.
That man be mine, who, like the Colonel here,
Can top his character in every sphere;
Who can a thousand ways employ his wit,
Outpromise statesmen, and outcheat a cit;
Beyond the colors of a trav'ler paint,
And cant, and ogle too – beyond a saint.
The last disguise most pleased me, I confess;
There's something tempting in the preaching dress;
And pleased me more than once a dame of note,
Who loved her husband in his footman's coat.
To see one eye in wanton motions played,
Th'other to the heavenly regions strayed,
As if it for its fellow's frailties prayed.
But yet I hope, for all that I have said,
To find my spouse a man of war in bed.

The Curtain falls.

The End.

Susannah Centlivre (1667-1723)

Accounts of Susannah Centlivre's early life vary. Some describe her as daughter to a Rawkins, some a Freeman, some have her born poor, others, a gentlewoman of Lincolnshire stock, the daughter of a Parliamentarian whose estate was confiscated after the Restoration. (She frequently returned to Holbeach in Lincolnshire in later life.)

She certainly learnt some Latin as well as French, Dutch and Spanish. She may have run away from home at the age of 14, either with strolling players or with Anthony Hammond, a Cambridge undergraduate, who kept her dressed as a boy, pretended she was his young cousin and taught her swordplay, logic and rhetoric, until questions began to be asked about their relationship.

She apparently married a man called Fox when she was 16, but he died within the year and she remarried (to an officer named Carroll and published her earlier work as by Susannah Carroll after he was killed in a duel.) While working as an actress, famous for breeches parts, she met and married Joseph Centlivre, principal cook to Queen Anne.

She also published *Familiar and Courtly Letters Written by Monsieur Voiture* and other volumes of letters, poems including contributing to a collection of elegies on Dryden's death and possibly contributed to *The Female Tatler.* She enjoyed a wide circle of friends including the playwrights known as the 'Female Wits' – Catherine Trotter, Mary Pix and Delariviere Manley, as well as George Farquhar, Nicolas Rowe and Sir Richard Steele.

Based on the number of performances of her work, Centlivre can be viewed as one of the most successful British dramatists of all time with her comic intrigues proving enduringly popular until the twentieth century. Her plays include: *The Busy Body* (1710) which had over 400 performances and was republished many times during the next century; *The Wonder! A Woman Keeps a Secret* (1714) a favourite of Garrick; *The Gamester* (1705); *The Bassett Table* (1706); *Love at a Venture* (1706); *The Platonic Lady* (1707); *A Bickerstaff's Burial* (1710); *Marplot* (1711); *A Gotham Election* (1715); *A Wife Well Manag'd* (1715); *The Cruel Gift* (1717) and *The Artifice* (1723).

A Bold Stroke For A Wife was successfully produced at Lincoln's Inn Fields in 1718 and was revived recently in Chicago as part of The Alcyone Festival 2008 which staged plays by women ranging over nearly 1000 years.

De Monfort: a Tragedy

Joanna Baillie

First performed at Drury Lane Theatre on 29th April, 1800.

Men

De Monfort

Rezenvelt

Count Freberg, friend to De Monfort and Rezenvelt

Manuel, servant to De Monfort

Jerome, De Monfort's old landlord

Conrad, an artful knave

Bernard, a monk

Monks, gentlemen, officers, pages, etc.

Women

Jane De Monfort, sister to De Monfort

Countess Freberg, wife to Freberg

Theresa, servant to the Countess

Abbess, nuns, and a lay sister, ladies, etc.

Setting: a town in Germany.

ACT ONE, SCENE 1

Jerome's house. A large old-fashioned chamber.

JEROME *(off-stage)* This way, good masters.

Enter Jerome, bearing a light, and followed by Manuel, and servants carrying luggage.

JEROME   Rest your burthens here.
　This spacious room will please the marquis best.
　He takes me unawares; but ill prepar'd:
　If he had sent, e'en though a hasty notice,
　I had been glad.
MANUEL   Be not disturb'd, good Jerome;
　Thy house is in most admirable order;
　And they who travel o' cold winter nights
　Think homeliest quarters good.
JEROME   He is not far behind?
MANUEL   A little way.
　(to the servants) Go you and wait below till he arrive.
JEROME *(shaking Manuel by the hand)* Indeed, my friend,
　I'm glad to see you here;
　Yet marvel wherefore.
MANUEL   I marvel wherefore too, my honest Jerome:
　But here we are; pri'thee be kind to us.
JEROME   Most heartily I will I love your master:
　He is a quiet and a lib'ral man:
　A better inmate never cross'd my door.
MANUEL   Ah! but he is not now the man he was.
　Lib'ral he'll be. God grant he may be quiet.
JEROME   What has befallen him?
MANUEL   I cannot tell thee;
　But, faith, there is no living with him now.
JEROME   And yet, methinks, if I remember well
　You were about to quit his service, Manuel,
　When last he left this house. You grumbled then.
MANUEL   I've been upon the eve of leaving him
　These ten long years; for many times he is
　So difficult, capricious, and distrustful,
　He galls my nature – yet, I know not how,
　A secret kindness binds me to him still.
JEROME   Some who offend from a suspicious nature,

Will afterwards such fair confession make
As turns e'en the offence into a favour.
MANUEL   Yes, some indeed do so; so will not he:
He'd rather die than such confession make.
JEROME   Ay, thou art right; for now I call to mind
That once he wrong'd me with unjust suspicion,
When first he came to lodge beneath my roof;
And when it so fell out that I was prov'd
Most guiltless of the fault, I truly thought
He would have made profession of regret.
But silent, haughty, and ungraciously
He bore himself as one offended still.
Yet shortly after, when unwittingly
I did him some slight service, o' the sudden
He overpower'd me with his grateful thanks;
And would not be restrain'd from pressing on me
A noble recompense. I understood
His o'erstrain'd gratitude and bounty well,
And took it as he meant.
MANUEL   'Tis often thus.
I would have left him many years ago,
But that with all his faults there sometimes come
Such bursts of natural goodness from his heart,
As might engage a harder churl than I
To serve him still. – And then his sister too;
A noble dame, who should have been a queen.
The meanest of her hinds, at her command,
Had fought like lions for her, and the poor,
E'en o'er their bread of poverty, had bless'd her –
She would have griev'd if I had left my lord.
JEROME   Comes she along with him?
MANUEL   No, he departed all unknown to her,
Meaning to keep conceal'd his secret route;
But well I knew it would afflict her much,
And therefore left a little nameless billet,
Which after our departure, as I guess,
Would fall into her hands, and tell her all.
What could I do! O 'tis a noble lady!
JEROME   All this is strange – something disturbs his mind
Belike he is in love.

MANUEL   No, Jerome, no.
Once on a time I serv'd a noble master,
Whose youth was blasted with untoward love,
And he, with hope and fear and jealousy
For ever toss'd, led an unquiet life:
Yet, when unruffled by the passing fit,
His pale wan face such gentle sadness wore
As mov'd a kindly heart to pity him.
But Monfort, even in his calmest hour,
Still bears that gloomy sternness in his eye
Which powerfully repels all sympathy.
O no! Good Jerome, no, it is not love.
JEROME   Hear I not horses trampling at the gate?
(listening) He is arrived – stay thou – I had forgot –
A plague upon't! My head is so confus'd –
I will return i' the instant to receive him.

He exits hastily. A great bustle without. Exit Manuel with lights, and returns again, lighting in De Monfort, as if just alighted from his journey.

MANUEL   Your ancient host, my lord, receives you gladly
And your apartment will be soon prepar'd.
DE MONFORT   'Tis well.
MANUEL   Where shall I place the chest you gave in charge?
So please you, say, my lord.
DE MONFORT *(throwing himself into a chair)* Where e'er thou wilt.
MANUEL   I would not move that luggage till you came.
(pointing to certain things)
DE MONFORT   Move what thou wilt, and trouble me no more.

Manuel, with the assistance of other servants, sets about putting the things in order, and De Monfort remains sitting in a thoughtful posture. Enter Jerome bearing wine, etc. on a salver. As he approaches De Monfort, Manuel pulls him by the sleeve.

MANUEL *(aside to Jerome)* No, do not now; he will not be disturb'd.
JEROME   What! Not to bid him welcome to my house,
And offer some refreshment?
MANUEL   No, good Jerome.
Softly a little while: I pri'thee do.

Jerome walks softly on tiptoe, till he gets behind De Monfort, then peeping on one side to see his face.

JEROME *(aside to Manuel)* Ah, Manuel, what an alter'd man is here!
His eyes are hollow, and his cheeks are pale.
He left this house a comely gentleman.
DE MONFORT Who whispers there?
MANUEL 'Tis your old landlord, sir.
JEROME I joy to see you here – I crave your pardon –
I fear I do intrude –
DE MONFORT No, my kind host, I am obliged to thee.
JEROME How fares it with your honour?
DE MONFORT Well enough.
JEROME Here is a little of the fav'rite wine
That you were wont to praise. Pray honour me. *(fills a glass)*
DE MONFORT *(after drinking)* I thank you, Jerome,
'Tis delicious.
JEROME Ay, my dear wife did ever make it so.
DE MONFORT And how does she?
JEROME Alas, my lord! She's dead.
DE MONFORT Well, then she is at rest.
JEROME How well, my lord?
DE MONFORT Is she not with the dead, the quiet dead,
Where all is peace? Not e'en the impious wretch,
Who tears the coffin from its earthy vault,
And strews the mould'ring ashes to the wind,
Can break their rest.
JEROME Woe's me!
I thought you would have griev'd for her.
She was a kindly soul! Before she died,
When pining sickness bent her cheerless head,
She set my house in order –
And but the morning ere she breath'd her last,
Bade me preserve some flaskets of this wine,
That should the Lord de Monfort come again
His cup might sparkle still.
(De Monfort walks across the stage, and wipes his eyes.)
Indeed I fear I have distress'd you, sir;
I surely thought you would be griev'd for her.
DE MONFORT *(taking Jerome's hand)* I am, my friend.
How long has she been dead?
JEROME Two sad long years.
DE MONFORT Would she were living still!
I was too troublesome, too heedless of her.

JEROME   O no! She lov'd to serve you.

Loud knocking without.

DE MONFORT   What fool comes here, at such untimely hour,
  To make this cursed noise? *(To Manuel)* Go to the gate. *(Exit Manuel.)*
  All sober citizens are gone to bed;
  It is some drunkards on their nightly rounds,
  Who mean it but in sport.
JEROME   I hear unusual voices – here they come.

Re-enter Manuel, showing in Count Freberg and his lady, with a mask, in her hand.

COUNT FREBERG *(running to embrace De Monfort)*
  My dearest Monfort! Most unlook'd for pleasure!
  Do I indeed embrace thee here again?
  I saw thy servant standing by the gate,
  His face recall'd, and learnt the joyful tidings!
  Welcome, thrice welcome here!
DE MONFORT   I thank thee, Freberg, for this friendly visit,
  And this fair lady too. *(bowing to the lady)*
LADY   I fear, my lord,
  We do intrude at an untimely hour:
  But now, returning from a midnight mask,
  My husband did insist that we should enter.
COUNT FREBERG   No, say not so; no hour untimely call,
  Which doth together bring long absent friends.
  Dear Monfort, why hast thou so slily play'd,
  Coming upon us thus so suddenly?
DE MONFORT   O! Many varied thoughts do cross our brain,
  Which touch the will, but leave the memory trackless;
  And yet a strange compounded motive make,
  Wherefore a man should bend his evening walk
  To th' east or west, the forest or the field.
  Is it not often so?
COUNT FREBERG   I ask no more, happy to see you here
  From any motive. There is one behind,
  Whose presence would have been a double bliss:
  Ah! How is she? The noble Jane De Monfort.
DE MONFORT *(confused)* She is – I have – I left my sister well.
LADY *(to Freberg)* My Freberg, you are heedless of respect.
  You surely mean to say the Lady Jane.

COUNT FREBERG   Respect!
No, madam; Princess, Empress, Queen,
Could not denote a creature so exalted
As this plain appellation doth,
The noble Jane De Monfort.
LADY (*turning from him displeased, to Monfort*)
You are fatigued, my lord; you want repose;
Say, should we not retire?
COUNT FREBERG   Ha! Is it so ?
My friend, your face is pale; have you been ill?
DE MONFORT   No, Freberg, no; I think I have been well.
COUNT FREBERG (*shaking his head*) I fear thou hast not,
Monfort – Let it pass.
We'll re-establish thee: we'll banish pain.
I will collect some rare, some cheerful friends,
And we shall spend together glorious hours,
That gods might envy. Little time so spent
Doth far outvalue all our life beside.
This is indeed our life, our waking life,
The rest dull breathing sleep.
DE MONFORT   Thus, it is true, from the sad years of life
We sometimes do short hours, yea minutes strike,
Keen, blissful, bright, never to be forgotten;
Which, through the dreary gloom of time o'er past,
Shine like fair sunny spots on a wild waste.
But few they are, as few the heaven-fir'd souls
Whose magic power creates them. Bless'd art thou,
If, in the ample circle of thy friends,
Thou canst but boast a few.
COUNT FREBERG   Judge for thyself: in truth I do not boast.
There is amongst my friends, my later friends,
A most accomplish'd stranger: new to Amberg;
But just arriv'd, and will ere long depart:
I met him in Franconia two years since.
He is so full of pleasant anecdote,
So rich, so gay, so poignant is his wit,
Time vanishes before him as he speaks,
And ruddy morning through the lattice peeps
Ere night seems well begun.
DE MONFORT   How is he call'd?
COUNT FREBERG   I will surprise thee with a welcome face:
I will not tell thee now.

LADY *(to Monfort)* I have, my lord, a small request to make,
And must not be denied. I too may boast
Of some good friends, and beauteous country-women:
To-morrow night I open wide my doors
To all the fair and gay: beneath my roof
Music, and dance, and revelry shall reign:
I pray you come and grace it with your presence.
DE MONFORT   You honour me too much to be denied.
LADY   I thank you, sir; and in return for this,
We shall withdraw, and leave you to repose.
COUNT FREBERG *(to De Monfort)* Must it be so? Good night – sweet
sleep to thee!
DE MONFORT *(to Freberg)* Good night. *(To Lady)* Good night, fair lady.
LADY   Farewell!

Exit Freberg and Lady.

DE MONFORT *(to Jerome)* I thought Count Freberg had been now in
France.
JEROME   He meant to go, as I have been inform'd.
DE MONFORT   Well, well, prepare my bed; I will to rest.

Exit Jerome.

DE MONFORT *(aside)* I know not how it is, my heart stands back,
And meets not this man's love – Friends! Rarest friends!
Rather than share his undiscerning praise
With every table-wit, and book-form'd sage,
And paltry poet puling to the moon,
I'd court from him proscription, yea abuse,
And think it proud distinction.

ACT ONE, SCENE 2

A small apartment in Jerome's house: a table and breakfast set.
Enter De Monfort, followed by Manuel, and sits down by the table, with a
cheerful face.

DE MONFORT   Manuel, this morning's sun shines pleasantly:
These old apartments too are light and cheerful.
Our landlord's kindness has reviv'd me much:
He serves as though he lov'd me. This pure air
Braces the listless nerves, and warms the blood:
I feel in freedom here. *(filling a cup of coffee, and drinking)*

MANUEL   Ah! Sure, my lord,
No air is purer than the air at home.
DE MONFORT   Here can I wander with assured steps,
Nor dread, at every winding of the path,
Lest an abhorred serpent cross my way,
To move – *(stopping short)*
MANUEL   What says your honour?
There are no serpents in our pleasant fields.
DE MONFORT   Thinkst thou there are no serpents in the world,
But those who slide along the grassy sod,
And sting the luckless foot that presses them?
There are who in the path of social life
Do bask their spotted skins in Fortune's sun,
And sting the soul – Ay, till its healthful frame
Is chang'd to secret, fest'ring, sore disease,
So deadly is the wound.
MANUEL   Heav'n guard your honour from such horrid
scath!
They are but rare, I hope!
DE MONFORT *(shaking his head)* We mark the hollow eye, the wasted
frame,
The gait disturb'd of wealthy honour'd men,
But do not know the cause.
MANUEL   'Tis very true. God keep you well my lord!
DE MONFORT   I thank thee, Manuel, I am very well.
I shall be gay too, by the setting sun.
I go to revel it with sprightly dames,
And drive the night away. *(filling another cup and drinking)*
MANUEL   I should be glad to see your honour gay.
DE MONFORT   And thou too shalt be gay.
There, honest Manuel,
Put these broad pieces in thy leather purse,
And take at night a cheerful jovial glass.
Here is one too, for Bremer; he loves wine:
And one for Jacques: be joyful altogether.
Enter Servant.

SERVANT   My lord, I met e'en now, a short way off,
Your countryman the Marquis Rezenvelt.
DE MONFORT *(starting from his seat, letting the cup fall from his hand)*
Whom sayst thou?
SERVANT   Marquis Rezenvelt, an' please you.

DE MONFORT   Thou liest – it is not so – it is impossible!
SERVANT   I saw him with these eyes, plain as yourself.
DE MONFORT   Fool! 'Tis some passing stranger thou hast seen,
And with all hideous likeness been deceiv'd.
SERVANT   No other stranger could deceive my sight.
DE MONFORT (*dashing his clenched hand violently upon the table,
and overturning everything*) Heaven blast thy sight! It lights on
nothing good.
SERVANT   I surely thought no harm to look upon him.
DE MONFORT   What, dost thou still insist? He must it be?
Does it so please thee well? (*Servant endeavours to speak.*)
Hold thy damn'd tongue!
By heaven I'll kill thee! (*going furiously up to him*)
MANUEL (*in a soothing voice*) Nay, harm him not,
my lord; he speaks the truth;
I've met his groom, who told me certainly
His lord is here. I should have told you so,
But thought, perhaps, it might displease your honour.
DE MONFORT (*becoming all at once calm, and turning sternly
to Manuel*)
And how dar'st thou
To think it would displease me?
What is't to me who leaves or enters Amberg?
But it displeases me, yea e'en to frenzy,
That every idle fool must hither come,
To break my leisure with the paltry tidings
Of all the cursed things he stares upon.
(*Servant attempts to appeal – De Monfort stamps with his foot.*)
Take thine ill-favour'd visage from my sight,
And speak of it no more.
(*Servant exits.*)
And go thou too; I choose to be alone.

*Exit Manuel. De Monfort goes to the door by which they went out; opens
it, and looks.*

DE MONFORT   But is he gone indeed? Yes, he is gone.
(*He goes to the opposite door, opens it, and looks then gives loose to all
the fury of gesture, and walks up and down in great agitation.*)
It is too much: by heaven it is too much!
He haunts me – stings me – like a devil haunts –
He'll make a raving maniac of me – Villain!

The air wherein thou drawst thy fulsome breath
Is poison to me – Oceans shall divide us! *(pauses)*
But no; thou thinkst I fear thee, cursed reptile;
And hast a pleasure in the damned thought.
Though my heart's blood should curdle at thy sight,
I'll stay and face thee still.
(A knocking at the chamber door)
Ha! Who knocks there?

COUNT FREBERG *(without)* It is thy friend, De Monfort.

DE MONFORT *(opening the door)* Enter, then.

Enter Freberg.

COUNT FREBERG *(taking his hand kindly)* How art thou now?
How hast thou pass'd the night?
Has kindly sleep refresh'd thee?

DE MONFORT   Yes, I have lost an hour or two in sleep,
And so should be refresh'd.

COUNT FREBERG   And art thou not?
Thy looks speak not of rest. Thou art disturb'd.

DE MONFORT   No, somewhat ruffled from a foolish cause,
Which soon will pass away.

COUNT FREBERG *(shaking his head)* Ah no, De Monfort!
Something in thy face
Tells me another tale. Then wrong me not:
If any secret grief distract thy soul,
Here am I all devoted to thy love:
Open thy heart to me. What troubles thee?

DE MONFORT   I have no grief: distress me not, my friend.

COUNT FREBERG   Nay, do not call me so. Wert thou my friend,
Wouldst thou not open all thine inmost soul,
And bid me share its every consciousness?

DE MONFORT   Freberg, thou knowst not man; not nature's man,
But only him who, in smooth studied works
Of polish'd sages, shines deceitfully
In all the splendid foppery of virtue.
That man was never born whose secret soul,
With all its motley treasure of dark thoughts,
Foul fantasies, vain musings, and wild dreams,
Was ever open'd to another's scan.
Away, away! It is delusion all.

COUNT FREBERG   Well, be reserved then; perhaps I'm wrong.

DE MONFORT How goes the hour?
COUNT FREBERG 'Tis early still; a long day lies before us;
Let us enjoy it. Come along with me;
I'll introduce you to my pleasant friend.
DE MONFORT Your pleasant friend?
COUNT FREBERG Yes, him of whom I spake.
(taking his hand) There is no good I would not share with thee;
And this man's company, to minds like thine,
Is the best banquet feast I could bestow.
But I will speak in mystery no more;
It is thy townsman, noble Rezenvelt.
(De Monfort pulls his hand hastily from Freberg, and shrinks back.)
Ha! What is this?
Art thou pain-stricken, Monfort?
Nay, on my life, thou rather seemst offended:
Does it displease thee that I call him friend?
DE MONFORT No, all men are thy friends.
COUNT FREBERG No, say not all men. But thou art offended.
I see it well. I thought to do thee pleasure.
But if his presence be not welcome here,
He shall not join our company to-day.
DE MONFORT What dost thou mean to say? What is't to me.
Whether I meet with such a thing as Rezenvelt
To-day, to-morrow, every day, or never?
COUNT FREBERG In truth, I thought you had been well with him;
He prais'd you much.
DE MONFORT I thank him for his praise – Come, let us move:
This chamber is confin'd and airless grown.
(starting) I hear a stranger's voice.
COUNT FREBERG 'Tis Rezenvelt
Let him be told that we are gone abroad.
DE MONFORT No! Let him enter.
Who waits there? Ho! Manuel!
(Enter Manuel.)
What stranger speaks below?
MANUEL The Marquis Rezenvelt.
I have not told him that you are within.
DE MONFORT *(angrily)* And wherefore didst thou not? Let him ascend.

A long pause. De Monfort walking up and down with a quick pace.
Enter Rezenvelt, who runs freely up to De Monfort.

REZENVELT *(to De Monfort)* My noble marquis, welcome!
DE MONFORT   Sir, I thank you.
REZENVELT *(to Freberg)* My gentle friend, well met.
   Abroad so early?
COUNT FREBERG   It is indeed an early hour for me.
   How sits thy last night's revel on thy spirit?
REZENVELT   O, light as ever. On my way to you
   E'en now, I learnt De Monfort was arriv'd,
   And turn'd my steps aside; so here I am. *(bowing gaily to De Monfort)*
DE MONFORT   I thank you, sir *(proudly)*; you do me much
   honour .
REZENVELT   Nay, say not so; not too much honour surely,
   Unless, indeed, 'tis more than pleases you.
DE MONFORT *(confused)* Having no previous notice of your coming,
   I look'd not for it.
REZENVELT   Ay, true indeed; when I approach you next,
   I'll send a herald to proclaim my coming,
   And bow to you by sound of trumpet, marquis.
DE MONFORT *(to Freberg, turning haughtily from Rezenvelt with
   affected indifference)* How does your cheerful friend, that good old man?
COUNT FREBERG   My cheerful friend? I know not whom you mean.
DE MONFORT   Count Waterlan.
COUNT FREBERG   I know not one so nam'd.
DE MONFORT *(very confused)* O pardon me – it was at Basle I knew him.
COUNT FREBERG.   You have not yet inquir'd for honest Reisdale.
   I met him as I came, and mention'd you.
   He seem'd amaz'd; and fain he would have learnt
   What cause procur'd us so much happiness.
   He question'd hard, and hardly would believe;
   I could not satisfy his strong desire.
REZENVELT   And know you not what brings De Monfort here?
COUNT FREBERG   Truly I do not.
REZENVELT   O! 'Tis love of me.
   I have but two short days in Amberg been,
   And here with postman's speed he follows me,
   Finding his home so dull and tiresome grown.
COUNT FREBERG *(to De Monfort)*
   Is Rezenvelt so sadly miss'd with you?
   Your town so chang'd?
DE MONFORT   Not altogether so;
   Some witlings and jest-mongers still remain
   For fools to laugh at.

REZENVELT   But he laughs not, and therefore he is wise.
He ever frowns on them with sullen brow
Contemptuous; therefore he is very wise;
Nay, daily frets his most refined soul
With their poor folly to its inmost core;
Therefore he is most eminently wise.
COUNT FREBERG   Fy, Rezenvelt! You are too early gay.
Such spirits rise out with the ev'ning glass:
They suit not placid morn. *(To De Monfort who, after walking
impatiently up and down, comes close to his ear and lays hold of his
arm.)* What would you Monfort?
DE MONFORT   Nothing – what is't o'clock?
No, no – I had forgot – 'tis early still. *(turns away again)*
COUNT FREBERG *(to Rezenvelt)* Waltser informs me that you have
agreed
To read his verses o'er, and tell the truth. It is a dangerous task.
REZENVELT   Yet I'll be honest:
I can but lose his favour and a feast.

*Whilst they speak, De Monfort walks up and down impatiently and
irresolute: At last he pulls the bell violently. Enter Servant.*

DE MONFORT *(to Servant)* What dost thou want?
SERVANT   I thought your honour rung.
DE MONFORT   I have forgot – stay. Are my horses saddled?
SERVANT   I thought, my lord, you would not ride to-day,
After so long a journey.
DE MONFORT *(impatiently)* Well – 'tis good.
Begone! – I want thee not.

Exit Servant.

REZENVELT *(smiling significantly)* I humbly crave your pardon, gentle
marquis.
It grieves me that I cannot stay with you,
And make my visit of a friendly length.
I trust your goodness will excuse me now;
Another time I shall be less unkind.
(To Freberg) Will you not go with me?
COUNT FREBERG   Excuse me, Monfort, I'll return again.

Exit Rezenvelt and Freberg.

DE MONFORT *(alone, tossing his arms distractedly)*

Hell hath no greater torment for th' accurs'd!
Than this man's presence gives –
Abhorred fiend! He hath a pleasure too,
A damned pleasure in the pain he gives!
Oh! The side glance of that detested eye!
That conscious smile! That full insulting lip!
It touches every nerve: it makes me mad.
What, does it please thee? Dost thou woo my hate?
Hate shalt thou have! Determin'd deadly hate,
Which shall awake no smile. Malignant villain!
The venom of thy mind is rank and devilish,
And thin the film that hides it.
Thy hateful visage ever spoke thy worth:
I loath'd thee when a boy.
That men should be besotted with him thus!
And Freberg likewise so bewitched is,
That like a hireling flatt'rer at his heels
He meanly paces, off'ring brutish praise.
O! I could curse him too!

Exit.

ACT TWO, SCENE 1

A very splendid apartment in Count Freberg's house, fancifully decorated.
A wide folding door opened, shows another magnificent room lighted up
to receive company. Enter through the folding doors the Count and
Countess, richly dressed.

COUNT FREBERG (*looking round*) In truth, I like those decorations
    well:
    They suit those lofty walls. And here, my love,
    The gay profusion of a woman's fancy
    Is well display'd. Noble simplicity
    Becomes us less, on such a night as this,
    Than gaudy show.
LADY   Is it not noble then?
    (*He shakes his head.*)
    I thought it so;
    And as I know you love simplicity,
    I did intend it should be simple too.

COUNT FREBERG   Be satisfied, I pray; we want tonight
A cheerful banquet-house, and not a temple.
How runs the hour?
LADY   It is not late, but soon we shall be rous'd
With the loud entry of our frolic guests.

Enter a Page, richly dressed.

PAGE   Madam, there is a lady in your hall,
Who begs to be admitted to your presence.
LADY   Is it not one of our invited friends?
PAGE   No, far unlike to them; it is a stranger.
LADY   How looks her countenance?
PAGE   So queenly, so commanding, and so noble,
I shrunk at first in awe; but when she smil'd,
For so she did to see me thus abash'd,
Methought I could have compass'd sea and land
To do her bidding.
LADY   Is she young or old?
PAGE   Neither, if right I guess; but she is fair:
For Time hath laid his hand so gently on her,
As he too had been aw'd.
LADY   The foolish stripling!
She has bewitch'd thee. Is she large in stature?
PAGE   So stately and so graceful is her form,
I thought at first her stature was gigantic;
But on a near approach I found, in truth,
She scarcely does surpass the middle size.
LADY   What is her garb?
PAGE   I cannot well describe the fashion of it.
She is not deck'd in any gallant trim,
But seems to me clad in the usual weeds
Of high habitual state; for as she moves
Wide flows her robe in many a waving fold,
As I have seen unfurled banners play
With a soft breeze.
LADY   Thine eyes deceive thee, boy;
It is an apparition thou hast seen.
COUNT FREBERG (*starting from his seat, where he has been sitting during the conversation between the lady and the page*) It is an apparition he has seen,
Or it is Jane De Monfort. (*Exit hastily*)

LADY *(displeased)*   No; such description surely suits not her.
Did she inquire for me?

PAGE   She ask'd to see the lady of Count Freberg.

LADY Perhaps it is not she – I fear it is –
Ha! Here they come. He has but guess'd too well.

Enter Freberg, leading in Jane De Monfort.

COUNT FREBERG *(presenting her to Lady)* Here, madam,
welcome a most worthy guest.

LADY   Madam, a thousand welcomes! Pardon me;
I could not guess who honour'd me so far;
I should not else have waited coldly here.

JANE   I thank you for this welcome, gentle countess.
But take those kind excuses back again;
I am a bold intruder on this hour,
And am entitled to no ceremony.
I came in quest of a dear truant friend,
But Freberg has inform'd me –
(To Freberg) And he is well, you say?

COUNT FREBERG   Yes, well, but joyless.

JANE   It is the usual temper of his mind;
It opens not, but with the thrilling touch
Of some strong heart-string o' the sudden press'd.

COUNT FREBERG   It may be so, I've known him otherwise:
He is suspicious grown.

JANE   Not so, Count Freberg; Monfort is too noble.
Say rather, that he is a man in grief,
Wearing at times a strange and scowling eye;
And thou, less generous than beseems a friend,
Hast thought too hardly of him.

COUNT FREBERG *(bowing with great respect)* So will I say;
I'll own nor word nor will, that can offend you.

LADY   De Monfort is engag'd to grace our feast:
Ere long you'll see him here.

JANE   I thank you truly, but this homely dress
Suits not the splendour of such scenes as these.

COUNT FREBERG *(pointing to her dress)*
Such artless and majestic elegance,
So exquisitely just, so nobly simple,
Will make the gorgeous blush.

JANE *(smiling)* Nay, nay, be more consistent,
    courteous knight,
    And do not praise a plain and simple guise
    With such profusion of unsimple words.
    I cannot join your company tonight.
LADY   Not stay to see your brother?
JANE   Therefore it is I would not, gentle hostess.
    Here will he find all that can woo the heart
    To joy and sweet forgetfulness of pain;
    The sight of me would wake his feeling mind
    To other thoughts. I am no doating mistress;
    No fond distracted wife, who must forthwith
    Rush to his arms and weep. I am his sister:
    The eldest daughter of his father's house:
    Calm and unwearied is my love for him;
    And having found him, patiently I'll wait,
    Nor greet him in the hour of social joy,
    To dash his mirth with tears –
    The night wears on; permit me to withdraw.
COUNT FREBERG   Nay, do not, do not injure us so far!
    Disguise thyself, and join our friendly train.
JANE   You wear not masks to-night.
LADY   We wear not masks, but you may be concealed
    Behind the double foldings of a veil.
JANE *(after pausing to consider)* In truth, I feel a little so inclin'd.
    Methinks unknown, I e'en might speak to him,
    And gently prove the temper of his mind;
    (To Lady) But for the means I must become your debtor.
LADY   Who waits? *(Enter her woman.)*
    Attend this lady to my wardrobe,
    And do what she commands you.

Exit Jane and waiting-woman.

COUNT FREBERG *(looking after Jane, as she goes out, with admiration)*
    Oh! What a soul she bears!
    See how she steps!
    Nought but the native dignity of worth
    E'er taught the moving form such noble grace.
LADY   Such lofty mien, and high assumed gait,
    I've seen ere now, and men have call'd it pride.

COUNT FREBERG   No, 'faith! Thou never didst, but oft indeed
The paltry imitation thou hast seen.
(looking at her) How hang those trappings on thy motley gown?
They seem like garlands on a May-day queen,
Which hinds have dress'd in sport.

Lady turns away displeased.

COUNT FREBERG   Nay, do not frown; I spoke it but in haste;
For thon art lovely still in every garb.
But see, the guests assemble.

Enter groups of well-dressed people, who pay their compliments to Freberg and his Lady; and, followed by her, pass into the inner apartment, where more company appear assembling, as if by another entry.

COUNT FREBERG *(remains on the front of the stage with a friend or two)*
How loud the hum of this gay-meeting crowd!
'Tis like a bee-swarm in the noonday sun.
Music will quell the sound. Who waits without?
Music strike up.

Music. When it ceases, enter from the inner apartment Rezenvelt, with several gentlemen, all richly dressed.

COUNT FREBERG *(to those who just entered)*
What, lively gallants, quit the field so soon?
Are there no beauties in that moving crowd
To fix your fancy?
REZENVELT   Ay, marry are there! Men of ev'ry fancy.
May in that moving crowd some fair one find
To suit their taste, though whimsical and strange,
As ever fancy own'd.
Beauty of every cast and shade is there,
From the perfection of a faultless form,
Down to the common, brown, unnoted maid,
Who looks but pretty in her Sunday gown.
1st GENTLEMAN   There is, indeed, a gay variety.
REZENVELT   And if the liberality of nature
Suffices not, there's store of grafted charms,
Blending in one the sweets of many plants,
So obstinately, strangely opposite,
As would have well defied all other art
But female cultivation. Aged youth,

With borrowed locks, in rosy chaplets bound,
Clothes her dim eye, parch'd lips, and skinny cheek
In most unlovely softness;
And youthful age, with fat round trackless face,
The downcast look of contemplation deep
Most pensively assumes.
Is it not even so? The native prude,
With forced laugh, and merriment uncouth,
Plays off the wild coquette's successful charms
With most unskilful pains; and the coquette,
In temporary crust of cold reserve,
Fixes her studied looks upon the ground,
Forbiddingly demure.

COUNT FREBERG   Fy! Thou art too severe.

REZENVELT   Say, rather, gentle.
I' faith! The very dwarfs attempt to charm
With lofty airs of puny majesty;
While potent damsels, of a portly make,
Totter like nurslings, and demand the aid
Of gentle sympathy.
From all those diverse modes of dire assault,
He owns a heart of hardest adamant,
Who shall escape to-night.

COUNT FREBERG (to De Monfort, who has entered during Rezenvelt's speech, and heard the greatest part of it)
Ha, ha, ha, ha!
How pleasantly he gives his wit the rein,
Yet guides its wild career! (De Monfort is silent.)

REZENVELT (smiling archly) What, think you, Freberg,
The same powerful spell
Of transformation reigns o'er all to-night?
Or that De Monfort is a woman turn'd,
So widely from his native self to swerve,
As grace my folly with a smile of his?

DE MONFORT   Nay, think not, Rezenvelt, there is no smile
I can bestow on thee. There is a smile,
A smile of nature too, which I can spare,
And yet, perhaps, thou wilt not thank me for it. (smiles contemptuously)

REZENVELT   Not thank thee! It were surely most ungrateful
No thanks to pay for nobly giving me
What, well we see, has cost thee so much pain.

For nature hath her smiles of birth more painful
Than bitt'rest execrations.
COUNT FREBERG These idle words will lead us to disquiet,
Forbear, forbear, my friends! Go, Rezenvelt,
Accept the challenge of those lovely dames,
Who through the portal come with bolder steps
To claim your notice.

*Enter a group of ladies from the other apartment, who walk slowly
across the bottom of the stage, and return to it again. Rezenvelt shrugs up
his shoulders, as if unwilling to go.*

1st GENTLEMAN *(to Rezenvelt)* Behold in sable veil a lady comes,
Whose noble air doth challenge fancy's skill
To suit it with a countenance as goodly. *(pointing to Jane De Monfort,
who now enters in a thick black veil)*
REZENVELT Yes, this way lies attraction. *(To Freberg)*
With permission – *(going up to Jane)*
Fair lady, though within that envious shroud
Your beauty deigns not to enlighten us,
We bid you welcome, and our beauties here
Will welcome you the more for such concealment.
With the permission of our noble host
(taking her hand, and leading her to the front of the stage)
JANE *(to Freberg)* Pardon me this presumption, courteous sir;
I thus appear *(pointing to her veil)*, not careless of respect
Unto the generous lady of the feast.
Beneath this veil no beauty shrouded is,
That, now, or pain, or pleasure can bestow.
Within the friendly cover of its shade
I only wish, unknown, again to see
One who, alas, is heedless of my pain.
DE MONFORT Yes, it is ever thus. Undo that veil,
And give thy count'nance to the cheerful light.
Men now all soft and female beauty scorn,
And mock the gentle cares which aim to please.
It is most damnable! Undo thy veil,
And think of him no more.
JANE I know it well: e'en to a proverb grown,
Is lovers' faith, and I had borne such slight:
But he, who has, alas, forsaken me,
Was the companion of my early days,

My cradle's mate, mine infant play-fellow.
Within our op'ning minds, with riper years,
The love of praise and gen'rous virtue sprung:
Through varied life our pride, our joys were one;
At the same tale we wept: he is my brother.
DE MONFORT   And he forsook thee? –
No, I dare not curse him:
My heart upbraids me with a crime like his.
JANE   Ah! Do not thus distress a feeling heart.
All sisters are not to the soul entwin'd
With equal bands; thine has not watch'd for thee,
Wept for thee, cheer'd thee, shar'd thy weal and woe,
As I have done for him.
DE MONFORT (*eagerly*) Ah! Has she not?
By heav'n the sum of all thy kindly deeds
Were but as chaff pois'd against massy gold,
Compar'd to that which I do owe her love.
Oh, pardon me! I mean not to offend –
I am too warm – but she of whom I speak
Is the dear sister of my earliest love;
In noble, virtuous worth to none a second:
And though behind those sable folds were hid
As fair a face as ever woman own'd,
Still would I say she is as fair as thou.
How oft amidst the beauty-blazing throng,
I've proudly to th' inquiring stranger told!
Her name and lineage! Yet within her house,
The virgin mother of an orphan race
Her dying parents left, this noble woman
Did, like a Roman matron, proudly sit,
Despising all the blandishments of love;
While many a youth his hopeless love conceal'd,
Or, humbly distant, woo'd her like a queen.
Forgive, I pray you! O forgive this boasting!
In faith! I mean you no discourtesy.
JANE (*off her guard, in a soft natural tone of voice*)
Oh, no! Nor do me any.
DE MONFORT   What voice speaks now?
Withdraw, withdraw this shade!
For if thy face bear semblance to thy voice,
I'll fall and worship thee.

Pray! Pray undo! *(puts forth his hand eagerly to snatch away the veil,*
whilst she shrinks back and Rezenvelt steps between to prevent him)
REZENVELT   Stand off: no hand shall lift this sacred veil.
DE MONFORT   What, dost thou think De Monfort fall'n so low,
   That there may live a man beneath heav'n's roof,
   Who dares to say, he shall not?
REZENVELT   He lives who dares to say –
JANE *(throwing back her veil, much alarmed, and rushing between*
   them) Forbear, forbear!

Rezenvelt, very much struck, steps back respectfully, and makes her a low
bow. De Monfort stands for a while motionless, gazing upon her, till she,
looking expressively to him, extends her arms, and he, rushing into them,
bursts into tears. Freberg seems very much pleased.
The company then advancing from the inner apartment, gather about
them, and the scene closes.

ACT TWO, SCENE 2

De Monfort's apartments. Enter De Monfort, with a disordered air, and
his hand pressed upon his forehead, followed by Jane.

DE MONFORT   No more, my sister, urge me not again:
   My secret troubles cannot be reveal'd.
   From all participation of its thoughts
   My heart recoils: I pray thee be contented.
JANE   What, must I, like a distant humble friend,
   Observe thy restless eye, and gait disturb'd,
   In timid silence, whilst with yearning heart
   I turn aside to weep? O no! De Monfort
   A nobler task thy nobler mind will give;
   Thy true entrusted friend I still shall be.
DE MONFORT   Ah, Jane, forbear! I cannot e'en to thee.
JANE   Then, fy upon it! Fy upon it, Monfort!
   There was a time when e'en with murder stain'd,
   Had it been possible that such dire deed
   Could e'er have been the crime of one so piteous,
   Thou wouldst have told it me.
DE MONFORT   So would I now – but ask of this no more.
   All other trouble but the one I feel
   I had disclos'd to thee. I pray thee spare me.
   It is the secret weakness of my nature.

JANE   Then secret let it be; I urge no farther.
　　The eldest of our valiant father's hopes,
　　So sadly orphan'd, side by side we stood,
　　Like two young trees, whose boughs in early strength
　　Screen the weak saplings of the rising grove,
　　And brave the storm together –
　　I have so long, as if by nature's right,
　　Thy bosom's inmate and adviser been,
　　I thought through life I should have so remain'd,
　　Nor ever known a change. Forgive me, Monfort,
　　A humbler station will I take by thee:
　　The close attendant of thy wand'ring steps;
　　The cheerer of this home, with strangers sought;
　　The soother of those griefs I must not know:
　　This is mine office now: I ask no more.

DE MONFORT   Oh, Jane! Thou dost constrain me with thy love!
　　Would I could tell it thee!

JANE   Thou shalt not tell me. Nay I'll stop mine ears,
　　Nor from the yearnings of affection wring
　　What shrinks from utt'rance. Let it pass, my brother.
　　I'll stay by thee; I'll cheer thee, comfort thee:
　　Pursue with thee the study of some art,
　　Or nobler science, that compels the mind
　　To steady thought progressive, driving forth
　　All floating, wild, unhappy fantasies;
　　Till thou, with brow unclouded, smil'st again;
　　Like one who, from dark visions of the night,
　　When th' active soul within its lifeless cell
　　Holds its own world, with dreadful fancy press'd
　　Of some dire, terrible, or murd'rous deed,
　　Wakes to the dawning morn, and blesses heaven.

DE MONFORT   It will not pass away; 'twill haunt me still.

JANE   Ah! say not so, for I will haunt thee too;
　　And be to it so close an adversary,
　　That, though I wrestle darkling with the fiend, I shall o'ercome it.

DE MONFORT   Thou most gen'rous woman!
　　Why do I treat thee thus? It should not be –
　　And yet I cannot – O that cursed villain!
　　He will not let me be the man I would.

JANE What sayst thou, brother?
Oh! What words are these?
They have awak'd my soul to dreadful thoughts.
I do beseech thee, speak!
(He shakes his head, and turns from her; she following him)
By the affection thou didst ever bear me;
By the dear mem'ry of our infant days;
By kindred living ties, ay, and by those
Who sleep i' the tomb, and cannot cull to thee,
I do conjure thee, speak!
(He waves her off with his hand and covers his face with the other, still turning from her.)
Ah! Wilt thou not? *(assuming dignity)* Then, if affection, most unwearied love,
Tried early, long, and never wanting found,
O'er generous man hath more authority,
More rightful power than crown or sceptre give,
I do command thee.
(He throws himself into a chair, greatly agitated.)
De Monfort, do not thus resist my love.
Here I entreat thee on my bended knees. *(kneeling)*
Alas! My brother!

De Monfort starts up, and catching her in his arms, raises her up, then placing her in the chair, kneels at her feet.

DE MONFORT Thus let him kneel who should the abased be,
And at thine honour'd feet confession make!
I'll tell thee all – but, oh! thou wilt despise me.
For in my breast a raging passion burns,
To which thy soul no sympathy will own –
A passion which hath made my nightly couch
A place of torment; and the light of day,
With the gay intercourse of social man,
Feel like th' oppressive airless pestilence.
O Jane! Thou wilt despise me.
JANE Say not so:
I never can despise thee, gentle brother.
A lover's jealousy and hopeless pangs
No kindly heart condemns.
DE MONFORT A lover, sayst thou?
No, it is hate! Black, lasting, deadly hate!

Which thus hath driven me forth from kindred peace,
From social pleasure, from my native home,
To be a sullen wand'rer on the earth,
Avoiding all men, cursing and accurs'd.

JANE   De Monfort, this is fiend-like, frightful, terrible!
What being, by th' Almighty Father form'd,
Of flesh and blood, created even as thou,
Could in thy breast such horrid tempest wake,
Who art thyself his fellow?
Unknit thy brows, and spread those wrath-clench'd hands.
Some sprite accurs'd within thy bosom mates
To work thy ruin. Strive with it, my brother!
Strive bravely with it; drive it from thy breast;
'Tis the degrader of a noble heart:
Curse it, and bid it part.

DE MONFORT   It will not part. *(his hand on his breast)*
I've lodg'd it here too long:
With my first cares I felt its rankling touch;
I loath'd him when a boy.

JANE   Whom didst thou say?

DE MONFORT   Oh! That detested Rezenvelt!
E'en in our early sports, like two young whelps
Of hostile breed, instinctively reverse,
Each 'gainst the other pitch'd his ready pledge,
And frown'd defiance. As we onward pass'd
From youth to man's estate, his narrow art
And envious gibing malice, poorly veil'd
In the affected carelessness of mirth,
Still more detestable and odious grew.
There is no living being on this earth
Who can conceive the malice of his soul,
With all his gay and damned merriment,
To those, by fortune or by merit plac'd
Above his paltry self. When, low in fortune,
He look'd upon the state of prosp'rous men,
As nightly birds, rous'd from their murky holes,
Do scowl and chatter at the light of day,
I could endure it; even as we bear
Th' impotent bite of some half-trodden worm,
I could endure it. But when honours came,
And wealth and new-got titles fed his pride;

Whilst flatt'ring knaves did trumpet forth his praise,
And grov'ling idiots grinn'd applauses on him;
Oh! Then I could no longer suffer it!
It drove me frantic. – What! What would I give!
What would I give to crush the bloated toad,
So rankly do I loathe him!

JANE   And would thy hatred crush the very man
Who gave to thee that life he might have ta'en ;
That life which thou so rashly didst expose
To aim at his? Oh! This is horrible!

DE MONFORT   Ha! Thou hast heard it, then?
From all the world,
But most of all from thee, I thought it hid.

JANE   I heard a secret whisper, and resolv'd
Upon the instant to return to thee.
Didst thou receive my letter?

DE MONFORT   I did! I did! 'Twas that which drove me hither.
I could not hear to meet thine eye again.

JANE   Alas! That, tempted by a sister's tears,
I ever left thy house! These few past months,
These absent months, have brought us all this woe.
Had I remain'd with thee it had not been.
And yet, methinks, it should not move you thus.
You dar'd him to the field; both bravely fought;
He more adroit disarm'd you; courteously
Return'd the forfeit sword, which, so return'd,
You did refuse to use against him more;
And then, as says report, you parted friends.

DE MONFORT   When he disarm'd this curs'd, this worthless hand
Of its most worthless weapon, he but spar'd
From dev'lish pride, which now derives a bliss
In seeing me thus fetter'd, sham'd, subjected
With the vile favour of his poor forbearance;
While he securely sits with gibing brow,
And basely bates me like a muzzled cur
Who cannot turn again –
Until that day, till that cursed day,
I knew not half the torment of this hell,
Which burns within my breast. Heaven's lightnings blast him!

JANE   O this is horrible! Forbear, forbear!
Lest heaven's vengeance light upon thy head,
For this most impious wish.

DE MONFORT   Then let it light.
  Torments more fell than I have felt already
  It cannot send. To be annihilated,
  What all men shrink from; to be dust, be nothing,
  Were bliss to me, compar'd to what I am!
JANE   Oh! Wouldst thou kill me with these dreadful
  words?

DE MONFORT *(raising his hands to heaven)*
  Let me but once upon his ruin look,
  Then close mine eyes for ever!

*Jane, in great distress, staggers back, and supports herself upon the side
scene. De Monfort, alarmed, runs up to her with a softer voice.*

DE MONFORT   Ha! How is this? Thou'rt ill; thou'rt very pale.
  What have I done to thee? Alas, alas!
  I meant not to distress thee. – O my sister!
JANE *(shaking her head)* I cannot speak to thee.
DE MONFORT   I have kill'd thee.
  Turn, turn thee not away! Look on me still!
  Oh! Droop not thus, my life, my pride, my sister;
  Look on me yet again.
JANE   Thou too, De Monfort,
  In better days, wert wont to be my pride.
DE MONFORT   I am a wretch, most wretched in myself,
  And still more wretched in the pain I give,
  O curse that villain! That detested villain!
  He has spread mis'ry o'er my fated life:
  He will undo us all.
JANE   I've held my warfare through a troubled world,
  And borne with steady mind my share of ill;
  For thou wert then the helpmate of my toil.
  But now the wane of life comes darkly on,
  And hideous passion tears me from thy heart,
  Blasting thy worth. – I cannot strive with this.
DE MONFORT *(affectionately)* What shall I do?
JANE   Call up thy noble spirit;
  Rouse all the gen'rous energy of virtue;
  And with the strength of heaven-endued man,
  Repel the hideous foe. Be great; be valiant.
  O, if thou couldst! E'en shrouded as thou art

In all the sad infirmities of nature,
What a most noble creature wouldst thou be!
DE MONFORT   Ay, if I could: alas! Alas! I cannot.
JANE   Thou canst, thou mayst, thou wilt.
We shall not part till I have turn'd thy soul.

Enter Manuel.

DE MONFORT   Ha! Someone enters. Wherefore com'st thou
here?
MANUEL   Count Freberg waits your leisure.
DE MONFORT *(angrily)* Begone, begone I –
I cannot see him now.

Exit Manuel.

JANE   Come to my closet; free from all intrusion
I'll school thee there; and thou again shalt be
My willing pupil, and my gen'rous friend
The noble Monfort I have lov'd so long,
And must not, will not lose.
DE MONFORT   Do as thou wilt; I will not grieve thee more.

They exit.

ACT THREE, SCENE 1

*Countess Freberg's dressing room. Enter the Countess dispirited and out
of humour, and throws herself into a chair. Enter, by the opposite side,
Theresa.*

THERESA   Madam, I am afraid you are unwell;
What is the matter? Does your head ache?
LADY *(peevishly)* No,
'Tis not my head: concern thyself no more
With what concerns not thee.
THERESA   Go you abroad tonight?
LADY   Yes, thinkest thou I'll stay and fret at home?
THERESA   Then please to say what you would choose to wear–
One of your newest robes?
LADY   I hate them all.
THERESA   Surely that purple scarf became you well
With all those wreaths of richly-hanging flowers.

Did I not overhear them say, last night,
As from the crowded ball-room ladies pass'd
How gay and handsome in her costly dress
The Countess Freberg look'd ?

LADY   Didst thou o'erhear it?

THERESA   I did, and more than this.

LADY   Well, all are not so greatly prejudic'd.
All do not think me like a May-day queen,
Which peasants deck in sport.

THERESA   And who said this?

LADY (*putting her handkerchief to her eyes*) E'en my good lord, Theresa.

THERESA   He said it but in jest. He loves you well.

LADY   I know as well as thou he loves me well,
But what of that! He takes in me no pride:
Elsewhere his praise and admiration go
And Jane De Monfort is not mortal woman.

THERESA   The wondrous character this lady bears
For worth and excellence: from early youth
The friend and mother of her younger sisters,
Now greatly married, as I have been told,
From her most prudent care, may well excuse
The admiration of so good a man
As my good master is. And then, dear madam,
I must confess, when I myself did hear
How she was come through the rough winter's storm,
To seek and comfort an unhappy brother
My heart beat kindly to her.

LADY   Ay, ay, there is a charm in this I find:
But wherefore may she not have come as well
Through the wintry storms to seek a lover too?

THERESA   No, madam, no, I could not think of this.

LADY   That would reduce her in your eyes, mayhap,
To woman's level – Now I see my vengeance!
I'll tell it round that she is hither come
Under pretence of finding out De Monfort,
To meet with Rezenvelt. When Freberg hears it,
'Twill help, I ween, to break this magic charm.

THERESA   And say what is not, madam?

LADY   How canst thou know that I shall say what is not?
'Tis like enough I shall but speak the truth.

THERESA   Ah, no! There is –

LADY   Well, hold thy foolish tongue.
(Freberg's voice is heard without. After hesitating)
I will not see him now.

Lady exits. Enter Freberg by the opposite side, passing on hastily.

THERESA   Pardon, my lord; I fear you are in haste.
Yet must I crave that you will give to me
The books my Lady mention'd to you: she
Has charg'd me to remind you.
COUNT FREBERG   I'm in haste. *(passing on)*
THERESA   Pray you, my lord: your countess, wants them much:
The Lady Jane De Monfort ask'd them of her.
COUNT FREBERG *(returning instantly)* Are they for her?
I knew not this before.
I will, then, search them out immediately.
There is nought good or precious in my keeping,
That is not dearly honour'd by her use.
THERESA   My lord, what would your gentle countess say,
If she o'erheard her own request neglected,
Until supported by a name more potent?
COUNT FREBERG   Thinkst thou she is a fool, my good Theresa,
Vainly to please herself with childish thoughts
Of matching what is matchless – Jane De Monfort?
Thinkst thou she is a fool, and cannot see,
That love and admiration often thrive
Though far apart?

Re-enter Lady with great violence.

LADY   I am a fool, not to have seen full well,
That thy best pleasure in o'er-rating so
This lofty stranger, is to humble me,
And cast a dark'ning shadow o'er my head.
Ay, wherefore dost thou stare upon me thus?
Art thou asham'd that I have thus surpris'd thee?
Well mayst thou be so!
COUNT FREBERG   True; thou rightly sayst.
Well may I be asham'd: not for the praise
Which I have ever openly bestow'd
On Monfort's noble sister; but that thus,
Like a poor mean and jealous listener,
She should be found, who is Count Freberg's wife.

LADY   Oh, I am lost and ruin'd! Hated, scorn'd!
(pretending to faint)
COUNT FREBERG   Alas, I have been too rough!
(taking her hand and kissing it tenderly)
My gentle love! My own, my only love!
See, she revives again. How art thou, love?
Support her to her chamber, good Theresa.
I'll sit and watch by her. I've been too rough.

Exit Lady supported by Freberg and Theresa.

ACT THREE, SCENE 2

*De Monfort discovered sitting by a table reading. After a little time he lays down his book, and continues in a thoughtful posture.
Enter to him Jane De Monfort.*

JANE   Thanks, gentle brother. *(pointing to the book)*
Thy willing mind has rightly been employ'd:
Did not thy heart warm at the fair display
Of peace and concord and forgiving love?
DE MONFORT   I know resentment may to love be turn'd.
Though keen and lasting, into love as strong:
And fiercest rivals in th' ensanguin'd field
Have cast their brandish'd weapons to the ground,
Joining their mailed breasts in close embrace,
With generous impulse fir'd. I know right well
The darkest, fellest wrongs have been forgiven
Seventy times o'er from blessed heav'nly love:
I've heard of things like these; I've heard and wept.
But what is this to me?
JANE   All, all, my brother!
It bids thee too that noble precept learn,
To love thine enemy.
DE MONFORT   Th' uplifted stroke that would a wretch destroy,
Gorg'd with my richest spoil, stain'd with my blood;
I would arrest, and cry, "Hold! Hold! Have mercy."
But when the man most adverse to my nature,
Who e'en from childhood hath, with rude malevolence,
Withheld the fair respect all paid beside,
Turning my very praise into derision,

Who galls and presses me where'er I go,
Would claim the gen'rous feelings of my heart,
Nature herself doth lift her voice aloud,
And cry, "It is impossible!"
JANE *(shaking her head)* Ah, Monfort, Monfort!
DE MONFORT   I can forgive th' venom'd reptile's sting,
But hate his loathsome self.
JANE   And canst thou do no more for love of heaven?
DE MONFORT   Alas! I cannot now so school my mind
As holy men have taught, nor search it truly :
But this, my Jane, I'll do for love of thee;
And more it is than crowns could win me to,
Or any power but thine. I'll see the man.
Th' indignant risings of abhorrent nature;
The stern contraction of my scowling brows,
That like the plant whose closing leaves do shrink
At hostile touch, still knit at his approach;
The crooked curving lip, by instinct taught,
In imitation of disgustful things,
To pout and swell, I strictly will repress;
And meet him with a tamed countenance,
E'en as a townsman, who would live at peace,
And pay him the respect his station claims.
I'll crave his pardon too for all offence
My dark and wayward temper may have done.
Nay more, I will confess myself his debtor
For the forbearance I have curs'd so oft:
Life spar'd by him, more horrid than the grave
With all its dark corruption! This I'll do.
Will it suffice thee? More than this I cannot.
JANE   No more than this do I require of thee
In outward act, though in thy heart, my friend,
I hop'd a better change, and yet will hope.
I told thee Freberg had propos'd a meeting.
DE MONFORT   I know it well.
JANE   And Rezenvelt consents.
He meets you here; so far he shows respect.
DE MONFORT   Well, let it be; the sooner past the better.
JANE   I'm glad to hear you say so, for, in truth,
He has propos'd for it an early hour.
'Tis almost near his time; I came to tell you.

DE MONFORT　　　　What, comes he here so soon? Shame
on his speed!
It is not decent thus to rush upon me.
He loves the secret pleasure he will feel
To see me thus subdued.
JANE　　　　　　　O say not so! He comes with heart sincere.
DE MONFORT　　　　Could we not meet elsewhere? From home
– i' the fields,
Where other men – must I alone receive him?
Where is your agent, Freberg, and his friends,
That I must meet him here? *(He walks up and down, very much
disturbed.)*
Now! Didst thou say? – how goes the hour? – e'en now!
I would some other friend were first arriv'd.
JANE　　　　　　　See, to thy wish come Freberg and his dame.
DE MONFORT　　　　His lady too! Why comes he not alone?
Must all the world upon our meeting stare?

Enter Count Freberg and his Countess.

COUNT FREBERG　　A happy morrow to my noble marquis,
And his most noble sister!
JANE　　　　　　　Gen'rous Freberg,
Your face, methinks, forebodes a happy morn,
Open and cheerful. What of Rezenvelt?
COUNT FREBERG　　I left him at his home, prepar'd to follow:
He'll soon appear. *(To De Monfort)* And now, my worthy friend,
Give me your hand; this happy change delights me.

*De Monfort gives him his hand coldly, and they walk to the bottom of the
stage together, in earnest discourse, whilst Jane and the Countess remain
in the front.*

LADY　　　　　　　My dearest madam, will you pardon me?
I know Count Freberg's bus'ness with De Monfort,
And had a strong desire to visit you,
So much I wish the honour of your friendship;
For he retains no secret from mine ear.
JANE *(archly)*　　　Knowing your prudence – you are welcome, madam;
So shall Count Freberg's lady ever be.

*De Monfort and Freberg returning towards the front of the stage, still
engaged in discourse.*

COUNT FREBERG   He is indeed a man, within whose breast
Firm rectitude and honour hold their seat,
Though unadorned with that dignity
Which were their fittest garb. Now, on my life
I know no truer heart than Rezenvelt.
DE MONFORT   Well, Freberg, well, there needs not all this pains
To garnish out his worth: let it suffice;
I am resolv'd I will respect the man,
As his fair station and repute demand.
Methinks I see not at your jolly feasts
The youthful knight, who sang so pleasantly.
COUNT FREBERG   A pleasant circumstance detains him hence;
Pleasant to those who love high gen'rous deeds
Above the middle pitch of common minds;
And, though I have been sworn to secrecy,
Yet must I tell it thee.
This knight is near akin to Rezenvelt,
To whom an old relation, short while dead,
A good estate bequeathed, some leagues distant.
But Rezenvelt, now rich in fortune's store,
Disdain'd the sordid love of further gain,
And gen'rously the rich bequest resign'd
To this young man, blood of the same degree
To the deceas'd, and low in fortune's gifts,
Who is from hence to take possession of it:
Was it not nobly done?
DE MONFORT   'Twas right and hononrable.
This morning is oppressive, warm, and heavy:
There hangs a foggy closeness in the air;
Dost thou not feel it?
COUNT FREBERG   O no! To think upon a gen'rous deed
Expands my soul, and makes me lightly breathe.
DE MONFORT   Who gives the feast to-night?
His name escapes me.
You say I am invited.
COUNT FREBERG   Old Count Waterlan.
In honour of your townsman's gen'rous gift,
He spreads the board.
DE MONFORT   He is too old to revel with the gay.
COUNT FREBERG   But not too old is he to honour virtue.
I shall partake of it with open soul;

For, on my honest faith, of living men
I know not one, for talents, honour, worth,
That I should rank superior to Rezenvelt.
DE MONFORT   How virtuous he hath been in three short days!
COUNT FREBERG   Nay, longer, marquis; but my friendship rests
Upon the good report of other men,
And that has told me much.

De Monfort aside, going some steps hastily from Freberg, and rending his
cloak with agitation as he goes.

COUNT FREBERG   Would he were come! By heav'n I would he were!
This fool besets me so. *(Suddenly correcting himself, and joining the*
ladies, who have retired to the bottom of the stage, he speaks to
Countess Freberg with affected cheerfulness.)
The sprightly dames of Amberg rise by times,
Untarnish'd with the vigils of the night.
LADY   Praise us not rashly, 'tis not always so.
DE MONFORT   He does not rashly praise who praises you;
For he were dull indeed – *(stopping short, as if he heard something)*
LADY   How dull indeed?
DE MONFORT   I should have said –
It has escap'd me now – *(listening again, as if he heard something)*
JANE *(to De Monfort)*   What, hear you aught?
DE MONFORT *(hastily)* 'Tis nothing.
LADY *(to De Monfort)* Nay, do not let me lose it so, my lord.
Some fair one has bewitch'd your memory,
And robs me of the half-form'd compliment.
JANE   Half-utter'd praise is to the curious mind
As to the eye half-veiled beauty is,
More precious than the whole. Pray pardon him.
Some one approaches. *(listening)*
COUNT FREBERG   No, no, it is a servant who ascends;
He will not come so soon.
DE MONFORT *(off his guard)* 'Tis Rezenvelt: I heard his well-known foot,
From the first staircase, mounting step by step.
COUNT FREBERG   How quick an ear thou hast for distant sound!
I heard him not.

De Monfort looks embarrassed, and is silent. Enter Rezenvelt.
De Monfort, recovering himself, goes up to receive Rezenvelt, who meets
him with a cheerful countenance.

DE MONFORT *(to Rezenvelt)* I am, my lord, beholden to you greatly.
  This ready visit makes me much your debtor.
REZENVELT   Then may such debts between us, noble marquis,
  Be oft incurr'd, and often paid again!
  (To Jane) Madam, I am devoted to your service,
  And ev'ry wish of yours commands my will.
  (To Countess) Lady, good morning.
  (To Freberg) Well, my gentle friend,
  You see I have not linger'd long behind.
COUNT FREBERG   No, thou art sooner than I look'd for thee.
REZENVELT   A willing heart adds feather to the heel,
  And makes the clown a winged Mercury.
DE MONFORT   Then let me say, that, with a grateful mind,
  I do receive these tokens of good will;
  And must regret, that, in my wayward moods,
  I have too oft forgot the due regard
  Your rank and talents claim.
REZENVELT   No, no, De Monfort,
  You have but rightly curb'd a wanton spirit,
  Which makes me too neglectful of respect.
  Let us be friends, and think of this no more.
COUNT FREBERG   Ay, let it rest with the departed shades
  Of things which are no more; whilst lovely concord,
  Follow'd by friendship sweet, and firm esteem,
  Your future days enrich. O heavenly friendship!
  Thou dost exalt the sluggish souls of men,
  By thee conjoin'd, to great and glorious deeds;
  As two dark clouds, when mix'd in middle air,
  With vivid lightnings flash, and roar sublime.
  Talk not of what is past, but future love.
DE MONFORT *(with dignity)* No, Freberg, no, it must not
  (To Rezenvelt) No, my lord, I will not offer you an hand of concord,
  And poorly hide the motives which constrain me.
  I would that, not alone, these present friends,
  But ev'ry soul in Amberg were assembled,
  That I, before them all, might here declare
  I owe my spared life to your forbearance. *(holding out his hand)*
  Take this from one who boasts no feeling warmth,
  But never will deceive.

*Jane smiles upon De Monfort with great approbation, and Rezenvelt
runs up to him with open arms.*

REZENVELT   Away with hands! I'll have thee to my breast.
  Thou art, upon my faith, a noble spirit!
DE MONFORT *(shrinking back from him)* Nay, if you please, I am not
  so prepar'd –
  My nature is of temperature too cold –
  I pray you pardon me
  (Jane's countenance changes)
  But take this hand, the token of respect;
  The token of a will inclin'd to concord;
  The token of a mind, that bears within
  A sense impressive of the debt it owes you:
  And cursed be its power, unnerv'd its strength,
  If e'er again it shall be lifted up
  To do you any harm!
REZENVELT   Well, be it so, De Monfort, I'm contented;
  I'll take thy hand, since I can have no more.
  (carelessly) I take of worthy men whate'er they give.
  Their heart I gladly take, if not their hand;
  If that too is withheld, a courteous word,
  Or the civility of placid looks:
  And, if e'en these are too great favours deem'd,
  Faith, I can set me down contentedly
  With plain and homely greeting, or "God save ye!"
DE MONFORT *(aside, starting away from him some paces)*
  By the good light, he makes a jest of it!

Jane seems greatly distressed, and Freberg endeavours to cheer her.

COUNT FREBERG *(to Jane)* Cheer up, my noble friend; all will go well;
  For friendship is no plant of hasty growth.
  Though rooted in esteem's deep soil, the slow
  And gradual culture of kind intercourse
  Must bring it to perfection.
  (To the Countess) My love, the morning, now, is far advanc'd;
  Our friends elsewhere expect us; take your leave.
LADY *(to Jane)*   Farewell, dear madam, till the evening hour.
COUNT FREBERG *(to De Monfort)* Good day, De Monfort.
  (To Jane) Most devoutly yours.
REZENVELT *(to Freberg)* Go not too fast, for I will follow you.

Exit Freberg and his lady.

REZENVELT *(to Jane)* The Lady Jane is yet a stranger here:

She might, perhaps, in this your ancient city
Find somewhat worth her notice.

JANE   I thank you, marquis, I am much engag'd;
I go not out to-day.

REZENVELT   Then fare ye well! I see I cannot now
Be the proud man who shall escort you forth,
And show to all the world my proudest boast
The notice and respect of Jane de Monfort.

DE MONFORT *(aside impatiently)* He says farewell, and goes not!

JANE *(to Rezenvelt)* You do me honour.

REZENVELT   Madam, adieu! *(To Jane)* Good morning, noble
marquis.

*Jane and De Monfort look expressively to one another, without speaking,
and then exit severally.*

ACT FOUR, SCENE 1

*A hall or antechamber, with the folding doors of an inner apartment
open, which discovers the guests rising from a banquet. They enter and
pass over the stage, and exit; and after them enter Rezenvelt and Freberg.*

COUNT FREBERG Alas, my Rezenvelt!
I vainly hop'd the hand of gentle peace,
From this day's reconciliation sprung,
These rude unseemly jarrings had subdu'd;
But I have mark'd, e'en at the social board,
Such looks, such words, such tones, such untold things,
Too plainly told, 'twixt you and Monfort pass,
That I must now despair.
Yet who could think, two minds so much refin'd,
So near in excellence, should be remov'd.
So far remov'd, in gen'rous sympathy?

REZENVELT   Ay, far remov'd indeed!

COUNT FREBERG And yet, methought, he made a noble effort,
And with a manly plainness bravely told
The galling debt he owes to your forbearance.

REZENVELT   Faith! So he did, and so did I receive it;
When, with spread arms, and heart e'en mov'd to tears,
I frankly proffer'd him a friend's embrace:

And, I declare, had he as such receiv'd it,
I from that very moment had forborne
All opposition, pride-provoking jest,
Condemning carelessness, and all offence;
And had caress'd him as a worthy heart,
From native weakness such indulgence claiming.
But since he proudly thinks that cold respect,
The formal tokens of his lordly favour,
So precious are, that I would sue for them
As fair distinction in the public eye,
Forgetting former wrongs, I spurn it all.
And but that I do bear that noble woman,
His worthy, his incomparable sister,
Such fix'd, profound regard, I would expose him;
And, as a mighty bull, in senseless rage,
Rous'd at the baiter's will, with wretched rags
Of ire-provoking scarlet, chafes and bellows,
I'd make him at small cost of paltry wit,
With all his deep and manly faculties,
The scorn and laugh of fools.

COUNT FREBERG   For heaven's sake, my friend, restrain your wrath!
For what has Monfort done of wrong to you,
Or you to him, bating one foolish quarrel,
Which you confess from slight occasion rose,
That in your breasts such dark resentment dwells,
So fix'd, so hopeless?

REZENVELT   O! From our youth he has distinguish'd me
With ev'ry mark of hatred and disgust.
For e'en in boyish sports I still oppos'd
His proud pretensions to pre-eminence;
Nor would I to his ripen'd greatness give
That fulsome adulation of applause
A senseless crowd bestow'd.
Though poor in fortune,
I still would smile at vain assuming wealth:
But when unlook'd-for fate on me bestow'd
Riches and splendour equal to his own,
Though I, in truth, despise such poor distinction,
Feeling inclin'd to be at peace with him,
And with all men beside, I curb'd my spirit,
And sought to soothe him. Then, with spiteful rage,

From small offence he rear'd a quarrel with me,
And dar'd me to the field. The rest you know.
In short, I still have been th' opposing rock,
O'er which the stream of his o'erflowing pride
Hath foam'd and fretted. Seest thou how it is?
COUNT FREBERG   Too well I see, and warn thee to beware.
Such streams have oft, by swelling floods surcharg'd,
Borne down, with sudden and impetuous force,
The yet unshaken stone of opposition,
Which had for ages stopp'd their flowing course.
I pray thee, friend, beware.
REZENVELT   Thou canst not mean – he will not murder me?
COUNT FREBERG   What a proud heart,
With such dark passion toss'd,
May, in the anguish of its thoughts, conceive,
I will not dare to say.
REZENVELT   Ha, ha! Thou knowst him not.
Full often have I mark'd it in his youth,
And could have almost lov'd him for the weakness:
He's form'd with such antipathy, by nature,
To all infliction of corporeal pain,
To wounding life, e'en to the sight of blood,
He cannot if he would.
COUNT FREBERG   Then fie upon thee!
It is not gen'rous to provoke him thus.
But let us part: we'll talk of this again.
Something approaches. – We are here too long.
REZENVELT   Well, then, to-morrow I'll attend your call.
Here lies my way. Good night.

Rezenfelt exits. Enter Conrad.

CONRAD   Forgive, I pray, my lord, a stranger's boldness.
I have presum'd to wait your leisure here,
Though at so late an hour.
COUNT FREBERG   But who art thou?
CONRAD   My name is Conrad, sir,
A humble suitor to your honour's goodness,
Who is the more embolden'd to presume,
In that De Monfort's brave and noble marquis
Is so much fam'd for good and gen'rous deeds.
COUNT FREBERG   You are mistaken, I am not the man.

CONRAD   Then, pardon me: I thought I could not err;
   That mien so dignified, that piercing eye
   Assur'd me it was he.
COUNT FREBERG   My name is not De Monfort, courteous stranger;
   But, if you have a favour to request,
   I may, with him, perhaps, befriend your suit.
CONRAD   I thank your honour, but I have a friend
   Who will commend me to De Monfort's favour:
   The Marquis Rezenvelt has known me long,
   Who, says report, will soon become his brother.
COUNT FREBERG   If thou wouldst seek thy ruin from De Monfort,
   The name of Rezenvelt employ, and prosper;
   But, if aught good, use any name but his.
CONRAD   How may this be?
COUNT FREBERG   I cannot now explain.
   Early to-morrow call upon Count Freberg;
   So am I call'd, each burgher knows my house,
   And there instruct me how to do you service.
   Good night. *(Exit.)*
CONRAD *(alone)* Well, this mistake may be of service to me:
   And yet my bus'ness I will not unfold
   To this mild, ready, promise-making courtier;
   I've been by such too oft deceiv'd already.
   But if such violent enmity exist
   Between De Monfort and this Rezenvelt,
   He'll prove my advocate by opposition.
   For if De Monfort would reject my suit,
   Being the man whom Rezenvelt esteems,
   Being the man he hates, a cord as strong,
   Will he not favour me? I'll think of this.

Exit.

ACT FOUR, SCENE 2

*A lower apartment in Jerome's house, with a wide, folding glass door,
looking into a garden, where the trees and shrubs are brown and leafless.
Enter De Monfort with a thoughtful frowning aspect, and paces slowly
across the stage, Jerome, following behind him, with a timid step.
De Monfort hearing him, turns suddenly about.*

DE MONFORT *(angrily)* Who follows me to this sequester'd room?
JEROME   I have presum'd, my lord.
  'Tis somewhat late:
  I am inform'd you eat at home to-night;
  Here is a list of all the dainty fare
  My busy search has found; please to peruse it.
DE MONFORT   Leave me: begone! Put hemlock in thy soup,
  Or deadly night-shade, or rank hellebore,
  And I will mess upon it.
JEROME   Heaven forbid!
  Your honour's life is all too precious, sure.
DE MONFORT *(sternly)* Did I not say begone?
JEROME   Pardon, my lord, I'm old, and oft forget.
DE MONFORT *(looking after him, as if his heart smote him)*
  Why will they thus mistime their foolish zeal,
  That I must be so stern?
  O, that I were upon some desert coast!
  Where howling tempests and the lashing tide
  Would stun me into deep and senseless quiet;
  As the storm-beaten trav'ller droops his head,
  In heavy, dull, lethargic weariness,
  And, 'mid the roar of jarring elements,
  Sleeps to awake no more.
  What am I grown? All things are hateful to me. *(Enter Manuel.)*
  (stamping with his foot) Who bids thee break upon my privacy?
MANUEL   Nay, good my lord! I heard you speak aloud,
  And dreamt not surely that you were alone.
DE MONFORT   What, dost thou watch, and pin thine ears to holes,
  To catch those exclamations of the soul,
  Which heaven alone should hear?
  Who hir'd thee, pray?
  Who basely hir'd thee for a task like this?
MANUEL   My lord, I cannot hold. For fifteen years
  Long-troubled years, I have your servant been,
  Nor hath the proudest lord in all the realm,
  W'ith firmer, with more honourable faith
  His sov'reign serv'd, than I have served you;
  But if my honesty be doubted now,
  Let him who is more faithful take my place,
  And serve you better.
DE MONFORT   Well, be it as thou wilt. Away with thee
  Thy loud-mouth'd boasting is no rule for me
  To judge thy merit by.

Enter Jerome hastily, and pulls Manuel away.

JEROME   Come, Manuel, come away; thou art not wise.
The stranger must depart and come again,
For now his honour will not be disturb'd.

Exit Manuel sulkily.

DE MONFORT   A stranger, saidst thou? *(drops his handkerchief)*
JEROME   I did, good sir, but he shall go away;
You shall not be disturb'd.
(stooping to lift the handkerchief)
You have dropp'd somewhat.
DE MONFORT *(preventing him)* Nay, do not stoop, my friend,
I pray thee not!
Thou art too old to stoop.
I'm much indebted to thee. – Take this ring –
I love thee better than I seem to do.
I pray thee do it – thank me not. – What stranger?
JEROME   A man who does most earnestly intreat
To see your honour; but I know him not.
DE MONFORT   Then let him enter.

Exit Jerome. A pause. Enter Conrad.

DE MONFORT   You are the stranger who would speak with me?
CONRAD   I am so far unfortunate, my lord.
That, though my fortune on your favour hangs,
I am to you a stranger.
DE MONFORT   How may this be? What can I do for you?
CONRAD   Since thus your lordship does so frankly ask
The tiresome preface of apology
I will forbear, and tell my tale at once.
In plodding drudgery I've spent my youth,
A careful penman in another's office;
And now, my master and employer dead,
They seek to set a stripling o'er my head,
And leave me on to drudge, e'en to old age,
Because I have no friend to take my part.
It is an office in your native town,
For I am come from thence, and I am told
You can procure it for me. Thus, my lord,
From the repute of goodness which you bear,
I have presum'd to beg.

DE MONFORT   They have befool'd thee with a false report.

CONRAD   Alas! I see it is in vain to plead,
Your mind is prepossess'd against a wretch,
Who has, unfortunately for his weal,
Offended the revengeful Rezenvelt.

DE MONFORT   What dost thou say?

CONRAD   What I, perhaps, had better leave unsaid.
Who will believe my wrongs if I complain?
I am a stranger, Rezenvelt my foe,
Who will believe my wrongs?

DE MONFORT (*eagerly catching him by the coat*) I will believe them!
Though they were base as basest, vilest deeds,
In ancient record told, I would believe them!
Let not the smallest atom of unworthiness
That he has put upon thee be conceal'd.
Speak boldly, tell it all; for, by the light!
I'll be thy friend, I'll be thy warmest friend,
If he has done thee wrong.

CONRAD   Nay, pardon me, it were not well advis'd,
If I should speak so freely of the man
Who will so soon your nearest kinsman be.

DE MONFORT   What canst thou mean by this?

CONRAD   That Marquis Rezenvelt
Has pledg'd his faith unto your noble sister,
And soon will be the husband of her choice.
So I am told, and so the world believes.

DE MONFORT   'Tis false! 'Tis basely false!
What wretch could drop from his envenom'd tongue
A tale so damn'd? – It chokes my breath (*stamping with his foot*)
What wretch did tell it thee?

CONRAD   Nay, everyone with whom I have convers'd
Has held the same discourse. I judge it not.
But you, my lord, who with the lady dwell,
You best can tell what her deportment speaks;
Whether her conduct and unguarded words
Belie such rumour.

De Monfort pauses, staggers backwards, and sinks into a chair; then starting up hastily.

DE MONFORT   Where am I now? 'Midst all the cursed thoughts,
That on my soul like stinging scorpions prey'd,

This never came before – Oh, if it be!
The thought will drive me mad. – Was it for this
She urg'd her warm request on bended knee?
Alas! I wept, and thought of sister's love,
No damned love like this.
Fell devil! 'Tis hell itself has lent thee aid
To work such sorcery! *(pauses)* I'll not believe it.
I must have proof clear as the noonday sun
For such foul charge as this! Who waits without?
(paces up and down, furiously agitated)

CONRAD *(aside)*   What have I done? I've carried this too far.
I've rous'd a fierce ungovernable madman.

Enter Jerome.

DE MONFORT *(in a loud angry voice)* Where did she go, at such an
early hour,
And with such slight attendance?
JEROME   Of whom inquires your honour?
DE MONFORT   Why, of your lady. Said I not my sister.
JEROME   The Lady Jane, your sister?
DE MONFORT *(in a faltering voice)* Yes, I did call her so.
JEROME   In truth, I cannot tell you where she went.
E'en now, from the short beechen walk hard-by,
I saw her through the garden-gate return.
The Marquis Rezenvelt, and Freberg's countess,
Are in her company. This way they come,
As being nearer to the back apartments;
But I shall stop them, if it be your will,
And bid them enter here.
DE MONFORT   No, stop them not. I will remain unseen,
And mark them as they pass. Draw back a little.

*Conrad seems alarmed and steals off unnoticed. De Monfort grasps
Jerome tightly by the hand, and drawing back, with him two or three
steps, not to be seen from the garden, waits in silence, with his eyes fixed
on the glass door.*

DE MONFORT   I hear their footsteps on the grating sand:
How like the croaking of a carrion bird,
That hateful voice sounds to the distant ear!
And now she speaks – her voice sounds cheerly too –
Curs'd be their mirth! –

Now, now, they come; keep closer still! Keep steady! *(taking hold of
Jerome with both hands)*

JEROME   My lord, you tremble much.
DE MONFORT   What, do I shake?
JEROME   You do, in truth, and your teeth chatter too.
DE MONFORT   See! See they come! He strutting by her side.

*Jane, Rezenvelt, and Countess Freberg appear through the glass door,
pursuing their way up a short walk leading to the other wing of the
house.*

DE MONFORT   See, his audacious face he turns to hers;
Utt'ring with confidence some nauseous jest.
And she endures it too – Oh! This looks vilely!
Ha! Mark that courteous motion of his arm!
What does he mean? – He dares not take her hand!
(pauses and looks eagerly) By heaven and hell he does!
*(letting go his hold of Jerome, he throws out his hands vehemently,
and thereby pushes him against the scene)*
JEROME   Oh! I am stunn'd! My head is crack'd in twain:
Your honour does forget how old I am.
DE MONFORT   Well, well, the wall is harder than I wist.
Begone, and whine within.

*Exit Jerome, with a sad rueful countenance. De Monfort comes forward
to the front of the stage, and makes a long pause expressive of great
agony of mind.*

DE MONFORT   It must be so: each passing circumstance;
Her hasty journey here; her keen distress
Whene'er my soul's abhorrence I express'd;
Ay, and that damned reconciliation,
With tears extorted from me: Oh, too well!
All, all too well bespeak the shameful tale.
I should have thought of heaven and hell conjoin'd,
The morning star mix'd with infernal fire,
Ere I had thought of this –
Hell's blackest magic, in the midnight hour,
With horrid spells and incantation dire,
Such combination opposite unseemly,
Of fair and loathsome, excellent and base,
Did ne'er produce – But everything is possible,
So as it may my misery enhance!

Oh! I did love her with such pride of soul!
When other men, in gay pursuit of love,
Each beauty follow'd, by her side I stay'd;
Far prouder of a brother's station there,
Than all the favours favour'd lovers boast.
We quarrell'd once, and when I could no more
The alter'd coldness of her eye endure,
I slipp'd o'tip-toe to her chamber-door;
And when she ask'd who gently knock'd – Oh! Oh!
Who could have thought of this? *(throws himself into a chair, covers
his face with his hand, and bursts into tears.
After some time, he starts up from his seat furiously.)*
Hell's direst torment seize the infernal villain!
Detested of my soul! I will have vengeance!
I'll crush thy swelling pride – I'll still thy vaunting –
I'll do a deed of blood! – Why shrink I thus?
If by some spell or magic sympathy,
Piercing the lifeless figure on that wall
Could pierce his bosom too, would I not cast it?
(throwing a dagger against the wall)
Shall groans and blood affright me? No, I'll do it.
Though gasping life beneath my pressure heav'd,
And my soul shudder'd at the horrid brink,
I would not flinch. – Fie, this recoiling nature!
O that his sever'd limbs were strew'd in air,
So as I saw it not!

*Enter Rezenvelt from behind the glass door. De Monfort turns round, and on
seeing him, starts back, then drawing his sword, rushes furiously upon him.*

DE MONFORT   Detested robber! Now all forms are over;
Now open villainy, now open hate! Defend thy life!

REZENVELT   De Monfort, thou art mad.
DE MONFORT   Speak not, but draw. Now for thy hated life!

*They fight: Rezenvelt parries his thrusts with great skill, and at last
disarms him.*

DE MONFORT   Then take my life, black fiend, for hell assists
thee.
REZENVELT   No, Monfort, but I'll take away your sword,
Not as a mark of disrespect to you,
But for your safety. By tomorrow's eve

I'll call on you myself and give it back;
And then, if I am charg'd with any wrong,
I'll justify myself. Farewell, strange man!

Rezenfelt exits. De Monfort stands for some time quite motionless like one stupified. Enters to him a Servant: he starts.

DE MONFORT Ha! Who art thou?
SERVANT 'Tis I, an' please your honour.
DE MONFORT *(staring wildly at him)* Who art thou?
SERVANT Your servant Jacques.
DE MONFORT Indeed I knew thee not.
  Now leave me, and when Rezenvelt is gone,
  Return and let me know.
SERVANT He's gone already.
DE MONFORT How! Is he gone so soon?
SERVANT His servant told me
  He was in haste to go; as night comes on,
  And at the evening hour he purposes
  To visit some old friend, whose lonely mansion
  Stands a short mile beyond the farther wood
  In which a convent is of holy nuns
  Who chant this night a requiem to the soul
  Of a departed sister. For so well
  He loves such solemn music, he has order'd
  His horses onward by the usual road,
  Meaning on foot to cross the wood alone.
  So says his knave. Good may it do him, sooth!
  I would not walk through those wild dells alone
  For all his wealth. For there, as I have heard,
  Foul murders have been done, and ravens scream;
  And things unearthly, stalking through the night,
  Have scar'd the lonely trav'ller from his wits.
  (De Monfort stands fixed in thought.)
  I've ta'en your steed, an' please you from the field
  And wait your farther orders.
  (De Monfort heeds him not.)
  His hoofs arc sound, and where the saddle gall'd,
  Begins to mend. What further must be done?
  (De Monfort still heeds him not.)
  His honour heeds me not. Why should I stay?

DE MONFORT *(eagerly, as he is going)* He goes alone, saidst thou?
SERVANT   His servant told me so.
DE MONFORT   And at what hour?
SERVANT   He 'parts from Amberg by the fall of eve.
Save you, my lord! How chang'd your count'nance
Are you not well?
DE MONFORT   Yes I am well: begone,
And wait my orders by the city wall:
I'll wend that way, and speak to thee again.

*Exit Servant. De Monfort walks rapidly two or three times across the
stage; then seizes his dagger from the wall, looks steadfastly at its point,
and exits hastily.*

ACT FOUR, SCENE 3

*Moonlight. A wild path in a wood, shaded with trees. Enter De Monfort,
with a strong expression of disquiet, mixed with fear, upon his face,
looking behind him, and bending his ear to the ground, as if he listened to
something.*

DE MONFORT   How hollow groans the earth beneath my tread!
Is there an echo here? Methinks it sounds
As though some heavy footstep follow'd me.
I will advance no further.
Deep settled shadows rest across the path,
And thickly-tangled boughs o'erhang this spot.
O that a tenfold gloom did cover it,
That 'mid the murky darkness I might strike!
As in the wild confusion of a dream,
Things horrid, bloody, terrible do pass,
As though they pass'd not; nor impress the mind
With the fix'd clearness of reality.
(An owl is heard screaming near him.)
(starting) What sound is that? *(listens, and the owl cries again)*
It is the screech-owl's cry.
Foul bird of night! What spirit guides thee here?
Art thou instinctive drawn to scenes of horror?
I've heard of this. *(pauses and listens)*
How those fall'n leaves so rustle on the path,
With whisp'ring noise, as though the earth around me

Did utter secret things.
The distant river, too, bears to mine ear
A dismal wailing. O mysterious night!
Thou art not silent; many tongues hast thou.
A distant gath'ring blast sounds through the wood,
And dark clouds fleetly hasten o'er the sky:
O! That a storm would rise, a raging storm;
Amidst the roar of warring elements
I'd lift my hand and strike! But this pale light,
The calm distinctness of each stilly thing,
Is terrible. *(starting)* Footsteps, and near me too!
He comes! He comes! I'll watch him farther on –
I cannot do it here.

He exits. Enter Rezenvelt, and continues his way slowly from the bottom of the stage. As he advances to the front, the owl screams, he stops and listens, and the owl screams again.

REZENVELT   Ha! Does the night-bird greet me on my way?
How much his hooting is in harmony
With such a scene as this! I like it well.
Oft when a boy, at the still twilight hour,
I've leant my back against some knotted oak,
And loudly mimick'd him, till to my call
He answer would return, and, through the gloom,
We friendly converse held.
Between me and the star-bespangled sky,
Those aged oaks their crossing branches wave,
And through them looks the pale and placid moon.
How like a crocodile, or winged snake,
Yon sailing cloud bears on its dusky length!
And now transformed by the passing wind,
Methinks it seems a flying Pegasus.
Ay, but a shapeless band of blacker hue
Comes swiftly after –
A hollow murm'ring wind sounds through the trees;
I hear it from afar; this bodes a storm.
I must not linger here –
(A bell is heard at some distance.)
The convent bell. 'Tis distant still: it tells their hour of prayer.
It sends a solemn sound upon the breeze,
That, to a fearful superstitious mind,
In such a scene, would like a death-knell come. *(Exit.)*

ACT FIVE, SCENE 1

The inside of a convent chapel, of old Gothic architecture, almost dark: two torches only are seen at a distance, burning over a newly covered grave. Lightning is seen flashing through the windows, and thunder heard, with the sound of wind beating upon the building. Enter two monks.

1st MONK   The storm increases: hark how dismally
It howls along the cloisters. How goes time?
2nd MONK   It is the hour: I hear them near at hand:
And when the solemn requiem has been sung
For the departed sister, we'll retire.
Yet, should this tempest still more violent grow,
We'll beg a friendly shelter till the morn.
1st MONK   See, the procession enters: let us join.

The organ strikes up a solemn prelude. Enter a procession of nuns, with the abbess, bearing torches. After compassing the grave twice, and remaining there some time, the organ plays a grand dirge, while they stand round the grave.

Song by the Nuns:

    Departed soul, whose poor remains
    This hallow'd lowly grave contains;
    Whose passing storm of life is o'er,
    Whose pains and sorrows are no more;
    Bless'd be thou with the bless'd above,
    Where all is joy, and purity, and love!

    Let Him, in might and mercy dread,
    Lord of the living and the dead;
    In whom the stars of heav'n rejoice,
    And the ocean lifts its voice;
    Thy spirit, purified, to glory raise,
    To sing with holy saints his everlasting praise!

    Departed soul, who in this earthly scene
    Hast our lowly sister been,
    Swift be thy way to where the blessed dwell!
    Until we meet thee there, farewell! farewell!

Enter a young pensioner, with a wild terrified look, her hair and dress all scattered, and rushes forward amongst them.

ABBESS   Why com'st thou here, with such disorder'd looks,
   To break upon our sad solemnity?
PENSIONER   Oh! I did hear through the receding blast,
   Such horrid cries! They made my blood run chill.
ABBESS   'Tis but the varied voices of the storm,
   Which many times will sound like distant screams:
   It has deceiv'd thee.
PENSIONER   O no, for twice it call'd, so loudly call'd,
   With horrid strength, beyond the pitch of nature;
   And murder! Murder! Was the dreadful cry.
   A third time it return'd with feeble strength,
   But o' the sudden ceas'd, as though the words
   Were smother'd rudely in the grappled throat,
   And all was still again, save the wild blast
   Which at a distance growl'd.
   Oh! It will never from my mind depart!
   That dreadful cry, all i' the instant still'd:
   For then, so near, some horrid deed was done,
   And none to rescue.
ABBESS   Where didst thou hear it?
PENSIONER   In the higher cells,
   As now a window, open'd by the storm,
   I did attempt to close.
1st MONK   I wish our brother Bernard were arriv'd;
   He is upon his way.
ABBESS   Be not alarm'd; it still may be deception.
   'Tis meet we finish our solemnity,
   Nor show neglect unto the honour'd dead.

She gives a sign, and the organ plays again: just as it ceases, a loud knocking is heard without.

ABBESS   Ha! Who may this be? Hush!
   Knocking heard again.
2nd MONK   It is the knock of one in furious haste.
   Hush! hush! What footsteps come? Ha! Brother Bernard.

Enter Bernard bearing a lantern.

1st MONK   See, what a look he wears of stiffen'd fear!
   Where hast thou been, good brother?
BERNARD   I've seen a horrid sight! *(All gathering round him and speaking at once)* What hast thou seen?

BERNARD   As on I hasten'd, bearing thus my light,
  Across the path, not fifty paces off;
  I saw a murder'd corpse, stretch'd on his back,
  Smear'd with new blood, as though but freshly slain.
ABBESS   A man or woman was't?
BERNARD   A man, a man!
ABBESS   Didst thou examine if within its breast
  There yet were lodg'd some small remains of life?
  Was it quite dead?
BERNARD   Nought in the grave is deader.
  I look'd but once, yet life did never lodge
  In any form so laid.
  A chilly horror seiz'd me, and I fled.
1st MONK   And does the face seem all unknown to thee?
BERNARD.   The face! I would not on the face have look'd
  For e'en a kingdom's wealth, for all the world!
  O no! the bloody neck, the bloody neck! *(shaking his head and*
  shuddering with horror)

Loud knocking heard without.

SISTER   Good mercy! Who comes next?
BERNARD   Not far behind
  I left our brother Thomas on the road;
  But then he did repent him as he went,
  And threatened to return.
2nd MONK   See, here he comes.

Enter Brother Thomas, with a wild terrified look.

1st MONK   How wild he looks!
BERNARD *(going up to him eagerly)* What, hast thou seen it too?
THOMAS   Yes, yes! It glared upon me as it pass'd.
BERNARD   What glared upon thee? *(All gathering round*
  Thomas, and speaking at once) O! What hast thou seen?
THOMAS   As striving with the blast I onward came,
  Turning my feeble lantern from the wind,
  Its light upon a dreadful visage gleam'd,
  Which paus'd and look'd upon me as it pass'd;
  But such a look, such wildness of despair,
  Such horror-strained features, never yet
  Did earthly visage show. I shrank and shudder'd.
  If a damn'd spirit may to earth return,
  I've seen it.

BERNARD	Was there any blood upon it?
THOMAS	Nay, as it pass'd, I did not see its form;

Nought but the horrid face.

BERNARD	It is the murderer.
1st MONK	What way went it?
THOMAS	I durst not look till I had pass'd it far.

Then turning round, upon the rising bank,
I saw, between me and the pale sky,
A dusky form, tossing and agitated.
I stopp'd to mark it; but, in truth, I found
'Twas but a sapling bending to the wind,
And so I onward hied, and look'd no more.

1st MONK But we must look to 't; we must follow it:
Our duty so commands. *(to 2nd Monk)* Will you go, brother?
(to Bernard) And you, good Bernard?

BERNARD	If I needs must go.
1st MONK	Come, we must all go.
ABBESS	Heaven be with you, then!

Exit monks.

PENSIONER Amen! Amen! Good heav'n, be with us all!
O what a dreadful night!

ABBESS Daughters, retire; peace to the peaceful dead!
Our solemn ceremony now is finish'd.

They exit.

ACT FIVE, SCENE 2

A large room in the convent, very dark. Enter the Abbess, the young pensioner bearing a light, and several nuns; She sets down the light on a table at the bottom of the stage, so that the room is still very gloomy.

ABBESS They have been longer absent than I thought:
I fear he has escap'd them.

1st NUN	Heaven forbid!
PENSIONER	No, no, found out foul murder ever is,

And the foul murderer too.

2nd NUN The good Saint Francis will direct their search;
The blood so near this holy convent shed
For threefold vengeance calls.

ABBESS   I hear a noise within the inner court –
   They are return'd *(listening)*; and Bernard's voice I hear:
   They are return'd.
PENSIONER   Why do I tremble so?
   It is not I who ought to tremble thus.
2nd NUN   I hear them at the door.
BERNARD *(without)*   Open the door, I pray thee, Brother Thomas;
   I cannot now unhand the prisoner.
   *(All speak together, shrinking back from the door, and staring upon
   one another.)* He is with them!

*A folding door at the bottom of the stage is opened, and enter Bernard,
Thomas, and the other two monks, carrying lanterns in their hands, and
bringing in De Monfort. They are likewise followed by other monks. As
they lead forward De Monfort, the light is turned away, so that he is seen
obscurely; but when they come to the front of the stage, they turn the
light side of their lanterns on him at once, and his face is seen in all the
strengthened horror of despair, with his hands and clothes bloody.
The Abbess and nuns speak at once, and start back.*

ABBESS/NUNS   Holy saints be with us!
BERNARD *(to Abbess)* Behold the man of blood!
ABBESS   Of misery too; I cannot look upon him.
BERNARD *(to nuns)*   Nay, holy sisters, turn not thus away.
   Speak to him, if, perchance, he will regard you:
   For from his mouth we have no utt'rance heard,
   Save one deep groan and smother'd exclamation,
   When first we seiz'd him.
ABBESS *(to De Monfort)* Most miserable man, how art thou thus?
   (pauses) Thy tongue is silent, but those bloody hands
   Do witness horrid things. What is thy name?
DE MONFORT *(roused, looks steadfastly at the Abbess for some time;
   then speaking in a short hurried voice)* I have no name.
ABBESS *(to Bernard)*   Do it thyself; I'll speak to him no more.
PENSIONER   O holy saints! That this should be the man
   Who did against his fellow lift the stroke,
   Whilst he so loudly call'd —
   Still in my ears it rings: O murder! Murder!
DE MONFORT *(starting)* He calls again!
PENSIONER   No, he did call, but now his voice is still'd.
   'Tis past.
DE MONFORT   'Tis past.

PENSIONER   Yes, it is past! Art thou not he who did it?

De Monfort utters a deep groan, and is supported from falling by the monks. A noise is heard without.

ABBESS   What noise is this of heavy lumb'ring steps,
     Like men who with a weighty burden come?
BERNARD   It is the body: I have orders given
     That here it should be laid.

Enter men bearing the body of Rezenvelt, covered with a white cloth, and set it down in the middle of the room: they then uncover it. De Monfort stands fixed and motionless with horror, only that a sudden shivering seems to pass over him when they uncover the corpse. The Abbess and nuns shrink back and retire to some distance, all the rest fixing their eyes steadfastly upon De Monfort. A long pause.

BERNARD *(to De Monfort)* Seest thou that lifeless corpse,
     those bloody wounds?
     See how he lies, who but so shortly since
     A living creature was, with all the powers
     Of sense, and motion, and humanity!
     Oh! What a heart had he who did this deed!
1st MONK *(looking at the body)* How hard those teeth
     against the lips are press'd,
     As though he struggled still.
2nd MONK   The hands too, clench'd: nature's last fearful
     effort.

De Monfort still stands motionless. Brother Thomas then goes to the body, and raising up the head a little, turns it towards De Monfort.

THOMAS   Knowst thou this ghastly face?
DE MONFORT *(putting his hands before his face in violent perturbation)*
     Oh, do not! do not! Veil it from my sight!
     Put me to any agony but this!
THOMAS   Ha! Dost thou then confess the dreadful deed.
     Hast thou against the laws of awful heaven
     Such horrid murder done? What fiend could tempt thee?
     (pauses, and looks steadfastly at De Monfort)
DE MONFORT   I hear thy words, but do not hear their sense –
     Hast thou not cover'd it?
BERNARD *(to Thomas)* Forbear, my brother, for thou seest right well
     He is not in a state to answer thee.

Let us retire and leave him for awhile.
These windows are with iron grated o'er;
He is secur'd, and other duty calls.
THOMAS   Then let it be.
BERNARD *(to monks, etc)* Come, let us all depart.

Exit Abbess and nuns, followed by the monks, one monk lingering a little behind.

DE MONFORT   All gone! *(perceiving the monk)* O stay thou here!
MONK   It must not be.
DE MONFORT   I'll give thee gold; I'll make thee rich in gold,
    If thou wilt stay e'en but a little while.
MONK   I must not, must not, stay.
DE MONFORT   I do conjure thee!
MONK   I dare not stay with thee. *(going)*
DE MONFORT   And wilt thou go? *(catching hold of him eagerly)*
    O! Throw thy cloak upon this grisly form!
    The unclos'd eyes do stare upon me still.
    O do not leave me thus!

Monk covers the body, and exits.

DE MONFORT *(alone, looking at the covered body, but at a distance)*
    Alone with thee! But thou art nothing now.
    'Tis done, 'tis number'd with the things o'er past;
    Would! Would it were to come! –
    What fated end, what darkly gathering cloud
    Will close on all this horror?
    O that dire madness would unloose my thoughts,
    And fill my mind with wildest fantasies,
    Dark, restless, terrible! Aught, aught but this!
    (pauses and shudders)
    How with convulsive life he heav'd beneath me,
    E'en with the death's wound gor'd! O horrid, horrid!
    Methinks I feel him still — What sound is that?
    I heard a smother'd groan — It is impossible!
    (looking steadfastly at the body)
    It moves! It moves! The cloth doth heave and swell.
    It moves again! I cannot suffer this
    Whate'er it be, I will uncover it.
    (runs to the corpse, and tears off the cloth in despair)
    All still beneath.

Nought is there here but fix'd and grizzly death,
How sternly fixed! Oh! Those glazed eyes!
They look upon me still. *(shrinks back with horror)*
Come, madness! Come unto me, senseless death!
I cannot suffer this! Here, rocky wall,
Scatter these brains, or dull them!

*He runs furiously, and dashing his head against the wall, falls upon the
floor. Enter two monks hastily.*

1st MONK	See: wretched man, he hath destroy'd himself.
2nd MONK	He does but faint. Let us remove him hence.
1st MONK	We did not well to leave him here alone.
2nd MONK	Come, let us bear him to the open air.

Exit, bearing out De Monfort.

ACT FIVE, SCENE 3

*Before the gates of the convent. Enter Jane De Monfort, Freberg, and
Manuel. As they are proceeding towards the gate, Jane stops short and
shrinks back.*

COUNT FREBERG Ha! Wherefore? Has a sudden illness seiz'd thee?
JANE No, no, my friend. — And yet I am very faint —
I dread to enter here.
MANUEL Ay, so I thought:
For, when between the trees, that abbey tower;
First show'd its top, I saw your countenance change.
But breathe a little here: I'll go before,
And make inquiry at the nearest gate.
COUNT FREBERG Do so, good Manuel —
(Manuel goes and knocks at the gate.)
Courage, dear madam: all may yet be well.
Rezenvelt's servant, frighten'd with the storm,
And seeing that his master join'd him not,
As by appointment, at the forest's edge,
Might be alarm'd, and give too ready ear
To an unfounded rumour.
He saw it not; he came not here himself.

JANE *(looking eagerly to the gate, where Manuel talks with the porter)*
Ha! See, he talks with someone earnestly.
And seest thou not that motion of his hands?
He stands like one who hears a horrid tale.
Almighty God! *(Manuel goes into the convent.)*
He comes not back; he enters.
COUNT FREBERG   Bear up, my noble friend.
JANE   I will, I will! But this suspense is dreadful.

*A long pause. Manuel re-enters from the convent, and comes forward
slowly with a sad countenance.*

JANE   Is this the face of one who bears good tidings?
O God! His face doth tell the horrid fact:
There is nought doubtful here.
COUNT FREBERG   How is it, Manuel?
MANUEL   I've seen him through a crevice in his door:
It is indeed my master. *(bursting into tears)*

*Jane faints and is supported by Freberg. Enter Abbess and several nuns
from the convent, who gather about her, applying remedies. She recovers.*

1st NUN   The life returns again.
2nd NUN   Yes, she revives.
ABBESS *(to Freberg)*   Let me entreat this noble lady's leave
To lead her in. She seems in great distress:
We would with holy kindness soothe her woe,
And do by her the deeds of Christian love.
COUNT FREBERG   Madam, your goodness has my grateful thanks.

Exit, supporting Jane into the convent.

ACT FIVE, SCENE 4

*De Monfort is discovered sitting in a thoughtful posture. He remains so
for some time. His face afterwards begins to appear agitated, like one
whose mind is harrowed with the severest thoughts; then, starting from
his seat, he clasps his hands together, and holds them up to heaven.*

DE MONFORT   O that I ne'er had known the light of day!
That filmy darkness on mine eyes had hung,
And clos'd me out from the fair face of nature!
O that my mind in mental darkness pent,
Had no perception, no distinction known,

Of fair or foul, perfection or defect,
Nor thought conceiv'd of proud pre-eminence!
O that it had! O that I had been form'd
An idiot from the birth! A senseless changeling,
Who eats his glutton's meal with greedy haste,
Nor knows the hand which feeds him –
(pauses, then in a calmer sorrowful voice)
What am I now? How ends the day of life?
For end it must; and terrible this gloom,
This storm of horrors that surrounds its close.
This little term of nature's agony
Will soon be o'er, and what is past is past;
But shall I then, on the dark lap of earth
Lay me to rest, in still unconsciousness,
Like senseless clod that doth no pressure feel
From wearing foot of daily passenger;
Like a steep'd rock o'er which the breaking waves
Bellow and foam unheard? O would I could!

Enter Manuel, who springs forward to his master, but is checked upon perceiving De Monfort draw back and look sternly at him.

MANUEL   My lord, my master! O my dearest master!
(De Monfort still looks at him without speaking.)
Nay, do not thus regard me, good my lord!
Speak to me: am I not your faithful Manuel?
DE MONFORT *(in a hasty broken voice)* Art thou alone?
MANUEL   No, sir, the Lady Jane is on her way;
She is not far behind.
DE MONFORT *(tossing his arm over his head in all agony)*
This is too much! All I can bear but this!
It must not be – Run and prevent her coming.
Say, he who is detain'd a prisoner here
Is one to her unknown. I now am nothing.
I am a man of holy claims bereft;
Out of the pale of social kindred cast;
Nameless and horrible —
Tell her De Monfort far from hence is gone
Into a desolate and distant land,
Ne'er to return again. Fly, tell her this;
For we must meet no more.

Enter Jane De Monfort, bursting into the chamber and followed by Count Freberg, Abbess, and several nuns.

JANE   We must! We must! My brother, O my brother!

De Monfort turns away his head and hides his face with his arm. Jane stops short, and, making a great effort, turns to Count Freberg, and the others who followed her, and with an air of dignity stretches out her hand, beckoning them to retire. All retire but Count Freberg who seems to hesitate.

JANE   And thou too, Freberg: call it not unkind.

Exit Count Freberg. Jane and De Monfort only remain.

JANE   My hapless Monfort!

De Monfort turns round looks sorrowfully upon her. She opens her arms to him, and he, rushing into them, hides his face upon her breast, and weeps.

JANE   Ay, give thy sorrow vent; here mayst thou weep.
DE MONFORT *(in broken accents)* Oh! This, my sister, makes me feel again
   The kindness of affection.
   My mind has in a dreadful storm been tost;
   Horrid and dark – I thought to weep no more –
   I've done a deed – But I am human still.
JANE   I know thy suff'rings: leave thy sorrow free!
   Thou art with one who never did upbraid;
   Who mourns, who loves thee still.
DE MONFORT   Ah! Sayst thou so? No, no; it should not be.
   (shrinking from her) I am a foul and bloody murderer,
   For such embrace unmeet: O leave me! Leave me!
   Disgrace and public shame abide me now;
   And all, alas! Who do my kindred own,
   The direful portion share. – Away, away!
   Shall a disgrac'd and public criminal
   Degrade thy name, and claim affinity
   To noble worth like thine? – I have no name –
   I'm nothing now, not e'en to thee: depart.

She takes his hand, and grasping it firmly, speaks with a determined voice.

JANE   De Monfort, hand in hand we have enjoy'd
  The playful term of infancy together;
  And in the rougher path of ripen'd years
  We've been each other's stay. Dark low'rs our fate,
  And terrible the storm that gathers o'er us;
  But nothing, till that latest agony
  Which severs thee from nature, shall unloose
  This fix'd and sacred hold. In thy dark prison-house;
  In the terrific face of armed law;
  Yea, on the scaffold, if it needs must be,
  I never will forsake thee.
DE MONFORT *(looking at her with admiration)*
  Heav'n bless thy gen'rous soul, my noble Jane!
  I thought to sink beneath this load of ill,
  Depress'd with infamy and open shame;
  I thought to sink in abject wretchedness:
  But for thy sake I'll rouse my manhood up,
  And meet it bravely; no unseemly weakness,
  I feel my rising strength, shall blot my end,
  To clothe thy cheek with shame.
JANE   Yes, thou art noble still.
DE MONFORT   With thee I am; who were not so with thee?
  But, ah! my sister, short will be the term:
  Death's stroke will come, and in that state beyond,
  Where things unutterable wait the soul,
  New from its earthly tenement discharg'd,
  We shall be sever'd far.
  Far as the spotless purity of virtue
  Is from the murd'rer's guilt, far shall we be.
  This is the gulf of dread uncertainty
  From which the soul recoils.
JANE   The God who made thee is a God of mercy:
  Think upon this.
DE MONFORT *(shaking his head)* No, no! This blood! This blood!
JANE   Yes, e'en the sin of blood may be forgiv'n,
  When humble penitence hath once aton'd.
DE MONFORT *(eagerly)* What, after terms of lengthen'd misery,
  Imprison'd anguish of tormented spirits,
  Shall I again, a renovated soul,
  Into the blessed family of the good
  Admittance have? Thinkst thou that this may be?

Speak, if thou canst: O speak me comfort here!
For dreadful fancies, like an armed host,
Have push'd me to despair, It is most horrible –
O speak of hope! If any hope there be.

*Jane is silent, and looks sorrowfully upon him; then clasping her hands,
and turning her eyes to heaven, seems to mutter a prayer.*

DE MONFORT   Ha! Dost thou pray for me? Heav'n hear thy prayer!
I fain would kneel – Alas! I dare not do it.
JANE   Not so! All by th' Almighty Father form'd,
May in their deepest misery call on Him.
Come kneel with me, my brother.

*She kneels and prays to herself. He kneels by her, and clasps his hands
fervently, but speaks not. A noise of chains clanking is heard without, and
they both rise.*

DE MONFORT   Hearest thou that noise? They come to interrupt us.
JANE *(moving towards a side door)* Then let us enter here.
DE MONFORT *(catching hold of her with a look of horror)* Not there –
not there – the corpse – the bloody corpse!
JANE   What, lies he there? – Unhappy Rezenvelt!
DE MONFORT   A sudden thought has come across my mind;
How came it not before? Unhappy Rezenvelt!
Sayst thou but this?
JANE   What should I say? He was an honest man;
I still have thought him such, as such lament him. *(De Monfort utters a
deep groan.)* What makes this heavy groan?
DE MONFORT   It hath a meaning.

*Enter Abbess and monks, with two officers of justice carrying fetters in
their hands to put upon De Monfort.*

JANE *(starting)*   What men are these?
1st OFFICER   Lady, we are the servants of the law,
And bear with us a power, which doth constrain
To bind with fetters this our prisoner. *(pointing to De Monfort)*
JANE   A stranger uncondemn'd? This cannot be.
1st OFFICER   As yet, indeed, he is by law unjudg'd,
But is so far condemn'd by circumstance,
That law, or custom sacred held as law,
Doth fully warrant us, and it must be.

JANE　　　　　　　　　Nay, say not so; he has no power t'escape:
　　Distress hath bound him with a heavy chain;
　　There is no need of yours.
1st OFFICER　　　　　We must perform our office.
JANE　　　　　　　　　O! Do not offer this indignity!
1st OFFICER　　　　　Is it indignity in sacred law.
　　To bind a murderer? *(to 2nd Officer)* Come, do thy work.
JANE　　　　　　　　　Harsh are thy words, and stern thy harden'd brow;
　　Dark is thine eye; but all some pity have
　　Unto the lust extreme of misery.
　　I do beseech thee! If thou art a man. *(kneeling to him)*

De Monfort, roused at this, runs up to Jane, and raises her hastily from the ground then stretches himself up proudly.

DE MONFORT　　　　Stand thou erect in native dignity;
　　And bend to none on earth the suppliant knee,
　　Though cloth'd in power imperial. To my heart
　　It gives a feller gripe than many irons.
　　(holding out his hands) Here, officers of law, bind on those shackles;
　　And, if they are too light, bring heavier chains,
　　Add iron to iron; load, crush me to the ground:
　　Nay, heap ten thousand weight upon my breast,
　　For that were best of all.

A long pause, whilst they put irons upon him. After they are on, Jane looks at him sorrowfully, and lets her head sink on her breast. De Monfort stretches out his hand, looks at them, and then at Jane; crosses them over his breast, and endeavours to suppress his feelings.

1st OFFICER *(to De Monfort)* I have it, too, in charge to move you hence,
　　Into another chamber more secure.
DE MONFORT　　　　Well, I am ready, sir.

Approaching Jane, whom the abbess is endeavouring to comfort, but to no purpose.

DE MONFORT　　　　Ah! Wherefore thus, most honour'd and most dear?
　　Shrink not at the accoutrements of ill,
　　Daring the thing itself. *(endeavouring to look cheerful)*
　　Wilt thou permit me with a gyved hand?
　　(She gives him her hand, which he raises to his lips.)
　　This was my proudest office.

Exit De Monfort, leading out Jane.

ACT FIVE, SCENE 5

*An apartment in the convent, opening into another room, whose low
arched door is seen at the bottom of the stage. In one corner a monk is
seen kneeling. Enter another monk, who, on perceiving him, stops till he
rises from his knees, and then goes eagerly up to him.*

1st MONK   How is the prisoner?
2nd MONK *(pointing to the door)* He is within, and the strong hand of death
    Is dealing with him.
1st MONK   How is this, good brother?
    Methought he brav'd it with a manly spirit;
    And led, with shackled hands, his sister forth,
    Like one resolv'd to bear misfortune bravely.
2nd MONK   Yes, with heroic courage, for a while
    He seem'd inspir'd; but soon depress'd again,
    Remorse and dark despair o'erwhelm'd his soul:
    And, from the violent working of his mind,
    Some stream of life within his breast has burst;
    For many a time, within a little space,
    The ruddy tide has rush'd into his mouth.
    God grant his pains be short!
1st MONK   How does the lady?
2nd MONK   She sits and bears his head upon her lap,
    Wiping the cold drops from his ghastly face
    With such a look of tender wretchedness,
    It wrings the heart to see her.
    How goes the night?
1st MONK   It wears, methinks, upon the midnight hour.
    It is a dark and fearful night; the moon
    Is wrapp'd in sable clouds; the chill blast sounds
    Like dismal lamentations. Ay, who knows
    What voices mix with the dark midnight winds?
    Nay, as I pass'd that yawning cavern's mouth,
    A whisp'ring sound, unearthly, reach'd my ear,
    And o'er my head a chilly coldness crept.
    Are there not wicked fiends and damned sprites,
    Whom yawning charnels, and th' unfathom'd depths
    Of secret darkness, at this fearful hour,
    Do upwards send, to watch, unseen, around
    The murd'rer's death-bed, at his fatal term,
    Ready to hail with dire and horrid welcome,
    Their future mate? – I do believe there are.

2nd MONK   Peace, peace! God of wisdom and of mercy,
    Veils from our sight – Ha! Hear that heavy groan.

A groan heard within.

1st MONK   It is the dying man. *(another groan)*
2nd MONK   God grant him rest! *(listening at the door)*
    I hear him struggling in the gripe of death.
    O piteous heaven! *(goes from the door)*
    (Enter Brother Thomas from the chamber.)
    How now, good brother?
THOMAS   Retire, my friends. O many a bed of death
    With all its pangs and horrors I have seen,
    But never aught like this! Retire, my friends!
    The death-bell with its awful signal give,
    When he has breath'd his last.
    I would move hence, but I am weak and faint:
    Let me a moment on thy shoulder lean. Oh, weak and mortal man!
    (leans on 2nd Monk. A pause.)

Enter Bernard from the chamber.

2nd MONK *(to Bernard)* How is your penitent?
BERNARD   He is with Him who made him; Him, who knows
    The soul of man: before whose awful presence
    Th' unsceptred tyrant stands despoil'd and helpless,
    Like an unclothed babe. *(Bell tolls.)* The dismal sound!
    Retire, and pray for the blood-stained soul:
    May heav'n have mercy on him! *(Bell tolls again. They exit.)*

ACT FIVE, SCENE 6

A hall or large room in the convent. The bodies of De Monfort and Rezenvelt are discovered laid out upon a low table or platform, covered with black. Count Freberg, Bernard, Abbess, monks and nuns attending.

ABBESS *(to Freberg)*   Here must they lie, my lord, until we know
    Respecting this the order of the law.
COUNT FREBERG   And you have wisely done, my rev'rend mother.
    (goes to the table, and looks at the bodies, but without uncovering them)
    Unhappy men! Ye, both in nature rich,
    With talents and with virtues were endued.
    Ye should have lov'd, yet deadly rancour came,

And in the prime and manhood of your days
Ye sleep in horrid death. O direful hate!
What shame and wretchedness his portion is,
Who, for a secret inmate, harbours thee!
And who shall call him blameless, who excites,
Ungen'rously excites, with careless scorn,
Such baleful passion in a brother's breast,
Whom heav'n commands to love? Low are ye laid:
Still all contention now – Low are ye laid:
I lov'd you both, and mourn your hapless fall.

ABBESS   They were your friends, my lord?
COUNT FREBERG   I lov'd them both. How does the Lady Jane?
ABBESS   She bears misfortune with intrepid soul.
I never saw in woman, bow'd with grief;
Such moving dignity.
COUNT FREBERG   Ay, still the same.
I've known her long: of worth most excellent;
But in the day of woe she ever rose
Upon the mind with added majesty,
As the dark mountain more sublimely tow'rs
Mantled in clouds and storm.

Enter Manuel and Jerome.

MANUEL (*pointing*)   Here, my good Jerome, here's a piteous sight.
JEROME   A piteous sight! Yet I will look upon him:
I'll see his face in death. Alas, alas!
I've seen him move a noble gentleman!
And when with vexing passion undisturb'd,
He look'd most graciously. (*lifts up in mistake the cloth from the body
of Rezenvelt, and starts back with horror*)
Oh! This was the bloody work! Oh! oh, oh, oh!
That human hands could do it! (*drops the cloth again*)
MANUEL   That is the murder'd corpse;
here lies De Monfort. (*going to uncover the other body*)
JEROME (*turning away his head*) No, no! I cannot look upon him now.
MANUEL   Didst thou not come to see him?
JEROME   Fy! Cover him – inter him in the dark –
Let no one look upon him.
BERNARD (*to Jerome*) Well dost thou show the abhorrence nature feels
For deeds of blood, and I commend thee well.
In the most ruthless heart compassion wakes

For one, who, from the band of fellow man,
Hath felt such cruelty. *(uncovering the body of Rezenvelt)*
This is the murder'd corpse: *(uncovering the body of De Monfort)*
But see, I pray!
Here lies the murderer. What thinkst thou here?
Look on those features, thou hast seen them oft,
With the last dreadful conflict of despair,
So fix'd in horrid strength.
See those knit brows; those hollow sunken eyes;
The sharpen'd nose, with nostrils all distent;
That writhed mouth, where yet the teeth appear,
In agony, to gnash the nether lip.
Thinkst thou, less painful than the murd'rer's knife
Was such a death as this ?
Ay, and how changed too those matted locks!

JEROME   Merciful heaven! His hair is grizly grown,
Chang'd to white age, that was, but two days since,
Black as the raven's plume. How may this be?

BERNARD   Such change, from violent conflict of the mind,
Will sometimes come.

JEROME   Alas, alas! Most wretched!
Thou wert too good to do a cruel deed,
And so it kill'd thee. Thou hast suffer'd for it.
God rest thy soul! I needs must touch thy hand
And bid thee long farewell. *(laying his hand on De Monfort)*

BERNARD   Draw back, draw back: see where the lady comes.

*Enter Jane De Monfort. Count Freberg, who has been retired by himself
at the bottom of the stage, now steps forward to lead her in, but checks
himself on seeing the fixed sorrow of her countenance, and draws back
respectfully. Jane advances to the table, and looks attentively at the
covered bodies. Manuel points out the body of De Monfort, and she gives
a gentle inclination of the head, to signify that she understands him. She
then bends tenderly over it, without speaking.*

JEROME *(to Jane, as she raises her head)* Oh, madam, my good lord!

JANE   Well says thy love, my good and faithful Manuel:
But we must mourn in silence.

MANUEL   Alas! The times that I have followed him!

JANE   Forbear, my faithful Manuel. For this love
Thou hast my grateful thanks; and here's my hand:
Thou hast lov'd him, and I shall remember thee.

Where'er I am, in whate'er spot of earth
I linger out the remnant of my days,
I will remember thee.

MANUEL   Nay, by the living God! Where'er you are
There will I be. I'll prove a trusty servant:
I'll follow you, even to the world's end.
My master's gone; and I indeed am mean
Yet will I show the strength of nobler men:
Should any dare upon your honour'd worth
To put the slightest wrong. Leave you, dear lady!
Kill me, but say not this! *(throwing himself at her feet)*

JANE *(raising him)* Well, then! Be thou my servant, and my friend.
Art thou, good Jerome, too, in kindness come?
I see thou art. How goes it with thine age?

JEROME   Ah, madam! Woe and weakness dwell with age:
Would I could serve you with a young man's strength!
I'd spend my life for you.

JANE   Thank you, worthy Jerome.
O! Who hath said, the wretched have no friends?

COUNT FREBERG   In every sensible and gen'rous breast
Affliction finds a friend; but unto thee,
Thou most exalted and most honourable,
The heart in warmest adoration bows,
And even a worship pays.

JANE   Nay, Freberg! Freberg! Grieve me not, my friend.
He, to whose ear my praise most welcome was,
Hears it no more! And, oh, our piteous lot!
What tongue will talk of him? Alas, alas!
This more than all will bow me to the earth,
I feel my misery here.
The voice of praise was wont to name us both:
I had no greater pride.

She covers her face with her hand, and bursts into tears. Here they all hang about her: Count Freberg supporting her tenderly, Manuel embracing her knees, and old Jerome catching hold of her robe affectionately. Bernard, Abbess, monks and nuns likewise gather round her, with looks of sympathy. Enter two Officers of Law.

1st OFFICER   Where is the prisoner?
Into our hands he straight must be consigned.

BERNARD   He is not subject now to human laws;
The prison that awaits him is the grave.

1st OFFICER Ha! Sayst thou so? There is foul play in this.
MANUEL *(to officer)* Hold thy unrighteous tongue, or hie thee hence,
  Nor in the presence of this honour'd dame,
  Utter the slightest meaning of reproach.
1st OFFICER I am an officer on duty call'd,
  And have authority to say, "How died he?"
  (Here Jane shakes off the weakness of grief, and repressing Manuel,
  who is about to reply to the officer, steps forward with dignity.)
JANE Tell them by whose authority you come,
  He died that death which best becomes a man
  Who is with keenest sense of conscious ill
  And deep remorse assail'd, a wounded spirit.
  A death that kills the noble and the brave,
  And only them. He had no other wound.
1st OFFICER And shall I trust to this?
JANE Do as thou wilt:
  To one who can suspect my simple word
  I have no more reply. Fulfil thine office.
1st OFFICER No, lady, I believe your honour'd word,
  And will no further search.
JANE I thank your courtesy: thanks, thanks to all;
  My rev'rend mother, and ye honoured maids;
  Ye holy men, and you, my faithful friends;
  The blessing of the afflicted rest with you!
  And He, who to the wretched is most piteous,
  Will recompense you. – Freberg, thou art good;
  Remove the body of the friend you lov'd:
  'Tis Rezenvelt I mean. Take thou this charge:
  'Tis meet, that with his noble ancestors
  He lie entomb'd in honourable state.
  And now I have a sad request to make,
  Nor will these holy sisters scorn my boon;
  That I, within these sacred cloister walls,
  May raise a humble, nameless tomb to him,
  Who, but for one dark passion, one dire deed,
  Had claim'd a record of as noble worth,
  As e'er enrich'd the sculptur'd pedestal.

They exit.
The Curtain falls.
The End.

Joanna Baillie (1762-1851)

A Scottish poet and playwright, she was born at Bothwell, Lanarkshire, the third of three children of Dorothea (Hunter) and James Baillie, a junior minister at Hamilton, who later became Professor of Divinity at Glasgow University, a distant, undemonstrative father. As a child she was said to have been a tomboy, who loved outdoor sports, and though not studious, was known for her ability to make up stories and poems. She was later sent to boarding-school in Glasgow where she wrote plays and stage-managed theatricals.

After her father's death, her uncle, Dr George Hunter, became the children's guardian and on Hunter's death, Joanna's brother Matthew, who had also trained as a doctor, inherited a house in London, requiring the family to move south to Hampstead. Joanna is now recognized as an influence on her literary contemporaries such as Byron, Wordsworth, Scott and Shelley.

She published *Fugitive Verses* in 1790 and in 1798 the first volume of *A Series of Plays*, anonymously. They were well-received, the majority of reviewers assuming the author was a man. *De Monfort* was produced at Drury Lane where it ran for only 8 performances. It was recently revived at The Orange Tree Theatre in Richmond, England in May, 2008.

"Joanna Baillie's 1798 tragedy was a big hit in its day and a starring vehicle for both John Philip Kemble and Edmund Kean, and you can see why. Its central character gets to suffer and then rise above his suffering in an attempt to be honourable and then sink into madness and then be overwhelmed by guilt ... And even if such melodramatic excess is not to most modern tastes, and ... (despite what I assume is extensive cutting) it all goes on a bit too long, still we once again must thank the Orange Tree for rediscovering a lost play and re-introducing us to a lost playwright of unquestionable power."   www.theatreguidelondon.co.uk

Rutherford and Son

by Githa Sowerby

First performed at the Court Theatre, London, on 31st January 1912.

CHARACTERS
Ann
Mary
Janet
John
Richard
John Rutherford
Martin
Mrs. Henderson

Scene: Living room in John Rutherford's house. Two days elapse between Acts One and Two. One night between Acts Two and Three.

ACT ONE

John Rutherford's house stands on the edge of the moor, far enough from the village to serve its dignity and near enough to admit of the master going to and from the Works in a few minutes – a process known to the household as 'going across'. The living room, in which the family life has centred for generations, is a big square room furnished in solid mahogany and papered in red, as if to mitigate the bleakness of a climate that includes five months of winter in every year. There is a big table in the middle of the room covered with a brown cloth at which the family take their meals. An air of orderliness pervades the room, which perhaps accounts for its being extremely uncomfortable. From above the heavy polished sideboard the late John Rutherford looks down from his frame and sees the settle and armchair on either side of the fire, the marble clock on the mantelpiece, the desk with its brass inkstand and neatly arranged bundles of papers precisely as he saw them in life.

On this particular evening in December, Ann Rutherford is sitting by the fire alternately knitting and dozing. She is a faded, querulous woman of about 60, and wears a black dress with a big flat brooch and a cap with lilac ribbons. Mary Rutherford, a gentle delicate-looking woman of 26, is seated on the settle opposite to her making a baby's cap; she is bending forward to catch the light of the fire on her work, for the lamp has not yet been brought in.

Presently Janet comes in carrying a silver basket and a pair of carpet slippers. She is a heavy dark woman, some ten years older than Mary, with an expressionless tired face and monotonous voice. All her movements are slipshod and aimless, and she seldom raises her eyes. She is dressed in a dark dress of some warm material with white collar and cuffs.

JANET *(glancing at the clock)* He's not back yet.

ANN   No ... If you mean your father.

JANET *(folding up the brown cloth preparatory to laying the table)* Who else should I mean?

ANN   You might mean anyone ... You always talk about he and him, as if there was no one else in the house.

JANET   There isn't.

ANN   Answer me back, that's the way. *(Janet makes no reply. She puts the silver basket on the table and comes to the fire with the slippers.)* There – put his slippers down to warm. The Committee room's cold as ice, and he'll come in like the dead.

MARY *(looking up from her work for a moment)* I believe it's going to freeze tonight – the chimneys are flaring so.

Janet drops the shoes one by one on to the hearthrug without stooping.

ANN   They'll never warm there! I never seed sic a feckless lass. *(stoops laboriously and sets them up against the fender.)* Is the dinner all right?

JANET   Susan's let the pie get burnt, but I've scraped the top off – he won't notice. The girdle cake's as tough as leather. She'll have to do a fresh one – if there's time.

ANN   You might ha' seen to things a bit.

JANET   I have. There wouldn't ha' been a pie at all if I hadn't. The oven damper's gone wrong.

ANN   Answer me – answer yer aunt! You and your dampers – and there you are a-laying the table and ye know weel enough yer father's forbid you to do things like a servant.

JANET What else is there to do? I can't sit and sew all day.

ANN I'm sure I'm never done finding fault from morning to night with one thing and another.

JANET Don't then.

ANN And a nice thing if I didn't! Nothing ever done in the house unless I see to it – that's what it comes to.

JANET *(spreading the cloth)* You'll drop your stitches.

ANN You never stir yourself, nor Mary neither, for that matter.

MARY I can't do much else with Tony to look after, Miss Rutherford.

JANET There's no need for her to do anything. It's not her business.

ANN Nor anybody's business, it seems to me. *(subsiding)* I don't know what's come to Susan nowadays, she's that daft – a head like a sieve, and that clumsy-handed.

JANET Susan's got a man.

ANN Well, I never!

JANET That's what she says. It's one of the men at the Works. He hangs about on his way home from the night shift – when she ought to be doing the rooms ... Susan's happy ... that's why she forgot to take the milk out of the can. There's no cream for the pudding.

ANN And he's so particular about his cream.

JANET He'll have to do without for once. And what with the pie burnt – and the girdle cake like leather, if he comes in before the other's ready – I should think we'll have a fair evening.

She leaves the room.

ANN Eh, dearie – dearie. Sic doings!

MARY *(absorbed in her cap)* Never mind, Miss Rutherford.

ANN Never mind! It's well for you to talk.

MARY Janet'll see that it's all right. She always does, though she talks like that.

ANN Her and her sulky ways. There's no doing anything with her of late. She used to be bad enough as a lass, that passionate and hard to drive. She's ten times worse now she's turned quiet.

MARY Perhaps she's tired with the long walks she takes. She's been out nearly two hours this afternoon in the rain.

ANN *(turning to her knitting)* What should she have to put her out – except her own tempers.

MARY *(trying to divert her attention)* Miss Rutherford, look at Tony's
    cap; I've nearly finished it.

ANN *(still cross)*   It's weel enough. Though what he wants wi' a lot
    o' bows standing up all over his head passes me.

MARY   They're butterfly bows.

ANN   Butterfly bows! And what'll butterfly bows do for
    'n? They'll no keep his head warm.

MARY   But he looks such a darling in them. I'll put it on
    tomorrow when I take him out, and you'll see.

ANN   London ways – that's what it is.

MARY   Do north-country babies never have bows on
    their caps?

ANN   Not in these parts. And not the Rutherfords
    anyway. Plain and lasting – that's the rule in this family, and we bide by
    it, babies and all. But you can't be expected to know, and you like a
    stranger in the hoose.

*Janet comes in carrying a lamp and a loaf on a trencher, which she puts
on the table.*

MARY   I've been here nearly three months.

ANN   And this very night you sit wasting your time
    making a bit of trash fit for a monkey at a fair. A body would think you
    would ha' learned better by now.

JANET *(quietly)*   What's the matter with Mary now?

ANN   We can talk, I suppose, without asking your
    leave?

JANET   It was you that was talking. Let her be.

ANN   And there you've been and put the loaf on as if it
    was the kitchen – and you know weel enough that gentlefolk have it set
    round in bits.

JANET   Gentle folk can do their own ways.

She goes out to fetch the knives.

ANN *(gets up laboriously and goes to the table)* I'll have to do it myself as
    usual. *(She cuts the bread and sets it round beside the plates.)*

MARY *(who has gone to the window and is looking out at the winter
    twilight)* If I'm a stranger, it's you that makes me so.

ANN   Ye've no cause to speak so, lass … I'm not blamin'
    you. It's no' your fault that you weren't born and bred in the north
    country.

MARY   No. I can't change that … I wonder what it's like
    here when the sun shines!

ANN *(who is busy with the bread)* Sun?

MARY It doesn't look as if the summer ever came here.

ANN If ye're looking for the summer in the middle o' December ye'll no' get it. Ye'll soon get used to it. Ye've happened on a bad autumn for your first, that's all.

MARY My first.

ANN Ye're a bit saft wi' livin' in the sooth, nae doubt. They tell me there's a deal of sunshine and wickedness in them parts.

MARY The people are happier, I think.

ANN Mebbees. Bein' happy'll make no porridge.

She goes back to her chair.

MARY I lived in Devonshire when I was a child, and everywhere there were lanes. But here – it's all so old and stern – this great stretch of moor, and the fells – and the trees – all bent one way, crooked and huddled.

ANN *(absorbed in her knitting)* It's the sea wind that does it.

MARY The one that's blowing now?

ANN Aye.

MARY *(with a shiver)* Shall I draw the curtains?

ANN Aye.

Mary draws the curtains. After a silence she speaks again gently.

MARY I wonder if you'll ever get used to me enough to – like me?

ANN *(with the north-country dislike of anything demonstrative)* Like you! Sic a question – and you a kind of a relation.

MARY Myself, I mean.

ANN You're weel enough. You're a bit slip of a thing, but you're John's wife, and the mother of his bairn, and there's an end.

MARY Yes, that's all I am!

She takes up her work again.

ANN Now you're talking.

MARY *(sewing)* Don't think I don't understand. John and I have been married five years. All that time Mr Rutherford never once asked to see me; if I had died, he would have been glad.

ANN I don't say that. He's a proud man, and he looked higher for his son after the eddication he'd given him. You mustn't be thinking such things.

MARY *(without bitterness)* Oh, I know all about it. If I hadn't been Tony's mother, he would never have had me inside his house. And if I hadn't been Tony's mother, I wouldn't have come. Not for anything in the world … It's wonderful how he's picked up since he got out of those stuffy lodgings.

ANN *(winding up her wool)* Well, Mr Rutherford's in the right after all.

MARY   Oh yes. He's in the right.

ANN   It's a bitter thing for him that's worked all his life to make a place i' the world to have his son go off and marry secret-like. Folk like him look for a return from their bairns. It's weel known that no good comes of a marriage such as yours, and it's no wonder that it takes him a bit of time to make up his mind to bide it. *(getting up to go)* But what's done's done.

Young John Rutherford comes in while she is speaking. He is delicate-looking and boyish in speech and manner – attractive, in spite of the fact that he is the type that has been made a gentleman of and stopped half-way in the process.

JOHN *(mimicking her tone)* So it is, Aunt Ann. Dinner's late, isn't it?

ANN   He's not back yet. He's past his time. I'm sure I hope nothing's happened.

JOHN   What should have happened?

ANN   Who's to tell that he hasn't had an accident. Things do happen.

JOHN   They do indeed. He may have jumped into a furnace.

ANN   Ah, you may joke. But you never know. You never know.

She wanders out, with the vague intention of seeing to the dinner.

JOHN   Cheery old soul, Aunt Ann. No one's ever five minutes late but she kills and buries them. *(pause)* What's she been saying to you?

MARY *(sewing)*   She's been talking about – us.

JOHN   I should have thought that subject was about threadbare by now. *(pause)* What's she say?

MARY   The usual things. How angry your father still is, and how a marriage like ours never comes to good –

JOHN   Oh, rot. Anyway, we needn't talk about it.

She looks quickly up at him and her face changes.

MARY	Someone's always talking about it.
JOHN	Who is?
MARY	Miss Rutherford – any of them. Your father

would, if he ever spoke to me at all. He looks it instead.

JOHN   Oh, nonsense; you imagine things. The Guv'nor's like that with us all – it's always been so; besides, he doesn't like women – never notices them. *(trying to make it all right)* Look here, I know it's rather beastly for you just now, but it'll be all right in time. Things are going to change, so don't you worry, little woman.

MARY   What are we going to do?

JOHN   Do? What should we do?

MARY   Anything. To get some money of our own. To make some sort of life for ourselves, away from here.

JOHN   You wait till I get this invention of mine set going. As for getting away, please remember it was you who insisted on coming. I never wanted you to.

MARY   I had to come. Tony was always ailing in London.

JOHN   You never left me alone till I'd crawled to the Guv'nor and asked to come back.

MARY   What else was there left to do? You couldn't find work –

JOHN   If you'd had patience and waited, things would have been all right.

MARY   I've waited five years. I couldn't go on earning enough when Tony came.

JOHN *(sulkily)*   Well, you couldn't expect me to ask the Guv'nor to keep us all three. And if I had stayed in London with you instead of coming back when he gave me the chance, what good would it have done? I'd have missed the biggest thing of my life – I know that ... Anyway, I do hate this going back over it all. Beastly, sordid –

MARY *(looking before her)* I couldn't go on. I'd done it so long – long before you knew me. Day after day in an office. The crowded train morning and night – bad light – bad food – and because I did that my boy is small and delicate. It's been nothing else all along – the bare struggle for life. I sometimes think that it's the only reality in the world.

JOHN *(ill-humoured)*   Whether it's the only reality or not, I call it a pretty deadly way of looking at things.

MARY   It is deadly. I didn't know how deadly till I began to care for you and thought it was going to be different.

JOHN   The old story.

MARY   No, no, we won't look back. But oh, John, I do so
dreadfully want things for Tony. *(John begins to move about the room.)*
I didn't mind when there was only ourselves. But when he was coming I
began to think, to look at the other children – children of people in our
position in London – taught to work before they'd had time to learn
what work means – with the manhood ground out of them before ever
it came. And I thought how that was what we had to give our child, you
and I … When your father forgave you for marrying me, and said you
might come here, it seemed like a chance. And there's nothing, nothing
– except this place you call home.

JOHN   Hang it all –

MARY   Oh, I know it's big – there's food and warmth,
but it's like a prison! There's not a scrape of love in the whole house.
Your father! – No one's any right to be what he is – never questioned,
never answered back – like God! And the rest of you just living round
him – neither children, nor men and women – hating each other.

JOHN *(turning to look at her with a sort of wonder)* Don't exaggerate.
Whatever has set you off talking like this?

MARY   Because I'm always thinking about it.

JOHN   You've never had a home of your own, and you
don't make excuses for family life – everybody knows it's like that more
or less.

MARY   And you've lived with it always – you can't see it
as I do.

JOHN   I do see it. And it's jolly unpleasant – I'm not
arguing about that –

MARY   Don't you see that life in this house is
intolerable?

JOHN   Well, frankly, no, I don't. That is, I don't see why
you should find it so. It's all very well to abuse my people, and I
sympathise with you in a way – no one dislikes them more than I do. I
know Janet's got a filthy temper, and Aunt Ann – well, she hasn't
moved on with the rest of us, poor old soul, that's the long and the short
of it. As for the Guv'nor – it's no use beginning to apologise for *him*.

MARY   Apologise!

JOHN   Well, that's about what you seem to expect. I've
told you I quite see that it isn't over pleasant for you, and you might
leave it at that, I think. You do drive at one so … and you seem to forget
how ill I've been.

MARY   I don't forget. But don't you see we may go on
like this for twenty years doing nothing?

JOHN Do you suppose I wouldn't have done something? Do you suppose I didn't mean to do something, if I hadn't been knocked over just at the critical moment? *(injured)* Do you suppose I wouldn't rather have been working than lying on my back all these weeks?

MARY *(quietly)* How about all the other weeks?

JOHN Good heavens, what more could I do than I have done? Here have I hit on a thing worth thousands – a thing that any glass-maker would give his ears to have the working of. And you talk to me about making money – and a life of our own. Good Lord! We're going to be rich – rich, once it's set going.

MARY *(unimpressed)* Have you told Mr Rutherford about it?

JOHN Yes. At least, I've told him what it is … I haven't told him how it's done – naturally … He won't listen to me – it's like talking to a lump of granite. He'll find he'll have to listen before long … I've set Martin on to him.

MARY Why Martin?

JOHN Because he helped me to work it out. And because he happens to be the one person in the world the Guv'nor ever listens to.

MARY *(looking up)* He trusts Martin, doesn't he? Absolutely.

JOHN Oh, Lord! Yes. Martin can do no wrong. The Guv'nor'll listen to him all right.

MARY *(resuming her work)* When is he going to tell him?

JOHN Oh, directly he gets a chance. He may have done it already.

MARY *(putting down her sewing)* Today? Then Martin really believes there's something in it?

JOHN *(indignantly)* Something in it! My dear Mary, I know you don't mean to be, but you are most fearfully irritating. Here have I told you over and over again that I'm going to make my fortune, and because someone else agrees with me you're kind enough to believe what I say. One would think you had no faith in me.

MARY *(giving it up as hopeless)* I'm sorry. We won't talk of it any more. I've said it all so often – said it till you're sick of hearing it, and it's no good.

JOHN Molly, don't be cross … I don't mean to be a brute, but it is a bit disappointing, isn't it? When I really have found the right thing at last, to find you so lukewarm about it. Because it really is this time. It'll change everything; and you shall do what you like and enjoy yourself as much as you want to – and forget all about those filthy years in Walton Street. *(He comes to her and puts his arm round her.)* There, don't be a little fool. What are you making?

MARY	A cap for Tony.
JOHN	Dear little beggar, isn't he?
MARY	Yes ... Don't say things to please me, John.
JOHN	I'm not. I do think he's a dear little beggar.

(pleased with himself) We'll be as happy as kings by and by.

MARY	As happy as we were at first?
JOHN	Happier – we'll have money.
MARY	We couldn't be happier. *(sits with her hands in*

her lap, her mouth wistful) What a pair of babies we were, weren't we?

JOHN   Oh, I don't know.

MARY   What – blunderers! I thought it was so different – and I dare say you did, too, though you never said so. I suppose it's really true what they think here – that we'd no business to marry and have a child when we'd nothing to give him when he came.

JOHN	What a little worrit you are.
MARY	I do worry, John – you don't know how much.
JOHN	But what about?
MARY	Tony.
JOHN	You funny little thing. Surely there's time enough

to think about Tony; he's just four months old.

MARY   Yes, but to me – I suppose every woman thinks about her baby like that – till he's a boy and a man and a child all in one – only he never grows old. *(in a practical tone)* How long will it take?

JOHN   How long will what take?

MARY   Your invention. *(looks up quickly)* I mean – don't be cross – will it be months – or years before it *pays*?

JOHN *(moving away)* I really can't say – it depends. If the Guv'nor has the sense to see things my way – it depends. *(He takes a cigarette.)*

MARY   I see. You will work at it, won't you? *Make* it go?

JOHN *(striking a light)* There's no work to be done. All I've got to do is to sit down and let someone pay for it.

MARY   Sit down? It seems so much to us, doesn't it? *Everything –*

JOHN *(who has burnt his finger)* It means my getting the whip-hand of the Guv'nor for once in my life. *(irritably)* And it means my getting away from your incessant nagging at me about the kid – and money.

MARY   John!

JOHN *(sharply)*   After all, it isn't very pleasant for me having you dependent on the Guv'nor and being reminded of it every other day. I don't choose this kind of life, I can tell you. If you're sick of it, God knows I am.

While he is speaking Ann drifts into the room again.

ANN There you are – smoking again; and you know what the doctor said. Mary, tell him he's not to.

MARY John must do as he likes.

JOHN I must have something; my nerves are all on edge.

ANN Weel, ye can't expect to be right all of a sudden. When I think o' the Sunday night ye was so bad, I never thought to see ye standin' there now.

JOHN (*injured*) I shouldn't worry about that. I don't suppose anyone would have been much the worse if I had pegged out.

ANN Whatever makes you say a thing like that?

JOHN Mary. Yes, you do, Mary. To hear you talk one would think I was no good. How do you suppose I've made an invention if I were the rotter you think me?

MARY I didn't say that – I didn't say that.

ANN An invention's weel enough if you're not mistaken.

JOHN Mistaken!

ANN Ah, but older people nor you make mistakes. There was old Green – I mind him fiddlin' on wi' a lot of old cogs and screws half his time, trying to find oot the way to prevent a railway train going off the line. And when he did find it and took it to show it to some one as knawed aboot such things, it was so sartin sure not to go off the line that the wheels wouldn't turn roond at all. A poor, half-baked body he was, and his wife without a decent black to show herself in o' Sundays.

JOHN I'll undertake that my wheels will go round.

ANN If it's such a wonderful thing, why hasn't someone thought of it afore? Answer me that.

JOHN You might say that of any new idea that ever came into the world.

ANN Of course, if you set up to know more about glass-making than your father that's been at it ever since he was a bairn ...

JOHN It isn't a case of knowing. I've a much better chance because I don't know. It's the duffers who get hold of the best things – stumble over them in the dark, as I did. It makes my blood run cold to think how easily I could have missed it, of all the people who must have looked straight at it time after time, and never seen it. (*contemptuously*) Hullo, Dick!

Richard Rutherford has come in from the hall. He wears the regulation clergyman's clothes and looks older than John, though he is in reality the younger by a couple of years. He is habitually overworked, and his face has the rather pathetic look of an overweighted youth that finds life too much for its strength. His manner is extremely simple and sincere, which enables him to use priggish phrases without offence. He comes to the table while John is speaking, looks from him to Ann, then at the butter, sugar, and bread in turn.

DICK *(very tired)*	Dinner?
JOHN *(mimicking him)*	Not imminent.
DICK	Will it be long?
ANN *(crossly)*	Ye'll just have to bide quiet till it comes.
DICK *(gently)*	Ah! ... In that case I think I'll just –

He takes a piece of bread and moves towards the door.

ANN   You look fair done.

DICK   I've had a tiring day. *(To Mary)* Where is Janet?

MARY   In the kitchen. *(She looks at him intently.)* Why did you ask? Do you want her?

DICK *(uncertainly)*   No, no. I thought she might have gone out. It's best for her not to go out after dark.

ANN   You can't sit in your room i' this cold.

DICK   I'll put on a coat. It's quiet there.

JOHN   You'll have time to write your sermon before he comes in, I dare say.

DICK *(simply)*   Oh, I've done that, such as it is.

He leaves the room, eating his bread as he goes.

JOHN *(irritably)*   This is a damned uncomfortable house. I'm starving.

ANN   It's Committee day.

JOHN   He'll be having the whole Board on his toes as usual, I suppose.

ANN   That Board'll be the death of him. When I think of the old days when he'd no one to please but himself!

JOHN   He's stood it for five years. I wouldn't – being badgered by a lot of directors who know as much about glass-making as you do.

ANN   That's all very well. But when you borrow money you've got to be respectful one way and another. If he hadn't gone to the Bank how would Rutherford's ha' gone on?

JOHN *(who has taken up the newspaper and is half reading it as he talks)*
Why should it go on?

ANN *(sharply)* What's that?

JOHN Why didn't he sell the place when he could have made a decent profit?

ANN *(scandalised)* *Sell* Rutherford's? Just you let your father hear you.

JOHN I don't care if he does. I never can imagine why he hangs on – working his soul out year after year.

ANN *(conclusively)* It's his *duty! (She resumes her knitting.)*

JOHN Duty – rot! He likes it. He's gone on too long. He couldn't stop and rest if he tried. When I make a few thousands out of this little idea of mine I'm going to have everything I want, and forget all about the dirt and the ugliness, the clatter and bang of the machinery, the sickening hot smell of the furnaces – all the things I've hated from my soul.

ANN *(who has become absorbed in a dropped stitch)* Aye weel ... there's another strike at Rayner's, they tell me.

JOHN Yes. Eight hundred men. That's the second this year.

ANN You don't think it'll happen here, do you?

JOHN I can't say. They're smashing things at Rayner's.

ANN It'll no' come here. The men think too much of your father for that.

JOHN I'm not so sure.

ANN There was the beginnings of a strike once, years ago, and he stopped it then. The men at the furnaces struck work – said it was too hard for 'n. And your father he went doon into the caves and took his coat off afore them all, and pitched joost half as much coal again as the best of'em – now!

JOHN Yes, that's the sort of argument they can see – it catches hold of the brute in them. If the Guv'nor had sat quietly in his office and sent his ultimatum through the usual channels, he would have been the owner of Rutherford's, and the strike would have run its course. Shovelling coal in his shirt with his muscles straining, and the sweat pouring off him, he was 'wor John' – and there's three cheers for his fourteen stone of beef and muscle. That was all very well – thirty years ago.

ANN And what's to hinder it now?

JOHN Oh, the Guv'nor was a bit of a hero then – an athlete, a runner. The men who worked for him all the week crowded to see him run on Saturday afternoons, Martin's told me. But when all's said and done, Rutherford's is a money-making machine. And the Guv'nor's the only man who doesn't know it. He's getting old.

ANN *(crossly)*   To hear you talk, a body would think we were all going to die tomorrow. Your father's a year younger nor me – now! And a fine up-standing man forbye.

JOHN *(who is looking at himself in the glass above the mantelpiece)* Oh, he knows how to manage a pack of savages.

ANN   There's not one of 'em today or thirty years ago but'll listen to him.

JOHN   He'd knock anyone down who didn't.

Janet comes in with a tray and begins to set cups and saucers on the table.

ANN   They all stood by him when the trouble came, every one of 'em. And he's climbed up steady ever since, and never looked ahint him. And now you've got your invention it'll no be long now – if it's all you think it. Ah, it 'ud be grand to see Rutherford's like old times again.

JOHN   Rutherford's ... *(He speaks half seriously, half to tease Ann.)* Aunt Ann, have you ever in your life – just for a moment at the back of your mind – wished Rutherford's at the bottom of the Tyne?

Ann gazes at him in silence. When she speaks again it is as to a foolish child.

ANN   Are you taking your medicine reg'lar?

JOHN   Yes. But have you ever heard of Moloch? No – Well, Moloch was a sort of a god – some time ago, you know, before Dick and his kind came along. They built his image with an ugly head ten times the size of a real head, with great wheels instead of legs, and set him up in the middle of a great dirty town. *(Janet, busy at the table, stops to listen, raising her eyes almost for the first time.)* And they thought him a very important person indeed, and made sacrifices to him – human sacrifices – to keep him going, you know. Out of every family they set aside one child to be an offering to him when it was big enough, and at last it became a sort of honour to be dedicated in this way, so much so, that the victims gave themselves gladly to be crushed out of life under the great wheels. That was Moloch.

There is a silence. Janet speaks eagerly.

JANET   Where did you get that?

JOHN	Get what?
JANET	What you've been saying.
JOHN	Everybody knows it.
JANET	Dedicated – we're dedicated – all of us – to

Rutherford's. And being respected in Grantley.

ANN   Talk, talk – chatter, chatter. Words never mended nothing that I knows on.

JOHN *(who is tired of the subject)* Talk – if I hadn't you to talk to, Aunt Ann, or Mary, I think I'd talk to the doorpost.

JANET *(who has slipped back into her dull listlessness)* And just as much good would come of it, I dare say.

ANN   And who are you to say it? You got no book-learning like him – and no invention neither.

JANET *(who is laying forks round the table)* How do you know he's got an invention?

ANN   Because he says so, o' course – how else? It's a secret.

JANET   John always had a secret. He used to sell them to me when we were little. And when I'd given him whatever it was he'd taken a fancy to, there was no secret. Nothing worth paying for, anyway.

ANN *(as if they were children)* Now, now. Don't quarrel.

JANET   We're not quarrelling.

JOHN   Yes, we are. And you began it.

JANET   I didn't. I only said what anyone can see. *(scornfully)* *You* make an invention. Likely.

JOHN   A lot you know about it.

JANET   If you did, you'd muck it somehow, just as you do everything.

ANN *(querulously)*   Bairns! Bairns! One would think you'd never growed up.

JOHN *(angrily to Janet)* I wish you'd keep quiet if you can't say anything decent. You never open your mouth except to say something dis-agreeable. First there's Mary throwing cold water, then you come in.

JANET   I'm not any more disagreeable than anyone else. We're all disagreeable if it comes to that. All except Susan.

ANN   Susan's not one of the family! A common servant lass.

JANET   Like me.

ANN *(using the family threat)* Just you let your father hear you.

JANET   We do the same things.

ANN   Susan's *paid* for it. Whoever gave you a farthing?

JANET *(bitterly)*   Aye!
ANN   Has she made another girdle cake?
JANET   I didn't notice. She's probably talking to her
young man at the gate.
JOHN   Susan with a young man!
ANN   Yes, indeed – a nice thing, and her turned forty.
JOHN   Ugliest woman I ever saw bar none. Who is it?
Not Martin surely! *(Janet stops suddenly and looks at him.)* I've
noticed he's been making excuses to come about lately, and he's taken
the cottage at the Tarn.
JANET *(with a sudden stillness)* It isn't Martin.
JOHN   Well, if it is, the Guv'nor would soon put a stop to
it.
JANET   Put a stop to what?
JOHN   Martin getting married – if it's that he's after.
JANET   What right's he to interfere?
JOHN   Right – nonsense. Martin practically lives at the
Works as it is. If he had a wife he'd get to be just like the other men –
hankering after going home at the proper time, and all that.
ANN *(preparing to leave the room)* You and your gossip – and the dinner
spoiling every minute. *(with a parting shot at Janet)* It's a good thing
nobody's married you – a nice hoose you'd make without me to look to
everything.

She fusses out.

JOHN   Married! Cheer up, Janet! Thirty-five last
birthday, isn't it?
MARY   John!
JANET *(her voice hard)* No, it isn't. It's thirty-six.
JOHN   You'll make a happy home for someone yet. No
one's asked you so far, I suppose?
JANET   Who's there been to ask me?
JOHN   Oh, I don't know. I suppose you have been kept
pretty close. Other girls manage it, don't they?
JANET   I don't know other girls.
JOHN   Mary caught me.
JANET   I don't know anybody – you know that. No one in
Grantley's good enough for us, and we're not good enough for the other
kind.
JOHN   Speak for yourself.

JANET   Oh, we're all alike; don't you fret. Why hasn't young Squire Earnshaw invited you to shoot with him again? He did once – when none of his grand friends were there.

John pretends not to hear.

JANET   I know why.

JOHN   Oh, you know a lot, don't you?

JANET   It was because you pretended – pretended you knew the folk he talked about, because you'd shown them over the Works once when father was away. Pretended you said 'parss' for pass every day. I heard you. And I saw the difference. Gentlemen are natural. Being in company doesn't put them about. They don't say 'thank you' to servants neither, not like you do to Susan.

JOHN   Oh, shut up, will you?

JANET   I wouldn't pretend, whatever I did – mincing round like a monkey.

ANN (*coming in from the kitchen*) Now, now. That's the door, isn't it?

They all listen. A voice is heard outside, then the outer door opens.

JOHN   Father.

JANET   Martin.

There is the sound of a stick being put into the umbrella stand then John Rutherford comes in, followed by Martin. He is a heavily-built man of sixty, with a heavy lined face and tremendous shoulders – a typical north countryman. There is a distinct change in the manner of the whole family as he comes in and walks straight to his desk as if the door had scarcely interrupted his walk. Martin is a good-looking man of the best type of working man. Very simple in manner and bearing – about forty years of age. He touches his forelock to the family and stands beside the door with nothing servile in either action.

RUTHERFORD (*talking as he comes in*) … and it's got to be managed somehow. Lads are wanted and lads'll have to be found. Only six out of the seventeen shops started the first shift o' Monday.

MARTIN   Grey couldn't start at all last week for want o' lads.

RUTHERFORD   What's got them? Ten years ago you could have had fifty for the asking, and taken your pick. And now here's the work waiting to be done, and half the hands we want to do it lounging about Grantley with their hands in their breeches pockets, the beggars. What do they think they're bred for?

MARTIN   There's too many of 'em making for the towns, that's it. It's lighter work.

RUTHERFORD   Just remind me to give the men a word o' wages time o' Saturday. They got to keep their lads at home as long as they're wanted at Rutherford's. *(turning papers and a bunch of keys out of his pocket on to the desk)* The new lear man's shaping all right then.

MARTIN   Dale? Knows as much aboot a pot-arch as I knows aboot a flying-machine.

RUTHERFORD   Why didn't you tell me before?

MARTIN   I thought I'd wait to give him a trial. I took a look at the flues myself to make sure it wasn't them at fault. He can't get the heat up properly, and the pots are put into the furnaces afore they're furnace heat. They'll all be broke one o' these days.

RUTHERFORD   We'd better take on Ford.

MARTIN   He finishes at Cardiff on Saturday.

RUTHERFORD   He'll do, I suppose?

MARTIN *(feeling in his pocket and pulling out a leather purse or bag)* You couldn't get a better man for the job in all Tyneside. There's the ten pound young Henderson had out o' the cash-box.

He counts it out on the desk.

RUTHERFORD   What! He's given it up?

MARTIN   Aye. Leastways, I took it off him.

RUTHERFORD   Has he owned to it?

MARTIN   Sure enough. Said he hadn't gone for to do it. Cried like a bairn, he did.

JOHN *(from his armchair by the fire)* Henderson? Has he been stealing?

MARTIN   Aye, Mr. John. I caught him at it i' the office – at dinner time when there's nobody much aboot – wi' his hands i' the box.

JOHN   Dirty little sweep! Have you kicked him out?

RUTHERFORD *(pausing with his hand on his cash-box)* I suppose there's no doubt he's a bad 'un?

MARTIN   Bred and born.

RUTHERFORD   No use giving him another chance.

MARTIN   Throwed away on the likes o' him.

RUTHERFORD *(locking the box and putting it in a drawer)* Ah ... Well, if he comes back, turn him away. Everything ready for the pot-setting in the morning?

MARTIN   Aye, sir. The night shift'll set four when they stop, and the other shift'll set the others a bit later.

RUTHERFORD   You'll be there to see them do it?

MARTIN Surely.

RUTHERFORD *(with a curious softening in his voice)* When'll you get your rest?

MARTIN Plenty of time for that, sir.

RUTHERFORD *(crossing to the fire)* We'll have you on strike one o' these days, Martin.

MARTIN *(turning to go)* Not me, sir. When you begin to spare yourself you can begin to think about sparing me. And next week things'll go easier ... Is that all for the night, sir?

RUTHERFORD *(wearily)* Aye. Good night to ye. *(He has taken his pipe from the rack above the mantelpiece and is filling it.)* You've further to go now ye're in the Tarn Cottage.

There is a slight pause before Martin replies.

MARTIN Aye. A bit, mebbee.

RUTHERFORD *(lighting his pipe)* I – should ha' – thought you'd had done better to stick to your old one – near at hand; but you know your own business best.

MARTIN It's weel enough.

ANN Now Martin's here, can he no take a look at the range? Susan canna get the oven to go.

JANET *(to Ann)* The oven's all right.

RUTHERFORD *(with a complete change of voice and manner)* Now what's that got to do with Martin?

ANN *(subsiding)* He could tell Baines to send up a man i' the mornin'.

RUTHERFORD That's not Martin's business – you must send word to Baines himself.

MARTIN I could easy take a look at it while I'm here, sir. It 'ud save you sending.

RUTHERFORD *(wearily)* Oh, all right. If you want a job.

ANN Janet, go and show Martin.

Martin turns at the door and looks for her to pass out before him.

JANET *(standing motionless)* Susan can show him.

Martin goes, closing the door.

RUTHERFORD Any letters?

ANN *(flurried)* Yes. They're somewheres. Janet –

RUTHERFORD *(with the sudden irritation of a tired man)* Bless me, can't I have a simple thing like that done for me? How often have I said to put them in one place and stick to it? *(Janet discovers the letters on the small table by the door and brings them to him. He sits on the settle and stretches out his legs.)* Here, take them off for me. I'm dead beat. *(After a moment's silent revolt she kneels and begins to unlace his boots. He looks at her bent sullen face.)* Ah! Sulky, are ye? *(She makes no answer.)* 'Ud like to tell me to take them off myself, I dare say. And I been working the day long for you. *(getting irritated at her touch)* Spoilt – that's what you are, my lass. *(opening a letter)* What's this? A polite letter from the vicar, eh? Damn polite – a new organ – that's his trouble – thinks I'd like to help pay for it. *(He throws it across the hearth-rug to John.)* There's a job for you – you're idle enough. Write and tell His Reverence to go to the devil and ask him for an organ. Or mebbe Richard'll like to do it, as he's his curate. *(To Janet)* Let be, let be.

He takes his boots off painfully one with the other.

ANN *(plaintively)*   I'm sure the vicar came in pleasant enough not a week gone, and asked for 'ee –

RUTHERFORD   Asked for my money, you mean. They're civil enough when they want anything, the lot of them. *(To Janet – sarcastically, as she carries the boots away.)* Thank 'ee kindly.

He gets up and puts his slippers on. Ann speaks in a flurried whisper to John.

ANN   John, you've got your father's chair.

JOHN *(gets up)*   Sorry.

RUTHERFORD *(drags the chair up to the table, and sits down as if he were tired out. He looks at John with a curiously interested expression as he lounges across.)* Feeling better?

JOHN *(uneasy and consequently rather swaggering)* Oh, I'm still a bit shaky about the knees.

RUTHERFORD   You'll be coming back to work, I suppose. There's plenty to be done. How's the little lad?

JOHN   I don't know – all right, I suppose. Isn't he, Mary?

MARY   Mr Rutherford asked you.

JOHN   But I don't know.

Rutherford looks at Mary, she at him; there is a pause.

RUTHERFORD *(busy with his letters)* I thought Gibson had forbidden you to smoke?

John rebels for a moment, then throws his cigarette into the fire, with an action like a petted child.

JOHN	I must do something.
RUTHERFORD	What have you been busy with today? ... This –

metal o' yours? Eh?

JOHN (*evasively*)	Aunt Ann's been talking about it.
ANN (*meaning well*)	We've joost been saying how it'll all come right

now – all the bother. John'll do it – Rutherford's 'll be itself again.

RUTHERFORD	Martin tells me you've hit on a good thing – a big

thing ... I've got to hear more about it, eh?

JOHN	If you like.
RUTHERFORD	What's that?

He looks up slowly under his eyebrows – a long curious look, as if he saw the first possibility of opposition.

JOHN (*going over to the fireplace*) Can't we have dinner?	
ANN	You're getting back your appetite. That's a good

sign.

RUTHERFORD	Dinner can wait. (*He sweeps a space clear on the

table and puts his letters down. Janet presently sits down resigned to a family row. Mary listens throughout intently, her eyes constantly fixed on John.*) I'm a business man, and I like to know how I stand. (*launching at John*) Now – what d 'ye mean?

JOHN	I don't understand you, sir.
RUTHERFORD	What's there to understand?
JOHN (*his manner gradually slipping into that of a child afraid of its father*) Well, I've been away from the Works for two months. Before we	

begin to talk about the other thing, I'd like to know what's doing.

RUTHERFORD	What's that got to do with it? You never have

known what's doing.

JOHN	I think I ought to be told – now.
RUTHERFORD	Now! That's it, is it? You want a bone flung to

your dignity! Well, here it is. Things are bad.

JOHN	Really bad?
RUTHERFORD	For the present. These colliery strikes one on top

of another, for one thing. Rayner's drew the ponies out of the pit this afternoon.

JOHN	It'll about smash them, won't it?
RUTHERFORD	Mebbee. The question is how it affects us.
JOHN	Oh! We get coal from them?
RUTHERFORD	I should have thought you'd ha' picked up that

much – in five years.

JOHN	Stoking isn't my business.

RUTHERFORD   You might have noticed the name on the trucks –
you see it every day of your life. Well, yes – we get our coal from them
... What then?

JOHN   Well – what's going to happen? *How* bad is it?

RUTHERFORD   I said – bad for the present. The balance-sheet
for the year's just been drawn up and shows a loss of four thousand on
last year's working. It's not a big loss, considering what's been against
us – those Americans dumping all that stuff in the spring – we had to
stop that little game, and it cost us something to do it. Then the price of
materials has gone up, there's a difference there. *(irritably, answering
his own thoughts)* It's not *ruin*, bless us – it's simply a question of work
and sticking together; but the Bank's rather more difficult to manage
than usual. There's not one of 'em would sacrifice a shilling of their own
to keep the old place going – they want their fees reg'lar. That's their
idea of the commercial enterprise they're always talking about. It's the
pulse they keep their finger on – when it misses a beat, they come
crowding round with their hands up like a lot of damned old women ...
Well, well! Something's wanted to pull things together ... Now – this
idea of yours. Martin tells me it's worth something.

JOHN *(nettled)*   Worth something? It's worth thousands a year to
anyone who works it properly.

RUTHERFORD *(with his half smile)* Thousands! That's a fair margin.
(drily) What's your calculation in figures?

JOHN   That depends on the scale it's worked on.

RUTHERFORD *(as to a child)* Yes – so I supposed. What's your
preliminary cost?

JOHN *(getting nervous)* Nothing – as far as I know. I can't say for certain
– something like that.

RUTHERFORD   Something like nothing; and on something like
nothing you're going to show a profit of thousands a year on a single
metal. *(drily)* Sounds like a beautiful dream, doesn't it? About your cost
of working now – that should run you into something?

JOHN *(who is getting annoyed)* Thirty per cent less than what you're
working at now.

RUTHERFORD   Indeed ... May I ask where and how you've
carried out your experiments?

JOHN *(uneasily)*   I didn't mention it to you. A year ago I got a
muffle furnace. I've worked with it from time to time, in the old pot-loft.

RUTHERFORD   Paid for it by any chance?

JOHN   Not yet.

RUTHERFORD   How did you manage for coals now?

JOHN　　　　　　　I – took what I wanted from the heap.

RUTHERFORD　　　Ah, and your materials – I suppose you took what you wanted of those too? Well, I've no objection, if you can make it good. *(suddenly)* What's your receipt?

JOHN　　　　　　　I haven't – I'm not prepared to say.

There is a silence. Ann lowers her knitting with an alarmed look.

RUTHERFORD *(heavily)* A week or two ago in this room you told me it was perfected – ready for working tomorrow.

JOHN　　　　　　　Yes – I told you so.

RUTHERFORD *(suppressed)* What d'ye mean? ... Come, come, sir – I'm your father, I want an answer to my question – a plain answer, if you can give one.

JOHN *(in a high-pitched, nervous voice)* I – I'm a business man, and I want to know where I stand. *(Rutherford breaks into a laugh.)* Oh, you turn me into an impudent schoolboy, but I'm not. I'm a man, with a thing in my mind worth a fortune.

ANN　　　　　　　John! *(asserting her authority)* You must tell your father.

JOHN *(very excited)*　　I shan't tell him till I've taken out my patent, so there!

There is a pause – Rutherford stares at his son.

RUTHERFORD *(heavily)* What d'ye mean?

JOHN　　　　　　　I mean what I say. I want my price.

RUTHERFORD　　　Your price – *your* price? *(bringing his fist down on the table)* Damn your impudence, sir. A whippersnapper like you to talk about your price.

JOHN *(losing his temper)* I'm not a whippersnapper. I've got something to sell and you want to buy it, and there's an end.

RUTHERFORD　　　To buy? To sell? And this to your father?

JOHN　　　　　　　To any man who wants what I've made.

There is a dead silence on this, broken only by an involuntary nervous movement from the rest of the family. Then Rutherford speaks without moving.

RUTHERFORD　　　Ah! So that's your line, is it? ... This is what I get for all I've done for you ... This is the result of the schooling I give you.

JOHN *(with an attempt at a swagger)* I suppose you mean Harrow.

RUTHERFORD　　　It was two hundred pound – that's what I mean.

JOHN　　　　　　　And you gave me a year of it!

RUTHERFORD   And a lot of good you've got of it ... What ha' you
done with it? Idled your time away wi' your books o' poetry when you
should ha' been working. Married a wife who bears you a bairn you
can't keep. *(at a movement from Mary)* Aye – hard words mebbee.
What will you do for your son when the time comes? I've toiled and
sweated to give you a name you'd be proud to own – worked early and
late, toiled like a dog when other men were taking their ease – plotted
and planned to get my chance, taken it and held it when it come till I
could ha' burst with the struggle. Sell! You talk o' selling to me, when
everything you'll ever make couldn't pay back the life I've given to you!

JOHN   Oh, I know, I know.

ANN   You mustn't answer your father, John.

JOHN   Well, after all, I didn't ask to be born.

RUTHERFORD   Nor did the little lad, God help him.

JOHN *(rapidly)*   Look here, Father – why did you send me to
Harrow?

RUTHERFORD   Why? To make a gentleman of you, and because I
thought they'd teach you better than the Grammar School. I was
mistaken.

JOHN   They don't turn out good clerks and office boys.

RUTHERFORD   What's that?

JOHN   I've been both for five years. Only I've had no
salary.

RUTHERFORD   You've been put to learn your business like any
other young fellow. I began at the bottom – you've got to do the same.
There'll not be two masters at Rutherford's while I'm on my legs.

JOHN   That's it, that's it. You make a servant of me.

RUTHERFORD   What do you suppose your work's worth to
Rutherford's? Tell me that.

JOHN   What's that matter now? I've done with it. I've
found a way out.

RUTHERFORD   A way out – of what?

JOHN *(rather taken aback)* Well – you don't suppose I'd choose to live
here all my life?

ANN *(taking it personally)* And why not, pray?

RUTHERFORD   Your father has lived here, and your grandfather
before you. It's your inheritance – can't you realise that? – what you've
got to come to when I'm underground. We've made it for you, stone by
stone, penny by penny, fighting through thick and thin for close on a
hundred years.

JOHN Well, after all, I can't help what you and grandfather chose to do.

RUTHERFORD *Chose* to do! There's no chose to do. The thing's there. You're my son – my son that's got to come after me.

JOHN Oh, it's useless. Our ideas of life are utterly different.

RUTHERFORD Ideas of life! What do you know about life?

JOHN Oh, nothing, of course.

RUTHERFORD If you did, you'd soon stop having ideas about it. Life! I've had nigh on sixty years of it, and I'll tell you. Life's *work* – keeping your head up and your heels down. Sleep, and begetting children, rearing them up to work when you're gone – that's life. And when you know better than the God who made you, you can begin to ask what you're going to get by it. And you'll get more work and six foot of earth at the end of it.

JOHN And that's what you mean me to do, is it?

RUTHERFORD It's what you've got to do – or starve. You're my son – you've got to come after me.

JOHN Look here, Father. You tell me all this. Just try and see things my way for once. Take the Works. I know you've done it all, built it up, and all that – and you're quite right to be proud of it. But I – I don't like the place, that's the long and the short of it. It's not worth my while. After all, I've got myself to think of – my own life. If I'd done that sooner, by Jove! I'd have been a jolly sight better off. I'd not have married, for one thing. *(with a glance at Mary)* Not that I regret that. You talk about what you did when you were young. You've told me the sort of time you've had – nothing but grind, grind, since the time you could do anything. And what have you got by it? What have you got? I have myself to think of. I want a run for my money – your money, I suppose it is – other fellows do. And I've made this thing myself, off my own bat – and – and – *(ending lamely)* – I don't see why I shouldn't have a look in ... On my own account ...

There is an uncomfortable silence.

RUTHERFORD *(in a new tone)* You're going to take out a patent, you say?

JOHN *(taking this as friendly)* Yes.

RUTHERFORD Know anything about Patent Law?

JOHN Well, no – not yet.

RUTHERFORD It's very simple, and wonderfully cheap – three pound for three years. At the end of three years, you can always extend the time if you want to – no difficulty about that.

JOHN Oh, no.

RUTHERFORD   But you can't patent a metal.
JOHN   I don't see why not.
RUTHERFORD   What's the use if you do?
JOHN   It's the same as anything else. I take out a patent
for a certain receipt, and I can come down on anyone who uses it.
RUTHERFORD   And prove that they've used it?
JOHN   They have to find out what it is first. It's not
likely I'm going to give the show away. *(pause)*
RUTHERFORD   But you want to sell, you say.
JOHN   Yes.
RUTHERFORD   How are you going to do that without giving it
away? ... Suppose you go to one of the big chaps – Miles of Cardiff, for
example. 'Here you are,' you say. 'I've got an idea worth a fortune. Give
me a fortune and I'll tell you what it is.' He's not going to buy a pig in a
poke any more than I am. People have a way of thinking they're going
to make their fortunes, d'ye see? But those people aren't generally the
sort you let loose in your glasshouse.
JOHN   Of course, I shall make inquiries about all that.
I can't say till I know.
RUTHERFORD   Do you remember a little thing of mine – an
invention you would call it. Did ye ever happen to see it?
JOHN   Yes. Martin showed it to me once.
RUTHERFORD   What's your opinion of that now – as a business
man?
JOHN   Of course, it had the makings of a good thing –
anyone could see that.
RUTHERFORD   Nobody did. I was nineteen at the time – a lad.
Like you, I hadn't the money to run it myself. Clinton, the American
people, got hold of it, and sold seven hundred thousand the first six
months in New York alone. *(He gets up and addresses the room,
generally.)* Dinner in ten minutes.
JOHN   Surely you could have got someone to take it up –
an obvious thing like that?
RUTHERFORD *(drily)* That's how it worked out in my case. *(He moves
slowly to the door.)*
JOHN   You don't believe I can do what I say.
RUTHERFORD   I can't tell – nor can you.
JOHN *(high-handed)* Oh, very well then. What are we talking about?
RUTHERFORD   You undertake to produce ordinary white metal
at a third of the usual cost – that's it, isn't it? You've worked this out in
a muffle furnace. My experience of muffle furnaces is that they're

excellent for experimenting in a very small way. A child can hit on an idea for a metal – provided he's materials at his command, and knows a bit about chemistry. But no man living can estimate the cost of that idea until it's worked out on a big scale. Your receipt, as it stands, isn't worth the paper it's written on.

As Rutherford moves again towards the door John makes a movement to stop him.

JOHN   Father, look here. Here's an offer.

RUTHERFORD   Thank you kindly.

JOHN   If you'll let me have a pot in one of the big furnaces for a trial – I swear to you, on my honour, I'll let you see the result without touching it, after I've put in the materials. You can clay the pots up – seal them, if you like. Let me do it tomorrow; I can't stand hanging on like this.

RUTHERFORD   Tomorrow! Impossible.

JOHN   Why not?

RUTHERFORD   You can't come down to the Works in this weather. You'd catch cold, and be laid up again.

JOHN   The day after then – next week – or, why not? – let Martin do it.

RUTHERFORD   Martin? *(He turns to look at John, struck by a new thought.)*

JOHN   Why not? He can do it as well as I can.

RUTHERFORD   Martin? ... He knows then?

JOHN *(surprised)* Why, he talked to you about it, didn't he?

RUTHERFORD   Yes, yes. But – he's got the receipt?

JOHN   Yes – there's no difficulty at all. Let him mix the metal and clay her up, and you can open her yourself. Then you'll see. You'll take Martin's word for it, I suppose? Only, for Heaven's sake, give me a fair chance.

RUTHERFORD *(moving suddenly)* Fair chance be damned, sir. You've said your say, and I've said mine. Think it over!

He goes out, leaving John standing staring after him.

JOHN *(under his breath as the door closes)* Oh, go to the devil!

ANN   For shame to speak so. Just let him hear you. And there, dinner'll be as dry as a bone, and I've waited so long I don't feel as if I could touch a morsel. You might keep your business till we'd had something to eat, I think. *(She hurries out.)*

JANET *(with a sort of admiration)* Now you've done it.

JOHN   Done it! I've jolly well let him know what I think
– and high time, too. *(brokenly)* It isn't fair – it isn't fair. Old bully.
What am I going to do?

JANET *(dropping into her usual tone)* What you've always done, I
suppose.

JOHN   What's that?

JANET   Say you're sorry. It's the soonest way back.

JOHN   I'm not going back. Sooner than give in, I'll
starve. I don't care. I'll go to London, Canada, anywhere. He shan't have
me, to grind the life out of me by inches – and he shan't have my metal.
If he thinks he's going to pick my brains and give me nothing for it, he'll
find himself jolly well mistaken. I don't care. Once and for all, I'm going
to make a stand. And he can jolly well go to the devil.

Mary speaks for the first time, in a low voice.

MARY   What are you making a stand for?

JOHN *(stopping to look at her)* Good Lord, Mary, haven't you been
listening?

MARY   Yes, I've been listening. You said you wanted
your price. What is your price?

JANET   All the profits and none of the work – that's
John's style. *(She sits on settle, her chin on her hands.)*

JOHN   A lot you know about it.

Mary speaks again.

MARY   If you get your price, what will you do with it?

JANET   He won't get it.

JOHN *(to Janet)*   Do you suppose I'm going to sit down under his
bullying?

JANET   You've done it all your life.

JOHN   Well, here's an end of it then.

JANET   No one ever stands out against father for long –
you know that – or else they get so knocked about they don't matter any
more. *(She looks at Mary, who has made an involuntary movement.)*
Oh, I don't mean he hits them – that's not his way.

JOHN   Oh, don't exaggerate.

JANET   Exaggerate – look at mother! You were too young
– I remember – *(To Mary)* You've been here nigh on three months.
If you think you're going to change this house with your soft ways,
you're mistaken. Nothing'll change us now – nothing. We're made that
way – set – and we've got to live that way. *(slowly)* You think you can

make John do something. If ever he does it'll be for fear of father, not
for love of you.

JOHN What do you mean? *(in a high voice)* If you think
I'm going to give in –

JANET You've said that three times. I know you're going
to give in.

JOHN Well, I'm not – so there.

JANET What will you do then?

JOHN That's my business. Curse Rutherford's! Curse it!

JANET *(to Mary)* That's what he'll do. That's what he's been doing
these five years. And what's come of it? He's dragged you into the life
here – and Tony – that's all ... I knew all the time you'd have to come in
the end, to go under, like the rest of us.

MARY *(quickly)* No, no –

JANET Who's going to get you out of it? ... John? ...
You're all getting excited about this metal. I don't know whether it's
good or bad, but anyway it doesn't count. In a few days John'll make
another row for us to sit round and listen to. In a few days more he'll
threaten father to run away. He can't, because he's nothing separate
from father. When he gives up his receipt, or whatever it is, it'll go to
help Rutherford's – not you or me or anyone, just Rutherford's. And
after a bit he'll forget about it – let it slide like the rest of us. We've all
wanted things, one way and another, and we've let them slide. It's no
good standing up against father.

JOHN Oh, who listens to you? Come along, Mary.
(moving to the door) Disagreeable old maid!

He goes out. Mary stands in the same place looking at Janet.

MARY Oh, Janet, no one's any right to be what he is –
no one's any right.

JOHN *(calling from the hall)* Mollie! I want you. *(irritably)* Mollie!

MARY Coming! *(She follows him.)*

*Janet remains in the same attitude – her chin on her hands, staring
sullenly before her. Suddenly she bows her face in her arms and begins to
cry. Martin comes in from the kitchen on his way out. As he reaches the
door leading to the hall, he sees her and stops.*

MARTIN *(in a whisper)* My lass!

She starts and gets up quickly.

JANET Martin! Martin!

He blunders over to her and takes her in his arms with a rough movement, holding her to him – kisses her with passion and without tenderness, and releases her suddenly. She goes to the fireplace, and leans her arms on the mantelpiece, her head on them – he turns away with his head bent. They stand so.

MARTIN (*as if the words were dragged from him*) Saturd'y night – he's away to Wickham – at the Tarn ... Will ye come?

JANET　　　Yes.

Martin goes to the door at back. As he reaches it Rutherford comes into the room with some papers in his hand. In crossing between the two, he stops suddenly as if some thought had struck him.

MARTIN　　　　　Good night, sir.

RUTHERFORD　　　Good night. (*He stands looking at Janet till the outer door shuts.*) Why don't you say good night to Martin? It 'ud be more civil – wouldn't it?

JANET　　　　　I have said it. (*Their eyes meet for a moment – she moves quickly to the door.*) I'll tell Susan you're ready.

Rutherford is left alone. He stands in the middle of the room with his papers in his hand motionless, save that he turns his head slowly to look at the door by which Martin has gone out.

ACT TWO

It is about nine o'clock in the evening. The lamp is burning on the large table. Bedroom candlesticks are on the small table between the window and door. Rutherford is sitting at his desk. He has been writing, and now sits staring in front of him with a heavy brooding face. He does not hear Dick as he comes in quietly and goes to the table to light his candle – then changes his mind, looks at his father, and comes to the fire to warm his hands. He looks, as usual, pale and tired. Rutherford becomes suddenly aware of his presence, upon which Dick speaks in a gentle, nervous tone.

DICK　　　　　I should rather like to speak to you, if you could spare me a minute.

RUTHERFORD　　What's the matter with *you*?

DICK　　　　　The matter?

RUTHERFORD　　You're all wanting to speak to me nowadays –

what's wrong with things? ... *(taking up his pen)* What's the bee in your bonnet?

DICK *(announcing his news)* I have been offered the senior curacy at St. Jude's, Southport.

RUTHERFORD   Well – have you taken it?

DICK *(disappointed)*   I could not do so without your consent. That's what I want to speak to you about – if you could spare me a minute.

RUTHERFORD *(realising)* Ah! That means you're giving up your job here?

DICK   Exactly.

RUTHERFORD   Ah ... Just as well, I dare say.

DICK   You will naturally want to know my reasons for such a step. *(He waits for a reply and gets none.)* In the first place, I have to consider my future. From that point of view there seems to be a chance of – of more success. And lately – I have had it in my mind for some time past – somehow my work among the people here hasn't met with the response I once hoped for ... I have done my best – and it would be ungrateful to say that I had failed utterly when there are always the few who are pleased when I drop in ... But the men are not encouraging.

RUTHERFORD   I dare say not.

DICK   I have done my best. Looking back on my three years here, I honestly cannot blame myself; and yet – failure is not the less bitter on that account.

RUTHERFORD *(almost kindly)* Well – perhaps a year or two at a Theological College wasn't the best of trainings for a raw hell like Grantley. It always beats me – whenever a man thinks it's his particular line to deal with humanity in the rough, he always goes to school like a bit of a lad to find out how to do it.

DICK   Ah! You don't understand.

RUTHERFORD   You mean I don't see things your way – well, that's not worth discussing. *(He goes back to his writing.)*

DICK   I have sometimes wondered if your not seeing things my way has had anything to do with my lack of success among your people. For they are your people.

RUTHERFORD   What d'ye mean?

DICK *(sincerely)*   Not only the lack of religious example on your part – even some kind of Sunday observance would have helped – to be more in touch – but all through my ministry I have been conscious of your silent antagonism. Even in my active work – in talking to the men, in visiting their wives, in everything – I have always felt that dead weight against me, dragging me down, taking the heart out of all I do and say, even when I am most certain that I am right to do and say it. *(He ends rather breathlessly.)*

RUTHERFORD *(testily)* What the devil have you got hold of now?

DICK   Perhaps I haven't made it clear what I mean.

RUTHERFORD *(deliberately)* I've never said a word against you or for you. And I've never heard a word against you or for you. Now! ... As for what you call your work, I don't know any more about it than a bairn, and I haven't time to learn. I should say that if you could keep the men out of the public houses and hammer a little decency into the women it might be a good thing. But I'm not an expert in your line.

DICK *(bold in his conviction)* Father – excuse me, but sometimes I think your point of view is perfectly deplorable.

RUTHERFORD   Indeed! Frankly, I don't realise the importance of my point of view or of yours either. I got my work to do in the world – for the sake o' the argument, so have you – we do it or we don't do it. But what we think about it either way, doesn't matter.

DICK *(very earnestly)*   It matters to God.

RUTHERFORD   Does it? – Now run along – I'm busy.

DICK   This is all part of your resentment – your natural resentment – at my having taken up a different line to the one you intended for me.

RUTHERFORD   Resentment – not a bit. Wear your collar-stud at the back if you like, it's all one to me. You can't make a silk purse out of a sow's ear – you were no good for my purpose, and there's an end. For the matter o' that, you might just as well never ha' been born – except that you give no trouble either way ... Where's John?

DICK   I don't know. His candle is here ... I am still absolutely convinced that I chose the better part.

RUTHERFORD   Probably. There are more ways than one of shirking life, and religion's one of them. If you want my blessing, here it is. As long as you respect my name and remember that I made a gentleman of ye, ye can go to the devil in your own way.

DICK   Then I have your consent to accept St. Jude's?

RUTHERFORD *(writing)* Aye. Just ring the bell before you go. I want my lamp.

Dick does so, depressed and disappointed. On his way to his candle he hesitates.

DICK   By the way – I'm forgetting – Mrs Henderson wants to see you.

RUTHERFORD	And who is Mrs Henderson?
DICK	William's mother.
RUTHERFORD	William? ... The chap who's been pilfering my

money? Oh, that matter's settled.

DICK	Oh! ... Yes.
RUTHERFORD	Good night. Did you ring?
DICK	Yes. I rang. Good night. *(There is a silence,*

broken by the scratching of Rutherford's pen. Dick summons up his courage and speaks again.) I'm afraid I told Mrs Henderson she might call tonight.

RUTHERFORD	Did ye now?
DICK	Yes.
RUTHERFORD	And what the devil did ye do that for, if one may

inquire?

DICK She is one of my parishioners – in my district. She came to me – asked my help.

RUTHERFORD Told you the usual yarn, I suppose. More fool you, to be taken in by it. I can't see her.

DICK We don't know that it isn't true. The boy has been led astray by bad companions to bet and gamble. It's a regular gang – George Hammond's one, Fade's another.

RUTHERFORD I know them. Two of the worst characters and the best workers we've got.

DICK However that may be, the mother's in great grief, and I promised to intercede with you to give her son another chance.

RUTHERFORD Then you'd no business to promise anything of the kind. The lad's a young blackguard. Bless my soul – look at the head he's got on him! As bad an egg as you'll find in all your parish, and that's saying a good deal.

DICK I'm afraid it is – God help them. But – *(A series of slow heavy knocks on the outer door are heard, ending with a belated single one.)* I'm afraid that *is* Mrs Henderson.

RUTHERFORD *(going on with his writing)* Aye, it sounds like her hand. Been drowning her trouble, mebbee.

DICK *(after another knock)* Well. She's here.

RUTHERFORD You'd better go and tell her to go away again.

DICK Yes. *(He makes an undecided move towards the door; stops.)* The woman ought to have a fair hearing.

RUTHERFORD *(losing patience)* Fair hearing! She's badgered Martin till he's had to turn her out, and on the top of it all you come blundering in with your talk of a fair hearing.

He gets up and swings to the door, pushing Dick aside.

RUTHERFORD   Here – let be.

DICK *(speaking with such earnestness that Rutherford stops to look at him)* Father – one moment ... Don't you think – don't you think it might be better to be friendly with her? To avoid unpleasantness? And gossip afterwards – ?

RUTHERFORD   What? God help you for a fool, Richard. One would think I'd nothing to do but fash myself about this young blackguard and speak soft to his mother. *(He goes out into the hall and is heard opening the door.)* Now, Mrs Henderson – you've come about your lad. You've had my answer.

Mrs Henderson is heard speaking apparently on the mat.

MRS HENDERSON   Oh, if you please, sir – if you could just see your way to sparin' me a minute I'd take it kindly, that I would. And I come all the way from home on me two feet – and me a poor widder woman.

She drifts imperceptibly just inside the room. She is a large and powerful woman with a draggled skirt and a shawl over her head, and she is slightly drunk. Rutherford follows her in and stands by the open door, holding the handle.

RUTHERFORD   Well, then, out with it. What ha' ye got to say?

MRS HENDERSON   It's my lad Bill as has been accused o' takin' your money –

RUTHERFORD   Ten pounds.

MRS HENDERSON   By Mr Martin, sir.

RUTHERFORD   What then?

MRS HENDERSON   And not another living soul near to say the truth of it.

RUTHERFORD   Martin's my man, Mrs Henderson. What he does, he does under my orders. Besides, Martin and your son both say he took it. They've agreed about it.

MRS HENDERSON   Aye, when he was scared out of his life he owned to it. I'm not denying he owned to it –

RUTHERFORD   Oh, that's it, is it? He wants to go back on it? Why did he give up the money?

MRS HENDERSON   He was that scared, sir, o' being sent to the gaol and losing his place and all, what wi' Mr Martin speaking that harsh to him, and all, and him a bit of a lad –

RUTHERFORD   I see. In that case I owe him ten pounds?

MRS HENDERSON   Eh?

RUTHERFORD I've took ten pounds off him, poor lad, all his honest savings mebbe. Good night, Mrs Henderson.

MRS HENDERSON Ah, Mr Rutherford, sir, don't 'ee be hard on us – don't 'ee now. We all got summat to be overlooked – every one on us when ye get down to it – and there's not a family harder working nor more respected in Grantley. Mr Richard here'll speak for us.

RUTHERFORD Speak for them, Richard.

DICK I ... I do believe they are sincerely trying to do better.

RUTHERFORD Just so – better not rake up bygones. My time's short, Mrs Henderson, and you've no business to come up to the house at this time o' night, as you know well enough.

MRS HENDERSON Aye, sir, begging your pardon. I'm sure I'd be the last to intrude on you and the family if it warn't for –

RUTHERFORD I dare say. What did Martin say to you when you intruded into the glasshouse?

MRS HENDERSON What did he say to me?

RUTHERFORD (*impatiently*) Aye.

MRS HENDERSON (*fervently*) Far be it from me to repeat what he did say. God forbid that I should dirty my mouth wi' the words that man turned on me! Before the men too, and half of 'em wi' their shirts off and me a decent woman. (*violently*) 'Hawd yer whist,' I says to 'n. 'Hawd yer whist for a shameless –'

RUTHERFORD That'll do, that'll do – that's enough. You can take what Martin said from me. The matter's ended. (*Dick makes an appealing movement.*) Five years ago your son was caught stealing coppers out o' the men's coats – men poorer than himself. Don't forget that. I knew about it well enough. I gave him another chance because he was a young 'un, and because you ought to ha' taught him better.

MRS HENDERSON Me? Taught him better! That I should ever hear the like!

RUTHERFORD I gave him another chance. He made the most of it by robbing me the first time he thought he was safe not to be caught. Every man's got a right to go to the devil in his own way, as I've just been telling Mr Richard here, and your son Bill's old enough to choose his. I don't quarrel with him for that. But lads that get their fingers in my till are no use to me. And there's an end!

DICK Father! If you talk to her like this –

RUTHERFORD It's you that's brought her to hear me – you must take the consequences.

DICK No one is wholly bad – we have no right to say the lad is past hope, to condemn him utterly.

MRS HENDERSON Thank 'ee kindly, Mr Richard, sir – it's gospel truth every word of it. My son's as good a son as ever a lone woman had, but he's the spittin' image of his father, that easily led. And now to have him go wrong and all through keeping bad company and betting on the racing – just as he might ha' laid a bit on you, sir, in your young days and won his money too, sir, along o' your being sartain sure to win.

RUTHERFORD Well, I would have done my best to get him his money. But if I'd lost he'd ha' had to take his beating and pay up like a man and no whining about it. You take an interest in running?

MRS HENDERSON (*fervently*) Aye, sir, and always has done ever since I was a bit lass. And many's the Saturday me and my old man's gone down to the ground to see you run.

RUTHERFORD You don't happen to have heard who's won the quarter-of-a-mile at Broughton, do you?

DICK   Father!

MRS HENDERSON I did hear as it was Dawson, sir, as I was passing.

RUTHERFORD Ah. Shepherd was overtrained. What time did he do – Dawson?

MRS HENDERSON I don't know, sir.

RUTHERFORD I made him a shade worse than six under at his trial. Shepherd should have been that.

DICK   Father, please! Do let us talk this matter out seriously.

RUTHERFORD Seriously? What more?

DICK   You see, it is as I said. I am sure Mrs Henderson will answer for her son's good conduct if you will consent to take him back – won't you, Mrs Henderson? Just this once. Your kindness may make all the difference, reform him altogether, who knows? He's had his lesson and I hate to preach, but – there is such a thing as repentance.

RUTHERFORD (*drily*) That's all right. You say what you think! And don't misunderstand me. I've no objection to Bill Henderson repenting, but I won't have him doing it in my Works, d'ye see? There's nothing spreads so quick as a nice soft feeling like that, and – who knows – we might have half-a-dozen other young blacklegs at the same game? Now, Mrs Henderson, go home like a sensible woman and send your lad away from Grantley. He'll soon find his feet if he's a mind to go straight. Keep him clear o' the pit towns – put him on a farm somewhere, where there aren't so many drinks going. And if I were you, (*looking at her*) why not go with him yourself?

MRS HENDERSON (*after a pause, suddenly truculent*) Me? Me leave Grantley? Me go to a place where I'm not respected and not a friend to speak for me? In Grantley I was born and in Grantley I'll live, like yourself. And beggin' your pardon, though you are the master, I'll joost take the liberty o' choosin' my own way.

RUTHERFORD   Quite right – quite right. When you've lived and had your bairns and got drunk in a place you're apt to get attached to it. I'm that way myself. But it's just as well to change your drinks once in a while. It's only a friendly word of advice I'm giving you. Take it or leave it.

MRS HENDERSON (*bridling*) And so I will take it or leave it. Much obliged to 'ee.

RUTHERFORD   And now go home, like a good woman.

MRS HENDERSON (*tossing her head with an unsteady curtsey*) And so I will, and a lot I got for my trouble – thank 'ee for nothing.

RUTHERFORD   Thank me for not prosecuting your son, as I might ha' done.

MRS HENDERSON (*working herself up*) Prosecute! Prosecute my son! And why didn't ye do it? Ye darena' – that's why. You're feared o' folks talkin' – o' things said i' the court. And ye took and hided him and him a bit of a lad, and not a decent woman in Grantley but's crying shame on ye!

RUTHERFORD (*good-humouredly*) Now, Richard, this is where you come in. You brought her here.

MRS HENDERSON (*very shrill*) You let him off easy, did you? You give him another chance, did you? My lad could ha' had you up for assault – that's what he'd ha' done if he'd had a mind, and quite right too. It's him that's let you off, mind that. And you may thank your devil's luck you're not up afore the magistrate this next Assizes that ever is, and printed in the paper for all the countryside to mock at.

RUTHERFORD   Go on, Richard. She's your parishioner. Turn her out.

MRS HENDERSON   Him turn me out? A bit of a preaching bairn no stronger nor a linty – him with his good noos and his sojers-o'-Christ-arise! Whee was it up and ran away from old Lizzie Winter like a dawg wi' a kettle tied to his tail?

RUTHERFORD (*quietly without turning*) We'll have all your secrets in a minute. Are you going, Mrs Henderson?

MRS HENDERSON   I'll go when it pleases me, and not afore!

He gets up and moves towards her in a threatening manner.

MRS HENDERSON *(retreating)* Lay hands on me! Lay hands on a
helpless woman! I'll larn ye! I'll larn ye to come on me wi' yer high
ways. Folks shall hear tell on it, that they shall, and a bit more besides.
I'll larn ye, sure as I'm a living creature ... I'll set the police on ye, sure
as I'm a living woman ...

RUTHERFORD *(to Dick, contemptuously)* Hark to that – hark to it.

MRS HENDERSON   You think yourself so grand wi' your big hoose,
and your high ways. And your grandfather a potman like my own. You
wi' your son that's the laughing-stock o' the parish, and your daughter
that goes wi' a working man ahint your back! And so good night to 'ee.

*The outer door bangs violently. There is a pause. Dick speaks in a voice
scarcely audible.*

DICK   What was that? ... She said something – about
Janet.

RUTHERFORD *(impatiently)* Good God, man – don't stand staring
there as if the house had fallen.

DICK *(shaking)*   I told you to be careful– I warned you – I knew
how it would be.

RUTHERFORD   Warned me! You're fool enough to listen to what
a drunken drab like that says!

DICK   She's not the only one –

RUTHERFORD *(looking at him)* What d'ye mean? What's that?

DICK   People are talking. I've – heard things ... It isn't
true – it can't be – it's too dreadful.

RUTHERFORD   Heard things – what ha' ye heard?

DICK   It isn't true.

RUTHERFORD   Out with it.

DICK   Lizzie Winter that time – called out something. I
took no notice, of course ... Three nights ago as I was coming home –
past a public-house – the men were talking. I heard something then.

RUTHERFORD   What was it you heard?

DICK   There was his name, and Janet's. Then one of
them – George Hammond, I think it was – said something about having
seen him on the road to the Tarn late one evening with a woman with a
shawl over her head – Martin!

RUTHERFORD   Martin!

DICK *(trying to reassure himself)* It's extremely unlikely that there is any
truth in it at all. Why, he's been about ever since we were children.
A servant, really. No one's ever thought of the possibility of such a
thing. They will gossip, and one thing leads to another. It's easy to put

two and two together and make five of them. That's all it is, we'll find. Why, even I can recall things I barely noticed at the time – things that might point to its being true – if it weren't so utterly impossible.

RUTHERFORD *(hoarsely)* Three nights gone. In this very room –

DICK What? *(running on again)* They've seen some one like Janet, and started the talk. It would be enough.

RUTHERFORD *(speaking to himself)* Under my roof –

DICK After dark on the road with a shawl – all women would look exactly alike ... It's a pity he's taken the Tarn Cottage.

RUTHERFORD *(listening again)* Eh?

DICK I mean it's a pity it's happened just now.

RUTHERFORD A good mile from the works.

DICK You can't see it from the village.

RUTHERFORD A good mile to walk, morn and night.

DICK No one goes there.

RUTHERFORD A lone place – a secret, he says to himself. Martin ...

He stands by the table, his shoulders stooped, his face suddenly old. Dick makes an involuntary movement towards him.

DICK Father! Don't take it like that, for heaven's sake – don't look so broken.

RUTHERFORD Who's broken ... *(He makes a sign to Dick not to come near.)* Him to go against me. You're only a lad – you don't know. You don't know.

John comes into the room, evidently on his way to bed.

JOHN *(idly)* Hullo! *(stops short, looking from one to the other)* What's the matter?

RUTHERFORD *(turning on him)* And what the devil do *you* want?

JOHN Want? – nothing ... I thought you were talking about me, that's all.

RUTHERFORD About you, damn you – go to bed, the pair o' ye.

DICK Father –

RUTHERFORD Go to bed. There's men's work to be done here – you're best out o' the way. *(He goes to his desk and speaks down the tube.)* Hulloh there – Hulloh!

DICK Wouldn't it be better to wait to talk things over? Here's John – you may be able to settle something – come to some arrangement.

RUTHERFORD   Who's that? Gray – has Martin gone home?
Martin! Tell him to come across at once – I want him. Aye – to the house
– where else? Have you got it? Tell him at once.

JOHN *(suspicious)*   I rather want a word with Martin myself. I think
I'll stay.

RUTHERFORD   You'll do as you're bid.

JOHN   What do you want Martin for at this time of night?

RUTHERFORD   That's my business.

JOHN   About my metal –

RUTHERFORD   Your metal! What the devil's your metal got to do
with it? *(breaks off)*

JOHN *(excited)*   Martin's got it. You know that. You're sending for
him. Martin's honest – he won't tell you.

DICK   Here's Janet.

*Janet has come in in answer to the bell and stands by the door sullen and
indifferent, waiting for orders.*

JANET   Susan's gone to bed. *(As the silence continues,
she looks round.)* The bell rang.

DICK *(looking at Rutherford)* Some time ago. The lamp – father wanted
his lamp.

She goes out.

JOHN *(rapidly)*   It's no use going on like this, settling nothing
either way. Sooner or later we've got to come to an understanding …
(Dick makes a movement to stop him.) Oh, shut up, Dick!

RUTHERFORD   I want to have it clear. You heard what I said,
three days past?

JOHN   Yes, of course.

RUTHERFORD   You still ask your price?

JOHN   I told you – the thing's mine – I made it.

RUTHERFORD *(to John)* You've looked at it – fair and honest.

DICK   Oh, what is the use of talking like this now?
Father! You surely must see – under the circumstances – it isn't right –
it isn't decent.

JOHN   It's perfectly fair and just, what I ask. It benefits
us both, the way I want it. You've made your bit. Rutherford's has served
its purpose – and it's coming to an end – only you don't see it, Guv'nor.
Oh, I know you're fond of the old place and all that – it's only natural-
but you can't live forever – and I'm all right – if I get my price …

RUTHERFORD   So much down for yourself – and the devil take
Rutherford's.

JOHN	You put it that way –
RUTHERFORD	Yes or no?
JOHN	Well – yes.

A knock is heard at the outer door.

DICK	That's Martin, Father –
JOHN	I'll stay and see him – I may as well.
RUTHERFORD	Tomorrow – tomorrow I'll settle wi' ye.

John looks at him in amazement. Dick makes a sign to him to come away; after a moment he does so.

JOHN (*turning as he reaches the door*) Thanks, Guv'nor – I thought you'd come to see things my way.

They go out.

RUTHERFORD   Come in.

Martin comes in, cleaning his boots carefully on the mat – shuts the door after him and stands cap in hand. Rutherford sits sunk in his chair, his hands gripping the arms.

MARTIN   I came up as soon as I could get away. (*pause*)

RUTHERFORD (*as if his lips were stiff*) You've stayed late.

MARTIN   One o' the pots in Number Three Furnace ran down, and I had to stay and see her under way.

RUTHERFORD   Sit down ... Help yourself.

MARTIN   Thank 'ee, sir. (*He comes to the table and pours out some whisky, then sits with his glass resting on his knee.*) Winter's setting in early.

RUTHERFORD   Aye –

MARTIN   There's a heavy frost. The ground was hardening as I came along ... They do say as Rayner's'll be working again afore the week's out.

RUTHERFORD   Given in – the men?

MARTIN   Ay – the bad weather'll have helped it. Given a fine spell the men 'ud ha' hung on a while longer – but the cold makes 'em think o' the winter – turns the women and bairns agin them.

RUTHERFORD   Ah!

MARTIN   I thought you'd like to hear the coal 'ud be coming in all right, so I just went over to have a word wi' White the Agent this forenoon. (*He drinks, then as the silence continues, looks intently at Rutherford.*) You sent for me?

Janet comes in carrying a reading-lamp. She halts for a moment on seeing Martin. He gets up awkwardly.

MARTIN *(touching his forelock)* Evenin'.
JANET　　　　　　　Good evening.

She sets the lamp on the desk. Rutherford remains in the same position till she goes out, closing the door. There is a moment's silence, then Martin straightens himself, and they look at each other.

MARTIN *(hoarsely)*　You're wanting summat wi' me?
RUTHERFORD　　　　I want the receipt of Mr John's metal.
MARTIN *(between amazement and relief)* Eh?
RUTHERFORD　　　　You've got it.
MARTIN　　　　　　Ay –
RUTHERFORD　　　　Then give it me.
MARTIN　　　　　　I cannot do that, sir.
RUTHERFORD　　　　What d'ye mean?
MARTIN　　　　　　It's Mr John's own – what belongs to him – I
canna do it.
RUTHERFORD　　　　On your high horse, eh, Martin? You can't do a
dirty trick – *you* can't, eh?
MARTIN　　　　　　A dirty trick. Ye'll never be asking it of me – you
never will –
RUTHERFORD　　　　I am asking it of ye. We've worked together five
and twenty years, master and man. You know me. You know what there
is'll stop me when I once make up my mind. I'm going to have this
metal, d'ye understand. Whether Mr John gives it me or I take it, I'm
going to have it.
MARTIN　　　　　　It's Mr John's own; if it's ever yourn, he must
give it to ye himself. It's not for me to do it. He's found it, and it's his to
do what he likes wi'. For me to go behind his back – I canna do it.

They look at each other then Rutherford gets out of his chair and begins to pace up and down with his hands behind him. He speaks deliberately, with clumsy gestures and an air of driving straight to a goal.

RUTHERFORD　　　　Sit down ... Look how we stand. We've seven
years' losing behind us, slow and sure. We've got the Bank that's poking
its nose into this and that, putting a stop to everything that might put
us on our legs again – because o' the risk ... Rutherford's is going down
– down – I got to pull her up somehow. There's one way out. If I can
show the directors in plain working that I can cover the losses on the
first year and make a profit on the second, I've got 'em for good and all.

MARTIN   That's so – and Mr John'll see it, and ye'll come
to terms –

RUTHERFORD   Mr John's a fool. My son's a fool – I don't say it
in anger. He's a fool because his mother made him one, bringing him up
secret wi' books o' poetry and such-like trash – and when he'd grown a
man and the time was come for me to take notice of him, he's turned
agin me –

MARTIN   He'll come roond – he's but a bit lad yet –

RUTHERFORD   Turned agin me – agin me and all I done for him
– all I worked to build up. He thinks it mighty clever to go working
behind my back – the minute he gets the chance he's up on the hearth-
rug dictating his terms to me. He knows well enough I've counted on his
coming after me. He's all I got since Richard went his ways – he's got
me there ... He wants his price, he says – his price for mucking around
with a bit of a muffle furnace in his play-hours – that's what it comes to.

MARTIN   Ay – but he's happened on a thing worth a bit.

RUTHERFORD   Luck! Luck! What's he done for it? How long has
he worked for it – tell me that – an hour here and a bit there – and he's
got it! I've slaved my life long, and what have I got for it? Toil and weariness. That's what I got – bad luck on bad luck battering on me – seven
years of it. And the worst bit I've had yet is that when it turns it's put
into my son's hands to give me or not, if you please, as if he was a lord.

MARTIN   He'll come roond – lads has their notions – we all
want to have things for ourselves when we're young, all on us –

RUTHERFORD   Want – want – lad's talk! What business has he
to want when there's Rutherford's' going to the dogs?

MARTIN   That canna be, it canna – he'll have to see
different.

RUTHERFORD   When it's too late. Look here, Martin, we can't go
on – you know that as well as I do – leastways you've suspected it. Ten
years more as things are'll see us out. Done with! Mr. John's made this
metal – a thing, I take your word for it, that's worth a fortune. And
we're going to sit by and watch him fooling it away – selling it for a
song to Miles or Jarvis, that we could break tomorrow if we had half a
chance. And they'll make on it, make on it – while Rutherfords'll grub
on as we've been grubbing for the last seven years. I'm speaking plain
now – I'm saying what I wouldn't say to another living man. We can't
go on. You've been with me through it all. You've seen me do it. You've
seen the drag and the struggle of it – the days when I've nigh thrown up
the sponge for very weariness – the bit o' brightness that made me go
on – the times when I've stood up to the Board, sick in the heart of me,

with nothing but my will to turn 'em this way or that. And at the end of it – I come up against this – a bit o' foolishness – just foolishness – and all that I done'll break on that – just that.

MARTIN   Nay – nay –

RUTHERFORD   I'm getting old, they say – old – there's new ways in the trade, they say. And in their hearts they see me out of it – out o' the place I built afore they learnt their letters, many of 'em –

MARTIN   That'll never be.

RUTHERFORD   Why not – when you've got but to put your hand in your pocket to save the place and you don't do it. You're with them – you're with the money-grubbing little souls that can't see beyond the next shilling they put in their pockets, that's content to wring the old place dry, then leave it to the rats – you're with a half-broke puppy like Mr John that wants to grab his bit for himself and clear out. Twenty-five years ... and you go snivelling about what Mr John thinks of ye – what's right for you to do. Everybody for himself – his pocket or his soul, it's all one. And Rutherford's loses her chance through the lot o' ye. Blind fools!

MARTIN   You blame me – you put me i' the wrong. It's like as if I'd have to watch the old place going down year by year, and have it on my mind that I might ha' saved her. But Mr John's got his rights.

RUTHERFORD   You think I'm getting this metal for myself against Mr John?

MARTIN   I'm loath to say it.

RUTHERFORD   Answer me –

MARTIN   Mr John'll see it that way.

RUTHERFORD   Stealing like, out o' his pocket into mine. When men steal, Martin, they do it to gain something. If I steal this, what'll I gain by it? If I make money, what'll I buy with it? Pleasure mebbee? Children to come after me – glad o' what I done? Tell me anything in the wide world that'd bring me joy, and I'll swear to you never to touch it.

MARTIN   If you think what you're saying, it's a weary life you got to face.

RUTHERFORD   If you give it to me, what'll you gain by it? Not a farthing shall you ever have from me – no more than I get myself.

MARTIN   And what'll Mr John get for it?

RUTHERFORD   Rutherford's – when I'm gone. *(after a silence)* He'll thank you in ten years – he'll come to laugh at himself – him and his price. He'll see the Big Thing one day mebbee, like what I've done. He'll see that it was no more his to keep than 'twas yours to give nor mine to take ... It's Rutherford's ... Will you give it to me?

MARTIN *(facing him)* If I thought that we'd make a farthing out of it, either on us –

RUTHERFORD   Will ye give it me –

Martin stands looking at him, then slowly begins to feel in his pockets.

RUTHERFORD   Got it – on you?

MARTIN *(taking out a pocket-book)* He'll never forgi' me, Mr John won't – never i' this world ... It should be somewheres. He'll turn agin me – it'll be as if I stole it.

RUTHERFORD   Got it?

MARTIN   Nay, I mun' ha' left it up hame. Ay, I call to mind now – I locked it away to keep it safe.

RUTHERFORD   Can ye no' remember it? Think, man – think!

MARTIN   Nay, I canna be sure. I canna call the quantities to mind.

RUTHERFORD *(violently)* Think – think – you must know!

MARTIN *(wonderingly)* I can give it 'ee first thing i' the morning.

RUTHERFORD   I want it tonight ... No, no – leave it – you might get it wrong – better make sure – bring it up in the morning. Good night to 'ee – good night. And remember – I take your word to bring it – no going back, mind ye –

MARTIN   Nay, nay. *(turning to go)* I doubt if Mr John'll ever see it in the way you do. If you could mebbee explain a bit when he hears tell of it – put in a word for me, belike –

RUTHERFORD   I'm to bed.

MARTIN   I take shame to be doing it now.

RUTHERFORD   Off wi' ye – off wi' ye – wi' your conscience so delicate and tender. Keep your hands clean, or don't let anyone see them dirty – it'll do as well.

MARTIN   He worked it out along o' me. Every time it changed he come running to show me like a bairn wi' a new toy.

RUTHERFORD   It's for Rutherford's.

MARTIN   Aye, for Rutherford's – Good night, sir.

He goes out. After a pause, Janet comes in to put things straight for the night. She goes into the hall and is heard putting the chain on the outer door – comes back, locking the inner door – then takes the whisky decanter from the tray and locks it in the sideboard, laying the key on the desk. Rutherford stands on the hearth-rug. As she takes up the tray he speaks.

RUTHERFORD   How long has this been going on atween you and Martin?

She puts the tray down and stands staring at him with a white face.

JANET	How long?
RUTHERFORD	Answer me.
JANET	September – about when Mary and Tony came.

(There is a long silence. When it becomes unbearable she speaks again.) What are you going to do? *(He makes no answer.)* You must tell me what you're going to do?

RUTHERFORD	Keep my hands off ye.
JANET	You've had him here.
RUTHERFORD	That's my business.

JANET *(speaking in a low voice as if she were repeating a lesson)* It wasn't his fault. It was me. He didn't come after me. I went after him.

RUTHERFORD	Feel proud o' yourself?
JANET	You can't punish him for what isn't his fault. If

you've got to punish anyone, it's me …

RUTHERFORD	How far's it gone?

JANET *(after a pause)*   Right at first. I made up my mind that if you ever found out, I'd go right away, to put things straight. *(She goes on presently in the same toneless voice.)* He wanted to tell you at the first. But I knew it would be no use. And once we'd spoken – every time was just a little more. So we let it slide … It was I said not to tell you.

RUTHERFORD	Martin … that I trusted as I trust myself.
JANET	I'll give him up.
RUTHERFORD	You can't give him back to me. He was a straight

man. What's the good of him now? You've dragged the man's heart out of him with your damned woman's ways.

She looks at him.

JANET	You haven't turned him away – you couldn't do that!
RUTHERFORD	That's my business.
JANET	You couldn't do that – not Martin …
RUTHERFORD	Leave it – leave it … Martin's my servant, that I

pay wages to. I made a name for my children – a name respected in all the countryside – and you go with a working-man. Tomorrow you leave my house. D'ye understand. I'll have no light ways under my roof. No one shall say I winked at it. You can bide the night. Tomorrow when I come in, I'm to find ye gone … Your name shan't be spoke in my house … Never again.

JANET   Yes. *(stands looking down at the table, then slowly moves to go, her feet dragging – stops for a moment and says in a final tone, almost with a sigh of relief)* Then there'll be no need for anybody to know it was Martin –

RUTHERFORD	No need to know. Lord, you drive me crazy! With all Grantley telling the story – my name in every public house.
JANET	When I'm gone. *(looking up)* What did you say?
RUTHERFORD	It's all over the place by now. Richard's heard it – your own brother ... You've been running out o' night, I suppose. Somebody's seen.
JANET	What's Dick heard?
RUTHERFORD	What men say about women like you. They got a word.
JANET	The men ... O God!
RUTHERFORD	Aye – you say that now the thing's done – you'll whine and cry out now you done your worst agin me.
JANET	Let me be.
RUTHERFORD	You're going to put things straight, are ye – you're going to walk out comfortable wi' your head up and your fine talk.
JANET	I'm ready to stand by it.
RUTHERFORD	It's not you that's got to stand by it – it's me! What ha' you got to lose? Yourself, if you've a mind to. That's all. It's me that's to be the laughing-stock – the Master whose daughter goes wi' a working-man like any Jenny i' the place –
JANET	Oh! You stand there! *To* drive me mad –
RUTHERFORD	That'll do – that'll do. I've heard enough. You've confessed, and there's an end.
JANET	Confessed? As if I'd stolen something. *(brokenly)* You put it all on to me, every bit o' the wrong.
RUTHERFORD	Ah, you'll set to and throw the blame on Martin now. I thought we'd come to it.
JANET	No, no. I've taken that. But ... you make no excuse ... You think of this that I've done separate from all the rest – from all the years I done as you bid me, lived as you bid me.
RUTHERFORD	What's that to do wi' it? I'm your father! I work for 'ee ... I give 'ee food and clothes for your back! I got a right to be obeyed – I got a right to have my children live respectable in the station where I put them. You gone wrong. That's what you done. And you try to bring it up against me because I set you up i' the world. Go to bed!
JANET	Oh, you've no pity ... *(makes a movement to go, then turns again as if for a moment)* I was thirty-six. Gone sour. Nobody'd ever come after me. Not even when I was young. You took care o' that. Half of my life was gone, well-nigh all of it that mattered ... What have I had of it, afore I go back to the dark? What have I had of it? Tell me that. Tell me!

RUTHERFORD Where's the man as 'ud want you wi' your sulky ways?

JANET I've sat and sewed – gone for a walk – seen to the meals – every day – every day ... That's what you've given me to be my life – just that!

RUTHERFORD Talk, talk, talk! Fine words to cover up the shame and disgrace you brought on me –

JANET On you?

RUTHERFORD Where'd you ha' been if I hadn't set you up?

JANET Down in the village – in amongst it, with the other women – in a cottage – happy mebbee.

RUTHERFORD *(angrily)* I brought you up for a lady as idle as you please – you might ha' sat wi' your hands afore you from morn till night if ye'd had a mind to.

JANET Me a lady? What do ladies think about, sitting the day long with their hands before them? What have they in their idle hearts?

RUTHERFORD What more did you want, in God's name?

JANET Oh, what more! The women down there know what I wanted ... with their bairns wrapped in their shawls and their men to come home at night time. I've envied them – envied them their pain, their poorness – the very times they hadn't bread. Theirs isn't the dead empty house, the blank o' the moors; they got something to fight, something to be feared of. They got life, those women we send cans o' soup to out o' pity when their bairns are born. Me a lady! With work for a man in my hands, passion for a man in my heart! I'm common – common.

RUTHERFORD It's a lie! I've risen up. You can't go back on it – my children can't go back.

JANET Who's risen – which of us?

RUTHERFORD You say that because you've shamed yourself, and you're jealous o' them that keep decent like gentlefolk –

JANET Dick – that everyone laughs at? John – with his manners?

RUTHERFORD Whisht wi' your wicked tongue!

JANET Who's Mary? A little common work-girl – no real gentleman would ha' looked at ... You think you've made us different by keeping from the people here. We're just the same as they are! Ask the men that work for you – ask their wives that curtsey to us in the road. Do you think they don't know the difference? We're just the same as they are – common, every one of us. It's in our blood, in our hands and faces; and when we marry, we marry common –

RUTHERFORD	Marry! Common or not, nobody's married you
that I can see –	
JANET	Leave that – don't you say it!
RUTHERFORD	It's the truth, more shame to 'ee.

JANET *(passionately)*   Martin loves me honest. Don't you come near! Don't you touch that! ... You think I'm sorry you've found out – you think you've done for me when you use shameful words on me and turn me out o' your house. You've let me out o' gaol! Whatever happens to me now, I shan't go on living as I lived here. Whatever Martin's done, he's taken me from you. You've ruined my life, you with your getting on. I've loved in wretchedness, all the joy I ever had made wicked by the fear o' you ... *(wildly)* Who are you? Who are you? A man – a man that's taken power to himself, power to gather people to him and use them as he wills – a man that'd take the blood of life itself and put it into the Works – into Rutherford's. And what ha' you got by it – what? You've got Dick, that you've bullied till he's a fool – John, that's waiting for the time when he can sell what you've done – and you got me – me to take your boots off at night – to well-nigh wish you dead when I had to touch you ... Now! ... Now you know!

ACT THREE

It is about eleven o' clock on the following morning. Janet is sitting at the table with a shawl about her shoulders talking in low tones to Mary, who is opposite.

JANET *(after a pause)*	You mean that you guessed?
MARY	Yes.
JANET	You knew all the time, and you didn't tell? Not
even John?	
MARY	Why should I tell him?
JANET	I would ha' told Martin if it had been you.
MARY	Not John.
JANET	It was good of you. You've always been better to
me than I've been to you.	
MARY	What are you going to do?
JANET	He says I'm to go. He's to come in and find me
gone, and no one's to speak of me any more. Not John, nor Dick,	
nor Aunt Ann – I'm never to set foot in this room again. Never to lock	
up and give him the keys last thing. Never to sit the long afternoon	

through in the window, till the chimneys are bright in the dark. I've done what women are shamed for doing – and all the night I've barely slept for the hope in my heart.

MARY   Hope?

JANET   Of things coming. I had a dream – a dream that I was in a place wi' flowers, in the summer time, white and thick like they never grow on the moor – but it was the moor – a place near Martin's cottage. And I dreamt that he came to me with the look he had when I was a little lass, with his head up and the lie gone out of his eyes. All the time I knew I was on my bed in my room here – but it was like as if sweetness poured into me, spreading and covering me like the water in the tarn when the rains are heavy in the fells.

MARY   Is Mr Rutherford very angry?

JANET   He won't never hear my name again. Oh, last night I said things to him, when he blamed me so – things he can't never forget. I was wild – mad with the bitterness of it. He made it all ugly with the things he said. I told him what I never looked to tell him, though I'd had it in my heart all these years. All the time I was speaking I was dead with shame that he should know, and I had to go on. But afterwards – it was as if I'd slipped a burden, and I was glad he knew, glad that Dick heard it in the street, glad that he sneaked of me behind my back – glad! For, when I'd got over the terror of it, it came to me that this was what we'd been making for ever since you came without knowing it, that we were to win through to happiness after all, Martin and I, and everything come right. Because I've doubted. Men's lives are different to ours. And sometimes, when we've stolen together, and afterwards I've seen his face and the sadness of it, I've wondered what I had to give him that could count against what he'd lost.

MARY   But that's done with now.

JANET   Yes! That's why I dreamt of him so last night. It was as if all that was best in me was in that dream – what I was as a bairn, and what I'm going to be. He couldn't help but love me. It was a message – I couldn't have thought of it by myself. It's something that's come to me, here. *(putting her hands on her breast)* Part of me.

Mary looks at her with a new understanding. After a pause she speaks again, very gently.

MARY   Where are you going when Martin comes for you?

JANET   I don't know yet. He'll say what to do.

MARY   Have you got your things ready?

JANET (*as if she scarcely heard*) Yes.

MARY   I could see to them for you.

JANET   They're all ready. I put them together early in the
box mother had. (*She breaks off, listening.*)

MARY   Janet, if ever the time should be when you want
help – and it does happen sometimes even to people who are very
happy – remember that I'll come when you ask me – always.

JANET   He's coming now! (*She sits listening, her eyes
bright. Mary goes out quietly, closing the door.*)

JANET (*very tenderly*) Martin! (*He stands in the doorway, his cap in his
hands, his head bent. He looks spent, broken, and at the sight of him
the hope dies slowly out of her face.*)

MARTIN   Is Mr John about?

JANET   I don't know.

MARTIN   I mun see 'n. I got summat to say to 'n.

JANET   He's down at the Works mebbee –

MARTIN   I canna seek him there – I got summat to say to 'n.

JANET ,   You could give a message.

MARTIN   Nay. It's summat that's got to be said to his face
– like a man.

JANET   Have you nothing to say to me, Martin – to my
face like a man?

MARTIN   What should there be to say betwixt you and me?
It's all said long since.

JANET   He's turned you away?

He raises his eyes and looks at her for the first time.

MARTIN   Aye. You've said it. What I've been trying to tell
myself these three months past. Turned away I am, sure enough.
Twenty-five year. And in a minute it's broke. Wi' two words.

JANET   He'll call you back. He can't do without you,
Martin. He's done it in anger like he was last night. He'll call you back.

MARTIN   He never calls no one back. He's a just man, and
he's in the right of it. Anger – there's no anger in a face that's twisting
like a bairn's – white as if it was drained o' the blood. There's no anger
in a man that stands still where he is, when he might ha' struck and
killed and still been i' the right.

Janet gets up slowly and goes to the fire.

JANET   Come and get warm by the fire. It's a bitter cold
morning. Come and get warm.

He moves slowly across and sits on the settle. She kneels beside him, takes his hands and begins to rub them.

JANET *(as if he were a child)* Your hands are as cold, as cold – like frozen. It's all fresh and new to you now, my dear, the surprise of it. It'll pass – and by-and-by you'll forget it – be glad, mebbee. Did you get your breakfast?

MARTIN   Aye.

JANET   What have you been doing – since?

MARTIN   Walking – walking. Upon the fell I been – trying to get it clear –

JANET   On the fell, in such weather! That's why you're so white and weary. You should have come to me, my honey – you should ha' come straight to me. I would ha' helped you, my dear – out of my love for 'ee.

MARTIN   There's no help.

JANET   You say that now because your heart's cold with the trouble. But it'll warm again – it'll warm again. I'll warm it out of my own heart, Martin – my heart that can't be made cold, not if he killed me. Why, last night he was just the same with me as he's been with you. I know it all – there's nothing you feel that I don't know. We'll face it together, you and me, equal – and by-and-by it'll be different. What we done was for love – people give up everything for love, Martin; every day they say there's someone in the world that does it. Don't 'ee take on so – don't 'ee.

MARTIN *(brokenly)*   I'd rather ha' died than he turn me away. I'd ha' lost everything in the world to know that I was true to 'n, like I was till you looked at me wi' the love in your face.

JANET   Everything in the world ... I gave you joy – joy for the toil he gave you, softness for his hardness.

MARTIN *(without bitterness)* Aye, you were ready. And you gave the bitter with the sweet. Every time there was him to face, wi' a heart like lead.

JANET   It was a power – a power that came, stronger than us both.

MARTIN   You give me the word.

JANET   You took away my strength. *(There is a silence. He sits looking dully at the fire.)* Anyone might think me light. It isn't true. I never had anyone but you, never. All my life I've been alone. When I was a little lass I wasn't allowed to play with the other bairns, and I used to make signs to tell them I wanted to. You'd never have known I loved you if I hadn't given you the word – and all our happiness, all that's been between us, we'd never have had it –

gone through our lives seeing each other, speaking words that didn't matter, and grown old and never known what was sleeping in our hearts under the dullness. I wasn't light. It was only that I couldn't be shamed for you.

MARTIN Nay, nay, it was a great love ye gave me – you in your grand hoose wi' your delicate ways. But it's broke me.

JANET But – it's just the same with us. Just the same as ever it was.

MARTIN Aye. But there's no mending, wi' the likes o' him.

JANET What's there to mend? What's there to mend except what's bound you like a slave all the years? You're *free* – free for the first time since you were a lad mebbee – to make a fresh start.

MARTIN A fresh start? Wi' treachery and a lyin' tongue behind me?

JANET With our love that nothing can break. Oh, my dear, I'll help 'ee. Morning, noon, and night I'll work for 'ee, comfort 'ee. We'll go away from it all, you and me together. We'll go to the south, where no one's heard tell of Rutherford's or any of us. I'll love 'ee so. I'll blind your eyes wi' love so that you can't look back.

MARTIN (*looking up*) Aye. There's that.

JANET We'll begin again. We'll be happy – happy. You and me, free in the world! All the time that's been'll be just like a dream that's past, a waiting time afore we found each other – the long winter afore the flowers come out white and thick on the moors-

MARTIN He'll be lookin' to me to right ye. He'll be lookin' for that.

JANET To right me?

MARTIN Whatever's been, they munna say his daughter wasn't made an honest woman of. He'll be lookin' for that.

There is a silence. She draws back slowly, dropping her hands.

JANET What's he to do with it?

He looks at her, not understanding.

JANET Father – what's he to do with it?

MARTIN It's for him to say – the Master.

JANET Master!

MARTIN What's come to ye, lass?

JANET It's time you left off doing things because of him. You're a free man. He's not your master any more.

MARTIN What's wrong wi' ye?

JANET   You'll right me because of him. You'll make an
honest woman of me because he's looking for it. He can't make you do
as he bids you now. He's turned you away. He's not your master any
more. He's turned you away.

MARTIN   Whisht – whisht. *(He sinks his head in his
hands.)* Nay, but it's true. I'll never do his work again. But I done it too
long to change – too long.

JANET   He's done with you – that's how much he cares. I
wouldn't ha' let you go, not if you'd wronged me.

MARTIN   Twenty-five years ago he took me from nothing.
Set me where I could work my way up – woke the lad's love in me till I
would ha' died for him – willing. It's too long to change.

JANET *(passionately)*   No – no.

MARTIN   I'll never do his work no more; but it's like as if
he'd be my master just the same – till I die –

JANET   No, no, not that! You mustn't think like that! You
think he's great because you've seen him at the Works with the men –
everybody doing as he bids them. He isn't great – he's hard and cruel –
cruel as death.

MARTIN   What's took you to talk so wild?

JANET *(holding him)*   Listen, Martin. Listen to me. You've worked all
your life for him, ever since you were a little lad. Early and late you've
been at the Works – working – working for him.

MARTIN   Gladly!

JANET   Now and then he gie you a kind word – when you
were wearied out mebbe – and your thoughts might ha' turned to what
other men's lives were, wi' time for rest and pleasure. You didn't see
through him, you wi' your big heart, Martin. You were too near to see,
like I was till Mary came. You worked gladly, mebbe – but all the time
your life was going into Rutherford's – your manhood into the place he's
built. He's had you, Martin – like he's had me, and all of us. We used to
say he was hard and ill-tempered. Bad to do with in the house – we fell
silent when he came in – we couldn't see for the little things – we
couldn't see the years passing because of the days. And all the time it was
our lives he was taking bit by bit – our lives that we'll never get back.

MARTIN   What's got ye to talk so wild?

He moves from her as she talks and clings to him.

JANET   Now's our chance at last! He's turned us both
away, me as well as you. We two he's sent out into the world together.
Free. He's done it himself, of his own will. It's ours to take, Martin –

our happiness. We'll get it in spite of him. He'd kill it if he could.

MARTIN   Whisht, whisht! You talk wild!

JANET   Kill it, kill it! He's gone nigh to it as it is. *(as he makes a movement to rise)* Martin, Martin, I love 'ee. I'm old – with the lines on my face – but it's him that's made me so. I'm bitter-tongued and sharp – it's him that's killed the sweetness in me, starved it till it died. He's taken what should have been yours to have your joy of. Stolen it – remember that – and say he's in the right! Say it when you wish me young and bonny. Say it as I shall when I look in your face for the love that can't wake for me.

MARTIN   Bide still! Bide still!

JANET   I wouldn't ha' turned against you, not if you'd nigh killed me – and you set his love up against mine! Martin!

He gets up, not roughly, but very wearily, and moves away from her.

MARTIN   It bain't the time, it bain't the time. I been a bad servant. Faithless. We can twist words like we done all along to make it seem different, but there it stands. Leave him, when you talk to me. Leave him ... Mebbee he's had his mind full of a big work when you've took a spite at him.

JANET   Ah!

MARTIN   Womenfolk has their fancies, and mebbee they don't know the harshness that's in the heart of every man that fights his way i' the world when he comes into the four walls of his bit hoose of a night and sees the littleness of it. *(standing by the table)* I'm a plain man with no book larning, and mebbee I don't see far. But I've watched the Master year in year out, and I never seed him do a thing, nor say a thing, that he warn't in the right of. And there's not a man among them that can say different. *(taking up his cap)* I'll be seekin' Mr John.

JANET *(speaks in a dull, toneless voice, kneeling where he left her)* He says I have to be gone by the time he comes in. Where am I to go to?

He turns to look at her with a puzzled face.

MARTIN   Aye. There's that.

JANET   Where am I to go?

MARTIN   It would be best to go a bit away – where ye wouldna' be seen for a while.

JANET   Where's a place – far enough?

MARTIN   There's Horkesley – up the line. Or Hillgarth yonder. He's not likely to be knawed thereaboots.

JANET   I haven't any money.

Martin slowly counts out some coins on the table.

MARTIN   It'll be a hard life for you, and you not used to it.
Work early and late – wi' a bairn mebbe. Bitter cold i' the winter
mornings wi' the fire to light and the breakfast to get, and you not used
to it; we mun just bide it, the pair on us. Make the best of it. I've saved
two hundred pounds. There'll be summat to get along whilst I look for a
job. Afterwards we mun just bide it.

There is a silence.

JANET (*without bitterness*) Take up your money.
MARTIN (*puzzled*)   It's for you, lass.
JANET   Take up your money. I'll have no need of it.

After a moment he picks it up and returns it to his pocket.

JANET (*still kneeling*) After all, you'd give the world to ha' been true to
him – you'd give me, that you said was the world. He'd have you back if
it wasn't for me. He needs you for the Works. If I was out of it there'd
be no more reason – you'd go back, and people would think it all a
mistake about you and me. Gossip. After a bit he'd forget and be the
same. Because he needs you for the Works. Men forgive men easy
where it's a woman, they say, and you could blame me, the pair of you.
Me that gave you the word.

Mary comes in hurriedly.

MARY   John's coming. He's coming across from the
Works.

*Martin turns to face the door. Janet does not move. John comes in excited
and nervous.*

JOHN (*awkwardly*)   Hullo! (*He looks at Janet and speaks to Martin.*)
What are you here for?
MARTIN   Mr John – I summat to say to you – summat I
must say afore I go.
JOHN   You'd better keep quiet, I should think. Oh, I
know! I've been with the Guv'nor, and he's told me plain enough. You'd
better keep quiet.
MARY   John, you must listen.
JOHN   I tell you I know! The less we talk about it the
better; I should think you would see that – the whole beastly,
disreputable business. I can't stay – I can't talk calmly, if you can – I'm
better out of it. (*He makes for the door. Martin stops him.*)

MARTIN   Mr John ... You been wi' the Master. What was it he told you – plain enough?

JOHN *(significantly)*   What was it!

MARTIN   Did he tell you he'd got your metal?

John looks at him.

JOHN   Are you mad?

MARTIN   I've give it him – I took it him this morning, and when he got it safe he turned me away. That's what I got to say.

JOHN *(sharply)*   I don't believe it! You can't have! You haven't got the quantities!

MARTIN   The paper I took the last trial we made –

JOHN *(his voice high-pitched with excitement)* Don't – don't play the fool.

MARTIN   I'm speaking God's truth, and you'd best take it. Yesterday night he sent for me – and I give it him, because he asked me for it. He was i' the right, yesterday night – I don't call to mind how. And just now I give it him. That's what I got to say.

John stands staring at him speechless. Martin, having said what he came to say, turns to go. Mary, suddenly realising what it all means, makes an involuntary movement to stop him.

MARY   Martin! You've given the receipt to Mr Rutherford! He's got it – he'll take the money from it! ... You're sure of what you say, Martin? You haven't made a mistake?

MARTIN   Mistake?

MARY   You may have got it wrong – the quantities, or whatever it is. It all depends on that, doesn't it? The least slip would put it all wrong, wouldn't it?

MARTIN *(tired out and dull)* There's no mistake.

MARY *(with a despairing movement)* Oh! You don't know what you've done!

JOHN *(almost in tears)* He knows well enough – you knew well enough. You're a thief – you're as bad as he is – you two behind my back. It was mine – the only chance I had. Damn him! Damn him! You've done for yourself, that's one thing – you're done for! You'll not get anything out of it now, not a farthing. He's twisted you round his finger, making you think you'd have the pickings, has he? And then thrown you out into the street for a fool and worse. You're done for! ... You've worked with me, seen it grow. I never thought but to trust you as I trusted myself – and you *give it away* thinking to make a bit behind my back! You'll not get a farthing now – not a farthing – you're done for.

MARTIN   Hard words, Mr John, from you to me. But I done it, and I mun bide by it.

JOHN   Oh, clear out – don't talk to me. By *heaven*! I'll be even with him yet.

MARTIN   I done it – but it bain't true what you think, that I looked to make a bit. I give it to him, but I had no thought o' gain by what I done ... It's past me – it's all past me – I canna call it to mind, nor see it plain. But I know one thing, that I never thought to make a penny. *(suddenly remembering)* It was for Rutherford's – that's what he said – I mind it now. He said, for Rutherford's – and I seed it yesterday night. It was as clear as day – yesterday night.

No one answers. After a moment he goes out. As the outer door closes John suddenly goes to Rutherford's desk and begins pulling out drawers as if searching for something.

MARY *(watching him)*   What are you doing?

JOHN   Where's the key, curse it!

MARY *(sharply)*   You can't do that!

JOHN   Do what? I'm going to get even.

MARY   Not money! You can't take his money!

JOHN *(unlocking the cash box)* Just be quiet, will you? He's taken all I have. *(He empties the money out on to the desk; his hands shaking.)* Fifteen – twenty – twenty-three. And it's twenty-three thousand he owes me more like, that he's stolen. Is there any more – a sixpence I've missed, that'll help to put us even? Twenty-three quid – curse him! And he stood and talked to me not an hour ago, and all the time he *knew*! He's mean, that's what he is – *mean* and petty-minded. No one else could have done it – to go and get at Martin behind my back because he knew I was going to be one too many for him.

MARY *(imploringly)*   Put it back! Oh, put it back!

JOHN   Oh, shut up, Mollie.

MARY   Don't take it, John.

JOHN   I tell you it's mine, by right – you don't understand ... How am I to get along if I don't?

MARY   You've not got to do this, John – for Tony's sake. I don't care what he's done to you – you've not got to do it.

JOHN   Don't make a tragedy out of nothing. It's plain common sense! *(angrily)* And don't look at me as if I were stealing. It's mine, I tell you. I only wish there were a few thousands – I'd take them!

MARY   John, listen to me. I've never seriously asked you to do anything for me in my life. Just this once – I ask you to put that money back.

JOHN   My dear girl, don't be so foolish –

MARY (*compelling him to listen to her*) Listen! You're Tony's father! I
can't help it if you think I'm making a tragedy out of what seems to you
a simple thing. One day he'll know – someone'll tell him that you stole
money – well then, that you took money that wasn't yours, because you
thought you had the right to it. What will it be like for him? Try and
realise – we've no right to live as we like – we've had our day together,
you and I – but it's past, and we know it. He's what matters now – and
we've got to live decently for him – keep straight for him –

JOHN (*answering her like an angry child*) Then *do* it! I've had enough –
I'm sick of it.

*Janet, who all this time has been kneeling where Martin left her, gets up
suddenly, stumbling forward as if she were blind. The other two stop
involuntarily and watch her as she makes for the door, dragging her
shawl over her head. As the outer door shuts on her, Mary with a half-cry
makes a movement to follow her.*

MARY   Janet!

JOHN   Oh, let her be!

MARY (*facing the door*) Where's she going to?

JOHN   I'm not going to argue – I've done that too long –
listening to first one and then another of you. What's come of it? You
wouldn't let me go out and sell the thing while it was still mine to sell. I
might have been a rich man if I'd been let to go my own way! You were
always dragging me back, everything I did – with your talk. Tony –
you're perpetually cramming him down my throat, till I'm sick of the
very name of the poor little beggar. How much better off is he for your
interfering? Give up this and give up that – I've lost everything I ever
had by doing as you said. Anybody would have bought it, anybody! And
made a fortune out of it – and there it is, lost! Gone into Rutherford's,
like everything else. Damn the place! Damn it! Oh, let him wait! I'll be
even with him. I came back once because I was a soft fool – this time I'll
starve sooner.

MARY   You're going away?

JOHN   Yes, I'm going for good and all.

She stands looking at him.

MARY   Where are you going to?

JOHN   London – anywhere. Canada, probably – that's
the place to strike out on your own –

MARY   You mean to work then?

JOHN *(impatiently)*   Of course. We can't live for ever on twenty-three quid.

MARY   What are you going to work at?

JOHN   Anything – as long as I show him –

MARY   But what – what?

JOHN   Oh, there'll be something. Damn it, Mary, what right have you to catechise?

MARY   Don't, please. I'm not catechising; I want to know. It's a question of living. What are you going to do when you've spent what you've got?

JOHN *(trying not to look shamefaced as he makes the suggestion)* You could go back to Mason's for a bit – they'd be glad enough to have you.

MARY   Go back?

JOHN *(resentfully)*   Well, I suppose you won't mind helping for a bit till I see my way. What was the screw you got?

MARY   Twenty-five.

JOHN   That would help if the worst came to the worst.

MARY   We lived on it before.

JOHN   We could put up at the same lodgings for a bit. They're cheap.

MARY   Walton Street.

JOHN *(loudly)*   Anyway, I'm going to be even with him – I'll see him damned before I submit. I've put up with it long enough for your sake – I'm going to get a bit of my own back for once. After all, I'm his son – you can't count Dick; when I'm gone he'll begin to see what he's lost. Why, he may as well *sell* Rutherford's outright – with no one to come after him. He's worked for that – all his life! Lord! I'd give something to see his face when he comes in and asks for me!

Mary makes no answer, as there is indeed none to make. She speaks again, not bitterly, but as one stating a fact.

MARY   So that's your plan. *(There is a silence, in which he cannot meet her eyes. She repeats, without hope.)* John, once more – from my soul I ask you to do what I wish.

JOHN *(impatiently)*   What about?

MARY   The money. To put it back. *(He makes a movement of desperate irritation.)* No, don't answer just for a moment. You don't know how much depends on this – for us both. Our future life – perhaps our last chance of happiness together – you don't know what it may decide.

JOHN I tell you, you don't understand. *(There is a blank silence. He moves uncomfortably.)* You can't see. What's twenty-three quid!

She makes a despairing movement.

MARY *(in a changed voice)* I'm afraid you'll find it rather a burden having me and Tony – while you're seeing your way, I mean.

JOHN A burden? You? Why, you've just said you could help at Mason's –

MARY I can't go out all day and leave Tony.

JOHN Old Mrs What's-'er-name would keep an eye on him.

MARY It would free you a good deal if we weren't with you.

JOHN Of course if you won't do anything to help –

MARY *(after a pause)* How would it be if you went alone? Then – when you've seen your way – when you've made enough just to live decently – you could write and we could come to you. Somewhere that would do for Tony – wherever it may be.

JOHN In a month or two.

MARY In a month or two.

JOHN *(awkwardly)* Well, perhaps it would be better – as you suggest it. I really don't exactly see how I'm going to manage the two of you ... You mean – stay on here in the meantime.

MARY Yes – stay on here.

JOHN But the Guv'nor – I'm afraid it'll be pretty rotten for you without me.

MARY That's all right.

JOHN *(irritably)* All these stupid little details – we lose sight of the real issue. That's settled, then.

MARY Yes – settled. *(She moves, passing her hand over her eyes.)* How are you going?

JOHN *(relieved)* What's the time now? Close on twelve!

MARY You're not thinking of going now – at once!

JOHN There's the one o'clock train. I'll get old Smith to drive me to the Junction – it doesn't stop.

MARY There won't be time to pack your things.

JOHN Send them after me.

MARY You've no food to take with you.

JOHN That doesn't matter; I'll get some on the way.

MARY *(suddenly)* You can't go like this! We must talk – we can't end it all like this.

JOHN I must – I didn't know it was so late – he'll be in to dinner. Cheer up, dear, it's only for a little while. I hate it too, but it wouldn't do for him to find me here. It would look – weak.

MARY No, no – you're right – you mustn't meet – it would do no good. *(She stands undecided for a moment, then goes quickly into the hall and brings his overcoat.)* It's bitter cold. And it's an open trap, isn't it?

JOHN I shall be all right. *(She helps him on with the coat.)* It won't be long – the time'll pass before you know where you are; it always does – I haven't time to see the kid – it's the only thing to be done – other fellows make their fortunes every day, why shouldn't I?

MARY *(as if he were a child)* Yes, yes, why shouldn't you?

JOHN Something'll turn up – and I've got the devil's own luck at times – you'll see. I've never had a chance up to now. Some day you'll believe in me. *(He sees her face and stops short.)* Mollie – !

He takes her in his arms. She breaks down, clinging to him.

MARY Oh, my dear – if I could!

JOHN *(moved)* I will do it, Mollie – I swear I will. Something'll turn up, and it'll all come right – we'll be as happy as kings, you see if we aren't. Don't, dear, it's only for a little while ... Well then – will you come with me now?

MARY No, no, that can't be. Go, go – he'll be in directly. Go now.

She goes with him to the outer door. Ann Rutherford comes in on her way through the room.

ANN Who is it's got the door open on such a day? And the wind fit to freeze a body's bones! *(The outer door is heard closing. Mary comes in slowly, very pale.)* Come in, come in, for the Lord's sake. *(looking at her)* What be ye doing out there?

MARY He's gone.

ANN *(cross with the cold)* Gone, gone, this one and that – John? And what'll he be gone for? I never seed such doings, never!

MARY Shall I make up the fire?

ANN And you all been and let it down. Nay, nay, I'll do it myself. It'll not be up for ten minutes or more. Such doings. What'll he be gone for?

MARY He's had a quarrel with his father.

ANN *(putting logs on, half-whimpering)* A fine reason for making folks talk – bringing disgrace on the house, and all Grantley talking, and tomorrow Sunday – I never seed the like, never!

MARY	It's no use crying.
ANN	It's weel enough for you to talk – you bain't one

of the family, a stranger like you. You don't know. When you've come
up i' the world and are respected, there's nothing pleases folk better
than to find something agin you. What am I to say when I'm asked after
my nevvy? Tell me that. And him gone off without so much as a change
to his back – it aren't respectable. And there's Janet not ten minutes
since gone along the road wi' her shawl over her head like a common
working lass. Where it's to end, I'm sure I can't tell.

MARY	Perhaps it is ended.
ANN	Perhaps half the work's left and the house upset.

Susan'll be giving notice just now – her and her goings on. As if lasses
weren't hard enough to get – and there's dinner and all –

MARY	Do you want the table laid?
ANN	It'd help – though you've no call to do it – you

got your own troubles – the little lad'll be wanting you mebbee.

MARY	He's still asleep. I'll leave the door open and then

I shall hear him. (*She opens the door, listening for a moment before
she comes back into the room.*)

ANN	Janet'll be back mebbee afore you've finished.

Such doings – everything put wrong. I'll go and fetch the bread. (*She
wanders out, talking as she goes.*)

*Mary takes the red cloth off the table, folds it, takes the white one from
the drawer in the sideboard, and spreads it. As she is doing so Rutherford
comes in. He stands looking at her for a moment, then comes to the fire.*

RUTHERFORD (*as he passes her*) Dinner's late.
MARY (*going on with her work*) It'll be ready in a few minutes.
RUTHERFORD   It's gone twelve.

*She makes no answer. He takes his pipe off the chimney-piece and begins
to fill it. As he is putting his tobacco-pouch back into his pocket his eyes
fall on the table; he stops short.*

RUTHERFORD	You've laid a place short. (*raising his voice*) D'ye

hear me, you've laid a –

MARY	No.

*She goes to the sideboard and spreads a cloth there. He stands motionless
staring at the table.*

RUTHERFORD	Gone. Trying to frighten me, is he? Trying a bit o'

bluff – he'll show me, eh? And all I got to do is sit quiet and wait for
him to come back – that's all I got to do.

MARY *(quietly)*   He won't come back.

RUTHERFORD   Won't he! He'll come back right enough when he feels the pinch – he'll come slinking back like a whipped puppy at nightfall, like he did afore. I know him – light – light-minded like his mother afore him. *(He comes to his desk and finds the open cash box.)* Who's been here? Who's been here? *(He stands staring at the box till the lid falls from his hand.)* Nay – he'll not come back, by God!

MARY *(hopelessly)*   He thought he had the right – he believed he had the right after you'd taken what was his.

RUTHERFORD   I'd sooner have seen him in his grave.

MARY   He couldn't see.

RUTHERFORD   Bill Henderson did that because he knowed no better. And my son knowed no better, though I made a gentleman of him. Set him up. I done with him – done with him.

He drops heavily into the armchair beside the table and sits staring before him. After a long silence he speaks again.

RUTHERFORD   Why haven't you gone too, and made an empty house of it?

MARY   I'm not going.

RUTHERFORD   Not going, aren't you? Not till it pleases you, I take it – till he sends for you?

MARY   He won't send for me.

RUTHERFORD *(quickly)* Where's the little lad?

MARY   Asleep upstairs. *(After a pause, she speaks again in level tones.)* I've lived in your house for nearly three months. *(He turns to look at her.)* Until you came in just now you haven't spoken to me half-a-dozen times. Every slight that can be done without words you've put upon me. There's never a day passed but you've made me feel that I'd no right here, no place.

RUTHERFORD   You'll not die for a soft word from the likes o' me.

MARY   Now that I've got to speak to you, I want to say that first – in case you should think I'm going to appeal to you, and in case I should be tempted to do it.

RUTHERFORD   What ha' ye got to ask of me?

MARY   To ask – nothing. I've a bargain to make with you.

RUTHERFORD *(half truculent)* Wi' me?

MARY   You can listen – then you can take it or leave it.

RUTHERFORD   Thank ye kindly. And what's your idea of a bargain?

MARY A bargain is where one person has something to sell that another wants to buy. There's no love in it – only money – money that pays for life. I've got something to sell that you want to buy.

RUTHERFORD What's that?

MARY My son. *(Their eyes meet in a long steady look. She goes on deliberately.)* You've lost everything you have in the world. John's gone – and Richard – and Janet. They won't come back. You're alone now and getting old, with no one to come after you. When you die Rutherford's will be sold – somebody'll buy it and give it a new name perhaps, and no one will even remember that you made it. That'll be the end of all your work. Just – nothing. You've thought of that. I've seen you thinking of it as I've sat by and watched you. And now it's come ... Will you listen?

RUTHERFORD Aye.

She sits down at the other end of the table, facing him.

MARY It's for my boy. I want – a chance of life for him – his place in the world. John can't give him that, because he's made so. If I went to London and worked my hardest I'd get twenty-five shillings a week. We've failed. From you I can get what I want for my boy. I want – all the good common things: a good house, good food, warmth. He's a delicate little thing now, but he'll grow strong like other children. I want to undo the wrong we've done him, John and I. If I can. Later on there'll be his schooling – I could never save enough for that. You can give me all this – you've got the power. Right or wrong, you've got the power ... That's the bargain. Give me what I ask, and in return I'll give you – him. On one condition. I'm to stay on here. I won't trouble you – you needn't speak to me or see me unless you want to. For ten years he's to be absolutely mine, to do what I like with. You mustn't interfere – you mustn't tell him to do things or frighten him. He's mine. For ten years more.

RUTHERFORD And after that?

MARY He'll be yours.

RUTHERFORD To train up. For Rutherford's? You'd trust your son to me?

MARY Yes.

RUTHERFORD After all? After Dick, that I've bullied till he's a fool? John, that's wished me dead?

MARY In ten years you'll be an old man; you won't be able to make people afraid of you any more.

RUTHERFORD   Ah! Because o' that? And because I have the
  power?
MARY   Yes. And there'll be money for his clothes – and
  you'll leave the Works to him when you die.

There is a silence. He sits motionless, looking at her.

RUTHERFORD   You've got a fair notion of business – for a
  woman.
MARY   I've earned my living. I know all that that teaches
  a woman.
RUTHERFORD   It's taught you one thing – to have an eye to the
  main chance.
MARY   You think I'm bargaining for myself?
RUTHERFORD   You get a bit out of it, don't you?
MARY   What?
RUTHERFORD   A roof over your head – the shelter of a good
  name – your keep – things not so easy to come by, my son's wife, wi' a
  husband that goes off and leaves you to live on his father's charity.
  (There is a pause.)
MARY *(slowly)*   There'll be a woman living in the house – year
  after year, with the fells closed round her. She'll sit and sew at the
  window and see the furnace flare in the dark; lock up, and give you the
  keys at night –
RUTHERFORD   You've got your bairn.
MARY   Yes, I've got him! For ten years. *(They sit silent.)*
  Is it a bargain?
RUTHERFORD   Aye. *(She gets up with a movement of relief. As
  he speaks again she turns, facing him.)* You think me a hard man. So I
  am. But I'm wondering if I could ha' stood up as you're standing and
  done what you've done.
MARY   I love my child. That makes me hard.
RUTHERFORD   I used to hope for my son once, like you do for
  yours now. When he was a bit of a lad I used to think o' the day when
  I'd take him round and show him what I had to hand on. I thought he'd
  come after me – glad o' what I'd done. I set my heart on that. And the
  end of it's just this – an empty house – we two strangers, driving our
  bargain here across the table.
MARY   There's nothing else.
RUTHERFORD   You think I've used him badly? You think I've
  done a dirty thing about this metal?
MARY   It was his.

RUTHERFORD   I've stolen it behind his back and I'm going to make money out of it?

MARY   I don't know – I don't know.

RUTHERFORD   It'll come to your son.

MARY   Yes.

RUTHERFORD   Because I done that he'll have his chance, his place i' the world. What would ha' gone to the winds, scattered and useless, 'll be his. He'll come on, young and strong, when my work's done, and Rutherford's 'll stand up firm and safe out o' the fight and the bitterness – Rutherford's that his grandfather gave his life to build up.

MARY *(stopping him with a gesture)* Hush!

RUTHERFORD What is it? *(They both listen.)* The little lad. He's waking!

Mary runs out. The room is very silent as Rutherford sits sunk in his chair, thinking.

The Curtain falls.

The End.

Githa Sowerby (1876-1970)

Githa was born and grew up at Low Fell, Gateshead and later at Chollerton, Northumberland. She was the daughter of glass manufacturer John G. Sowerby, whose Gateshead based company, Sowerby and Co. had been passed down from his father and grandfather. In 1896, following financial problems and clashes with the Company Directors, the Sowerbys moved south to Colchester.

Githa was the second of five daughters and had one brother, the eldest child, John Lawrence. Githa moved to London in 1905 where she became active in the Fabian Society and wrote short stories and children's books illustrated by her sister Millicent including a series of *Little Plays for Little People* (1910).

In 1912, aged 36, she married Major John Kendall (1869-1952) a poet, playwright and journalist, who had served in the Indian army. Her other plays include the one-act *Before Breakfast* (published,1913); *Jinny* (unpublished, 1914); a revised *A Man and Some Women* (unpublished, 1914); *Sheila* (unpublished, 1917); *The Stepmother* (1924, published by The Women's Press in Toronto, 2008, alongside a revival directed by Joanna Falk for The Shaw Festival) and *The Policeman's Whistle* (unpublished, 1934).

Rutherford and Son opened at The Royal Court Theatre in 1912, receiving considerable acclaim from the critics who assumed the author to be male. It later transferred to the West End and New York. It has since been translated into many languages.

It was revived for Northern Stage in Newcastle in 2009, with a production directed by Richard Beecham.

The Chalk Garden

Enid Bagnold

First performed at the Ethel Barrymore Theatre, New York, on 26th October 1955.

CHARACTERS

Miss Madrigal, the 1st Applicant
Maitland, the manservant
A Little Lady, the 2nd Applicant
3rd Lady, the 3rd Applicant
Laurel
Mrs St Maugham, her grandmother
Nurse
Olivia, Laurel's mother
The Judge
Pinkbell, unseen but not unfelt

ACT ONE

A morning in June. Time – the present.

The sitting room of Mrs St Maugham's house in Sussex. The house, built on lime and chalk soil, is close to a village by the sea. The sitting room is also used for luncheon, the main dining room is probably under dust sheets. The room has a look of the country, also of vigour and culture and is much lived in. Through a wide arch and up two steps, is the hall, staircase and passage to the drawing-room. At the head of the stairs is a small curtained arch leading to the bedrooms.

A door Right of the staircase leads to the butler's pantry, the kitchen, etc. The front door is downstage in the hall and the outside of it is visible through a window down Left in the room. Up Centre is a glass-panelled door giving access to the garden, and large casement windows are Right

*of the door. Up Right is a door leading to the conservatory and thence
again to the garden. Down Right is a door leading to 'Pinkbell's' room. In
front of the window up Centre is a large table littered with gardening
paraphernalia, a watering-can, a tin of nicotine insecticide, etc. A desk,
with a house telephone is up Right. There is a small table down Right, and
a couch. An armchair stands Centre with an occasional table Left of it.
There is a small console table under the window down Left. The setting
has four upright chairs normally placed one at the desk, one down Left,
one below the arch Left and one in the hall. Built-in bookshelves are down
Right and Left of the door up Centre. Outside the windows up Centre
there is a garden wall and gate with a distant view of the Sussex Downs
beyond. Over the window up Centre and over the door down Right are
shelves set with books, pictures, etc. At night the room is lit by electric
candle wall-brackets above and below the arch Left, and a table-lamp on
the desk.*

*When the Curtain rises, the four upright chairs are set diagonally in a
row Left Centre, facing down Right. Miss Madrigal is seated on the
upstage chair. She is an enigmatical, contained woman, neat and non-
committal in dress, with fine eyes and a high aquiline look. She has the
still look of an eagle at rest upon a rock. Her mackintosh is over the back
of her chair, her handbag is on the chair immediately below her and her
zip-bag is on the floor beside the chair on which she is seated. On the chair
with her handbag is a feather boa. Almost immediately the Little Lady
appears outside the front door Left and rings the bell. She is a little, bird-
like woman. Maitland, the manservant, wearing a white jacket, enters
from the pantry, crosses the hall to the front door and opens it. The Little
Lady comes in rapidly, like a bird over a lawn, stops quickly, then moves
on quickly below the line of chairs to Centre.*

LITTLE LADY *(aflutter)*   Good morning. May one sit?

*Maitland nods and exits up Right to the garden. She sits on the chair next
but one to Miss Madrigal, removes her gloves and places them with her
handbag beside Madrigal's bag on the vacant chair between them. She
hides her hands, looks at them and hides them again. It is a trick of hers.*

LITTLE LADY   Lovely blowy weather. *(There is no answer.)*
    Are you too here for the interview? *(Miss Madrigal looks towards the
    Little Lady.)* As I came in – I saw a lady going out – *(confidentially)* in
    a temper.

*The 3rd Lady, whose beauty is decayed, sails in by the front door. She
wears a chiffon scarf on her head. Maitland enters up Right.*

MAITLAND *(to the 3rd Lady)* Who let *you* in?

3RD LADY　　　　　The front door stood wide open – so humane. *(She moves down Left. To the others)* Good morning. How do you do?

MAITLAND *(moving in front of the couch)* Have you a letter?

3RD LADY *(taking a letter from her handbag and facing Maitland)* I wouldn't have come, dear, if I hadn't had a letter. *(She waves it at him.)* Are you the butler?

MAITLAND　　　　　I am the manservant.

3RD LADY　　　　　A world of difference! *(She replaces the letter in her bag and removes her scarf.)* In my days it was thought common to wear a white coat. A relic of our occupation in India. Now over. *(She turns to the others.)* In those days only worn in Cheltenham. *(She moves above the table Left of the armchair and waves a coy finger.)* In those days – in the Hill Stations – I was thought to have extraordinary charm. *(She turns suddenly to Maitland.)* Is this a house where there are gentlemen?

MAITLAND *(stiffly)*　　　I am not to give information.

3RD LADY *(putting her scarf on the back of the armchair)* But you have only to nod. *(She moves to the table up Centre and fingers the things on it.)* Gardening gloves – nicotine for wood lice ... Is your lady going up in the world? Or coming down? *(She moves down Left of the armchair. To the Little Lady)* One has to be so careful.

MAITLAND *(outraged)*　　Mrs St Maugham has a house in Belgrave Square!

3RD LADY　　　　　But you are left in the country, I suppose, when she goes up for the Season?

MAITLAND *(shortly)*　　Madam is past the Season. Take a chair, please.

3RD LADY　　　　　Where are the entertaining rooms?

MAITLAND　　　　　They are under dust sheets.

3RD LADY *(picking up her scarf and turning to the others)* Not that I am applying for the post, you know – not really!

LITTLE LADY *(gasping)*　Not applying?

3RD LADY　　　　　I came – *(crosses to the hall)* I came to have a peep. *(improvising)* So nostalgic ...

MAITLAND *(crossing to the 3rd Lady)* Where are you off to?

3RD LADY *(tying the scarf round her hair, mockingly)* Such a wind out! So rough and rude in summer.

MAITLAND　　　　　But you're not going?　　　　.

3RD LADY *(teasing him but it is the truth)* I could not think of staying in a house – where there is not even a nephew.

She moves towards the front door.

MAITLAND *(following 3rd Lady into the hall)* But what shall I tell her?
3RD LADY *(with ancient mischief)* That people who advertise are never quite of one's world.

The 3rd Lady exits by the front door. Maitland exits to the pantry. Laurel enters down the stairs. She is aged sixteen, is dressed in a summer dress, and wears a most unsuitable amount of jewellery. She stands in the archway Left and surveys the others with an unruffled, contemplative stare.

LAUREL   My grandmother had one hundred and seven answers. *(The two Ladies turn and look at Laurel. There is a short silence. She moves behind the chairs and stands.)* I mean to her advertisement for someone to look after me. *(She plays with her jewellery.)*
LITTLE LADY *(rising, propitiatory)* You are the young lady who requires a companion? *(Her poor nervous hand steals out.)*
LAUREL *(crossing and standing below the armchair)* I never shake hands. It's so animal. *(The Little Lady sinks back on to her chair. Laurel looks at the two Ladies.)* So one of you has come to look after me? We were expecting four applicants – the ones my grandmother selected from the letters. So now there are only two to choose from. *(To the Little Lady)* What are your qualifications?
LITTLE LADY *(anxious, leaning forward)* Frobel-trained. Long ago. But Frobel-trained. *(almost in a whisper)* And patience.
LAUREL   Would you have patience with me?
LITTLE LADY   I am so fond of young people.
LAUREL   I set fire to things. I am not allowed alone, except in the garden.
LITTLE LADY *(carrying on bravely)* Such lovely weather for the garden. *(She rises and crosses above Laurel to Right of her.)* The advertisement said 'with handicraft'. I am clever with my fingers. I am fond of making pretty things. *(coy)* Now – can *you* make a lampshade?
LAUREL *(insolent)*   All the lampshades here are made already.
LITTLE LADY *(moving above Laurel to Left of her, confidential)* Will you tell me, dear, of what does the family consist?
LAUREL *(matter of fact, without emphasis)* Of my grandmother. Of me. And Maitland. *(She points to the ceiling.)* And the terrible old man upstairs. And his hospital nurse.
LITTLE LADY *(horrified)* Your – grandfather?
LAUREL   Mr Pinkbell was always the butler. Now he has a stroke.

LITTLE LADY *(glancing towards the pantry door)* Who was that, then?
LAUREL That was Maitland. He wears a grocer's coat. You get them for a guinea. Mr Pinkbell, of course, used to wear a black one, and have a footman.
LITTLE LADY But is there no one else?
LAUREL Oh, we are rich. *(She crosses below the chairs to Left of them.)* If we have only one servant it is part of my grandmother's newest theory about life. She says true devotion is only to be got when a man is worked to death and has no rival. *(She fingers the feather boa distastefully.)* Maitland plays games with me so he has his hands full. *(She moves down Left.)*
LITTLE LADY *(moving to her chair)* But have you no mother?
LAUREL *(leaning on the table down Left)* My mother married again. She married for love. *(The Little Lady resumes her seat.)* It has given me an adolescent repugnance to her. My case is practically in Freud. My grandmother will explain it to you. *(She fingers the pot-pourri bowl on the table down Left.)*
LITTLE LADY And who is your father?
LAUREL *(moving behind the Little Lady's chair)* My father shot himself when I was twelve. I was in the room. *(She turns to Madrigal and stands behind her chair.)* And what are your qualifications?
MADRIGAL *(turning a frosty eye on Laurel)* I prefer to wait for your grandmother.
LAUREL *(interested in this answer)* Are you Scotch?
MADRIGAL I was born in Barbados.
LAUREL Where do you live?
MADRIGAL *(after a pause)* In my room.
LAUREL *(crossing above Madrigal to Right of her)* How do you take to me?
MADRIGAL You are not what I am used to.
LAUREL I am fond of painting. Can you paint?
MADRIGAL What I cannot do is wait much longer.

A Lady appears outside the front door and rings the bell.

LAUREL *(moving to the door up Centre)* Oh, she'll come. Grandloo will come. She is working in the garden. She's a great gardener, but nothing grows for her. *(She moves down Right of Madrigal. Maitland enters from the pantry and goes to the front door.)* Do wait. You may be the one we are looking for.

Maitland hurries to the row of chairs and picks up the feather boa.

MAITLAND   She says she left this behind. *(He looks at Laurel.)* What are you doing wearing madam's necklaces? *(Laurel runs up Right. He crosses to Laurel.)* Off with them. You've been upstairs and I thought I'd left you happy in the garden. *(Laurel removes the jewellery and hands it to Maitland, but conceals a bracelet behind her back. The Little Lady rises, moves up Centre and looks out of the window.)* Out you go. *(He pushes her towards the door up Right.)* I've got a bonfire laid at the top there. You shall light it when I get a minute.

Laurel hands the bracelet to Maitland and exits up Right. Maitland runs to the front door and hands the boa to the Lady. The Lady exits. Maitland closes the front door.

LITTLE LADY *(to Madrigal, distractedly)* Do you think it's all true?
MADRIGAL   I should think it unlikely.

Maitland crosses and puts the jewellery in a cigar box on the table.

LITTLE LADY *(to Madrigal and also glancing at Maitland)* For the interview – when the interview – ought we to be together?
MAITLAND *(turning, box in hand)* One of you ladies can wait in the drawing–room. It's dust-sheeted but there's a chair. *(He turns and puts the box on the table.)*
LITTLE LADY *(moving at speed to the chairs)* One must be fair! Let it be me! *(She reaches over for her handbag. Madrigal picks up her own handbag and puts it on her lap. She picks up her gloves and bag.)* This lady – was before me. *(She crosses quickly to the hall. To Madrigal)* When you're ready, you just call, dear.

The Little Lady makes for the passage to the drawing room, then unseen, turns and exits quickly by the front door.

MAITLAND *(turning)*   Whew!
MADRIGAL   She's a little light-fingered.
MAITLAND *(moving and looking on the table Left of the armchair)* That one? Oh!
MADRIGAL   No more than a box of matches or the *Tatler*.
MAITLAND   Do you know her?
MADRIGAL   No. But I have met those hands before. Many times.
MAITLAND   Met her hands? *(He crosses to the hall and looks off Left)* She's gone! Out of the front door. *(He takes a bowl of flowers from the table in the hall and comes into the room.)*
MADRIGAL *(as to herself)* They were none of them solid applicants.

MAITLAND *(moving behind Madrigal)* But they wrote to Madam.

MADRIGAL It's how they spend their days. They answer advertisements.

MAITLAND *(moving to the table down Left)* Not meaning to take the job.

He puts the bowl on the table down Left and picks up a writing pad.

MADRIGAL *(absently)* They are always in two minds. It makes a change for them – *(at her own words she goes a bit off track)* and then, too, she has a garden.

MAITLAND *(crossing above the chairs to Centre)* It's you who have two minds, it seems. *(He eyes her anxiously.)* Don't *you* be flitting. *(He crosses to the desk.)* If there's nobody here – after all the advertising – who do you think's going to get the brunt?

MADRIGAL *(to herself)* I cannot hope to be acceptable – at the first undertaking.

MAITLAND *(putting the pad on the desk)* You don't need to worry. *(He picks up four opened letters from the desk.)* Madam's up a tree. Today's the deadline.

MADRIGAL *(prim and yet nervous)* There's an urgency?

MAITLAND *(crossing to Centre)* Madam's mad for the child. She's got her daughter coming. A shy lady. A nice one. But there's wheels within wheels. If you ask me, madam's afraid she'll take the child ... *(He puts the letters on the table Left of the armchair.)*

MADRIGAL *(interrupting)* The *child's* outlandish!

MAITLAND Only what madam makes her. I can explain her. Nurse and Nanny I bin to her.

MADRIGAL In a house like this – would I be suitable?

MAITLAND She'll take you. Madam loves the Unusual! It's a middle-class failing – she says – to run away from the Unusual.

MRS ST MAUGHAM *(off in the garden, calling)* Maitland! *(She calls again, nearer.)* Maitland! Maitland!

MAITLAND *(moving to Right of the table)* Madam.

Mrs St Maugham, wearing her hat and gardening gloves, appears outside the window up Centre. She is an old, over-powering, once beautiful, ex-hostess of London Society.

MRS ST MAUGHAM Maitland. *(She looks in the open window.)* Are my teeth on the shelf? My bottom teeth.

MAITLAND *(searching on the shelf)* There's nothing.

MRS ST MAUGHAM Then I must have left them in the greenhouse. *(Mrs St Maugham disappears to Right.)*

MAITLAND *(finding the teeth)* Oh, wait, madam – here they are – wrapped in a handkerchief.

Maitland exits up Right, and re- enters almost immediately. Mrs St Maugham follows him on. Madrigal rises respectfully and moves behind her chair, looking at Mrs St Maugham.

MAITLAND *(as he enters)* There's a dentist taken the empty house by the Church. *(He stands by the armchair.)* He might make you comfortable.

MRS ST MAUGHAM *(sweeping to Right of Maitland)* I've tried all the dentists. *(She removes her gloves.)* You can't fit false teeth to a woman of character. *(She puts her gloves on the table up Centre and removes her hat.)* As one grows older and older, the appearance becomes such a bore. *(She sees Madrigal.)* Good morning. *(To Maitland, displeased)* But I was expecting four applicants!

MAITLAND   Four came. Three have gone.

MRS ST MAUGHAM   And one wrote me such a good letter. Gone!

MAITLAND   But I've kept this one.

MRS ST MAUGHAM *(to Madrigal)* Shall we sit? *(She gives her hat to Maitland.)* You can go, Maitland. *(She moves to the armchair.)*

Maitland exits to the pantry. Madrigal crosses and sits on the couch. With a sudden and alarming charm of manner as she seats herself in the armchair.

MRS ST MAUGHAM   Now, what questions do total strangers put to one another?

MADRIGAL *(colourlessly)* The name is Madrigal. *(Mrs St Maugham selects the "Madrigal" letter from the table.)* I am the daughter of the late Ronald Bentham Madrigal, Rajpootnah Hussars, Indian Army. He was the son of General Bentham Madrigal – the Honourable East India Company.

MRS ST MAUGHAM   No, no! That you can't be. The Honourable East India Company was dissolved in eighteen-sixty. I'm an expert. My great grandfather was Tarr Bethune, Governor of Madras, tried for corruption in eighteen fifty-nine and found guilty.

MADRIGAL *(calmly)*   My grandfather had my father at the age of seventy-five.

MRS ST MAUGHAM *(admitting the point)* That might make it possible. What experience have you?

MADRIGAL   I have small private means. I have not taken such a post before.

MRS ST MAUGHAM   Why do you apply to me?

MADRIGAL	The advertisement tempted me. I have been somewhat alone.
MRS ST MAUGHAM	You will be able, I suppose, to give me references?
MADRIGAL *(coldly)*	That will be difficult.
MRS ST MAUGHAM	What?
MADRIGAL	In fact, impossible.

A hospital Nurse in full uniform, enters down Right. She carries a breakfast tray with the remains of breakfast for one.

NURSE *(stiff, reproachful)* We've been ringing, Mrs St Maugham.
MRS ST MAUGHAM　　I heard nothing.
NURSE *(moving to the table up Centre, acidly)* Our breakfast tray was late again. *(She puts the tray on the table.)*
MRS ST MAUGHAM　　One can't have everything.
NURSE.　　　　　　　Mr Pinkbell says one should have a great deal more.

The Nurse flounces out down Right.

MRS ST MAUGHAM *(shutting her eyes)* One of his cross mornings. Now – ask *me* questions, Miss Madrigal.
MADRIGAL　　　　　Does one have a room to oneself?

Maitland enters from the pantry, crosses to the table up Centre and picks up the breakfast tray.

MRS ST MAUGHAM *(with her eyes still closed)* Life without a room to oneself is a barbarity. Luncheon here with me and my grand-daughter. *(Maitland crosses towards the pantry door.)* Your evening meal served in your room on a tray ...
MAITLAND *(stopping and turning)* That can't be done!
MRS ST MAUGHAM *(automatically)* 'Ma'am'
MAITLAND *(automatically)* Ma'am.
MRS ST MAUGHAM　　And why can't it? *(The telephone rings.)*
MAITLAND　　　　　Because I shall be busy serving at Madam's table.
MRS ST MAUGHAM　　I hear the telephone. *(Maitland exits to the pantry.)* Now – now – Miss Madrigal. We are so continuously interrupted. *(She pauses.)* Are you Church of England?
MADRIGAL *(whose mind is only on the telephone)* My religion is private. I should tell you – in case you should ask me to – I don't answer the telephone.

MRS ST MAUGHAM *(immediately interested)* For what reason?
MADRIGAL I prefer not to. *(She pauses then realizes by Mrs St Maugham's attitude that more explanation is needed.)* It disturbs me to join two worlds.
MRS ST MAUGHAM Which ... ?
MADRIGAL The outside and the inside one.

Maitland enters from the pantry and moves to Left of Mrs St Maugham.

MAITLAND *(to Mrs St Maugham)* They want you to open the village Summer Festival.
MRS ST MAUGHAM Are they holding on?
MAITLAND They are.
MRS ST MAUGHAM Ask them what attendance they can ensure. Last time I opened something there was nobody there.
MAITLAND Madam is so unpopular.
MRS ST MAUGHAM How do *you* know?
MAITLAND I hear it on all sides.
MRS ST MAUGHAM They tell you that when I send you down to the post. Give me my engagement book.
MAITLAND *(crossing to the desk)* That's last year's.
MRS ST MAUGHAM Give it me all the same. The dates are not so different.

Maitland takes the engagement book from the desk and returns to Left of Mrs St Maugham.

MRS ST MAUGHAM Have you lived in a village, Miss Madrigal? *(Maitland hands the book to Mrs St Maugham.)*
MADRIGAL *(mumbling)* No, Mrs St Maugham.
MRS ST MAUGHAM *(leafing vaguely through the book)* All the graces of life here go unvalued. In a village one is down to the bones of things. When I was at my height – though I lived here – I never knew them. They were waiting for my old age like wolves, it seems. *(To Maitland)* Tell them I won't open it. *(She returns the book to Maitland who puts the book on the desk and exits to the pantry.)* Now – where were we? My advertisement asks for handicraft. What handicraft do you suggest?
MADRIGAL I have ornamented a chapel.
MRS ST MAUGHAM With your needle?
MADRIGAL With my brush. I have painted a twining plant on the altar candles.
MRS ST MAUGHAM *(immediately interested)* But – as the candles burnt down, the painting must have melted away.

MADRIGAL *(ecstatic)* *That* was the beauty of it. Is this a quiet house?
MRS ST MAUGHAM Absolutely.

Wild screams are heard off in the garden. Maitland bursts in from the pantry.

MAITLAND *(rushing to the door)* That child again. *(Maitland exits.)*
MRS ST MAUGHAM *(calm)* It's my daughter's child. My grand-daughter. She's so fond of screaming.
MADRIGAL While I was waiting, a young girl passed through the room.
MRS ST MAUGHAM That was she. She lives with me. Did she say anything?
MADRIGAL *(colourless)* Nothing of consequence.
MRS ST MAUGHAM Not the suicide of her father?
MADRIGAL I think she mentioned it.
MRS ST MAUGHAM *(delighted)* Oh, Laurel – to make a drama. He died – poor man – of his liver. Oh I knew there would be something. She has a *need* for fantasy!
MADRIGAL *(as though it were a foible)* She does not care for the truth?
MRS ST MAUGHAM No. But I encourage her. She loves a small limelight. One must be tender with her. Alas, he died when she was three. Rich and a fine estate. Four Van Dykes and unique Sheraton furniture. *(bitterly)* Her mother's one success. *(She rises.)* But why speak of it? She married again.
MADRIGAL And where *is* her mother?
MRS ST MAUGHAM She follows the drum – as they say – in Arabia. Stationed abroad is the term, but I dislike military language. She is coming by ship. I am expecting her.
MADRIGAL *(rising)* Would you sooner postpone – ?
MRS ST MAUGHAM But she does not come here. I should be your employer.
MADRIGAL *(cautiously)* She *is* coming?
MRS ST MAUGHAM In front of the child – we don't mention it! She is coming. *(Madrigal resumes her seat on the couch.)* One does not know why, though I shrewdly suspect it. *(She picks up a framed photograph of Olivia from the table Left of the armchair.)* I have an unworldly daughter. She was always crying out after being simple. That's hard to understand! *(She replaces the photograph.)* It seems such a waste, with all the chances of life, to want to be simple. Privilege and power make selfish people – but gay ones ... *(She breaks off.)* Forgive me, Miss Madrigal, for being personal – but irritation is like a rash on the heart! *(She sits in the armchair.)*

MADRIGAL *(to change the subject)* The child – is she fond of her
stepfather?

MRS ST MAUGHAM *(indifferent)* I never asked. His rank is Colonel. My
grand-daughter has developed an interesting mother-hatred, which is
clearly explained in Freud. You have had experience? You feel
competent to deal with such things?

MADRIGAL *(dreamily)*   For the worse – or the better ...

MRS ST MAUGHAM   You seem absent in mind!

MADRIGAL *(pulling herself together)* Not in mind – but in manner.
(pursily) The child is naturally alienated – that a sex life has broken out
again in her mother.

MRS ST MAUGHAM   You put it well! Exactly! The child was
frenzied. When nothing would stop the wedding – she ran from the
hotel into the dark – *(There is a long buzz on the house telephone.)*

MADRIGAL   There seems to be a bell ringing.

*Mrs St Maugham rises and crosses to the house telephone on the desk,
speaking as she goes.*

MRS ST MAUGHAM   – and by some extraordinary carelessness she
was violated in Hyde Park at the age of twelve. It has upset her nerves.
(She lifts the receiver.) We are waiting as it were for calmer weather.
(into the telephone) You want me, Pinkbell? One moment ... *(She puts
her hand over the mouthpiece. To Madrigal)* Of course we put it less
strongly to her mother. Apart from certain fixations with regard to fire,
she is a charming, intelligent girl. I should welcome your impressions.
(into the telephone) What's that? ... I did. I ordered it. The Extract of
Humus – for the seed boxes ... It should have come ... I'll ring. I'll ring
and ask him. *(She is about to replace the receiver but is recalled by the
voice.)* I know! I know! But one can't have perfection, Pinkbell! *(She
replaces the receiver. To herself)* Oh – isn't jealousy terrible! *(She
moves to the table up Centre and picks up a handbell.)*

MADRIGAL *(with surprising force)* Yes!

MRS ST MAUGHAM   You made me jump. *(She moves to Left of the
table.)* He's my butler. Forty years my butler. Now he's had a stroke but
he keeps his finger on things. *(She rings the bell.)*

MADRIGAL *(automatically)* He carries on at death's door.

MRS ST MAUGHAM *(equally automatically)* His standards rule this
house.

MADRIGAL *(absently)*   You must be fond of him.

MRS ST MAUGHAM   Alas, no. He trains Maitland – but now
Maitland won't go near him. But I shall overcome it. He's so good with
the garden. *(She rings the bell.)*

MADRIGAL   Maitland?

MRS ST MAUGHAM   Pinkbell. He directs mine from his window. All butlers dream of gardening. (*She replaces the bell on the table.*) We spoke of references. Who will speak for you? (*She sits in the armchair.*)

MADRIGAL (*indifferently*) No one will speak for me. (*earnestly*) Extract of humus is too rich for summer biennials.

Maitland enters and crosses to Left of Mrs St Maugham.

MRS ST MAUGHAM   Has a bag of humus been delivered at the back door?

MAITLAND   There's a sack there.

MRS ST MAUGHAM   When did it come?

MAITLAND   Days ago.

MRS ST MAUGHAM   And you walk by it and ignore it. How do you know someone hasn't sent me a brace of pheasants! Mr Pinkbell says you must always report, and at once, everything that comes to the back door.

MAITLAND (*suddenly reaching his limit*) I won't take orders from the old bastard!

MRS ST MAUGHAM   Am I to have trouble with you, Maitland?

MAITLAND (*breaking*)   Oh, if I could please and be sure of myself.

MRS ST MAUGHAM (*quiet and menacing*) Maitland ...

MAITLAND   Oh, if things would go smoothly.

MRS ST MAUGHAM (*with deliberation and distinctiveness*) Maitland. (*Maitland looks at Mrs St Maugham*) Bring, me the Crème de Menthe and two glasses. (*Maitland's chest fills with emotion. He seems about to burst and rushes out to the pantry. She sits back in her chair and fans her face with her handkerchief.*) Touch and go. How frail is authority. What were you saying?

MADRIGAL   When?

MRS ST MAUGHAM   About humus and summer biennials.

MADRIGAL (*tonelessly, as though sleep-walking*) Don't pep up the soil before birth. It leads them on to expect (*To herself*) what life won't give them.

MRS ST MAUGHAM (*leaning forward*) Speak louder.

MADRIGAL (*with awkward and unstable loudness*) What life won't give them.

MRS ST MAUGHAM (*suddenly reminded*) What was that plant you painted on the candles?

MADRIGAL (*with inner pleasure as though she were eating a sweet*) Lapagaria. Sub-tropical. With waxy umbels.

MRS ST MAUGHAM   Lady Dorchester had it in her wedding bouquet
after the Battle of the Marne. I had forgotten it. Could I grow it in my
greenhouse?

MADRIGAL *(by rote)* It needs the early actinic rays. Exclude the sun
again at midday. Counteract the high lime content in your soil with
potash.

MRS ST MAUGHAM   Where did you learn about such things?

MADRIGAL   I was put in charge of –

MRS ST MAUGHAM   What?

MADRIGAL   – a garden.

*Maitland enters from the pantry, carrying, most correctly, a tray with a
bottle of Creme de Menthe and two glasses, and even a clean napkin over
his arm. He crosses to the table Left of the armchair, sets down the tray
with exactitude, then straightens himself.*

MAITLAND   I wish to give my notice.

MRS ST MAUGHAM *(with eyes like steel)* If I take it you will not get it
back again.

MAITLAND   I am prepared for that.

MRS ST MAUGHAM *(terrible)* Are you?

MAITLAND *(immediately broken)* You know I can't stand criticism.
Every time a word's said against me a month's work is undone.

MRS ST MAUGHAM   We all make mistakes.

MAITLAND *(passionately)* But nothing should be said about them.
Praise is the only thing that brings to life again a man that's been
destroyed. But, oh, if I leave – what will you do without me? *(Laurel is
heard off in the garden, screaming.)* And what will the child do?

Maitland runs off up Right.

MRS ST MAUGHAM *(smiling in triumph)* Do you know the secret of
authority, Miss Madrigal? Changes of mood. The Inexplicable. The
thunder, the lightning, and the sudden sun. He won't leave me. Will you
have a Crème de Menthe?

MADRIGAL *(stiffly)*   I never touch alcohol.

MRS ST MAUGHAM *(pouring a drink for herself)* Certainly he makes
scenes. But I like them. He has been a prisoner.

MADRIGAL   A prisoner!

MRS ST MAUGHAM   Five years. Now that there are no subject races,
one must be served by the mad, the sick, and those who can't take their
place in the outside world – and served I must be. *(She drinks.)*

Laurel rushes in up Right and stands by the door, looking out.

MRS ST MAUGHAM   Laurel!

LAUREL *(without turning)* One moment, Grandloo. One moment, darling – I'm watching the bonfire – I must see it die. *(She moves to Left of her.)* I put salt on it to turn the flame blue. *Blocks* of it.

MRS ST MAUGHAM *(taking Laurel's hand)* Who told you to put salt on it?

LAUREL   The old bastard – Mr Pinkbell.

MRS ST MAUGHAM   Not now, my darling. Superlatives only between ourselves.

LAUREL *(looking at the chairs Left)* Where are the others?

MRS ST MAUGHAM   *This* is Miss Madrigal.

LAUREL *(eager)*   Have you settled everything? *(She turns to Madrigal.)* Do you understand all about me?

MADRIGAL   Not yet.

LAUREL   Oh, can't we have the interview together? Shall I get the book that explains me?

MRS ST MAUGHAM   Not so fast. Externalize! Externalize, my darling! She has quaint self-delusions. You mustn't mind them. *(She sips her drink and puts the glass on the table Left of her chair.)*

Maitland enters up Right with his jacket over his arm. He gives Laurel a black look and exits to the pantry.

LAUREL   But you mustn't cross them. *(She looks over her shoulder at the departing Maitland.)*

MADRIGAL *(to Laurel)*   Are you an only child?

LAUREL   I am Delilah's daughter!

MRS ST MAUGHAM   Laurel has a poltergeist! Stones fall in the bedrooms, and words leap and change colour in her mouth like fishes! I, too, at her age ...

LAUREL   Wit often skips a generation.

MRS ST MAUGHAM   She is my parchment sheet on which I write. I hope she will remember my life and times. There seems no one else to do it.

LAUREL   *I* am your little immortality!

MRS ST MAUGHAM *(to herself with reality)* Those who eat too big a meal of life – get no monument. *(She holds Laurel at arm's length Left of her chair.)* You see how light my finger lies upon her. The child's a flower. She grows in liberty!

MADRIGAL   Weeds grow as easily.

MRS ST MAUGHAM   As I was saying –

LAUREL *(moving above the couch)* – before the interruption.

MRS ST MAUGHAM   Freedom is Captain here! Calm is its Lieutenant!

The Nurse rushes in down Right, leaving the door open.

NURSE   The madonna lilies have blown over!

MRS ST MAUGHAM *(rising)* Oh – great heavens – *(She moves up Centre.)* this mule of a garden! *Maitland! (She turns to the Nurse.)* He was to order the bamboos and he forgot them. Are they all down?

NURSE *(with triumph)* All. And not for want of warnings!

The Nurse exits down Right, closing the door behind her.

MRS ST MAUGHAM   Oh, my lilies! My lilies! One waits a year for them ...

Mrs St Maugham exits hurriedly up Centre. Laurel follows her to the door. Madrigal rises and moves to the door up Right. Maitland enters from the pantry.

MAITLAND   What was that I heard?

LAUREL   The calm of Grandloo.

MAITLAND   But what's happened?

MADRIGAL   There's been an accident in the garden.

MAITLAND *(to Laurel, denouncingly)* Fire! *(He moves to the door up Centre.)*

LAUREL *(stopping him)*   Wind. You didn't stake the lilies.

Maitland rushes to the door up Right and looks off.

MAITLAND *(frantic)*   Oh, are they down? The Nurse told me and I forgot! *(He moves Centre.)* How the old bastard will be crowing – !

MADRIGAL *(primly)*   Stake in May. *(She moves up Right of armchair.)*

MAITLAND *(turning on her fiercely)* They weren't full grown in May.

MADRIGAL   They should have been.

MAITLAND *(more fiercely)* Is that a criticism?

MADRIGAL *(quietly)*   So you are the gardener here as well?

MAITLAND *(excitedly)*   I'm everything! I'm the kingpin and the pivot and the manservant and the maidservant and the go-between – *(He turns on Laurel.)* and the fire extinguisher.

LAUREL   Prisoner Six–five–seven–four!

MAITLAND *(jumping to attention)* Sir!

LAUREL   Carry your bed-area and about turn! Through the corridor second door on the left and into your cell. *March!*

Maitland marches to Laurel, starts to salute but cannot make it.

MAITLAND   I'm all to pieces. I can't play it.

LAUREL *(sitting on the third chair Left Centre in mock tragic tones)* He
was five long years in prison, Miss Madrigal.
MADRIGAL *(politely)* Was it your first conviction?
MAITLAND Conviction! It was for my ideals. I was a
Conscientious Objector.
MADRIGAL *(prim)* And didn't you find it trying?
MAITLAND She says. 'Trying'! Five years! Five long years!
Given one chance to live and five years taken from it! An ant among a
thousand ants – and taking orders from ants!
MADRIGAL If it upsets you better not recall it.
MAITLAND Not recall it! It's stamped on my skin and at
the back of my eyes! It's in my legs when I walk up and down! In my
heart that sticks with fright when *she* gets angry!
MADRIGAL *(sententious)* But since you felt you had Right on your side?

*Maitland moves Madrigal's mackintosh on to her zip-bag then picks up
the two upstage chairs.*

MAITLAND 'Right on my side!' *That* didn't uphold me. I
went in there because I wouldn't take a life but before I came out I
would have killed a warder! *(He puts one chair below the arch Left and
the other in the hall.)*
MADRIGAL *(platitudinously)* All acts become possible.
MAITLAND *(over his shoulder)* What can *you* know of life?
MADRIGAL True, it's been sheltered.

*Laurel rises, moves to Left of the table and pours a glass of Crème de
Menthe.*

LAUREL All our lives are sheltered.
MAITLAND *(turning and seeing Laurel)* Don't do that! She'll be furious.

*He rushes at Laurel. Laurel tosses the drink down her throat before
Maitland can reach her.*

LAUREL Not with me. I'm not responsible.

*She puts the glass on the tray crosses above Madrigal and stands behind
the couch.*

MAITLAND *(to Madrigal)* You'll witness, miss. I didn't touch it. I have to
be on the ready for injustice in life.
LAUREL *(moving below the couch)* From me? From your little Laurel?
How touchy you are. *(She sits on the couch.)*

MAITLAND   I have soft ground and hard ground to my
feelings. You should mind where you step.

LAUREL *(in mock concern)* Have you taken your Luminol?

MAITLAND   That's it! That's it! *(He puts the mackintosh on
the upstage chair and the zip-bag beside it.)* Even a child knows a man
must take a sedative. But, coming from you, Laurel ...

LAUREL   *Miss* Laurel. I am a victim and you ought to
love me.

MAITLAND *(moving Centre, angrily)* I do love you – like the poor
mother who ought by rights and reasons to take a stick to you. *(He
crosses to the hall.)*

LAUREL   What do you expect from me? A child that's
been forsaken by its mother!

MAITLAND   That's as may be. That's as those think it to be.
I was found in a field but I don't make a fuss about it!

Maitland exits up the stairs.

LAUREL *(soapily)* Poor Maitland likes the Right – even when the Right
is wrong.

MADRIGAL *(platitudinously)* He has your interests at heart.

LAUREL *(with interest)*   Are you a hospital nurse?

MADRIGAL   Why do you ask?

LAUREL   You have that unmeaning way of saying things.

MADRIGAL *(after a second's pause and with a little formal manner of
adapting herself)* Now that we are alone am I to call you 'Laurel'?

LAUREL   It's my name.

MADRIGAL *(sitting beside Laurel on the couch)* And what are you
interested in – Laurel? I mean – apart from yourself?

LAUREL   What I don't like – is to be questioned.

MADRIGAL   I agree with you.

LAUREL   But I don't like to be agreed with – just in case
I might argue. And I don't like to be read aloud to unless I suggest it.
And if read aloud to – *I don't like emphasis!* And every morning I don't
like "*Good* morning" said. I can see for myself what sort of a day it is.

MADRIGAL   You sound as if you had lady companions
before. How did you get rid of them?

LAUREL   I tell Pinkbell.

MADRIGAL   He tells your grandmother. My mind works
more slowly than yours. But it was going that way.

LAUREL   You see, she loves to advertise. She loves what
comes out of it. It's like dredging in the sea, she says – so much comes
up in the net.

MADRIGAL	I – for instance?
LAUREL	Why not?
MADRIGAL	Doesn't she take a chance – that way?
LAUREL	No. She says you get more out of life by haphazard. By the way, if you want to get on with my grandmother – you must notice her eccentricity.
MADRIGAL	She is fond of that?
LAUREL	She adores it. The *tales* I let her tell me when I am in the mood!
MADRIGAL *(musing)*	Does she love you?
LAUREL	She would like to. *(confidentially)* She *thinks* she does! But I am only her remorse.
MADRIGAL	You try your foot upon the ice, don't you?
LAUREL	I find you wonderfully odd. Why do you come here?
MADRIGAL	I have to do something with my life ...
LAUREL	What life have you been used to?
MADRIGAL *(softly)*	Regularity. Punctuality. Early rising.
LAUREL	It sounds like a prison!
MADRIGAL	– and what are *you* used to?
LAUREL	Doing what I like. Have you been told why I am peculiar?
MADRIGAL	Something was said about it.
LAUREL	If you come here, we'll talk for hours and hours about it. And why I hate my mother!
MADRIGAL	I, too, hated my mother. I should say it was my stepmother.
LAUREL	Oh, that's just an ordinary hatred! Mine is more special.
MADRIGAL	The dangerous thing about hate is that it seems so reasonable.
LAUREL	Maitland won't let me say so, but my mother is Jezebel! She is so overloaded with sex that it sparkles. She is golden and striped – like something in the jungle.
MADRIGAL	You sound proud of her. Does she never come here?
LAUREL	To see me? Never! She's too busy with love. Just now she's in Arabia with her paramour.
MADRIGAL	With her ... ?
LAUREL *(vexed)*	If you pin me down, he is my stepfather. Have you read *Hamlet*? It tipped my mind and turned me against my mother.
MADRIGAL	Does she know you feel discarded?

LAUREL   I don't. I left *her.* *(She pauses.)* The night
   before she married – she forgot to say 'good night' to me. Do you think
   that sounds a little thing?

MADRIGAL *(passionately)* Oh, no! It lights up everything.

LAUREL *(looking at her)* Are you talking of *you*? Or of *me*?

MADRIGAL *(her hand on her breast)* When one feels strongly – it is
   always of me.

LAUREL   Oh, if you are not a spy sent by my mother, I
   shall enjoy you! Do you know about crime? Maitland and I share a
   crime library. Bit by bit we are collecting the *Notable Trial Series.*

MADRIGAL *(looking at her, in a low voice)* Don't you like detective
   stories better?

LAUREL   No, we like real murder. The trials. We act the
   parts.

MADRIGAL *(faintly)*   Which – trials have you got?

LAUREL   So far only Mrs Maybrick, Lizzie Borden and
   Dr. Crippen. But Maitland likes the murder*esses* better. He's half in love
   with them. Oh – if you come here –

MADRIGAL *(rising and picking up her gloves and handbag.)* Here!

LAUREL   Couldn't we act them together? *(Madrigal
   does not reply.)* Maitland is so slow I make him read the prisoner. *(She
   rises, crosses above Madrigal and stands above the chairs Left Centre.)*
   Why does the prisoner have so little to say – *(She waits.)* do you think?
   (She pauses. Madrigal does not reply.) What a habit you have – haven't
   you – of not answering.

*Madrigal, whose eyes have been fastened high up in the air, now lets
them travel down to look at Laurel.*

MADRIGAL *(low, with difficulty)* I made an answer.

LAUREL   Only to yourself, I think.

*Mrs St Maugham enters up Right. She carries a sheaf of lilies, some with
broken stems. Madrigal turns to face Mrs St Maugham. Laurel moves
behind the chairs Left Centre and goes down Left.*

MRS ST MAUGHAM   All gone! All! Oh – when things are killed in
   my garden it upsets me – as when I read every day in the newspapers
   that my friends die!

LAUREL   I should have thought as one got older one
   found death more natural. *(She sits on the downstage chair.)*

MRS ST MAUGHAM *(putting the lilies on the table)* Natural! It's as
   though the gods went rook-shooting when one was walking confident

in the park of the world – *(She moves below the armchair Centre.)* and there are pangs and shots, and one may be for me. Natural!

Madrigal picks up her mackintosh and zip-bag.

MADRIGAL *(involuntarily)* That is why a garden is a good lesson.

She crosses to the hall.

MRS ST MAUGHAM   What?
MADRIGAL *(stopping and turning)* – So much dies in it. And so often.
MRS ST MAUGHAM   It's not a lesson I look for. Take Miss Madrigal into the garden, Laurel.

Laurel rises and moves to Madrigal.

MADRIGAL   No, I think I must be going.
MRS ST MAUGHAM *(moving Centre)* I want you to see the garden.
MADRIGAL *(nervous)*   I'll write – I'll let you know...
MRS ST MAUGHAM   There is nothing to know yet.
MADRIGAL   I'd better not waste your time.
MRS ST MAUGHAM *(crossing to Madrigal)* And that great bag! *(She takes the zip-bag from Madrigal.)* No one will touch it here. *(She puts the bag on the table up Centre.)*

Laurel takes Madrigal's mackintosh and puts it on the chair in the hall. Madrigal exits up Centre. Laurel follows Madrigal, then darts back. Mrs St Maugham picks up the lilies and crosses to the hall.

LAUREL *(alone on the garden threshold, conspiratorially)* Grandloo – psst! What do you think?
MRS ST MAUGHAM   I never allow myself to think. I have another method.
LAUREL   But ...
MRS ST MAUGHAM   And while you are in the garden listen to her! She knows her subject.
LAUREL   But shall you take her?
MRS ST MAUGHAM   Certainly not! But before she goes I want her opinion on the garden.

Mrs St Maugham exits to the pantry. Laurel exits up Right. Olivia enters by the front door. She wears light travelling clothes, as from the East. One is just aware that she is pregnant. Maitland enters down the stairs. He carries a broom.

OLIVIA   I didn't telephone, Maitland. *(She crosses to Centre.)* I thought it better just to come. How is my mother?

MAITLAND *(leaning the broom against the banisters)* She has the health
of – *(grasping for the unexplainable in Mrs St Maugham's health)*
something in Nature.

OLIVIA	And my daughter?
MAITLAND	They're as thick as thieves, madam.
OLIVIA	Could you look for my mother?
MAITLAND	Madam was here ...

*Maitland collects the broom and exits to the pantry. Olivia moves up
Right Centre and puts her handbag on the table up Centre. Madrigal
enters up Centre and crosses to the hall for her mackintosh.*

OLIVIA *(sharply)*   Who are you?

MADRIGAL *(not looking at Olivia)* It makes no difference. *(She pauses,
picks up her mackintosh and crosses to the table.)* Perhaps I should tell
you – the field is free for you ... *(She turns to look at her.)*

OLIVIA	To see the child?
MADRIGAL	You have to see the grandmother first.
OLIVIA *(after a pause)*	Yes.

MADRIGAL   Looking at you, I wouldn't come here if there is
any other post open to you.

OLIVIA	Why?
MADRIGAL	Because the child will make hay of you.
OLIVIA	She *has* made hay of me.
MADRIGAL	Are you the mother?

OLIVIA   Yes. *(She looks towards the door up Right.)* Is
she out there?

MADRIGAL   Yes.

OLIVIA *(taking Madrigal's arm and urging her to the door up Right)*
Please – go out – keep her there ...

MADRIGAL   But I am a stranger.

OLIVIA   I know, but sometimes one speaks the truth to
a stranger. I'm not supposed to see her. First, I must see my mother.
(She steps close to Madrigal.) Please, go out ...

MRS ST MAUGHAM *(off calling)* Olivia!

OLIVIA *(urgently)*   Please.

MRS ST MAUGHAM *(off calling)* Olivia!

*Madrigal exits up Right, taking her mackintosh with her. Mrs St
Maugham enters from the pantry. Maitland follows her on.*

MRS ST MAUGHAM *(urgently)* Maitland – light a bonfire.

Maitland exits hurriedly up Centre.

MRS ST MAUGHAM   Olivia! *(She crosses to Centre.)* So soon!
But you're safe – that's all that matters.
OLIVIA   Mother! *(They embrace.)*
MRS ST MAUGHAM   Oh – let me look at you! How brown you are.
You look like an Arab. How is the desert, darling? I can almost *see* the
sand in your hair. *(She sits on the couch.)*
OLIVIA *(sitting in an armchair)* Mother – how's the child?
MRS ST MAUGHAM *(stung)* Ask for *me* – ask for *me*, Olivia.
OLIVIA   I do, I would, but you ran in like a girl. And not
a day older. As I came in – the standards *dripping* with roses. Oh, the
English flowers after the East!
MRS ST MAUGHAM   Let me tell you before we talk.
OLIVIA   Before we quarrel.
MRS ST MAUGHAM   No – not this time. I was going to say– that
I've missed you. If I'd known you were coming, I'd have driven up to see
you. Whatever – and in your condition – made you rush down here
without a word?
OLIVIA   I flew. I got here this morning.
MRS ST MAUGHAM   Like one of those crickets that leap from a
distance and fall at one's feet ... How do you do it?
OLIVIA *(removing her gloves)* By breakfasting in Baghdad and dining in
Kuffra and taking a taxi in England. We're on a Course. I wrote. Two
months at Aldershot.
MRS ST MAUGHAM   Aldershot! Oh – who would have thought you
would have taken on that look – so quickly – of the Colonel's Lady.
What was it they called it – Reveille. How are the bugles at dawn,
Olivia?
OLIVIA   We don't live in a camp.
MRS ST MAUGHAM   I feel sure you said you did.
OLIVIA   Never mind the camp. I want to talk to you.
MRS ST MAUGHAM   But why down here the very second you arrive
– and without warning.
OLIVIA   Mother – I've come about Laurel – don't put
me off any longer.
MRS ST MAUGHAM *(to distract from the main issue)* Did you wear that
scarf – on purpose to annoy me? What you wear is a language to me.
OLIVIA *(indignant)*   Oh – that's an old battle – and an old method.
MRS ST MAUGHAM   When I've *told* you – in letter after letter...
OLIVIA   It's time I saw for myself, Mother. For nine
years I shut the world out for her ...

MRS ST MAUGHAM *(rising)* Nine years of widowhood – might have been spent better. *(She crosses above the armchair.)* I have asked you *not* to come – but you *come*. I have asked you to warn me – but you ignore it. And how can you wear beige with your skin that colour!

OLIVIA   Does it never become possible to talk as one grown woman to another!

MRS ST MAUGHAM   The gap's lessening. After fifty I haven't grown much wiser. *(She moves up Centre.)* But at least I know what the world has to have – though one cannot pass anything on. When I count my ambitions and what you have made of them ...

OLIVIA   I did what you wanted.

MRS ST MAUGHAM   But *how* you resisted me. I was burning for you to cut ice in the world – yet you had to be *driven* out to gaiety. I had to beat you into beauty. You had to be lit – as one lights a lantern. Decked – like a maytree.

OLIVIA   Oh, can't we be three minutes together ...

MRS ST MAUGHAM *(moving down Centre)* Even your wedding dress you wore like wrapping paper. And where is it now – the success to which I pushed you? Laurel might have been a child these four years, playing in a high-walled park. *(She sits on the upstage chair Left Centre.)*

OLIVIA   And I might have been a widow, with deer gazing at me. But life isn't like that. You had for me the standards of another age. The standards of – Pinkbell.

MRS ST MAUGHAM   Plain, shy, obstinate, silent! But I won. I married you.

OLIVIA *(rising and moving to Right of Mrs St Maugham)* But you won't meet the man *I* married – the man I love!

MRS ST MAUGHAM   Love can be had any day. Success is far harder.

OLIVIA   You say that off the top of your head – where you wore your tiara.

MRS ST MAUGHAM   So you have found a tongue to speak with!

OLIVIA   I have found many things – and learned others. I have been warmed and praised and made to speak. Things come late to me. Love came late to me. Laurel was born in a kind of strange virginity. To have a child doesn't always make a mother. And you won't give up the image of me. Coltish – inept, dropping the china – picking up the pieces ...

MRS ST MAUGHAM   It was I who picked up the pieces.

OLIVIA *(passionately)*   I know. *But I'm without her.*

MRS ST MAUGHAM   You are going to have another child.

OLIVIA This child's the Unknown. Laurel's my daughter!

MRS ST MAUGHAM Who came to me! *(She rises.)* Who ran to me! As an asylum from her mother! *(She crosses to the armchair.)*

OLIVIA *(desperately)* Oh – you find such words to change things. You talk as if I were a light woman!

MRS ST MAUGHAM *(sitting in the armchair)* No, you are not light. You have never been a light woman. You are a dark, a mute woman. If there was lightness in you it was I who lent – it to you. And all that I did – gone.

OLIVIA *(with a step towards her)* Mother! Of a thousand thousand rows between you and me – and this not, I know, the last one – be on my side. Oh – for once be on my side. Help me ...

MRS ST MAUGHAM To what?

OLIVIA Help me to find her. Help me to take her back.

MRS ST MAUGHAM Take her back! *(lighting on an idea)* What, now? Just now – when I have such a companion for her. A woman of the highest character. Of vast experience. I have put myself out endlessly to find her!

OLIVIA She can help you to prepare her. When I come back for her ...

MRS ST MAUGHAM You mean before the baby's born? *That* will be an odd moment – won't it – to come for her.

OLIVIA *(passionately)* No! It's *why* I want her. Before I love the baby. *(She crosses to the couch.)* I can't sleep! I can't rest. I seem to myself to have abandoned her. *(She sits on the couch and faces front.)*

MRS ST MAUGHAM To her own grandmother! I am not a baby farmer or a headmistress or the matron of an orphanage ...

OLIVIA *(turning to Mrs St Maugham)* But she'll be a woman. And I'll never have known her.

MRS ST MAUGHAM It suited you when you first married that I should have her. Laurel came to me of her own free will – and I have turned my old age into a nursery for her.

OLIVIA And God has given you a second chance to be a mother.

MRS ST MAUGHAM *(rising)* Olivia! *(She crosses to Left of the chairs.)* Oh, there's *no one* who puts me in a passion like you do.

OLIVIA *(rising)* And no one who knows you so well. And knows today is hopeless ... *(makes to go)*

Madrigal enters up Right, on a high wave of indignation, matching the crescendo of the other two.

MADRIGAL (*pulling on a glove menacing and accusing*) Mrs St Maugham
– there must be some *mistake*. *This* is a chalk garden.
Who has tried to grow rhododendrons in a *chalk garden*?

MRS ST MAUGHAM (*crossing to Centre, taken aback*)
Rhododendrons? We put them in last Autumn. But they're unhappy.
(*She picks up a catalogue from the table and sits in the armchair.*)

MADRIGAL (*magnificent, stern*) They are *dying*. They are in pure lime.
Not so much as a little leaf-mould. There is no evidence of palliation.
(*She picks up her zip-bag from the table up Centre.*)

MRS ST MAUGHAM   Wait – wait! Where are you going?

MADRIGAL (*moving down Centre*) They should have had compost! But
the compost heap is stone-cold! Nothing in the world has been done for
them.

A gay scream is heard from the garden. Olivia moves up Right and looks off!

OLIVIA (*to Madrigal*)   Is that Laurel? She's screaming. What's the
matter?

MADRIGAL (*witheringly*) There is nothing the matter. She is dancing
round the bonfire with the manservant.

MRS ST MAUGHAM   I should have told you – *this* is Miss Madrigal
(*She opens the catalogue.*) Not so fast! I want to ask you – the bergamot
– and the gunnera ... (*Olivia collects her handbag.*)

MADRIGAL   Won't thrive on chalk.

MRS ST MAUGHAM   There's an East slope I can grow nothing on.

MADRIGAL (*crossing to the hall*) The soil can't give what it has not got.

OLIVIA (*crossing to Madrigal*) Don't go! The wind blows from the sea
here and growing things need protection.

MADRIGAL (*suddenly halted by the look on Olivia's face, in a low voice*)
... and the lilies have rust – there is black spot on the roses – and the
child is screaming in the garden.

MRS ST MAUGHAM   The *roses*! What would you have done for
them? Pinkbell ordered – and I sprayed them.

MADRIGAL (*magnificent, contemptuous*) With *what*, I wonder. You had
better have prayed for them.

Mrs St Maugham and Madrigal measure each other for a moment.

MADRIGAL   If you will accept me – (*She crosses to Mrs St
Maugham.*) I will take this situation, Mrs St Maugham.

Olivia moves quietly to the front door and exits.

MADRIGAL (*with a dry lightness*) You have been very badly advised – I
think – by Mr Pinkbell.

ACT TWO

The sitting room. Two months later. Before luncheon. When the curtain rises, the drop-leaf table from the hall is now standing Left Centre, fully opened. The two chairs Left Centre have been returned to their places. The occasional table Left of the armchair is now below the couch. On it are a seed catalogue, a rose in a small vase, a glass jam jar with water in it, and a small cigarette box. Laurel is seated on the couch with an old mahogany box of water colours. She is painting the rose, on a painting block. Two other sheets of paintings are on the floor at her feet. She is now dressed in a linen frock and sandals.

Maitland enters from the pantry, whistling, and wheeling a trolley laden with cutlery etc. for four, salt, pepper and a silver mustard pot, bread, butter, and an empty glass vase, also a bottle of turpentine and duster for polishing the luncheon table. He is in his shirt sleeves and wears a baize apron. He leaves the trolley in the hall, picks up the turpentine and duster and crosses to Laurel.

MAITLAND All alone? Whose idea is that?

LAUREL *(without looking up)* The Boss's.

MAITLAND *(sprinkling turpentine on the duster)* And not even burning the curtains?

LAUREL *(with dignity)* I am painting a flower.

MAITLAND Occupational therapy?

LAUREL *(looking up)* What was yours? Picking oakum?

MAITLAND Who would think you were weak in the head? You've given up screaming.

LAUREL My madness is older. It's too old for screaming.

MAITLAND *(glancing at her)* Why do you sham mad – dearest?

LAUREL *(in surprise)* 'Dearest'?

MAITLAND *(moving above the table Left Centre)* Only in a sad sort of way I have no dearest. *(He puts the bottle on the floor.)*

LAUREL You shouldn't be sorry for yourself. It unmans you.

MAITLAND *(polishing the table)* It's better than being vain and in love with the glory of one's misfortune. But I'll say this for you. The Boss has changed you.

LAUREL I'm her business and her vocation.

MAITLAND Oh – who could imagine that a maiden lady could know so much about life.

LAUREL She's no maiden lady. *(She looks round at him.)* Might she be a love child?

MAITLAND That's enough now. *(He goes to the trolley, collects the cutlery, etc., then lays four places on the table.)*

LAUREL How prudish you are. Look how she came to us – with nothing. A lady from a shipwreck. Her brush is new and her dresses. No box of shells by *her* bed – no mirror backed with velvet. Oh – she's cut off her golden past like a fish's tail. She's had a life of passion.

MAITLAND *(below the table Left Centre)* What words you use!

LAUREL *You* have a set of words you keep in a cage. Does she get any letters? Do you spy on her?

MAITLAND Who?

LAUREL Our duke's daughter, our hired companion.

MAITLAND *(now Right of the table)* If you are talking of *Miss* Madrigal, she never gets a letter.

LAUREL Don't you get a hint or a sound or a sigh out of her?

MAITLAND No. Do you?

LAUREL With me she's on guard. I can't surprise or ambush her. She watches me.

MAITLAND Whatever she does you're the better for it.

LAUREL Mr Pinkbell doesn't think so.

MAITLAND Poison he is – but influential.

LAUREL If you ask me rows are coming.

MAITLAND *(moving above the table)* I don't ask you. You're too set up with yourself and pleased as a peacock to be the bone of contention.

LAUREL She says he's the devil in charge. He's ordered rhododendrons. It took a *lorry* to deliver them!

MAITLAND *(turning to her)* What's that got to do with it?

LAUREL The Boss reversed the labels. She sent them back again.

MAITLAND *(turning to the table)* Whew – I'm for Miss Madrigal. I've no mercy on him.

LAUREL Poor Mr Pinkbell!

MAITLAND A man's no better when he's dying! *(He picks up the bottle of turpentine.)*

LAUREL What's in the bottle?

MAITLAND Turps. Turpentine.

LAUREL Give it to me. *(He gives the bottle and duster to Laurel.)*

MAITLAND   How did she take our having a visitor to lunch?

He gets the vase and the bread from the trolley and puts them on the table.

LAUREL   I was to wear this clean frock. Otherwise
nothing. *(She looks disdainfully at her frock.)* Straight as an envelope.
It looks so adolescent – and with a Judge coming.

MAITLAND   How do I call him? *(He gets the butter and
mustard pot from the trolley and puts them on the table.)*

LAUREL   A Judge is called M'Lord.

MAITLAND   Oh – I wish I could see it.

LAUREL   What?

MAITLAND *(moving above the armchair)* Him in his robes and his great
wig and all that happens.

LAUREL *(rubbing the inside of the paintbox lid with the turpentine
duster)* How you *dote* on justice!

MAITLAND   It's the machinery and the magnificence! It's
the grandness.

LAUREL *(slyly)*   In prison – was there grandness?

MAITLAND   No, I was brought up from a cell and saw none
of it.

*Mrs St Maugham enters up Centre. She carries a small bunch of Sweet
Williams.*

MRS ST MAUGHAM *(half fantasy, half memory)* Heavens, Maitland! Is
this a morning for daydreams! The gold toothpicks, the green-handled
ivory knives ...

MAITLAND   Locked away.

MRS ST MAUGHAM   And the key of the Safe! It's years since I've
seen it! We used to have celery with the Stilton –
and the Bristol finger bowls and the épergne –
and the sieve we served the Caraque on –
and those glasses for the brandy ...

MAITLAND   They broke.

MRS ST MAUGHAM *(moving above the table)* There was a gold cigar
box that played a tune King Edward gave me ...

LAUREL *(rising and moving Centre)* Is it gold? I used to keep a mouse in it.

MRS ST MAUGHAM   Go and get it. *(She puts the flowers in the vase
on the table Left Centre.)*

Maitland gets glasses from the trolley and puts them on the table.

LAUREL   I can't remember where I put it. But isn't the
man who's coming – *old*?

MRS ST MAUGHAM   Puppy?
LAUREL   The Judge!
MRS ST MAUGHAM   That's what I called him.
LAUREL   Can I wear ... ?
MRS ST MAUGHAM   Wear anything you like. I'm sick of white
things and innocence. *(The crack of a cricket ball against a bat is heard
off down Left.)* Oh! Are they playing out there with the hard ball again?
Can you identify them? *(Laurel runs to the chair down Left, jumps on it
and looks out of the window.)*
LAUREL   The one with the bat is the fishmonger's son.
MAITLAND   How do *you* know?
LAUREL *(waving out of the window)* He's looking at me.
MAITLAND   Get down now.
MRS ST MAUGHAM   Leave that to me, Maitland.
LAUREL *(getting down)*   It's time I looked at boys – or I won't get the
hang of it. *(She moves to the couch and sits.)*
MRS ST MAUGHAM *(moving to the window, taking no notice)* Every
summer – the boys with their cricket! Every summer a broken window!
MAITLAND *(setting out the glasses on the table)* Isn't it strange that *men*
play cricket.
MRS ST MAUGHAM *(turning)* And you an Englishman.
MAITLAND   At the Orphanage we played Rounders.
MRS ST MAUGHAM *(moving to the table, dismissing the whole
subject)* We shall want sherry before luncheon. Bring the sweet as well
as the dry. *(She looks at the table.)* Shouldn't there be two wine glasses
to each person?
MAITLAND   But there's only one wine.
MRS ST MAUGHAM   Put two. I forget the reason. Oh – and the
spoons *outside* the knives.
MAITLAND *(desperately)* You said the opposite last time.
MRS ST MAUGHAM   Never! *(She changes a spoon then a doubt
enters her mind.)* Someone must know. *(She crosses below the
armchair.)* I shall ask Pinkbell.
LAUREL   Pinkbell is sulking.

*Maitland goes to the trolley, gets the small plates and puts them on the
table.*

MRS ST MAUGHAM   Why?
LAUREL *(mocking)*   He is full of jealous rage about his enemy.
MRS ST MAUGHAM   What again! And where is she now?
LAUREL *(mocking)*   She is urging on the agapanthus lilies.

MRS ST MAUGHAM   She is *what?*

LAUREL   She is using diluted cow urine. One in seven.

MRS ST MAUGHAM *(moving to the door up Right, ecstatic)* Oh, I must go and see at once and watch how *that* is done.

Mrs St Maugham exits quickly up Right. Laurel, paintbox in hand, rises and moves above the couch.

LAUREL *(calling after Mrs St Maugham)* Keep behind the escalonia hedge. Every movement is watched. *(She turns to Maitland.)* The nurse came down this morning for the field glasses. Prisoner Six–five–seven–four!

MAITLAND   Sir. *(He takes two steps forward and salutes.)*

LAUREL *(moving to Left of the couch)* Do you know whose paintbox this is?

MAITLAND   Yours.

LAUREL   No. Come and look at it. *(She sits on the couch.) She* lent it to me. The Boss. *(She points inside the lid where she has been rubbing. Maitland kneels beside Laurel.)* Can you see where the letters are that are burnt in the wood there? Look – under the black mark. Under the smear of paint. It is 'C.D. –?'

MAITLAND   And 'W'. It is 'C.D.W.' *(He rises.)*

Madrigal appears outside the door up Centre. She wears an apron and carries a rug-basket, a trowel, a note-book and a pencil. She changes her shoes outside the door up Centre.

LAUREL   Take the turpentine! I don't want her to see it!

Maitland takes the bottle and duster and exits to the pantry. Madrigal comes in from the garden.

LAUREL   Oh! *(She rises and leaves the paintbox on the upstage end of the couch.)* Grandloo has just this minute gone to look for you. *(She sits in the armchair.)*

MADRIGAL *(in the doorway)* I caught sight of her – but I thought it best that we should not be seen together.

LAUREL   She's head over heels with excitement about our guest. Does one still mind when one is old – what men think?

MADRIGAL *(moving above the couch)* One never knows when one is old – for certain. *(She writes in her note-book.)*

LAUREL   She calls him 'Puppy'. I think she was once his mistress.

MADRIGAL   Do you know that?

LAUREL *(casual)*	No.
MADRIGAL	Then why do you say it?
LAUREL	Why does one say things? It's more fun.

Maitland enters from the pantry with four napkins.

MADRIGAL   If you pretend – and it's believed – where are you? *(She puts the note-book in the basket and puts the basket on the table.)*

LAUREL *(smiling)*   Where am I?

MAITLAND *(setting out the napkins on the table Left Centre)* Floating away. The only *hold* we have on this world is the truth. Oh, to think I'm to feed him! A man who's got so much power. *(Madrigal unties her apron.)*

LAUREL	We've never had a Judge here before.
MADRIGAL *(pausing)*	A Judge? Is the visitor that's coming a Judge?
MAITLAND	He's here for the Courts. He's on Circuit.
MADRIGAL	What's his name?

MAITLAND   It's in the newspapers. But the old bastard's got them. They are carried up to him. I only get to read them on the doorstep.

LAUREL   We can talk to him of murder.

MADRIGAL *(removing her apron and putting it on the table)* If you do that it will be a want of tact. It will bore him. *(She moves to Left of the couch.)* You and I will sit at a separate table for luncheon. Maitland will put us a small table here by the sofa.

MAITLAND *(turning to Madrigal)* Not two tables! Not with a guest! Oh – that can't be managed.

MADRIGAL *(swiftly changing her manner to one of treacherous interest)* You can manage anything. *(She moves to Right of Maitland.)* Tell us what surprise you've arranged for us. What are we going to eat?

MAITLAND *(setting out the last two napkins still upset)* Fortnum's have sent the cold cooked chickens. *(unable to resist)* I have carved them. I have ornamented them with mint leaves. There's a salad. Salad dressing.

MADRIGAL	Out of a bottle?
MAITLAND	Mrs St Maugham doesn't believe so.

MADRIGAL *(treacherously agreeing)* The bottled is *so much* better – but one must never say so.

MAITLAND *(surveying the table)* Oh, when I have something to do, something to create, everything is clear again.

MADRIGAL   You look ten years younger.

MAITLAND Oh – if we had guests oftener. The sense of rising to something!

Maitland exits to the pantry, taking the trolley with him.

LAUREL Poor Maitland. How you twist him round your finger. *(with a certain suspicious hostility)* Why do we sit separately from the guest, you and I?

MADRIGAL *(moving to the table Left Centre)* It used to be done at luncheon – in the best houses. *(She collects the cutlery, mats etc. from the two places set above and below the table and stacks them together.)*

LAUREL Had you a life in them? *(sharply)* Who is 'C.D.W.'? *(Madrigal, taken aback, is silent for a moment.)*

MADRIGAL My married sister.

LAUREL I thought you had been born unrelated.

MADRIGAL Did you?

LAUREL And now you have a sister.

MADRIGAL Yes.

LAUREL Suppose you were to drop down dead. To whom should we write?

MADRIGAL I shall not drop down dead.

The house telephone buzzes. Laurel rises, crosses to the telephone, lifts the receiver, listens a moment then covers the mouthpiece.

LAUREL *(to Madrigal)* Pinkbell! In a rage! *(She listens a moment, puts down the receiver and backs up Centre.)* He has practically stung me. He asked for you. Would you be afraid to speak to him? *(Madrigal crosses below Laurel to the desk and picks up the receiver.)*

MADRIGAL *(into the telephone)* Mr Pinkbell?... Yes, it is I, Miss Madrigal ...

Maitland enters from the pantry, carrying a tray with four wine glasses and a glass cloth. He stands listening.

MADRIGAL Ah – but on that I disagree ... The rhododendrons – *I* sent them back again ... *I* reversed the labels! And if I could I would reverse everything! And I may yet – we shall see ... No, I'm afraid on that you are wrong, Mr Pinkbell. Your facts are wrong – also your deductions! ... Yes, and alas it is the wrong time of year to plant them. And the wrong soil ... Not at all. Don't blame yourself. Amateur gardeners very often make that mistake. *(She replaces the receiver.)*

MAITLAND　　　　　　*Blame* himself!
MADRIGAL　　　　　　He made use of sarcasm. *(She crosses to the table Left Centre. Laurel stands above the armchair.)*
MAITLAND *(moving above the table)* My God, you shall have two tables. You shall have three if you like. And the breast off both the chickens. *(He puts two glasses on the table.)*

The Nurse enters down Right, glares at Madrigal, then exits up Right. The others watch her in silence.

LAUREL *(moving to the door)* He's sent the Nurse for Grandloo. *(She moves Centre.)* Now there'll be ructions!

Madrigal picks up the cutlery, mats etc. she had collected.

MAITLAND　　　　　　And with the Judge coming. In the newspapers they say it'll be a long trial. Why, miss! Haven't you read it?

Madrigal puts the cutlery etc. on Maitland's tray, then two glasses.

MADRIGAL　　　　　　Are all the glasses polished?
MAITLAND *(putting the tray on the chair Left)* D'you think – in Lewes prison –
MADRIGAL *(picking up a glass, gently)* There's a cloud on this one.
MAITLAND　　　　　　– this murderer – *(He crosses, takes the glass from Madrigal and polishes it.)* that's lying in his cell –
MADRIGAL *(with a change of voice)* No man is a murderer until he is tried.
MAITLAND　　　　　　– does the Judge look at him?
MADRIGAL　　　　　　The Judge never looks up. He seems to sleep. But it's the sleep of cruelty.
MAITLAND *(persisting)*　When he first *sees* the Judge...
MADRIGAL　　　　　　Why do you think only of the Judge? It's the jury they work on.
MAITLAND *(replacing the glass on the table)* But it seems when you read about such trials, that it must be the Judge.
MADRIGAL *(fiercely)*　Read more and you'll see it's neither. *(To herself)* But fate.
MAITLAND　　　　　　How can that be?
MADRIGAL　　　　　　Because when it starts, there's no free will any more.
MAITLAND *(earnestly)*　But they work, don't they, to get at the truth?
MADRIGAL　　　　　　Truth doesn't ring true in a Court of Law.
MAITLAND　　　　　　What rings true, then?

MADRIGAL *(to herself, trancelike)* The likelihood. The probability. They work to make things fit together. What the prisoner listens to there is not his life. It is the shape and shadow of his life. With the accidents of truth taken out of it. *(She shakes herself free from her trance.)* Time is getting on, Maitland.

MAITLAND *(hurrying to the pantry door)* Oh, what would that man in prison give to be as free as I!

Maitland exits to the pantry.

LAUREL *(moving to Right of the table)* So you've been to a trial?

MADRIGAL *(crossing to the couch)* I did not say I hadn't.

LAUREL *(moving to Left of Madrigal)* Why did you not say – when you know what store we both lay by it?

MADRIGAL *(picking up the paintings from the floor)* It may be I think you lay too much store by it. *(She puts the paintings on the table below the couch.)*

LAUREL *(relaxing her tone and asking as though an ordinary light question)* How does one get in?

MADRIGAL   It's surprisingly easy. *(She sits on the couch and picks up the paintbox.)*

LAUREL   Was it a trial for murder?

MADRIGAL *(closing the box)* It would have to be to satisfy you.

LAUREL   *Was* it a trial for murder?

MADRIGAL *(flicking up Laurel's painting block)* Have you finished that flower?

LAUREL *(yawning)*   As much as I can. I get tired of it. *(wandering to the window)* In my house – at home – there were so many things to do.

MADRIGAL   What was it like?

LAUREL   My home? *(She moves the small table by the couch and sets it Right of the armchair.)*

MADRIGAL   Yes.

LAUREL *(as though caught unaware)* There was a stream. And a Chinese bridge. And yew trees cut like horses. And a bell on the weathervane, and a little wood called mine ...

MADRIGAL   Who called it that?

LAUREL *(unwillingly moved)* She did. My mother. And when it was raining we made an army of her cream pots and a battlefield of her dressing-table – I used to thread her rings on safety pins ...

MADRIGAL   Tomorrow I will light that candle in the green glass candlestick and you can try to paint that.

LAUREL   That – paint the flame?

She collects the loose paintings and the jar of water and puts them on the table.

MADRIGAL   Yes.

LAUREL *(putting the vase and rose on the desk)* I'm tired of fire, too, Boss.

MADRIGAL *(putting the painting book on the downstage end of the couch)* Why do you sign your name a thousand times?

LAUREL   I am looking for which is me.

MADRIGAL   Shall we read?

LAUREL *(sitting on the desk chair)* Oh, I don't want to read.

MADRIGAL   Let's have a game.

LAUREL   All right. *(With meaning)* A guessing game.

MADRIGAL   Very well. Do you know one?

LAUREL *(rising and moving above the armchair)* Maitland and I play one called "The Sky's the Limit".

MADRIGAL   How do you begin?

Laurel takes the cushion from the armchair, puts it on the floor beside the couch and sits on it.

LAUREL   We ask three questions each but if you don't answer one, I get a fourth.

MADRIGAL   What do we guess about?

LAUREL   Let's guess about each other. We are both mysterious …

MADRIGAL *(sententious)* The human heart is mysterious.

LAUREL   We don't know the first thing about each other, so there are so many things to ask.

MADRIGAL   But we mustn't go too fast. Or there will be nothing left to discover. Has it got to be the truth?

LAUREL   One can lie. But I get better and better at spotting lies. It's so dull playing with Maitland. He's so innocent. *(Madrigal folds her hands and waits.)* Now! First question. Are you a – *maiden* lady?

MADRIGAL *(after a moment's reflection)* I can't answer that.

LAUREL   Why?

MADRIGAL   Because you throw the emphasis so oddly.

LAUREL   Right! You don't answer. So now I have an extra question. *(She pauses.)* Are you living under an assumed name?

MADRIGAL   No.

LAUREL   Careful! I'm getting my lie-detector working. Do you take things here at their face value?

MADRIGAL No.

LAUREL Splendid! You're getting the idea.

MADRIGAL *(warningly)* This is to be your fourth question.

LAUREL *(rising, moving Centre and turning)* Yes. Yes, indeed. I must think – I must be careful. *(She shoots her question hard at Madrigal.)* What is the full name of your married sister?

Madrigal covers the paintbox with her hand and stares for a brief second at Laurel.

MADRIGAL Clarissa Dalrymple Westerham.

LAUREL Is Dalrymple Westerham a double name?

MADRIGAL *(with ironical satisfaction)* You've *had* your questions.

LAUREL *(gaily accepting defeat)* Yes, I have. Now yours. You've only three unless I pass one. *(She resumes her seat on the cushion.)*

MADRIGAL *(after a pause)* Was your famous affair in Hyde Park on the night of your mother's marriage?

LAUREL *(wary)* About that time.

MADRIGAL What was the charge by the police?

LAUREL *(wary)* The police didn't come into it.

MADRIGAL *(airily)* Did someone follow you? And try to kiss you?

LAUREL *(off her guard)* Kiss me! It was a case of Criminal Assault.

MADRIGAL *(following that up)* How do you know – if there wasn't a charge by the Police?

LAUREL *(after a brief pause, triumphant)* That's one too many questions. *(She rises.)* *Now* for the deduction. *(She picks up the cushion, replaces it on the armchair and sits.)*

MADRIGAL You didn't tell me there was a deduction.

LAUREL I forgot. It's the whole point. Mine's ready.

MADRIGAL What do you deduce?

LAUREL *(taking a breath then fast, as though she might be stopped)* That you've changed so much you must have been something quite different. When you came here you were like a rusty hinge that wanted oiling. You spoke to yourself out loud without knowing it. You had been *alone*. You may have been a missionary in Central Africa. You may have escaped from a private asylum. But as a maiden lady you are an impostor. *(She changes her tone slightly; slower and more penetrating)* About your assumed name I am not so sure. *But you have no married sister.*

MADRIGAL *(lightly)* You take my breath away.

LAUREL *(leaning back in her chair as lightly)* Good at it, aren't I?

MADRIGAL *(gaily)* Yes, for a mind under a cloud.

LAUREL   Now for *your* deduction.

MADRIGAL *(rising)*   Mine must keep. *(She moves to the door down Right, taking the paintbox with her.)* .

LAUREL *(rising)*   But it's the game! Where are you going?

MADRIGAL *(pleasantly)* To my room. To be sure I have left no clues unlocked. *(She opens the door.)*

LAUREL   To your past life?

MADRIGAL   Yes. You have given me so much warning.

Madrigal exits down Right. Laurel, taken aback, stands for a moment looking after her, looks around the room, then moves to the table up Centre, picks up the handbell, rings it and stands waiting looking Right. Maitland rushes in from the pantry, putting on his jacket.

MAITLAND   Was it you? You're not supposed to ring it! *(He turns to go.)*

LAUREL   Maitland.

MAITLAND   I'm busy now. *(He is about to go but changes his mind and turns.) Now* what is it?

LAUREL *(conspiratorial)* The Boss! We played the game …

MAITLAND *(immediately caught)* You didn't dare! What did you ask her?

LAUREL   Nothing. And everything. No game would uncover her. But, Maitland – she knows about life.

MAITLAND   What sort of knowledge?

LAUREL *(looking towards the door down Right)* Something – intense. Something too dreadful. Something cut in stone over her mind – to warn you when you walk in.

MAITLAND *(wistful)*   I, too, had something dreadful happen to me.

LAUREL   But hers is more dreadful. That's why she has no weakness. Her eyes see through me. I'm a mouse to her.   .

MAITLAND *(moving below the table tenderly)* Are you afraid – poor dearest? Let Maitland speak to her.

LAUREL *(bidding for his co-operation)* You! Oh, *you* tell her. How they brought me back that night …

MAITLAND   Don't talk of it!

LAUREL   So small, such a little thing. How I cried. They should have called a doctor.

MAITLAND   It's what I said they should. I argued it. Madam's got her ways. I've got mine. Oh – she would have got the moon for you. But I was the one who put up with you – who fetched and carried, who read to you. You had the right to the best in the world. A lady's child!

LAUREL *(teasing)*   'The Colonel's Lady.'

MAITLAND *(instantly furious)* Not that again. I forbid you. Your own mother! *(He moves Left and picks up the tray.)*

LAUREL *(moving to Left of the armchair)* Mr Pinkbell says 'Judy O'Grady ...'

MAITLAND *(crossing to Left of Laurel)* I'll have none of it. Out with the devil in you. For shame! And just when I was talking nicely to you.

LAUREL   But I've told you what she is ...

MAITLAND   Not me you won't tell. That's got no mother. If your mother's black as soot you don't say so to me, girl.

LAUREL   I shall scream.

MAITLAND   Scream away! Now we've got the Boss to get after you. *(He crosses Left.)* Oh, the relief of it.

LAUREL *(crossing quickly below Maitland to Left of him, pleading)* No! No – be nice to me. How tough you get – suddenly.

MAITLAND   It comes over me. The Right comes up in me. Like when they tried to make a soldier of me. All of a sudden I *see* how things should be.

Mrs St Maugham enters up Right, carrying three tall stems of hollyhocks. The Nurse follows her on.

MRS ST MAUGHAM *(moving Centre to Maitland)* Cut the stems three inches shorter. Put them in the blue Italian vase and three aspirins at the bottom.

Maitland lamely takes the flowers and crosses to the pantry door. Laurel stands above the table Left Centre. Madrigal enters down Right. She carries a large gardening book. Maitland stops and remains standing with the flowers awkwardly in his arms. She moves below the armchair.

MRS ST MAUGHAM (to Madrigal) Oh. Oh, indeed! My ears are filled with poison. What has the Nurse been telling me! *(The Nurse exits down Right.)* The poor old man upstairs is crying with rage.

MADRIGAL *(calmly)*   I corrected him.

MRS ST MAUGHAM   But for forty years Pinkbell has never been corrected. He is the butler who was the standard of all London.

MADRIGAL   Let him take his standard from the garden. *(fast and ritualistic)* I corrected his ignorance of detail, dates, fundamentals, application of manure. *(She crosses to Centre.)* I spoke – not of his spoons and forks – but of his shallow knowledge of the laws of growth. You can leave the room, Maitland. *(She faces up Centre and opens her book.)*

MRS ST MAUGHAM　　　*That* should have been said by me. But go,
　　Maitland.

Maitland exits hurriedly with the tray and the flowers to the pantry.
Laurel moves down Left of the table Left Centre.

MRS ST MAUGHAM　　　Now – now, Miss Madrigal – this is a crisis.

MADRIGAL *(closing the book and turning, equally severe and majestic)*
　　Yes. *Now* you have to make your decision.

MRS ST MAUGHAM　　　I! I have!

MADRIGAL　　　*Now* you have to choose between us. *(There is*
　　a moment's silence. She takes a step towards Mrs St Maugham. With
　　low, ferocious accusation) Is Mr Pinkbell to let the moment pass –
　　when one should layer the clematis? When the gladioli should be lifted?
　　(She advances another step, menacingly) Has anyone planted the
　　winter aconites? And the pelargoniums? *Who* has taken cuttings? *(Mrs*
　　St Maugham sits on the couch. She pauses. With mounting indignation
　　and on a high enumerating voice.) And the red tobacco seed and the
　　zinnias and the seeds of the white cosmos for next year? Do you wish –
　　like an *amateur* – to buy them?

MRS ST MAUGHAM *(in a faltering voice)* I – always have – bought
　　them.

MADRIGAL *(at the height of her passion)* If that is how you wish to live I
　　am no party to it. It is not possible for me to hold communication with
　　minds brought up on bedding plants – bought at the greengrocer's –
　　dying in shallow boxes. Out there every corner is crying aloud. Must I
　　be dumb when you and I approach together the time of year when all
　　next summer must stand or fall by us. *(She crosses below the couch to*
　　the door Right and turns.) Have you time – before death – to throw
　　away season after season? *(She stands with her hand on the open*
　　door.)

MRS ST MAUGHAM　　　*What* have I let in here out of an
　　advertisement!

MADRIGAL *(over her shoulder)* The East Wind!

Madrigal exits, pulling the door sharply shut after her.

LAUREL *(crossing to Mrs St Maugham)* Oh – we shall lose her,
　　Grandloo. Don't sit there. Go after her. Oh, *think* what she knows about
　　the garden.

MRS ST MAUGHAM　　　I *am* thinking.

LAUREL　　　Oh – she will go if she says she will. You don't
　　want to lose her?

MRS ST MAUGHAM　　　For nothing on earth. I'd sooner strangle Pinkbell – but how is it to be *done!*

LAUREL　　　With a cord.

MRS ST MAUGHAM　　　How is the *reconciliation* to be done? And with a guest at luncheon.

LAUREL　　　Weave her in – as you say you used to do in London. Go after her. Promise her the Earth. Promise her the garden!

MRS ST MAUGHAM　　　The garden ... ? *(She gives a quick glance upwards at the ceiling, then rises and moves to the door down Right.)* But what shall I say to *him?*

LAUREL *(with a glance upwards)* You are not afraid of *him.*

MRS ST MAUGHAM　　　I have always – *(She opens the door.)* always been afraid of Pinkbell.

Mrs St Maugham exits down Right. Maitland enters from the pantry. He carries a vase with the hollyhocks in it.

LAUREL *(crossing to Maitland)* If we are to keep the Boss we must fight for her. *(She takes the vase from Maitland and puts it on the right end of the table up Centre.)*

MAITLAND　　　Fight for her. *(He moves the chair down Left and sets it Right of the table.)* Have *you* upset her?

The Judge is seen through the window, outside the front door. He wears country tweeds and a light overcoat.

LAUREL　　　I haven't. Not I. She and I understand each other. *(The Judge rings the doorbell.)* There the *bell.* *(She moves Centre.)*

MAITLAND *(glancing out of the window, ecstatic)* The *Judge!*

Maitland collects the chair Left, sets it Left of the table Left Centre, then goes into the hall and opens the front door. The Judge enters by the front door and crosses to Centre. Maitland follows him into the room.

LAUREL *(radiantly)*　　　Oh – the *Judge! (grandly)* Oh – we're all expecting you. *(She shakes hands with the Judge.)*

JUDGE *(smiling)*　　　All? *(He looks around but sees only Maitland.)*

LAUREL　　　I am. And Maitland.

MAITLAND *(nervous)*　　　Psssht!

LAUREL *(to Maitland)*　　　Take his coat.

Maitland jumps to it and helps the Judge to remove his coat.

LAUREL　　　And my companion, Miss Madrigal. And my grandmother.

Maitland puts the Judge's coat and hat on the chair in the hall.

JUDGE *(crossing below the armchair)* So you're the grandchild?
LAUREL   Maitland, bring the sherry. The dry and the
sweet remember.

Maitland exits to the pantry. Laurel motions to the Judge to sit.

JUDGE *(sitting in the armchair)* Not for me. I never drink at midday.
LAUREL *(moving to Left of the Judge)* But my grandmother was telling
me this morning you used to glory in your palate.
JUDGE   We change as we grow older. As you'll find,
little girl. *(He looks at Laurel.)* But she *isn't* a little girl.
LAUREL   I am sixteen. But backward.
JUDGE   Bless my soul! What am I to make of that!
LAUREL   Nothing. It's too long a story. *(She sits on the
chair Right of the table Left Centre.)*
JUDGE   Then you are Olivia's daughter? Shy Olivia.
LAUREL *(putting her finger to her lips)* Hush! We don't speak of her.
JUDGE   She is living, I hope, my dear child?
LAUREL   In sin, Judge.

Mrs St Maugham enters down Right. The Judge and Laurel rise.

MRS ST MAUGHAM *(crossing in a swirl to the Judge)* So you've met
her. The little girl of my little girl. No grandmother today. But, *Puppy* –
after twenty years! No longer *young*.

The Judge kisses Mrs St Maugham's hand. Laurel resumes her seat.

JUDGE   What do you expect when you measure me by
that unsuitable nickname. Am I late? I lost my confounded way.
MRS ST MAUGHAM   But you don't drive yourself?

*Maitland enters from the pantry. He carries a tray with two decanters of
sherry, one light and one dark, and two sherry glasses. He crosses, puts
the tray on the table Right of the armchair, then exits to the pantry.*

JUDGE   I do. *(Mrs St Maugham sits in the armchair.)*
I'm so poor. And much too old to be poor. *(He suddenly snatches his
handkerchief from his pocket.)* Oh – forgive me ... *(He is about to
sneeze.)*
MRS ST MAUGHAM *(pouring two glasses of sherry)* Have you a cold?
JUDGE   We won't pin it down. A trifle. An allergy. They
were threshing in the cornfields. *(He sneezes, then takes a large pair of
dark sunglasses from his pocket and puts them on.)* I can stand London
dust – but not the country!

LAUREL   But now we can't see you.

JUDGE   You will. Twenty minutes will cheat my old nose that we are back at the Old Bailey.

Maitland enters from the pantry with the trolley bearing an entrée dish of chicken, a bowl of salad and a bottle of wine in a cooler. Mrs St Maugham offers sherry to the Judge, who refuses it. Maitland exits to the pantry.

MRS ST MAUGHAM   Before we talk of the past – how do you find the present?

JUDGE *(moving to the door up Right and looking out)* Too busy. Too busy. One hasn't time to think one's getting nearer to God.

LAUREL *(whispering anxiously to Mrs St Maugham)* Have you made it right with her?

MRS ST MAUGHAM   Speak louder. Never whisper. *(To the Judge)* My Laurel has a companion. A charming woman. Able – but passionate. At war, just now, with Pinkbell.

LAUREL *(still anxious)*   Grandloo ...

MRS ST MAUGHAM   The door was closed, Sweet. One is not at one's best through mahogany. But I heard no sound of packing.

JUDGE *(moving above the couch)* Pinkbell. What it brings back! What incorruptible ritual. How I remember – after the summer glare of Piccadilly – the young man that I was – crossing your hall – like a pawn across a chessboard –

Maitland enters from the pantry with two dinner plates and a glass – cloth. He wipes the plates and puts them on the table Left Centre.

MRS ST MAUGHAM *(aside in a low voice to Laurel)* Had you better go and look for her? *(Laurel rises but only goes up Centre as the Judge continues.)*

JUDGE   – and how after the first and second footmen – one arrived at last at – Pinkbell. *He* stood at the foot of the stairs. The apprehension one had of his sour displeasure –

MAITLAND *(moving to Laurel under his breath)* Not him – he's not meaning. *(He lifts his chin slightly at the ceiling. Laurel puts a finger to her lips. Maitland exits hastily to the pantry.)*

JUDGE   – *his* severity, *his* corklike dryness – later on, when I had to rebuke the Public Eye, I remembered Pinkbell. *(discovering the fact with amusement.)* My demeanour on the Bench *is* Pinkbell's.

Maitland enters from the pantry. He carries a butler's tray on a stand, already set with two places. He stands it beside the trolley.

MAITLAND *(ready to burst drawing himself up and letting out the words like an explosion, with indignation)* Everything – now – is at your service – Madam.

MRS ST MAUGHAM   Simply. Simply. Times have changed, Maitland.

Madrigal sweeps in down Right, wrapped in an enigmatic mantle of silence, the temporary dressing gown of her anger and offence. She stands down Right, facing front. The Judge moves to Left of the armchair. Laurel moves and stands above the couch.

MRS ST MAUGHAM   Ah, here she is – our Miss Madrigal. How you have relieved me. *(Madrigal bows but without looking.)* Let me introduce you. My right hand. My *green* hand. The mistress of my garden. *(Madrigal does not respond. To the Judge apologetically)* She has a speciality for the Anonymous. *(louder)* Some sherry – Miss Madrigal?

MADRIGAL   No, thank you.

MRS ST MAUGHAM *(rising)* Then – shall we all sit down? *(She indicates the chair Left of the table Left Centre.)* Puppy! (*She moves above the table.*)

Maitland collects the butler's tray, stands it between the armchair and the couch, then stands Left of the armchair. The Judge crosses to Left of the table.

MRS ST MAUGHAM   But why this segregation?

LAUREL   The Boss's orders.

JUDGE *(to Laurel)*   Are you below the salt? Or are we?

LAUREL *(sitting on the couch Right of the butler's tray)* Miss Madrigal means this to be the schoolroom.

Madrigal crosses and sits in the armchair. The Judge sits Left of the table Left Centre.

MRS ST MAUGHAM   She is so witty! Now you can start, Maitland. You can give us your cold chicken. *(She sits Right of the table Left Centre. To the Judge)* I don't entertain any more. The fight's over. Even the table is laid with fragments of forgotten ritual.

Maitland serves chicken to Mrs St Maugham.

JUDGE   Faith is handed down that way.

MRS ST MAUGHAM   When Pinkbell is dead we shall not know why we use two glasses for one bottle.

MAITLAND *(serving chicken to the Judge)* And what about the wine, ma'am?

LAUREL   The Judge doesn't drink.

MRS ST MAUGHAM   And I have such a bottle of Chablis on the ice for you!

Maitland serves chicken to Madrigal and Laurel.

JUDGE   Alcohol in the middle of the day disperses the old brains I try to keep together.

LAUREL   But aren't *we* to have any?

MRS ST MAUGHAM   If we get flushed, Laurel, and too much at our ease ...

LAUREL   I think that will be nice.

Maitland goes to the trolley for the salad.

MRS ST MAUGHAM   The reverse, alas, is the truth. But bring it, Maitland. Bring the bottle. *(She tries to include Madrigal in the conversation by leaning towards her.)* And after lunch shall we show the Judge our roses? *(To the Judge)* Miss Madrigal has soil magic! *(She turns and leans towards Madrigal.)* Things grow for you – during the night.

Madrigal does not answer. Maitland serves salad to Mrs St Maugham.

LAUREL   You mustn't talk to us. We're invisible.

JUDGE   But you have ears?

LAUREL *(nodding)*   We overhear.

Maitland serves salad to the Judge.

MRS ST MAUGHAM   You'll overhear the flavour of the past. Life was full of great rules then. And we high women were terrible. Would you have youth back, Puppy?

Maitland hands the salad bowl to Madrigal, then goes to the trolley and takes the bottle of wine from the cooler. Madrigal serves salad to Laurel and herself.

JUDGE   No. For a man *youth* isn't the triumph.

MRS ST MAUGHAM   I'd have it back if I could – even life's reverses. *(She leans round to Madrigal.)* Wouldn't you, Miss Madrigal?

MADRIGAL *(high and sharp)* You have spilled the salt, Laurel.

Maitland screws the corkscrew into the cork.

MRS ST MAUGHAM   I was asking – do you think grief tastes more
sharply than pleasure on the palate?

MADRIGAL *(startled)*   I beg your pardon...

MRS ST MAUGHAM   You can do better than *that*, Miss Madrigal.

MADRIGAL   I have not the give and take – *(into her plate)*
of ordinary conversation.

MRS ST MAUGHAM   Show it to me, Maitland. *(Maitland shows her
the bottle, the corkscrew already in the cork.)* Now, open it. (Maitland
takes the bottle to the trolley and removes the cork.)*

JUDGE *(looking round at Maitland)* In that case – after luncheon you'll
have to let me close my eyes.

*Maitland moves below Mrs St Maugham and pours a little wine into her
glass.*

MRS ST MAUGHAM   What – sleep in the daytime?

JUDGE   That shocks you? *(The Judge pauses whilst
Mrs St Maugham sips and approves the wine.)* In my job old age is
part of the trappings. *(Maitland fills the Judge's glass.)*

MRS ST MAUGHAM   One gets old – all the same.

JUDGE   Judges don't age. Time decorates them. You
should come and hear me. Learned and crumpled like a roseleaf of
knowledge. I snuffle and mumble. I sham deaf. I move into Court with
the red glory of a dried saint carried in festival. *(Maitland fills Mrs St
Maugham's glass.)* By some manipulation my image bows right and left
to the Sheriffs ...

LAUREL *(to Maitland)* Maitland – psst – *this* is what you missed!

Maitland, behind Mrs St Maugham, smiles at Laurel.

JUDGE   What?

LAUREL   Maitland and I want to know...

MRS ST MAUGHAM *(warningly)* And – Miss Madrigal? Talk is a
partaking. Not a usurping.

LAUREL   But it's *Maitland* who collects the *Notable
Trial Series.*

JUDGE   Maitland?

MAITLAND *(shamed)* Maitland is myself, m'lord.

LAUREL   We read them aloud together, and we are
converting Miss Madrigal.

JUDGE   Ah.

*Maitland, still with the bottle, collects the salad bowl, takes it to the trolley
and stands listening. Laurel, napkin in hand, rises and moves down Centre.*

LAUREL But tell us, in plainer language, how you will enter Court tomorrow!

JUDGE In ermine. In scarlet. With a full-bottomed wig. Magnificent! Seeing me now as I am – *(He removes his glasses.)* you wouldn't know me. *(He puts the glasses in his pocket. Madrigal's wine glass falls to the ground and breaks.)*

MADRIGAL Oh!

MRS ST MAUGHAM What's the matter?

LAUREL *(crossing to the couch)* She broke her glass. *(She picks up the pieces of glass and puts them on the sherry tray.)*

MADRIGAL My hand knocked it.

MRS ST MAUGHAM Maitland will get you another. Another glass, please, Maitland.

MAITLAND *(gazing at the Judge)* There are no more here.

MRS ST MAUGHAM There are plenty in the pantry.

LAUREL Oh – don't make him leave the room while the Judge is talking.

MRS ST MAUGHAM I forgot. *(To the Judge)* Maitland has been in prison, Puppy.

JUDGE *(to Maitland)* Have you, indeed?

MAITLAND Five years, m'lord.

JUDGE *(blandly)* I hope not too unpleasant?

MAITLAND It's given me a fascination and a horror, m'lord, if you can understand. A little stage-struck.

JUDGE Dear me, I hope that's not the usual effect. It's supposed to be a deterrent.

MAITLAND *(waving the bottle a little wildly)* Yes and no. Yes and no. It's hard to explain ...

MRS ST MAUGHAM Don't try. Take my second glass and give some wine to Miss Madrigal. *(She hands a wine glass to Maitland.)*

LAUREL When she had one she wasn't offered any.

MAITLAND She doesn't drink, madam.

MRS ST MAUGHAM *(conveying a sense of rebuke to Madrigal)* One's palate is reborn every morning. Fill the glass.

Maitland puts the glass in front of Madrigal.

MADRIGAL I am not used to wine –

MRS ST MAUGHAM *(flinging this to Madrigal)* One must dissemble.

MADRIGAL – but today I will have some.

Maitland fills Madrigal's glass.

MRS ST MAUGHAM *(with meaning)* It helps one to hold up one's end –
at the table.

LAUREL *(holding out her glass)* And mine! Fill mine! Oh, Judge – go on!

Maitland fills Laurel's glass.

JUDGE   With what?

LAUREL   With tomorrow. *(She drinks.)*

*Maitland stops to pick up bits of broken glass and in doing so leaves the
bottle on Madrigal's table. From then on Madrigal fills her own glass
from time to time.*

MRS ST MAUGHAM   Heavens, Laurel! Talk is a thoroughbred. One
does not say 'go on' – as if it were a donkey.

*Maitland exits with the broken glass to the pantry. Laurel resumes her
seat at the table.*

JUDGE   First I am driven to church to pray.

LAUREL   To *pray!*

JUDGE   I pray against my faults. When you are as old
as I am and sit in a high place – everyone sees your faults except
yourself. I suspect I am vain. But I get no corroboration. I have my likes
and dislikes. Nobody should know that – but everybody knows it.

LAUREL   The Jury doesn't know it.

JUDGE   You are wrong. When the battle around the
prisoner is ended – the relationship is between me and the Jury. *Then*
comes the gamble. Wooden, inscrutable, as they sit hour after hour –
they grow a communal nose. They sniff out weaknesses. I may speak
seldom. But there's no neutrality even in the rarest words. Even in
silence. Long, long before I come to sum up, they will have taken
mysterious sides for and against me. I pray against bias. And against
vanity.

MADRIGAL *(in a low voice)* And – for charity?

*Mrs St Maugham rises and takes her plate to the trolley. Maitland enters
from the pantry with a dish of cheese biscuits and butter. He hands the
dish to Mrs St Maugham and takes her plate.*

JUDGE *(smiling his sharp old ears having overheard)* That's outside my
job. *(direct to Madrigal)* I am sorry – I have forgotten how they call
you?

MADRIGAL   The name is Madrigal.

She refills her glass.

JUDGE *(finishing with his plate)* I ignore the heart Miss Madrigal, and satisfy justice. *(Mrs St Maugham puts the cheese dish on the table. To Mrs St Maugham)* Every little line on my face is written by law, not life.

MRS ST MAUGHAM   Oh – to be bound up again, Puppy, as you are. To be involved – to be back in the hurly-burly ...

Maitland collects Madrigal's, Laurel's and the Judge's plates and exits with them to the pantry.

JUDGE   My life's not the hurly-burly. That's for the Counsel. *(Mrs St Maugham sits at the table.)* I'm the old creature with the memory. I have to remember the things they *said* they said – but didn't. I have to decide according to dry facts – when appealed to in a passion.

LAUREL *(rising and crossing to the Judge)* But *tomorrow*, Judge. *Tomorrow.*

MRS ST MAUGHAM   Stop badgering the Judge, Laurel.

JUDGE *(indulgently)*   No. Let her be. On to the Law Courts. At the gate my trumpeters knock three times. Then blow for my admittance. In a little room behind the Court I change my great wig for a small one.

Maitland enters from the pantry.

LAUREL *(breathlessly)*   Then ...?

The Judge is histrionic, but partly carried away by his own words, every one of which has an effect on Madrigal.

JUDGE   Then – garbed and toffed with medieval meanings, obscured by ritual, carrying the gloves of Justice and the cap of death – on a hollow knock – I go in.

LAUREL   And the prisoner ...

MRS ST MAUGHAM   For the grace of Heaven, Laurel, after such a speech you should have paused and clapped him.

The Judge helps himself to cheese, butter and biscuits.

LAUREL   But I want to ask a question.

MRS ST MAUGHAM   Not yet! I am trying to weave in ... Oh, whoever invented two tables. Can't one join them?

JUDGE   Not across fifty years. Not the Past and the Present.

LAUREL   But can I ask the Judge ... ?

MRS ST MAUGHAM   Ask then! And don't leave our friend out of everything. *(Madrigal drinks.)*

LAUREL *(moving behind the Judge and standing above the table)* I don't know *how* to include her – when I want to ask my own question.

MRS ST MAUGHAM   Ask Miss Madrigal.

LAUREL   But it's the *Judge* I'm asking. Judge – aren't you going to try a murderer tomorrow?

JUDGE *(grim)* That is not a subject for discussion.

MRS ST MAUGHAM   You see! You see how stiff he can be. You see the resemblance.

JUDGE   To whom?

MRS ST MAUGHAM *(delighted)* To Pinkbell! *(Madrigal drinks.)*

LAUREL *(moving behind the Judge)* But here, today, you are alone with us. No one will quote you. *(Pleadingly)* And we are mad on murder.

JUDGE   Murder is a sordid thing.

Madrigal refills her glass.

LAUREL   Oh – you don't think so. Murder cracks open the lives of people you don't know – like cracking open a walnut. Murder is a crisis. *What* must have gone before to make it so! Isn't it true that to you, Judge, everything is told for the first time?

JUDGE   In principle.

LAUREL   But Miss Madrigal says that the Judge isn't even interested. That he sleeps.

MADRIGAL   I said he *seemed* to sleep. *(She drinks.)*

JUDGE   With one eye open. Like a tiger.

MRS ST MAUGHAM *(to Madrigal)* Have you been to a trial, then?

LAUREL   She has. She told me.

MRS ST MAUGHAM   You defeat my purpose. Let *her* answer.

JUDGE *(to Madrigal politely)* Have you heard me in Court, Miss Madrigal?

MADRIGAL *(cautiously)* When I spoke to Laurel of judges it was in a general sense. *(She pauses.)* But I heard you on the Bench, Judge. *(She drinks.)*

JUDGE   I trust it was one of my better days.

MADRIGAL *(after a pause, ironic and high with wine and danger)* I think, if I remember – I would not have come to your conclusion.

MRS ST MAUGHAM *(to the Judge)* Miss Madrigal has such answers to life! *(To Madrigal. In quite a different tone, annoyed)* But *that* was a strange one.

JUDGE   Well, a Judge does not always get to the bottom of a case. *(He drinks.)*

MADRIGAL *(loudly)*   No. It takes the pity of God to get to the bottom of things.

MRS ST MAUGHAM *(rising)* That's enough. *(She crosses to the table Right of the armchair and picks up the box of cigarettes.)*

MADRIGAL *(over-riding)* You must forgive me. *You* insisted. *(She smiles and lifts her glass.)* It has removed the inhibitions. *(She fills her glass and drinks.)*

Maitland collects Mrs St Maugham's cheese plate.

MRS ST MAUGHAM *(loudly)* Bring the coffee on.

The Judge rises and crosses to Centre. Maitland takes the Judge's cheese plate, then exits with the trolley to the pantry. Laurel gets a box of matches from the table down Left and crosses to the Judge.

LAUREL When it's a murderer – what do you feel?

MRS ST MAUGHAM *(offering the box to the Judge)* What should he feel, Laurel? *(The Judge takes a cigarette. She crosses to Left of the table.)* Judges see prisoners by the million. *(She puts the box on the table.)*

LAUREL *(over-riding)* But you've got to say haven't you whether the man's to live or die? *(She crosses to Right of the Judge.)* Do you suffer? *(She strikes a match and lights the Judge's cigarette. Mrs St Maugham sits Left of the table Left Centre.)*

MADRIGAL *(wildly and inconsequentially)* Nobody will suffer. They all go into a dream together.

LAUREL *(turning to Madrigal)* Even the prisoner?

The Judge crosses and sits Right of the table Left Centre.

MADRIGAL *(with an air of reasonably explaining)* The prisoner *thinks* he is at the judgement seat of justice. A place where all motives are taken into account.

LAUREL And isn't it?

MADRIGAL *(loudly)* No. *(She drinks.)*

Mrs St Maugham rings the handbell loudly. Laurel takes the ashtray from the table Right of the armchair and puts it with the matches on the table Left Centre in front of the Judge.

LAUREL But, Judge, while he listens – if the truth is quite different – does he never cry out?

JUDGE He may write notes to his Counsel.

LAUREL Miss Madrigal says that when all has gone against him –

MADRIGAL *(half rising wildly)* I am quoted enough.

LAUREL   – that after the verdict –

MADRIGAL *(with a sudden drunken desire for accuracy)* But if quoted, quoted rightly ... *(She drinks.)*

LAUREL   – when he is asked 'Have you anything to say?'

MADRIGAL   The prisoner is punch drunk. And says nothing.

Maitland enters from the pantry. He carries a tray of coffee which he places on the table in front of Mrs St Maugham.

JUDGE   Not always. Some have said remarkable things. There comes to my mind a woman ... Have you the trial, Maitland, of Connie Dolly Wallis?

LAUREL   Of whom? *(She catches Maitland's pocket flap.)*

MAITLAND *(freeing himself, stammering)* I – I haven't all the volumes, m'lord. I haven't that one.

JUDGE   It wasn't one of my successes. But you should read it for what the woman said when she stood before me. It was just before I sentenced her. *(He thoughtfully fingers his chin.)* Fine eyes she had. I think I should remember them. A tall woman. With a face like an eagle. 'What I have been listening to in Court,' she said, 'is not my life. It is the shape and shadow of my life. With the accidents of truth taken out of it.' Fifteen years ago it must have been. It was my sixtieth birthday.

Mrs St Maugham pours the coffee.

LAUREL   What was she tried for, Judge?

JUDGE   Murder. One of those cases people read at breakfast. During those seven days ...

MADRIGAL   Nine – if I remember. A girl who lied. And when she told the truth it didn't save her.

The Judge looks at Madrigal, frowning, reminded of something, but baffled.

JUDGE *(after a pause)*   Have you been to many trials?

MADRIGAL *(after a pause)* One trial. One. *(She rises, glass in hand, with an instinct to escape and moves to Left of her table.)* But it isn't the *duplication* that makes the impression. It's the first time – the first time – the first time ...

A crash of breaking glass is heard, off Left.

MRS ST MAUGHAM   Quick, Maitland! It's the fishmonger's boy! It's the fishmonger's boy! See if you can catch him.

Maitland rushes out by the front door.

LAUREL *(to the Judge but with an awed glance at Madrigal)* Was she hung?

MRS ST MAUGHAM *(turning back to the coffee)* Hanged – my darling – when speaking of a lady.

ACT THREE

The sitting room. The same day. After luncheon.
The luncheon table is now back in the hall. The upright chairs are in their normal places. The armchair is Left Centre with a stool in front of it and the small table Right of it. A cup of coffee and a seed catalogue are on the table. When the Curtain rises, the Judge is in the armchair, his feet on the stool and his silk handkerchief over his face, dozing. Laurel enters from the pantry.

LAUREL *(crossing to Right of the Judge)* Judge – Judge – wake up. *(The Judge mumbles behind his handkerchief.)* If you have your teeth out I will turn my back. *(She turns and faces Right.)*

JUDGE *(whipping off his handkerchief and sitting up)* My teeth are my own, thank God.

LAUREL *(turning to him)* What have you been thinking of – under that handkerchief?

JUDGE   I am an old man – trying to sleep, Laurel.

LAUREL *(crossing above the Judge to Left of him, urgent)* What did she do?

JUDGE   Who?

LAUREL   In that case you were speaking of.

JUDGE   In my days young girls didn't pester old judges about murder.

LAUREL   You are old-fashioned.

JUDGE   You will be old-fashioned one day. It's more shocking than getting old. *(He pushes the stool aside with his foot.)*

LAUREL   Who died – that they should arrest her?

JUDGE   Her stepsister.

LAUREL *(moving the stool close to Left of the armchair)* How was it done? And why? Was it jealousy.

She sits on the stool.

JUDGE *(struggling to his feet and moving away Right)* If you are going
  to sit down, I am going to stand up.
LAUREL   Why, Judge, didn't they hang her?
JUDGE *(half turning)*   What's that? What are you talking about?
LAUREL *(rising and moving to the Judge)* I'm talking about the case you
  were mentioning.
JUDGE *(shortly)*   She was reprieved. There was a doubt.
LAUREL   Yours?
JUDGE *(shortly)*   Not mine. *(He moves above the couch.)*
  Enough has been said, I think.
LAUREL *(moving to Right of the Judge)* Where do they go when they
  come out – all your murderers – when they don't go to the gallows?
JUDGE *(turning to her)*   One doesn't – mercifully – know.
LAUREL   Do you remember them?
JUDGE   In some strange way they are catalogued. As I
  get older they don't always come to hand.
LAUREL *(insisting)*   But one *would* know them– by peculiar habits?
JUDGE   Perhaps. *(He moves up Centre.)* Some mark
  might lie upon them.
LAUREL *(moving to Right of the Judge)* If they took their country walks,
  for instance, back and forth, up and down, wearing out the carpet in
  their bedroom ...
JUDGE   What?
LAUREL   With a habit, like a sailor's, of walking in a
  confined space. Might it be *that,* Judge?

*Mrs St Maugham enters softly down the stairs, so as not to disturb the
Judge. She sees Laurel.*

MRS ST MAUGHAM   Laurel! He was to sleep, child. And now you
  have disturbed him.

Laurel moves to the door up Right and turns.

LAUREL *(with a sly smile)* I think he was disturbed already. *(She exits up
  Right.)*
MRS ST MAUGHAM   My Original! So elegant and gentle. What do
  you think of her?
JUDGE *(moving to Right of the table)* I am not fond of young girls.
MRS ST MAUGHAM *(moving to the table down Left and picking up a
  writing pad)* You are not? You used to be. It was unfortunate about
  her companion. But your fault, Puppy, for not drinking the wine at
  luncheon.

JUDGE *(moving below the armchair)* How did you discover her?

MRS ST MAUGHAM   I advertised. *(She crosses to Left of the Judge.)* I took a chance and was justified. Miss Madrigal came to me like rain from Heaven.

JUDGE   With references?

MRS ST MAUGHAM   I never listen to what one woman says of another. References are a want of faith – in one's own judgement. Finish your sleep, Puppy. Since you must have it.

Mrs St Maugham exits up the stairs. Madrigal appears outside the door up Centre. Seeing the Judge is alone she comes into the room. The Judge sits in the armchair and takes a small silver box of pills from his pocket.

MADRIGAL   I am sorry to disturb you ...

JUDGE *(wary, playing for time and needing the last link)* On the contrary – on the contrary ... *(He waves his small silver box.)* Old men are kept alive on tablets. *(He takes a pill and a sip of coffee.)*

MADRIGAL *(attempting to control herself and speak reasonably)* Of course you think – this is not where I ought to be. There would be no difficulty – I have private means. *(She moves in front of the couch.)* But it's an understandable job. So fitted to me. *(control going)* Do you believe in God? I thought God had given it to me. *(There is a pause. The Judge is silent.)* Oh – don't look at me as if I were a sad piece of news. A curiosity. *(She pauses, in agony.)* Why don't you *say* something?

JUDGE *(with a sudden crack of his fingers everything has cleared)* That's it!

MADRIGAL *(stopping short)* What?

JUDGE   Well – it has come to me.

MADRIGAL   Oh, God – I thought you *knew*.

JUDGE *(to himself)*   I must say – the coincidences at luncheon– in retrospect – are distasteful.

MADRIGAL *(aghast)*   If I hadn't come in ... *(She pauses. The Judge makes a wry little gesture.)* So – now what will you do?

JUDGE   I am an old man, Miss Madrigal, and very learned. I don't know.

MADRIGAL *(ironically)*   Judge – I can't wait seven hours twice! You sent me to meet my Maker on a Tuesday – but that was altered. I have done what they call 'time'. It was a lifetime. I don't know what you *can* do to me. *What* can you do to me?

JUDGE   I do not presume to judge you twice.

MADRIGAL   Oh, you would come to the same conclusion. Cleverer minds than mine could not convince you. But there's nothing to gain by talking. You came here by accident ...

JUDGE   I wish I hadn't.
MADRIGAL *(bitterly)*   What can it be to you?
JUDGE   Embarrassment. *(He rises.)* What in the name
of Heaven made you choose *this* occupation? With *your* history? In *this*
family?
MADRIGAL *(satirical)*   In 'this' family?
JUDGE *(testy)*   In *any* family. I remember the young woman.
And the lies she told. A Pathological Imaginer. *(He moves up Centre.)*
MADRIGAL *(moving down Centre)* One does not forget the plums in
one's speeches.
JUDGE   And now you have planted me – with ethical
perplexity. It's most unpleasant. And *human* perplexity. Old friends –
and a child to consider.
MADRIGAL *(turning to him)* It's the child I'm considering. When I came
here I thought I had met myself again. The cobwebs and the fantasies.
The same evasions. I could have slipped away ...
JUDGE *(moving up Right)* There are worse solutions.
MADRIGAL   But the child needs me. *If* I stay – will you tell
them who I am?
JUDGE *(turning to her)* Connie Dolly Wallis – what the devil am I to
do with you!
MADRIGAL   The name is Madrigal.
JUDGE *(moving below the couch, testily)* Of course you had to take a
name.
MADRIGAL   It's more than a name to me. I come of a stock
– who in some insensate way – *cannot* accept defeat. My father was
cashiered. And after forty years of appeals – reinstated. My grandfather
died upright on his feet. He said God wouldn't give a fallen general
houseroom. For fifteen years, and alone, I have hammered out what I
am. I did not know I was as dogged as any of them .
JUDGE   But even conceding ...
MADRIGAL   You need concede nothing to solitude. It is a
teacher.
JUDGE *(with a step towards her)* You were a girl of considerable feeling,
if I remember.
MADRIGAL   Not now. I am burnt out white – like the moon
– lunar.
JUDGE   Are you not – if I may gently say so –
somewhat a stranger to life?
MADRIGAL   The girl I was. *She* was the stranger.
JUDGE   You have greatly changed.

MADRIGAL *(ironically)* At our last meeting I died. It alters the appearance.

JUDGE *(crossing down Left, suddenly sorry for himself)* Dear me! Oh, dearie me! As if there were not quite enough – this week ahead of me.

MADRIGAL *(with a step towards him)* You would have been going. Why not leave?

JUDGE *(turning to her)* Because I belong to a guild of men – who feel responsibility. *(wryly)* And a deep distaste for situations.

MADRIGAL What shall you do?

JUDGE *(moving up Right Centre)* Don't badger me. I can't remember when I was so bothered. *(Madrigal puts her hand to her head. Sharply)* What's the matter?

MADRIGAL It is that – after being so long unknown – it makes my head swim to be known ...

Olivia enters by the front door.

OLIVIA *(standing on the steps Left)* Judge! I remember you.

She crosses to the Judge and shakes hands with him.

OLIVIA You used to be so kind to me when I was little. What was that odd name mother had for you? Puppy? I used to wonder at it.

JUDGE *(smiling at her)* You were that silent little girl.

Madrigal crosses down Right.

OLIVIA Yes, I was silent. *(She moves below the armchair. To Madrigal)* We met before – do you remember? I have come back as I said I would – to fetch my daughter ...

MADRIGAL To *fetch* her!

JUDGE *(moving above the couch, quickly intervening)* I have to go – can my car be of use, Miss Madrigal? *(in a low voice)* It would be simple.

OLIVIA *(breaking in)* Oh, don't go – don't go. I'm so glad you are here. It's so lucky.

JUDGE Lucky?

OLIVIA For me. For with you here I shall put things better.

JUDGE *(with his own special wry humour)* I ought to go. I am not good out of my setting.

OLIVIA Surely *you* are not afraid of life?

JUDGE On the contrary – the Law has made me nervous of life.

OLIVIA No, Judge! Please stay. It's the influence of a stranger.

Mrs St Maugham enters down the stairs.

OLIVIA   With a third person in the room my mother hears reason better.

MRS ST MAUGHAM   Don't count on it, Olivia! *(forestallingly)* I got your letter.

OLIVIA   But you don't read them. You never did. *(She crosses to her mother.)* We've had our orders. We leave tonight for Aden.

MRS ST MAUGHAM   Aden! Whoever heard of it! It flashed in history and is gone for ever. Disraeli – Bismarck – I can't remember. *(She moves down Left.)* See what comes of marrying an Army Officer.

Laurel enters up Centre.

OLIVIA   Laurel!

LAUREL   Have you come alone? *(She moves in front of the couch.)*

MRS ST MAUGHAM   We have a guest. No drama!

LAUREL *(turning to Olivia)* You haven't been for four years.

OLIVIA *(glancing at Mrs St Maugham in silent accusation)* But *now* I have come for you. *(She moves to Right of the table Centre.)* Oh – as I drove down here – all the hedges and the telegraph posts were saying – Laurel ...

LAUREL *(undercutting her)* Are you going to have a baby?

OLIVIA   Yes.

LAUREL *(sitting on the couch)* So there's no room for me.

The Judge moves up Right Centre.

OLIVIA *(with a step towards Laurel)* There's room. There's always been room. A heart isn't a house – with a room for each person, *(To Mrs St Maugham)* I can't wait any longer. *(To Laurel)* Come just as you are ...

MADRIGAL *(suddenly throwing her weight in on the side of Olivia)* I can pack her things.

LAUREL *(turning to Madrigal)* What are you up to, Boss?

MRS ST MAUGHAM *(crossing to the armchair)* You are so kind. But there's no need for packing. *(She sits in the armchair.)*

LAUREL *(to Madrigal, menacing)* Did you speak without thinking?

MADRIGAL   No.

LAUREL   But I've told you what she is. I've told you ...

MADRIGAL   And do you think I have believed you?

OLIVIA   There's a seat taken on the plane tonight ...

LAUREL *(furious, but with Madrigal)* And fly with you? Have you thought of the risk?

OLIVIA On the plane? One doesn't think of that.

LAUREL The risk that – if you take me – *(She looks out front.)* I might murder my stepsister.

JUDGE Are you mad!

Olivia turns and looks at Mrs St Maugham, then moves up Right of the armchair.

LAUREL *(gazing out front)* They say so.

MADRIGAL *(to the Judge)* Don't give her the triumph of your attention.

MRS ST MAUGHAM Laurel always uses wild words instead of weeping. *(To Olivia)* I knew that if she saw you we should have trouble with her.

MADRIGAL *(quietly)* You have missed your effect, Laurel. The moment is passing. Would you care to let it go?

LAUREL *(menacing)* The sky's the limit, Boss! The sky's the limit.

Olivia looks at Laurel.

MADRIGAL No time for games.

LAUREL I mean – *no* limit. I can say anything.

JUDGE *(sharply)* *I would not.*

LAUREL Shall I go on?

JUDGE *No.*

LAUREL Shall I?

MADRIGAL If you want your scene – take it.

LAUREL How calm you are!

MRS ST MAUGHAM Miss Madrigal has the calm of a woman in a million.

LAUREL She has the calm of a woman who has been a long time – alone.

MADRIGAL *(in a low voice)* So we are in for it?

LAUREL No. It can be played on the edge still.

MADRIGAL An edge is sharp. One must come down one side or the other.

MRS ST MAUGHAM You see – they are always at some amusing invention. They're inseparable. What game, my poppet?

LAUREL A game that two can play at.

Maitland enters from the pantry, carrying an empty tray. The Judge sits on the desk chair.

LAUREL   Maitland! Look! It's my mother.
MAITLAND *(moving down Left)* I know it's your mother.
MRS ST MAUGHAM   Must the whole house be gathered.
MAITLAND   I came for the coffee cup.

He crosses and collects the Judge's coffee cup from the table.

MRS ST MAUGHAM   Oh, no, you didn't. You came for curiosity.
You've a nose for a crisis like a basset for a wild hare.

Maitland crosses towards the hall.

LAUREL *(rising and crossing to Maitland)* Maitland! *Wait*, Maitland.
How did you know?
MAITLAND   She has been here before.
LAUREL *(suddenly realizing)* How deep you are. *(She moves to Left of
Mrs St Maugham and looks at her.)* I did not know that.
MAITLAND   But I am loyal to madam.

Maitland exits quickly to the pantry.

MRS ST MAUGHAM *(furious)* Loyal! Loyalty died with Queen Victoria.
(Olivia turns away from Mrs St Maugham.) Disregarded in my own
house. Disregarded. I am talking to *you*, Olivia.
OLIVIA *(turning to her)*   Each time I came you promised you would tell
her.
MRS ST MAUGHAM   I had my own reasons. You never would listen.
You were never like other girls. The Judge will remember – though
daughters forget everything. You remember, Puppy, how I tried with
her?
JUDGE   I remember only the result. The shy and gentle
daughter.
OLIVIA   Thank you, Judge. *(To Mrs St Maugham)* But
I am not staying any longer. I want to go ...
MRS ST MAUGHAM *(taking Laurel's hand)* But you'll not take Laurel. I
have a special knowledge of her. To me she is like a porcelain on a shelf
– cracked in some marvellous way for the better.
OLIVIA *(turning to the Judge)* My mother uses words in her special
fashion. For a phrase – she would make capital of anything.
MRS ST MAUGHAM   Charming – for a mother to hear. And in front
of an old friend. If – at a luncheon party – you want to have out the
damage of a lifetime ...
MADRIGAL *(with sudden violence)* Let's have it.
MRS ST MAUGHAM   What?

MADRIGAL *(moving in front of the couch)* I beg your pardon.

The Judge rises and stands behind the couch.

MRS ST MAUGHAM	Were you objecting?
MADRIGAL	Yes. I think the wine has cut the caution. *(The Judge gestures.)*
MRS ST MAUGHAM	Don't gesture at me, Puppy.
JUDGE	Anything may precipitate …
MRS ST MAUGHAM	What?
MADRIGAL	*Anything.*
JUDGE *(to Madrigal)*	Will you come into another room – and I will

advise you.

MADRIGAL *(turning to him)* No. Your advice is foreseen. That I must leave here – but it is the child who must leave. *(She turns.)* Laurel must go, Mrs St Maugham, go with her mother.

Olivia moves above the armchair to Left of it.

MRS ST MAUGHAM *(rising)* You take a great liberty.

Laurel moves down Left Centre.

MADRIGAL	Yes, now I have a sense of liberty.
MRS ST MAUGHAM	That is not what I meant.
MADRIGAL	No, but it is what I mean.
MRS ST MAUGHAM	This girl of special soil! Transplant her?
MADRIGAL	You have not a green thumb, Mrs St Maugham,

with a plant or a girl. This is a house where nothing good can be made of her.

MRS ST MAUGHAM	*My* house!
MADRIGAL	Your house. Why even your garden is

demented. By the mercy of God you do not keep an animal.

MRS ST MAUGHAM	You are mad! You are a monster!
MADRIGAL	No, I am a woman who has lost touch with

things. With indulgence. With excuses, with making merry over bad things. The light – and the shade – has been hammered out of me. I am as humourless as a missionary.

Mrs St Maugham sits in the armchair.

JUDGE	Why complicate life? The past is over.
MADRIGAL	If the past is useful, I shall not hesitate to use

it. What I have been has long been done with. *(To Laurel)* What you are is yet to come. Let's *finish* with the charade made here of affection.

MRS ST MAUGHAM	Stop the woman, Puppy! Stop her!
OLIVIA	But Miss Madrigal has something to say.
JUDGE	No, she hasn't.
MADRIGAL	Oh. I am not inexperienced. You must allow

me a certain bias.

JUDGE	Have a care.
MADRIGAL	I am beyond caring!
LAUREL	Boss, Boss, don't go too far.

MADRIGAL (*crossing to Laurel and taking her passionately by the shoulders*) Don't drive me to it. Who else can tell you that when the moment comes when truth might serve you – you will not make it sound. Or that the clarion note, the innocence will desert you ...

LAUREL (*crossing to Right Centre and facing Right*) But everybody *knows* about me. They *know* what happened.

MADRIGAL   They know what you have told them. You didn't stop the marriage, but you snatched the attention. Shall we now deprive your grandmother of your famous seduction?

Laurel turns to face the others.

MRS ST MAUGHAM	At *what* a moment!
MADRIGAL	One has to *find* a moment to say such things.

The Judge sits on the desk chair.

OLIVIA (*moving to Left of the armchair, to Madrigal*) But is that what she said? (*To Mrs St Maugham*) Is that what you have believed?

MADRIGAL   Wait. (*She crosses to Laurel.*) Let the child tell you.

LAUREL (*moving below the couch*) You were not there.

MADRIGAL   I did not need to be there. The story can be read backwards. (*She turns to Mrs St Maugham.*) What newspaper did the cook take in, I wonder.

OLIVIA	A child of twelve!
MADRIGAL	An only child is never twelve. (*She turns to*

Laurel) Do you cry?

LAUREL	No.
MADRIGAL	I should cry.
LAUREL	I am not near crying.

MADRIGAL (*sitting on the couch and taking Laurel's hand*) I should cry – with relief – that your mother wants you. (*She pauses.*) Be careful. Even a mother can't wait for ever.

OLIVIA (*to Madrigal*)   But *why* did she pretend? Why did she make it up?

MADRIGAL   Odd things are done for love.

Laurel runs to the door up Centre and stops, facing up stage.

OLIVIA   Give it up, Laurel. It isn't worth going on.

Laurel turns and moves to Madrigal, looks at Mrs St Maugham as she passes her.

LAUREL   Has it got to be the truth?
MADRIGAL *(half smiling)* One can lie – but truth is more interesting.
LAUREL   And you get better and better at spotting it.
    You win, Boss.

She looks at Olivia, runs to the stairs, then pauses. Olivia takes a step towards Madrigal, who rises.

MADRIGAL *(to Olivia, softly and urgently)* Quick! A straw would break it.

Olivia turns and crosses to the stairs. Laurel, when she sees Olivia coming, exits quickly up the stairs. Olivia follows her off. She crosses to the hall and calls up the stairs in an exhausted voice.

MADRIGAL   Your blue linen dress is folded in the top drawer. Look – for your yellow striped one.

She moves slowly down Left. The Judge rises and crosses to Mrs St Maugham.

MRS ST MAUGHAM *(gripping tooth and nail to the behaviour of a hostess as she lets fall the tin clatter of words to the Judge)* What a precipitation of melodrama – your visit's fallen on.

She glances towards the stairs, flame beginning to run in her tone.

MRS ST MAUGHAM   Blood is thicker than water I had thought, but it appears not.
JUDGE *(close to her)*   My dear – my dear old friend ...
MRS ST MAUGHAM *(rising, at height of passion)* If you were on your knees you wouldn't stop me. *(She turns to Madrigal.)* That was a black patch, Miss Madrigal. If there's a fire to be lit – you've set a match to it. *(Madrigal sits on the chair down Left.)* What collusion behind my back. *(To the Judge)* You've been a witness to it.
JUDGE   You two would be better talking alone, I think.

He moves towards the hall.

MRS ST MAUGHAM   Stay where you are, Puppy. Men are such
cowards. *(She moves above the armchair.)* In the name of discretion or
a cool head or some such nonsense – they leave one in the lurch ...

JUDGE   So much better – better not say anything.

MRS ST MAUGHAM   There's an undependability in high-minded
men. They sit – objective. When they should be *burning* beside one. But
– when things become personal ... *(She moves to Right of the Judge.)*
What would you say if your clerk put your wig on?

JUDGE *(unhappily)*   I should reflect at length, I expect, and decide
on inaction.

MRS ST MAUGHAM   So you would. But I've been robbed of my
grand-daughter!

MADRIGAL *(calmly)*   If you face facts, Mrs St Maugham, you are
tired of her.

MRS ST MAUGHAM *(faintly)* Be a man, Puppy! Put her out. Put her out
in the street for me. *(The Judge makes an unhappy movement of recoil.
She turns to Madrigal with mounting passion.)* The flaming
impudence! The infamy! And I – lavish. Trusting – leaning ... *(She
moves to Madrigal.)* But I've been leaning on a demon. In your heart –
every penny should have scalded you. I've been betrayed. Don't talk to
me of wages. You'll see none of them. *(She crosses above the armchair
to Right of it.)*

JUDGE *(moving to Madrigal)* Perhaps this is where I may be of some
use?

MADRIGAL *(smiling gently)* No, Judge. Not now. Fifteen years ago you
might have been.

MRS ST MAUGHAM   Do you dare to speak! What are these
innuendoes?

JUDGE *(in a low voice)* Least said, soonest mended. *(He sits on the
chair Left.)*

MRS ST MAUGHAM   Hints – since lunch – have been flying like
gnats from side to side of the room. Nobody tells me – in plain English
– anything. Have you two met before, then?

The Judge and Madrigal look first at each other then at Mrs St Maugham.

MADRIGAL *(matter of fact)* I was once sentenced to death by the Judge
here.

MRS ST MAUGHAM   Ah. *(She sinks into the armchair.)*

JUDGE *(rising)*   Ill-advised. Ill-advised.

He moves above the armchair.

MRS ST MAUGHAM *(rising robustly)* Oh! If I were not seventy – this would revive me. To *death*? But *there you are.*

MADRIGAL   Those who still live – have to be somewhere.

MRS ST MAUGHAM   If it were true – it's outrageous! And if I start putting two and three together – Good Heavens – how can you be living at all?

JUDGE   There was a doubt.

MRS ST MAUGHAM   What I doubt is my senses. *(She turns away Right Centre.)* The thing's impossible. Either I don't believe it – or it's quite private. Besides, if it were true it would be – most inconvenient. Oh – I would like the situation annulled. And the conversation put back ...

JUDGE   To where?

MRS ST MAUGHAM   To where it hadn't happened. *(She crosses to Madrigal.)* And at the interview how dared you – I let pass so many excellent applicants in favour of you!

The Judge moves to Right of the table Centre.

MADRIGAL *(mildly)*   No – really – it was not so.

MRS ST MAUGHAM *(struck by another thought)* And the references. The references I had – I am amazed. You must have forged them.

MADRIGAL   I gave you none.

MRS ST MAUGHAM   Why?

MADRIGAL *(simply)*   I had none.

JUDGE *(explaining mildly)* This lady came to you out of prison.

MRS ST MAUGHAM   Prison! I would have thought a University. Oh, you have been most satisfactory – *I thought* – but now a light is thrown – I'm growing more and more thunderstruck.

MADRIGAL   But ...

MRS ST MAUGHAM   Don't speak to me, if you please. *(She crosses to the couch)* You who come out of God-knows-what Ancient Publicity. Blazing – from heaven-knows-what lurid newspapers. A headline! A felon! And how can you lunch with me, Puppy, and know such things. Oh, I'm dumbfounded. *(She sits on the couch, exhausted.)* What's more, I've been defrauded. Go! Pack your bags. Pack your bags. Out of the house with you. *(She practically collapses.)*

Madrigal rises. Maitland, on a light wind of impatience, enters from the pantry. The Judge moves above the couch.

MAITLAND *(crossing below the armchair)* I can't wait – I can't wait forever. *(To Mrs St Maugham)* Is she – who we think she is?

MRS ST MAUGHAM *(with a faint groan)* She is.
MAITLAND *(turning suddenly to Madrigal)* Oh – Miss – oh Madam ...

Madrigal gives a tiny bow. Maitland gives a tiny bow in return.

MRS ST MAUGHAM   Heavens! What an anti-climax. What
veneration. One would think the woman was an actress.
MAITLAND   When one is a humble man one can't express
it. I think it is – to *think* – that after such a gale she is with us.
MRS ST MAUGHAM *(feebly)* That's enough, Maitland.
MAITLAND *(moving to Left of the armchair)* To have stood one's life
before the Judge here – if you'll pardon me, m'lord, even though you eat
your lunch like other men – making the same light talk ... *(The door
down Right opens. Sharply)* Here's the Nurse – all of a dither!

The Nurse rushes in down Right.

NURSE *(as she enters)* Mrs St Maugham ... *(She stops short at the sight
of the Judge.)*
MRS ST MAUGHAM *(in a daze)* We have friends now. It can wait,
Nurse.
NURSE *(moving behind the couch)* Mr Pinkbell is dead.
MRS ST MAUGHAM   You can go, Nurse. I'll attend to it later. *(The
Nurse, aghast, does not move.)* I say we *have friends*, Nurse.

The Nurse, horrified, exits down Right, leaving the door open.

JUDGE   But – good heavens – Pinkbell!
MRS ST MAUGHAM *(dazed)* He is in expert hands.
MAITLAND   But the poor old bastard. He has passed over.
MRS ST MAUGHAM *(coming to)* Is *that* what she said?
MAITLAND   They've downed him – stiff as a rod. He hasn't
tomorrow ... *(struck by a worse thought)* He *hasn't the rest of today!*
MRS ST MAUGHAM   Dead – and my Past goes with him.
JUDGE *(moving slowly behind the couch)* Dear me, dear me. I am
shocked. First to know he is alive. Then to learn that he isn't.
MRS ST MAUGHAM *(musing)* When I was a young woman he educated
me – my manner with distinguished foreigners. He saw to my Ascots.
He bought my wine in France for me. Is there an afterlife, Puppy?
JUDGE   I don't give judgements easily. But in this life
you will miss him. *(He takes her hand.)*
MRS ST MAUGHAM *(not looking at him)* Alas, no. *(She robustly
disposes of Pinkbell.)* Shall you come again, Puppy? When the
excitement of your week is over?

JUDGE Too much happens in this house – for an old man.

He releases her hand and moves above the couch.

MRS ST MAUGHAM I am coming with you to your car. *(She rises.)* Everyone – accusing everyone – has been tiring. *(With a full return to her old manner.)* Stay with her, Maitland, I shan't be long. Keep an eye on her.

Mrs St Maugham crosses and exits by the front door. Madrigal sits on the chair Left. The Judge signs to Maitland to get his hat and coat from the hall, then crosses to Madrigal. Maitland goes into the hall and picks up the Judge's hat and coat.

JUDGE *(to Madrigal)* After all – have you liked the life here?
MADRIGAL *(with an ironic smile)* It has a hollow quality – which soothes me.
JUDGE What shall you do?
MADRIGAL I shall continue to explore – the *astonishment* of living.
JUDGE *(holding out his hand)* Good bye, Miss Madrigal. *(Madrigal rises and shakes hands with the Judge.)* No man's infallible.

The Judge goes into the hall, takes his hat and coat from Maitland and exits by the front door. Madrigal resumes her seat. Maitland moves to Right of Madrigal.

MAITLAND *(in eager excitement)* Can I come where you're going? I will serve you. We could throw our five and fifteen years away from us. In the dustbin.
MADRIGAL *(smiling)* Not mine. *(She rises.)* Not *my* fifteen years. *(She crosses to the table up Centre.)* I value them. They made me.
MAITLAND *(following Madrigal, ecstatic)* Ah – that's the strength I hanker after. That's what I've been missing, I was born to worship the stars. But I've never known *which* stars – *(He spreads his arms wide.)* when the whole heaven's full of them.

Mrs St Maugham enters by the front door and comes into the room.

MAITLAND *(on the same note.)* I wish to give my notice.
MRS ST MAUGHAM Again! You choose such odd moments.

She moves to the table down Left.

MAITLAND *(moving to Right of the armchair)* I wish to accompany Miss Madrigal.

MRS ST MAUGHAM   Where to?

MAITLAND   Where she's going?

MRS ST MAUGHAM *(choosing a rose from the vase on the table down Left with irony)* Yet now you have it all your own way, Maitland.

MAITLAND *(wincing and glancing up at the ceiling)* Don't say that.

Madrigal collects her gardening book, apron and note-book from the table.

MRS ST MAUGHAM *(crossing to the door down Right)* I'll talk to you later – I must go up. *(Mrs St Maugham exits down Right, leaving the door open. As she goes)* 'Stiff as a rod – the poor old bastard.'

Madrigal instantly turns to Maitland, refers to her note-book and speaks in clear, articulated haste like someone leaving important messages they have hardly time to deliver.

MADRIGAL   Thin out the seedlings – as I showed you – the lilac wants pruning – and the rock rose and the pasque flower –

MAITLAND *(trying to interrupt)* But …

MADRIGAL *(rapidly, in case Mrs St Maugham should return before she has finished)* – tie in the wild grape. Cut the heads off the moss rose –

MAITLAND   But..

MADRIGAL *(moving to the desk taking no notice)* – the asphodel and the dew plant …

MAITLAND   But what's to become of *my* decision?

MADRIGAL *(in irritated despair that he does not listen)* Oh – don't give notice so often! It's a fidgety habit. *(She sits at the desk.)*

Laurel and Olivia enter down the stairs. Laurel wears a white straw hat. She carries an overcoat and a suitcase, which she leaves in the hall. Laurel crosses to Maitland. Olivia stands Left.

MAITLAND   You look a proper daughter.

LAUREL   You may kiss me, Maitland. *(Maitland kisses Laurel's brow. She turns to Olivia.)* Maitland loves me.

OLIVIA   Loves you?

LAUREL   I had to have someone – *someone* who thought the world of me.

OLIVIA   As I did?

LAUREL *(crossing to Olivia and taking her hand)* As you *do.*

Mrs St Maugham enters down Right, closing the door behind her.

MRS ST MAUGHAM   Leave us, Maitland.

Maitland crosses and exits to the pantry. Mrs St Maugham plays this scene magnificent, relentless, and, towards Laurel, dry and gruff. She moves in front of the couch.

MRS ST MAUGHAM   You were right, Olivia, when you said he – *(with a slight glance at the door down Right)* and I had the same standards. Well, Laurel – *now* you have a mother. It's not so rare. Every kitten has one.

LAUREL *(stepping forward, her hands behind her)* Have you often seen death before, Grandloo?

MRS ST MAUGHAM   Up to now I have managed to avoid it. *(Still rather sharp from several reasons, that she has been beaten in battle, also that Madrigal is in the room and she does not want Laurel near her.)* Don't begin badly. Where are your gloves?

LAUREL *(with a step forward, showing her gloves)* Grandloo ...

MRS ST MAUGHAM *(putting a hand to ward Laurel off; with a dryness to cover emotion)* No good byes. I'm too old for them.

OLIVIA   Go to the car, darling. *(She pauses.)* Begin by obeying.

Laurel goes into the hall, turns, exchanges a look with Madrigal, then collects her coat and suitcase and exits by the front door.

MRS ST MAUGHAM   Well, Olivia? What are you going to do with her? Teach her the right things? After I've taught her the wrong ones?

OLIVIA   You're like an old Freethinker – who finds he has a son a clergyman.

MRS ST MAUGHAM   Is that so terrible?

OLIVIA   No. But to you inscrutable. *(She takes a step forward.)* Why did you want her?

MRS ST MAUGHAM   Is it a crime to want to be remembered? *(Olivia turns to go, but stops and turns as Mrs St Maugham continues.)* The Pharaohs built the Pyramids for that reason.

OLIVIA *(in a low voice)*   Are the thoughts of a daughter – no sort of memorial?

MRS ST MAUGHAM *(unconquered)* Is that an obituary?

Olivia looks at Mrs St Maugham for a moment, gives a little defeated shake of her head and exits by the front door. She runs to the window down Left and calls robustly, the Old Adam in her still in full sway.

MRS ST MAUGHAM   Leave her hair long! It gives her the choice later.

She pauses.

MRS ST MAUGHAM *(louder)* Keep her bust high.

She waits a moment then turns, moves slowly behind the armchair and draws herself to her full height. Aridly, stoically.

MRS ST MAUGHAM   What do women do – in my case?
MADRIGAL *(moving to the desk)* They garden.
MRS ST MAUGHAM   But it seems I'm not very good at that, either.
    (She picks up the catalogue from the table) Are your things packed?
MADRIGAL *(moving to the door down Right, coldly)* I am a light-footed
    traveller.
MRS ST MAUGHAM *(moving below the table and holding out the
    catalogue)* Before you go, will you point out the white crinum?
    (Madrigal comes forward and takes the catalogue.)
    You, who have an impertinent answer to everything – is there an
    afterlife?

She sits in the armchair.

MADRIGAL   Certainly.
MRS ST MAUGHAM *(surprised)* You say – 'certainly'?
MADRIGAL *(looking through the catalogue)* One does not sit alone for
    fifteen years without coming to conclusions.
MRS ST MAUGHAM   Is there – affection in it?
MADRIGAL *(moving to Right of the table)* But you have been living all
    this while without affection. Haven't you noticed it?

*She hands the catalogue to Mrs St Maugham. To this there is no answer.
Mrs St Maugham reads aloud from the catalogue.*

MRS ST MAUGHAM   '... very rare – from the High Andes of Bolivia.
    Jasmine-like tubular flowers ...'
MADRIGAL   Don't waste your time. They are beyond you.
MRS ST MAUGHAM *(not raising her head)* It speaks wonderfully of the
    Uvularia.
MADRIGAL   When will you learn you live on chalk?
MRS ST MAUGHAM *(catalogue in lap, in the same tone)* I have made
    such a muddle of the heart. Will Olivia forgive me?
MADRIGAL   It is pointless to wonder. You have no choice
    how she will sum up. *(She pauses. Quietly)* She will live longer.
MRS ST MAUGHAM *(vexed)* Am I to die unloved?
MADRIGAL   If necessary. *I* was prepared to do it.
MRS ST MAUGHAM *(still looking out front)* The Unicorn Root –

She is really saying this because she is going to say something else. It is to gain time for herself.

MADRIGAL *(looking towards the garden)* – needs a sheltered spot. *(She moves down Right.)* You haven't one.

MRS ST MAUGHAM *(slowly)* If you stay here – you can grow windbreaks. *(She turns suddenly to Madrigal.) I must know one thing!*

MADRIGAL   What?

Mrs St Maugham, her face agleam and smiling with human curiosity, looks up at Madrigal.

MRS ST MAUGHAM   Did you do it?

MADRIGAL *(unperturbed and calm)* What learned men at the top of their profession couldn't find out in nine days – why should *you* know?

MRS ST MAUGHAM *(after a second's pause, looking down at the catalogue)* The Dierama – the Wand Flower ...

MADRIGAL *(with a strange still certainty which sits like a Nimbus on her)* It won't grow on chalk. *(She moves behind the armchair and puts her hand like a blessing on Mrs St Maugham's shoulder.)* But if I stay with you – and we work together – with potash – and a little granular peat – we can *make* it do so.

Mrs St Maugham looks up at Madrigal as –

the Curtain falls.

The End.

Enid Bagnold (1889-1981)

The daughter of an army officer father, Bagnold was born in Kent but spent part of her childhood in Jamaica. She grew up in an artistic upper-class environment and later studied art at the Walter Sickert School of Art. She worked as a nurse in World War I but was highly critical of the hospital administration and wrote about it in *Diary Without Dates* (1917). She married Sir Roderick Jones, the Head of Reuters News Agency in 1920, moved to Rottingdean in Kent and had four children.

Bagnold's biggest theatrical success was her adaptation of her novel *National Velvet*, later filmed with Elizabeth Taylor.

Besides *The Chalk Garden,* eight of her plays were performed including: *Lottie Dundass* (1942); *Poor Judas* (1951); *Gertie* (or *Little Idiot,* 1952); *The Last Joke* (1960); *The Chinese Prime Minister* (1964); *Call Me Jacky* (1967) and *A Matter of Gravity* (1978). She also wrote poetry and a number of novels including *The Difficulty of Getting Married* (1924) and notably *The Squire* (1938).

Her great grand-daughter, Samantha Cameron, is married to the leader of the UK Conservative Party, David Cameron.

Extract from *Top Girls* by Caryl Churchill

First performed at The Royal Court Theatre, London on 28th August, 1982.

* / See note on page 411

ACT THREE

A year earlier. Sunday evening. Joyce's kitchen. Joyce, Angie, Marlene. Marlene is taking presents out of a bright carrier bag. Angie has already opened a box of chocolates.

MARLENE	Just a few little things. / I've no memory for
JOYCE	There's no need.
MARLENE	birthdays have I, and Christmas seems to slip by. So I think I owe Angie a few presents.
JOYCE	What do you say?
ANGIE	Thank you very much. Thank you very much, Aunty Marlene.

She opens a present. It is the dress from Act One, new.

ANGIE	Oh look, Mum, isn't it lovely?
MARLENE	I don't know if it's the right size. She's grown up since I saw her. / I knew she was always tall for her age.
ANGIE	Isn't it lovely?
JOYCE	She's a big lump.
MARLENE	Hold it up, Angie, let's see.
ANGIE	I'll put it on, shall I?
MARLENE	Yes, try it on.
JOYCE	Go on to your room then, we don't want / a strip show thank you.
ANGIE	Of course I'm going to my room, what do you think? Look Mum, here's something for you. Open it, go on. What is it? Can I open it for you?
JOYCE	Yes, you open it, pet.
ANGIE	Don't you want to open it yourself? / Go on.
JOYCE	I don't mind, you can do it.
ANGIE	It's something hard. It's - what is it? A bottle. Drink is it? No, it's what? Perfume, look. What a lot. Open it, look, let's smell it. Oh it's strong. It's lovely. Put it on me. How do you do it? Put it on me.
JOYCE	You're too young.

| ANGIE | I can play wearing it like dressing up. |

ANGIE   I can play wearing it like dressing up.

JOYCE   And you're too old for that. Here, give it here,
I'll do it, you'll tip the whole bottle over yourself I and we'll have you
smelling all summer.

ANGIE   Put it on you. Do I smell? Put it on Aunty too. Put
it on Aunty too. Let's all smell.

MARLENE   I didn't know what you'd like.

JOYCE   There's no danger I'd have it already, / that's one
thing.

ANGIE   Now we all smell the same.

MARLENE   It's a bit of nonsense.

JOYCE   It's very kind of you Marlene, you shouldn't.

ANGIE   Now. I'll put on the dress and then we'll see.

Angie goes.

JOYCE   You've caught me on the hop with the place in a
mess. / If you'd let me know you was coming I'd have got

MARLENE   That doesn't matter.

JOYCE   something in to eat. We had our dinner
dinnertime. We're just going to have a cup of tea. You could have an
egg.

MARLENE   No, I'm not hungry. Tea's fine.

JOYCE   I don't expect you take sugar.

MARLENE   Why not?

JOYCE   You take care of yourself.

MARLENE   How do you mean you didn't know I was coming?

JOYCE   You could have written. I know we're not on the
phone but we're not completely in the dark ages, / we do have a
postman.

MARLENE   But you asked me to come.

JOYCE   How did I ask you to come?

MARLENE   Angie said when she phoned up.

JOYCE   Angie phoned up, did she?

MARLENE   Was it just Angie's idea?

JOYCE   What did she say?

MARLENE   She said you wanted me to come and see you. / It
was a couple of weeks ago. How was I to know that's a

JOYCE   Ha.

MARLENE   ridiculous idea? My diary's always full a couple of
weeks ahead so we fixed it for this weekend. I was meant to get here
earlier but I was held up. She gave me messages from you.

JOYCE	Didn't you wonder why I didn't phone you

myself?

MARLENE	She said you didn't like using the phone. You're

shy on the phone and can't use it. I don't know what you're like, do I.

JOYCE	Are there people who can't use the phone?
MARLENE	I expect so.
JOYCE	I haven't met any.
MARLENE	Why should I think she was lying?
JOYCE	Because she's like what she's like.
MARLENE	How do I know / what she's like?
JOYCE	It's not my fault you don't know what she's like.

You never come and see her.

MARLENE	Well I have now / and you don't seem over the

moon.*

JOYCE	Good.

*Well I'd have got a cake if she'd told me. *(pause.)*

MARLENE	I did wonder why you wanted to see me.
JOYCE	I didn't want to see you.
MARLENE	Yes. I know. Shall I go?
JOYCE	I don't mind seeing you.
MARLENE	Great, I feel really welcome.
JOYCE	You can come and see Angie any time you like,

I'm not stopping you. / You know where we are. You're the

MARLENE	Ta ever so.
JOYCE	one went away, not me. I'm right here where I

was. And will be a few years yet I shouldn't wonder.

MARLENE	All right. All right.

Joyce gives Marlene a cup of tea.

JOYCE	Tea.
MARLENE	Sugar? *(Joyce passes Marlene the sugar.)*

It's very quiet down here.

JOYCE	I expect you'd notice it.
MARLENE	The air smells different too.
JOYCE	That's the scent.
MARLENE	No, I mean walking down the lane.
JOYCE	What sort of air you get in London then?

Angie comes in, wearing the dress. It fits.

MARLENE	Oh, very pretty. / You do look pretty, Angie.
JOYCE	That fits all right.

MARLENE	Do you like the colour?
ANGIE	Beautiful. Beautiful.
JOYCE	You better take it off, / you'll get it dirty.
ANGIE	I want to wear it. I want to wear it.
MARLENE	It is for wearing after all. You can't just hang it up

and look at it.

ANGIE	I love it.
JOYCE	Well if you must you must.
ANGIE	If someone asks me what's my favourite colour

I'll tell them it's this. Thank you very much, Aunty Marlene.

MARLENE	You didn't tell your mum you asked me down.
ANGIE	I wanted it to be a surprise.
JOYCE	I'll give you a surprise / one of these days.
ANGIE	I thought you'd like to see her. She hasn't been

here since I was nine. People do see their aunts.

MARLENE	Is it that long? Doesn't time fly?
ANGIE	I wanted to.
JOYCE	I'm not cross.
ANGIE	Are you glad?
JOYCE	I smell nicer anyhow, don't I?

Kit comes in without saying anything, as if she lived there.

MARLENE	I think it was a good idea, Angie, about time. We

are sisters after all. It's a pity to let that go.

JOYCE	This is Kitty, / who lives up the road. This is

Angie's Aunty Marlene.

KIT	What's that?
ANGIE	It's a present. Do you like it?
KIT	It's all right. / Are you coming out?*
MARLENE	Hello, Kitty.
ANGIE	*No.
KIT	What's that smell?
ANGIE	It's a present.
KIT	It's horrible. Come on.*
MARLENE	Have a chocolate.
ANGIE	*No, I'm busy.
KIT	Coming out later?
ANGIE	No.
KIT *(to Marlene)*	Hello.

Kit goes without a chocolate.

JOYCE	She's a little girl Angie sometimes plays with

because she's the only child lives really close. She's like a little sister
to her really. Angie's good with little children.

MARLENE   Do you want to work with children, Angie? /
Be a teacher or a nursery nurse?

JOYCE   I don't think she's ever thought of it.

MARLENE   What do you want to do?

JOYCE   She hasn't an idea in her head what she wants to
do. Lucky to get anything.

MARLENE   Angie?

JOYCE   She's not clever like you.

Pause.

MARLENE   I'm not clever, just pushy.

JOYCE   True enough.

Marlene takes a bottle of whisky out of the bag.

JOYCE   I don't drink spirits.

ANGIE   You do at Christmas.

JOYCE   It's not Christmas, is it?

ANGIE   It's better than Christmas.

MARLENE   Glasses?

JOYCE   Just a small one then.

MARLENE   Do you want some, Angie?

ANGIE   I can't, can I?

JOYCE   Taste it if you want. You won't like it.

MARLENE   We got drunk together the night your grandfather
died.

JOYCE   We did not get drunk.

MARLENE   I got drunk. You were just overcome with grief.

JOYCE   I still keep up the grave with flowers.

MARLENE   Do you really?

JOYCE   Why wouldn't I?

MARLENE   Have you seen Mother?

JOYCE   Of course I've seen Mother.

MARLENE   I mean lately.

JOYCE   Of course I've seen her lately, I go every
Thursday.

MARLENE *(to Angie)* Do you remember your grandfather?

ANGIE   He got me out of the bath one night in a towel.

MARLENE   Did he? I don't think he ever gave me a bath.

Did he give you a bath, Joyce? He probably got soft in his old age. Did
you like him?

ANGIE	Yes of course.
MARLENE	Why?
ANGIE	What?
MARLENE	So what's the news? How's Mrs Paisley? Still

going crazily? / And Dorothy. What happened to Dorothy?*

ANGIE	Who's Mrs Paisley?
JOYCE	*She went to Canada.
MARLENE	Did she? What to do?
JOYCE	I don't know. She just went to Canada.
MARLENE	Well / good for her.
ANGIE	Mr Connolly killed his wife.
MARLENE	What, Connolly at Whitegates?
ANGIE	They found her body in the garden. / Under the

cabbages.

MARLENE	He was always so proper.
JOYCE	Stuck up git. Connolly. Best lawyer money could

buy but he couldn't get out of it. She was carrying on with Matthew.

MARLENE	How old's Matthew then?
JOYCE	Twenty-one. / He's got a motorbike.
MARLENE	I think he's about six.
ANGIE	How can he be six? He's six years older than me.

/ If he was six I'd be nothing, I'd be just born this minute.

JOYCE	Your aunty knows that, she's just being silly. She

means it's so long since she's been here she's forgotten about Matthew.

ANGIE	You were here for my birthday when I was nine. I

had a pink cake. Kit was only five then, she was four, she hadn't started
school yet. She could read already when she went to school. You
remember my birthday? / You remember me?

MARLENE	Yes, I remember the cake.
ANGIE	You remember me?
MARLENE	Yes, I remember you.
ANGIE	And Mum and Dad was there, and Kit was.
MARLENE	Yes, how is your dad? Where is he tonight? Up
	the pub?
JOYCE	No, he's not here.
MARLENE	I can see he's not here.
JOYCE	He moved out.
MARLENE	What? When did he? / Just recently?*
ANGIE	Didn't you know that? You don't know much.

JOYCE   * No, it must be three years ago. Don't be rude,
   Angie.
ANGIE   I'm not, am I Aunty? What else don't you know?
JOYCE   You was in America or somewhere. You sent a
   postcard.
ANGIE   I've got that in my room. It's the Grand Canyon.
   Do you want to see it? Shall I get it? I can get it for you.
MARLENE   Yes, all right.

Angie goes.

JOYCE   You could be married with twins for all I know.
   You must have affairs and break up and I don't need to know about any
   of that so I don't see what the fuss is about.
MARLENE   What fuss?

Angie comes back with the postcard.

ANGIE   'Driving across the states for a new job in L.A. It's
   a long way but the car goes very fast. It's very hot. Wish you were here.
   Love from Aunty Marlene.'
JOYCE   Did you make a lot of money?
MARLENE   I spent a lot.
ANGIE   I want to go to America. Will you take me?
JOYCE   She's not going to America, she's been to
   America, stupid.
ANGIE   She might go again, stupid. It's not something
   you do once. People who go keep going all the time, back and forth on
   jets. They go on Concorde and Laker and get jet lag. Will you take me?
MARLENE   I'm not planning a trip.
ANGIE   Will you let me know?
JOYCE   Angie, / you're getting silly.
ANGIE   I want to be American.
JOYCE   It's time you were in bed.
ANGIE   No it's not. / I don't have to go to bed at all
   tonight.
JOYCE   School in the morning.
ANGIE   I'll wake up.
JOYCE   Come on now, you know how you get.
ANGIE   How do I get? / I don't get anyhow.
JOYCE   Angie.
   Are you staying the night?
MARLENE   Yes, if that's all right. / I'll see you in the morning.

ANGIE	You can have my bed. I'll sleep on the sofa.
JOYCE	You will not, you'll sleep in your bed. / Think I
can't	
ANGIE	Mum.
JOYCE	see through that? I can just see you going to sleep
/ with us talking.	
ANGIE	I would, I would go to sleep, I'd love that.
JOYCE	I'm going to get cross, Angie.
ANGIE	I want to show her something.
JOYCE	Then bed.
ANGIE	It's a secret.
JOYCE	Then I expect it's in your room so off you go. Give
us a shout when you're ready for bed and your aunty'll be up and see	
you.	
ANGIE	Will you?
MARLENE	Yes of course. *(Angie goes. Silence.)*
It's cold tonight.	
JOYCE	Will you be all right on the sofa? You can / have
my bed.	
MARLENE	The sofa's fine.
JOYCE	Yes, the forecast said rain tonight but it's held off.
MARLENE	I was going to walk down to the estuary but I've
left it a bit late. Is it just the same?	
JOYCE	They cut down the hedges a few years back. Is
that since you were here?	
MARLENE	But it's not changed down the end, all the mud?
And the reeds? We used to pick them when they were bigger than us.	
Are there still lapwings?	
JOYCE	You get strangers walking there on a Sunday. I
expect they're looking at the mud and the lapwings, yes.	
MARLENE	You could have left.
JOYCE	Who says I wanted to leave?
MARLENE	Stop getting at me then, you're really boring.
JOYCE	How could I have left?
MARLENE	Did you want to?
JOYCE	I said how / how could I?
MARLENE	If you'd wanted to you'd have done it.
JOYCE	Christ.
MARLENE	Are we getting drunk?
JOYCE	Do you want something to eat?
MARLENE	No, I'm getting drunk.

JOYCE	Funny time to visit, Sunday evening.
MARLENE	I came this morning. I spent the day.
ANGIE *(off)*	Aunty! Aunty Marlene!
MARLENE	I'd better go.
JOYCE	Go on then.
MARLENE	All right.
ANGIE *(off)*	Aunty! Can you hear me? I'm ready.

Marlene goes. Joyce goes on sitting. Marlene comes back.

JOYCE	So what's the secret?
MARLENE	It's a secret.
JOYCE	I know what it is anyway.
MARLENE	I bet you don't. You always said that.
JOYCE	It's her exercise book.
MARLENE	Yes, but you don't know what's in it.
JOYCE	It's some game, some secret society she has with Kit.
MARLENE	You don't know the password. You don't know the code.
JOYCE	You're really in it, aren't you? Can you do the handshake?
MARLENE	She didn't mention a handshake.
JOYCE	I thought they'd have a special handshake. She spends hours writing that but she's useless at school. She copies things out of books about black magic, and politicians out of the paper. It's a bit childish.
MARLENE	I think it's a plot to take over the world.
JOYCE	She's been in the remedial class the last two years.
MARLENE	I came up this morning and spent the day in Ipswich. I went to see mother.
JOYCE	Did she recognise you?
MARLENE	Are you trying to be funny?
JOYCE	No, she does wander.
MARLENE	She wasn't wandering at all, she was very lucid thank you.
JOYCE	You were very lucky then.
MARLENE	Fucking awful life she's had.
JOYCE	Don't tell me.
MARLENE	Fucking waste.
JOYCE	Don't talk to me.

MARLENE   Why shouldn't I talk? Why shouldn't I talk to you?/
Isn't she my mother too?

JOYCE   Look, you've left, you've gone away, / we can do
without you.

MARLENE   I left home, so what, I left home. People do leave
home / it is normal.

JOYCE   We understand that, we can do without you.

MARLENE   We weren't happy. Were you happy?

JOYCE   Don't come back.

MARLENE   So it's just your mother is it, your child, you
never wanted me round, / you were jealous of me because I was the –

JOYCE   Here we go.

MARLENE   little one and I was clever.

JOYCE   I'm not clever enough for all this psychology / if
that's what it is.

MARLENE   Why can't I visit my own family / without all
this?*

JOYCE   Aah.

*Just don't go on about Mum's life when you haven't been to see her for
how many years. / I go and see her every week.*

MARLENE   It's up to me.

*Then don't go and see her every week.

JOYCE   Somebody has to.

MARLENE   No they don't. / Why do they?

JOYCE   How would I feel if I didn't go?

MARLENE   A lot better.

JOYCE   I hope you feel better.

MARLENE   It's up to me.

JOYCE   You couldn't get out of here fast enough.

MARLENE   Of course I couldn't get out of here fast enough.
What was I going to do? Marry a dairyman who'd come home pissed? /
Don't you fucking this fucking that fucking bitch

JOYCE   Christ.

MARLENE   fucking tell me what to fucking do fucking.

JOYCE   I don't know how you could leave your own child.

MARLENE   You were quick enough to take her.

JOYCE   What does that mean?

MARLENE   You were quick enough to take her.

JOYCE   Or what? Have her put in a home? Have some
stranger / take her would you rather?

MARLENE   You couldn't have one so you took mine.

JOYCE	I didn't know that then.
MARLENE	Like hell, / married three years.
JOYCE	I didn't know that. Plenty of people / take that long.
MARLENE	Well it turned out lucky for you, didn't it?
JOYCE	Turned out all right for you by the look of you. You'd be getting a few less thousand a year.
MARLENE	Not necessarily.
JOYCE	You'd be stuck here / like you said.
MARLENE	I could have taken her with me.
JOYCE	You didn't want to take her with you. It's no good coming back now, Marlene, / and saying –
MARLENE	I know a managing director who's got two children, she breast feeds in the board room, she pays a hundred pounds a week on domestic help alone and she can afford that because she's an extremely high-powered lady earning a great deal of money.
JOYCE	So what's that got to do with you at the age of seventeen?
MARLENE	Just because you were married and had somewhere to live –
JOYCE	You could have lived at home. Or live with me
MARLENE	Don't be stupid.
JOYCE	and Frank. / You said you weren't keeping it. You
MARLENE	You never suggested.
JOYCE	shouldn't have had it / if you wasn't going to keep it.
MARLENE	Here we go.
JOYCE	You was the most stupid, / for someone so clever you was the most stupid, get yourself pregnant, not go to the doctor, not tell.
MARLENE	You wanted it, you said you were glad, I remember the day, you said I'm glad you never got rid of it, I'll look after it, you said that down by the river. So what are you saying, sunshine, you don't want her?
JOYCE	Course I'm not saying that.
MARLENE	Because I'll take her / wake her up and pack now.
JOYCE	You wouldn't know how to begin to look after her.
MARLENE	Don't you want her?
JOYCE	Course I do, she's my child.
MARLENE	Then what are you going on about / why did I have her?

JOYCE   You said I got her off you / when you didn't –
MARLENE   I said you were lucky / the way it –
JOYCE   Have a child now if you want one. You're not old.
MARLENE   I might do.
JOYCE   Good.

Pause.

MARLENE   I've been on the pill so long / I'm probably
sterile.
JOYCE   Listen when Angie was six months I did get
pregnant and I lost it because I was so tired looking after your fucking
baby / because she cried so much – yes I did tell
MARLENE   You never told me.
JOYCE   you – / and the doctor said if I'd sat down all day
with
MARLENE   Well I forgot.
JOYCE   my feet up I'd've kept it and that's the only
chance I ever had because after that –
MARLENE   I've had two abortions, are you interested? Shall I
tell you about them? Well I won't, it's boring, it wasn't a problem. I
don't like messy talk about blood and what a bad
JOYCE   If I hadn't had your baby. The doctor said.
MARLENE   time we all had. I don't want a baby. I don't want
to talk about gynaecology.
JOYCE   Then stop trying to get Angie off of me.
MARLENE   I come down here after six years. All night you've
been saying I don't come often enough. If I don't come for another six
years she'll be twenty-one, will that be OK?
JOYCE   That'll be fine, yes, six years would suit me fine.

Pause.

MARLENE   I was afraid of this.
I only came because I thought you wanted ...
I just want ...

Marlene cries.

JOYCE   Don't grizzle, Marlene, for God's sake. Marly?
Come on, pet. Love you really. Fucking stop it, will you?
MARLENE   No, let me cry. I like it.

They laugh, Marlene begins to stop crying.

MARLENE	I knew I'd cry if I wasn't careful.
JOYCE	Everyone's always crying in this house. Nobody
takes any notice.	
MARLENE	You've been wonderful looking after Angie.
JOYCE	Don't get carried away.
MARLENE	I can't write letters but I do think of you.
JOYCE	You're getting drunk. I'm going to make some
tea.	
MARLENE	Love you.

Joyce gets up to make tea.

JOYCE	I can see why you'd want to leave. It's a dump
here.	
MARLENE	So what's this about you and Frank?
JOYCE	He was always carrying on, wasn't he? And if I

wanted to go out in the evening he'd go mad, even if it was nothing, a
class, I was going to go to an evening class. So he had this girlfriend,
only twenty-two poor cow, and I said go on, off you go, hoppit. I don't
think he even likes her.

MARLENE	So what about money?
JOYCE	I've always said I don't want your money.
MARLENE	No, does he send you money?
JOYCE	I've got four different cleaning jobs. Adds up.
There's not a lot round here.	
MARLENE	Does Angie miss him?
JOYCE	She doesn't say.
MARLENE	Does she see him?
JOYCE	He was never that fond of her to be honest.
MARLENE	He tried to kiss me once. When you were
engaged.	
JOYCE	Did you fancy him?
MARLENE	No, he looked like a fish.
JOYCE	He was lovely then.
MARLENE	Ugh.
JOYCE	Well I fancied him. For about three years.
MARLENE	Have you got someone else?
JOYCE	There's not a lot round here. Mind you, the

minute you're on your own, you'd be amazed how your friends'
husbands drop by. I'd sooner do without.

MARLENE	I don't see why you couldn't take my money.
JOYCE	I do, so don't bother about it.

MARLENE	Only got to ask.
JOYCE	So what about you? Good job?
MARLENE	Good for a laugh. / Got back from the US of A a bit.
JOYCE	Good for more than a laugh I should think.
MARLENE	wiped out and slotted into this speedy

employment agency and still there.

JOYCE	You can always find yourself work then.
MARLENE	That's right.
JOYCE	And men?
MARLENE	Oh there's always men.
JOYCE	No one special?
MARLENE	There's fellas who like to be seen with a high-

flying lady. Shows they've got something really good in their pants. But they can't take the day to day. They're waiting for me to turn into the little woman. Or maybe I'm just horrible of course.

JOYCE	Who needs them?
MARLENE	Who needs them? Well I do. But I need

adventures more. So on on into the sunset. I think the eighties are going to be stupendous.

JOYCE	Who for?
MARLENE	For me. / I think I'm going up up up.
JOYCE	Oh for you. Yes, I'm sure they will.
MARLENE	And for the country, come to that. Get the

economy back on its feet and whoosh. She's a tough lady, Maggie. I'd give her a job. / She just needs to hang in there. This country

JOYCE	You voted for them, did you?
MARLENE	needs to stop whining. / Monetarism is not stupid.
JOYCE	Drink your tea and shut up, pet.
MARLENE	It takes time, determination. No more slop. / And
JOYCE	Well I think they're filthy bastards.
MARLENE	who's got to drive it on? First woman prime

minister. Terrifico. Aces. Right on. / You must admit. Certainly gets my vote.

JOYCE	What good's first woman if it's her? I suppose

you'd have liked Hitler if he was a woman. Ms Hitler. Got a lot done, Hitlerina. / Great adventures.

MARLENE	Bosses still walking on the workers' faces? Still

Dadda's little parrot? Haven't you learned to think for yourself? I believe in the individual. Look at me.

JOYCE	I am looking at you.
MARLENE	Come on, Joyce, we're not going to quarrel over

politics.

JOYCE	We are though.
MARLENE	Forget I mentioned it. Not a word about the slimy

unions will cross my lips.

Pause.

JOYCE	You say Mother had a wasted life.
MARLENE	Yes I do. Married to that bastard.
JOYCE	What sort of life did he have? / Working in the

fields like

MARLENE	Violent life?
JOYCE	an animal. / Why wouldn't he want a drink?
MARLENE	Come off it.
JOYCE	You want a drink. He couldn't afford whisky.
MARLENE	I don't want to talk about him.
JOYCE	You started, I was talking about her. She had a

rotten life because she had nothing. She went hungry.

MARLENE	She was hungry because he drank the money. /

He used to hit her.

JOYCE	It's not all down to him. / Their lives were

rubbish. They

MARLENE	She didn't hit him.
JOYCE	were treated like rubbish. He's dead and she'll die

soon and what sort of life / did they have?

MARLENE	I saw him one night. I came down.
JOYCE	Do you think I didn't? / They didn't get to

America and

MARLENE	I still have dreams.
JOYCE	drive across it in a fast car. / Bad nights, they had

bad days.

MARLENE	America, America, you're jealous. / I had to get

out,

JOYCE	Jealous?
MARLENE	I knew when I was thirteen, out of their house,

out of them, never let that happen to me, / never let him, make my own
way, out.

JOYCE	Jealous of what you've done, you're ashamed of

me if I came to your office, your smart friends, wouldn't you, I'm
ashamed of you, think of nothing but yourself, you've got on, nothing's
changed for most people / has it?

MARLENE	I hate the working class / which is what you're

going

JOYCE	Yes you do.
MARLENE	to go on about now, it doesn't exist any more, it means lazy and stupid. / I don't like the way they talk. I don't
JOYCE	Come on, now we're getting it.
MARLENE	like beer guts and football vomit and saucy tits and brothers and sisters –
JOYCE	I spit when I see a Rolls Royce, scratch it with my ring / Mercedes it was.
MARLENE	Oh very mature –
JOYCE	I hate the cows I work for / and their dirty dishes with blanquette of fucking veau.
MARLENE	and I will not be pulled down to their level by a flying picket and I won't be sent to Siberia / or a loony bin
JOYCE	No, you'll be on a yacht, you'll be head of Coca Cola and you wait, the eighties is going to be stupendous all right because we'll get you lot off our backs –
MARLENE	just because I'm original. And I support Reagan even if he is a lousy movie star because the reds are swarming up his map and I want to be free in a free world –
JOYCE	What? / What?
MARLENE	I know what I mean / by that – not shut up here.
JOYCE	So don't be round here when it happens because if someone's kicking you I'll just laugh.

Silence.

MARLENE	I don't mean anything personal. I don't believe in class. Anyone can do anything if they've got what it takes.
JOYCE	And if they haven't?
MARLENE	If they're stupid or lazy or frightened, I'm not going to help them get a job, why should I?
JOYCE	What about Angie?
MARLENE	What about Angie?
JOYCE	She's stupid, lazy and frightened, so what about her?
MARLENE	You run her down too much. She'll be all right.
JOYCE	I don't expect so, no. I expect her children will say what a wasted life she had. If she has children. Because nothing's changed and it won't with them in.
MARLENE	Them, them. / Us and them?
JOYCE	And you're one of them.

MARLENE	And you're us, wonderful us, and Angie's us / and Mum and Dad's us.
JOYCE	Yes, that's right, and you're them.
MARLENE	Come on, Joyce, what a night. You've got what it takes.
JOYCE	I know I have.
MARLENE	I didn't really mean all that.
JOYCE	I did.
MARLENE	But we're friends anyway.
JOYCE	I don't think so, no.
MARLENE	Well it's lovely to be out in the country. I really must make the effort to come more often.

I want to go to sleep.

I want to go to sleep.

Joyce gets blankets for the sofa.

JOYCE	Goodnight then. I hope you'll be warm enough.
MARLENE	Goodnight. Joyce –
JOYCE	No, pet. Sorry.

Joyce goes. Marlene sits wrapped in a blanket and has another drink. Angie comes in.

ANGIE	Mum?
MARLENE	Angie? What's the matter?
ANGIE	Mum?
MARLENE	No, she's gone to bed. It's Aunty Marlene.
ANGIE	Frightening.
MARLENE	Did you have a bad dream? What happened in it? Well you're awake now, aren't you pet?
ANGIE	Frightening.

The End.

Note:

When one character starts speaking before another is finished, the point of interruption is marked /

If a speech follows on from an earlier line of dialogue rather than the line immediately before it, the continuation is marked *

Caryl Churchill (1938-)

Born in London, Churchill grew up in the Lake District and in Canada before studying English at Lady Margaret Hall, Oxford. She began writing in the 1960s, with student productions of her early plays and then radio plays for the BBC, while raising her three sons.

Churchill's stage works developed during the upsurge of alternative theatre companies of the late 1970s and she served as resident dramatist at the Royal Court Theatre from 1974-1975. Many plays were developed through workshops with feminist company Monstrous Regiment, such as *Vinegar Tom* (1976) and particularly the new writing collective, Joint Stock Theatre Company. Some of her plays were scripted as part of a company devising process, such as *Light Shining in Buckinghamshire* (1976); *Cloud Nine* (1979); *Fen* (1983), working in particular with director Max Stafford-Clark.

Open to experiment with form, her work has encompassed collaborations with opera and dance companies like Second Stride, such as *Lives of the Great Poisoners* (1991).

Other plays include: *Owners* (1972); *Traps* (1978); *Objections to Sex and Violence* (1975); *Serious Money* (1987); *Softcops* (1984); *Hot Fudge* (1989);*The Skriker* (1994); *Blue Heart* (1997); *Far Away* (2000); *A Number* (2002) and *Drunk Enough To Say I Love You* (2006).

In 1982, Churchill won an Obie Award for Playwriting for *Top Girls* and in 1983 *Top Girls* was the runner-up for the Susan Smith Blackburn Prize. *Top Girls* has been widely performed, published and translated and is now studied as part of the National Curriculum.

Polly Stenham, playwright:

"She was a big inspiration to me in terms of writing. I first came across her when they did *Top Girls* at school. I was about 14, and I thought: "What the f***'s this? This is brilliant." ... I think that was my first introduction to how far you could go.'

"Why Caryl Churchill is the Top Girl" *The Times,* September 1st, 2008

Stones in his Pockets

Marie Jones

First performed at The Lyric Theatre, Belfast on 3rd June, 1999.

CHARACTERS

Charlie Conlon, mid-thirties
Jake Quinn, mid-thirties

Charlie and Jake play all the other characters in the play:

Simon, first A.D. (Ambitious Dublin 4 type)
Aisling, third A.D., young, pretty, anxious to impress those above her, no interest in those beneath
Mickey, a local in his 70s, was an extra in *The Quiet Man*
Clem, the director, English, quiet nature, not much understanding of the local community
Sean, a young local lad
Fin, a young local, Sean's friend
Caroline Giovanni, American star
John, accent coach
Brother Gerard, local teacher
Dave, a crew member, Cockney
Jock Campbell, Caroline's security man, Scottish
Mr Harkin, Sean's father
Interviewer

Setting: A scenic spot near a small village in Co. Kerry

ACT ONE

Charlie stands front stage as if queuing up at a catering truck. Jake is lounging in the sun.

CHARLIE   I'll have the lemon meringue pie please ... I know I was up before but it's not for me ... it's for my mate ... yes he is, he is an extra I swear ... he can't come and get it himself because he has just sprained his ankle ... okay ... *(To man behind him)* Don't shuv there's plenty left ... *(To Caterer)* An accident report sheet? ... he only went over on it, it's not life threatening ... no he doesn't want a full dinner, he only wants the sweet ... *(To man behind him)* I know we are only meant to have one helping but it's not for me ... *(To Caterer)* Look, I don't know why he can eat a sweet and not his dinner if he's sick, what am I, a doctor or something ... the fella asked me to go and get him a helping of lemon meringue pie ... fine fine ... No problem. *(walks away)* Jesus Christ, the Spanish Inquisition to get a bloody pudding.

JAKE   They've got wise to the extras ... first couple of days ones were bringing their families down and feeding them too ... *(laughs)* My mate has sprained his ankle ... not very good was it ... have you Ballycastle men no imagination ...

CHARLIE   How do you know I am from Ballycastle?

JAKE   You were in the pub last night talking to a few of the locals ... small town, word gets round ... Jake Quinn ... how are you doin', Charlie?

CHARLIE   What is this, the caterer gettin' on like he was trained by the RUC and you by the Special Branch ... no fear of gettin' homesick anyway.

JAKE   How did you end up here?

CHARLIE *(furtively looks around him)* You mean you don't know ... was there a breakdown in intelligence?

JAKE   You're very jumpy.

CHARLIE   Have to be, man ... I'm on the run.

SIMON   Aisling, get this lot back to work. Use a cattle prod if you have to. What about these catering vans?

AISLING   Just moving them now, Simon. Thank you. *(gesturing to vehicles)*

SIMON   I'm going to get Miss Giovanni from her Winnebago now.

AISLING   Quiet everyone, settle ... please finish your lunch quickly before we lose the light ... the next shot is a close up on Maeve reacting to you ... then we will turn the camera and have you reacting to

Maeve ... remember what you are reacting to ... Maeve is telling you she will plead your case to her father ... remember your positions exactly and those of you who were wearing caps ... please put them on.

CHARLIE *(to Jake)* Was I wearing a cap, I can't remember.

JAKE *(smirks)* So you're on the run then.

CHARLIE Keep your voice down.

JAKE On the run.

CHARLIE Aye.

JAKE On the run from who?

CHARLIE The Boys ... understand.

JAKE Jesus ... no messin'.

CHARLIE Aye they weren't bad though, they give me a head start ... they says, Charlie, we will close our eyes and count to twenty and you run like the hammers ... I thought that it was very dacent.

JAKE *(to Charlie)* You don't have to tell me if you don't want to ... only making conversation.

CHARLIE Aye, sorry mate, it was the lemon meringue pie interrogation that got to me ... well I am on the run, sort of ... had a video shop that went bust ... them Extra Vision bastards ... I never heard one person in Ballycastle complain to me before them hures opened up ... you know ... if a video was out, the customers would take something else, no problem ... the big boys move in and gullible Charlie here thinks ... my customers are loyal.

JAKE Look out, here she comes ... You were just in front of me beside oul Mickey and you had your hat on.

CHARLIE Sure it doesn't matter.

MICKEY Oh it will surely matter, they will check thon Polaroid and see for sure who was wearing what and you don't want to be gettin' yourself in trouble with your one with the yoke on her ear ... you have to keep your nose clean for thon one has a gob on her that would turn milk.

CHARLIE *(puts his cap on)* Happy now, Mickey?

MICKEY Not me, fella, I'm only warning you, if you don't want to be replaced you do as you're bid ... just say nothin' and you will be forty quid a day the wiser, that's my motto, Jake.

JAKE Aye right, Mickey.

CHARLIE Right pain in the ass.

JAKE *(to Charlie)* My mother's third cousin. Do you know that man's famous. He's the last surviving extra on *The Quiet Man* ... but don't get him started. Where were we ... aye, the Extra Vision hures.

CHARLIE Aye ... I says to myself ... they won't desert me ...

my customers won't desert me ... I am one of them, support your own and all that ... fuck was I wrong ... *(mimics them)* Charlie, you have to have more than two copies of a video, Extra Vision has loads ... Charlie you want to see the range Extra Vision has ... then they stopped saying anything 'cos they just stopped coming ... so I got up one morning, ... all my plans for the future in a heap of out-of-date movies ... I couldn't start all over again ... started all over again so many times I've lost count ... this time I just couldn't do it ... so I closed the door on the shop ... videos still on the shelves, nothing touched ... threw the tent in the boot and decided to do Ireland ... what about you?

JAKE Well I can't follow that.

CHARLIE Ah don't mind me ... just thought I would get it all out at once, save the locals making it up for me ... oh and the other thing, my girlfriend dumped me too ... talk about kicking a man when he is on the floor ... and you'll not believe this.

JAKE She is going out with the manager of Extra Vision.

CHARLIE How did you know?

JAKE You told the story last night in the pub to a second cousin of mine.

CHARLIE Jesus, that's me and gin ... bad combo ... anyway, the place is coming down with Hollywood stars ... it's a who's who of who's bonked who, and me, Charlie Conlon, is a topic of conversation ...

JAKE We are used to that lot ... it's outsiders coming in and taking jobs we don't like.

CHARLIE Place is coming down with outsiders ... it's like a bloody circus ... there she is ... look ... me, Charlie Conlon only ten feet away from Caroline Giovanni ... I'd give her one alright.

Caroline and John, the dialect coach.

CAROLINE *(as she crosses)* Can I try the other earrings? These are too dingly-dangly. *(practises)* I will speak to my father, you have suffered enough.

JOHN You're doing great, Caroline ... remember always to soften the a; and elongate it ... I will speak to my father, you have suffered enough.

CAROLINE *(She repeats badly)* I will speak to my faaather, no ... I will speak to my fetherr ... shit ...

JOHN No Caroline, put your tongue behind your teeth.

CAROLINE Thaaather.

JOHN No ... no, your bottom teeth.

CAROLINE	Faaather ... fetthe ... fattther ... shit ... these people will think it sounds ridiculous.
JOHN	Don't worry ... Caroline ... Ireland is only one per cent of the market.
CAROLINE	I want to get it right, John.
CHARLIE *(to Jake)*	I love that, huh ... half of America here is playing Irish people and they say I am the outsider.
JAKE	They promised the extras would be local ... she is gorgeous.
CHARLIE	I got it fair and square ... saw the ad, extras wanted and they liked the look of me ... pitched my tent and here I am ... great money and free grub ... it's a gift ... Would you ... you know, give her one?
JAKE	No chance of getting near her.
SIMON	Right, let's go for this now. Good morning, Caroline, looking lovely this morning, love those earrings.
AISLING	Simon, will I bring Rory out yet?
SIMON	No ... it's bloody freezin' ... he will go crazy hangin' about.
AISLING	Does Maeve not need to see him ... you know, the big moment of electricity.
SIMON	No ... he comes over the hill just as she turns away from the mob. It's the next shot, *(flirting)* silly girl.
AISLING	I'll go get his blankets ... and have him stand by.
SIMON	Hey Aisling.
AISLING	Yes Simon.
SIMON	What do you call a Kerryman with brains?
AISLING	I don't know, Simon.
SIMON	Dangerous. *(They laugh.)*
AISLING	I don't get it Simon.
SIMON	You will, Aisling, you will.
CHARLIE *(to Jake)*	What are we supposed to do?
JAKE	Look at her lookin' at us looking dispossessed.
CHARLIE	Dispo what?
JAKE	Like this. *(Jake demonstrates.)*
SIMON	Happy to go, Caroline. Turnover, speed, mark it, alright Clem, ACTION.

They look dispossessed, music plays.

SIMON	Cut ... beautiful, Caroline ... Stay in your places 'til we check the gate. Someone get Caroline a cup of coffee.

JAKE *(to Charlie)*   Terrible bloody accent.

CHARLIE   Doesn't matter ... been that many film stars playing Irish leads, everybody thinks that's the way we talk now ... I have my own film here ...

JAKE   A film?

CHARLIE   Yeah ... I sat in my shop day after day watching movies and I says to myself ... Charlie, you could do that so I did ... here it is ... and here I am, right smack in the middle of the people that can make it happen ... I'll choose my moment and wey hey.

JAKE   I'm impressed, Charlie.

CHARLIE   Don't grovel, you will have to audition like the rest.

CAROLINE   It's not right, John ... I want it to be right ... the rhythm is wrong.

JOHN.   Fine, let's go to the pub tonight ... mix with the locals ... get a feel.

CAROLINE   Yeah ... yeah I will ... I think I would quite like that.

JOHN   ... but be careful, Caroline, you can't be too exact, you won't get away with it in Hollywood, they won't understand.

CAROLINE   Hollywood is shit, John ... a crock of shit ... look around this place ... God, it's just heaven on earth ... I love this place ... I'm third generation, you know, on my mother's side ... I do get a real feeling of belonging here, you know that. You people are so simple, uncomplicated, contented.

CHARLIE *(to Jake)*   It would founder you up here. That wind would cut the arse off ye.

JAKE   Be a while yet, have to turn the camera on us.

CHARLIE   So then it's us lookin' dispossessed, luking at her with loads of land.

JAKE   Nah, it's not us they want, it's the Blasket Islands.

CHARLIE *(looks around)* Bloody amazing.

JAKE   Yeah ... they'll get a big shot of the Blaskets and the peasants, then Rory comes over the hill behind us like he is walking out of the sea. When he has his line, the lot of us disappear, even the Blasket Islands.

AISLING   Quiet everyone ... settle ... that's a wrap for the extras ... we will pick this up tomorrow afternoon ... quiet, settle ... I want all the extras in the turf-digging scene in costume by seven a.m. tomorrow morning ... and make sure you leave all costumes in the community centre ... don't be tempted to go home in them ... quiet ...

settle ... that is all the men in scene 37 ... tomorrow at seven a.m. ... breakfast will be from six.

Charlie has his script in his hand.

CHARLIE *(to Aisling)*   Excuse me.

AISLING *(stops him with her hand as she speaks into her walkie-talkie)* ... Hi Simon ... Yeah Kurt is mad we're not getting to his scene ... he was psyched up for it ... right, will do ... cheers Simon.

CHARLIE   Excuse me ... *(She stops him from speaking.)*

AISLING   Come back, come back, come back. Listen carefully everyone ... slight change of plan, you will be picked up at six-thirty a.m. tomorrow and taken to the location by minibus so that means everyone in costume by six ... the minibus will leave from the community hall sharp at six-thirty ...

CHARLIE   Excuse me.

AISLING *(sharply)*   Yes.

Charlie bottles out and puts his script back in his pocket.

CHARLIE   Are the ones in the turf-diggin' scene the same ones as the ones in the cart the day?

AISLING   Well where was the cart going?

CHARLIE *(blank ... looks around for support ... but no one else seems to know)* I don't know.

AISLING   Taking the men to dig the turf ... *(stops him again)* ... Hi Simon ... right ... *(To Charlie)* Excuse me.

She leaves.

MICKEY   Don't start gettin' yourself noticed ... just keep your head down and go where they put you ... that's how to survive as an extra.

CHARLIE   It's the gettin' up at the scrake, Mickey, is the killer.

MICKEY   Sure what would you be going to bed for if you have to be up for the scrake?

CHARLIE   Aye dead on, Mickey ...

MICKEY   And don't be going home in them boots ... the continuity would cut the heels off you.

CHARLIE   I'll remember that, Mickey.

MICKEY *(to Charlie)*   Do you know I'm famous as I'm one of the few surviving extras on *The Quiet Man* ... John Wayne called me by my first name ... he would always refer to me as wee Mickey.

CHARLIE	Did you call him Duke?
MICKEY	No I did not, I give the man his place ... I might

one day.

JAKE	Hey Mickey, there's the forty quid man comin'.
MICKEY *(to Charlie)*	I'll catch you later.
JAKE	He will spend that in the pub and by the morning

he will owe twenty more and the morra night he will pay back the twenty straight off and by the end of the night the same thing ... I don't think that man's liver could survive another movie.

Interior changing room ... showers running etc.

They start to undress and get into their day clothes during the following dialogue ...

CHARLIE	Have you done this before?
JAKE	No but most of the town have, there was another

big movie a few years back ... the locals have got cute to it now ... a woman that runs a guest house in the town had all her rooms full for the first time ever, a whole summer with a No Vacancies sign up, she was delighted with herself ... this year she and her family are sleeping in a caravan at the bottom of the garden ... she let their rooms out too ... last time they loved the glamour and the attention with a few bob thrown in ... this time it's the money and the money and the money ... sad.

CHARLIE   Sad? ... now hold on a minute ... me going bust to Extra Vision is sad ... somebody making twice what they made last year is not sad ... you miffed 'cause you didn't get a part last time ... not luk Irish enough.

JAKE	Nah, I was in the States.
CHARLIE	What did you do there?
JAKE	This and that ... you know, bit of this, bit of that

... worked a few bars, waited a few tables.

CHARLIE	Not make your fortune.
JAKE *(sarcastically)*	No, came back here to be a film star.
CHARLIE	Tell ye what, this is the life.
JAKE	A background bog man ... dead glamorous.
CHARLIE	You have to start somewhere, if you keep your

nose clean there could be a nice wee part in mine ... could you handle a sub-machine-gun ... ? *(Jake mimes sub-machine gun action.)* Don't call me, I'll call you.

JAKE   You haven't a hope, Charlie, it's who you know in this business ... that Aisling one, you know the one with the walkie-talkie grafted onto her ear ... she is for the top that one ... Father is a director, wants to produce her own films ... and she will.

CHARLIE I suppose it wouldn't even cross her mind that she might not.

JAKE Definitely not.

CHARLIE She is only about twenty.

JAKE Makes you sick.

CHARLIE Yeah but if you've got it, doesn't matter if you're a nobody ... talent is talent ... it wins through in the end.

JAKE You don't believe that, do ya ... ?

CHARLIE *(sharply)* This is Charlie's day of good cheer, nothing or nobody is going to put me in Joe Depressos.

JAKE *(taken aback)* Wouldn't dream of it ...

CHARLIE Jesus ... look at that young fella, he has lost it.

JAKE That's young Sean Harkin, a second cousin of mine ... drugs ... pain in the arse ... I'm off to the jacks.

SEAN Jumped-up tart ... jumped-up fucking tart ...

CHARLIE Hey mate, settle yourself.

SEAN That hure, who does she think she is ... I need a job.

CHARLIE Well look at the state of you, this is big money, they can't take a chance on an extra messing it up.

SEAN I was fucking born diggin' turf and that hurin' slag is tellin' me to piss off.

CHARLIE She does have a point you know.

SEAN *(turns on him)* And who the fuck are you, Mr Brown Noser?

CHARLIE Nobody ... just, an extra.

SEAN *(as he staggers off)* You're a nobody, just like me and she won't give me a job.

JAKE Is he gone?

CHARLIE Yeah. Come on, Jake, I need a drink.

JAKE Aye, with you in a minute. Hey Fin, you're his mate, can you not talk to Sean?

FIN He came yesterday, but he was out of it and she told him to clear off. He was alright this morning and he asked me to put his name down. I told him to be here for two o'clock and he would get a start, but for fuck sake look at him.

JAKE What's he on, Fin?

FIN Whatever he can get his hands on.

JAKE Can ye not do something, say something ... he is killing himself.

FIN *(exiting)*   And say what, I mean what would you say, Jake,
  don't do them nasty drugs, and get a life?
CHARLIE   Come on, Jake. Are you alright?
JAKE   When he was a young buck, he used to look up to
  me, his Da's farm was next to ours ... followed me everywhere ... Come
  on, Charlie, I need that drink too.
CHARLIE   Don't let me drink gin ...

Bar scene: background Country and Western music.

JAKE   Another gin there, Kevin, and a couple of pints ...
  business is boomin' then Kevin ... a restaurant? ... sure you wouldn't get
  many in this town atin' out when they cud ate in ... of course the place
  will be comin' down with tourists after this one ...

Sean staggers up to Charlie.

SEAN   Hey Brown Noser, have ye anything on ye ... I can
  pay.
CHARLIE   Piss off, Sean.
SEAN   Please mate.
CHARLIE   I have nothin', clear off.
SEAN   Yis all think yis are movie stars, yis are nothing,
  I'm Sean Harkin and I am a somebody and I fuckin' know yis are all
  nothin' ... wankers.
CHARLIE   Away home son, your Ma wants ye.
SEAN   Tossers ... fuckin' tossers ... full a shit.

*He staggers away from him ... Charlie looks at him for that brief moment
... but doesn't want to think about it.*

JAKE   How is it goin' Sean? ... Look at him, seventeen
  and out of his head ... keep thinkin' I should have a talk with him ...
  (distracted)
CHARLIE *(a bit pissed)* ... You know mate, I was so depressed ... so
  depressed ... I just couldn't even lift my head ... you know it just gets to
  you physically like ... I luked at myself in the mirror and I says ...
  Charlie, you have lived on this planet for thirty-two years and what have
  you to show for your existence ...
JAKE   Maybe you should go on the pints, man.
CHARLIE   Sorry mate ... yeah stop this ... no, this is Charlie's
  day of good cheer. So, this woman in America, did she dump ye?
JAKE   Nah she wanted to marry me ... an ultimatum ...
  I couldn't do it ... I could just about look after myself ... Me stuck there

with a wife and kids to support and not a clue about the future ... a mate of mine went over the same time, he's got a wife and two kids ... he works two bars and a late-night restaurant ... what kind of life is that? ... So here I am on the dole and back living with the ma.

CHARLIE   Jesus, look who is sitting in that corner.

JAKE   Caroline Giovanni ... when did she come in?

CHARLIE   Mixing with the plebs ... I tell you there is not a man in here wouldn't give her one.

JAKE   There is not a man in here would get a look in.

CHARLIE   She might, you know ... for research purposes ... could be trying for a taste of the real thing.

JAKE   You've sex on the brain, man.

CHARLIE   It's not my brain that's the problem ... Jesus, look at the cut of Kevin the owner, he is practically salivating.

JAKE   You know what he will do, he will get the wife to make her a sandwich and when the restaurant opens he will have a big plaque saying ... 'Caroline Giovanni dined here' ... I was right, there's Bridget haring off into the kitchen.

CHARLIE *(watching her go)* Go on ye girl ye.

JAKE   Jesus, man, look at her, she is so sexy.

CHARLIE   Bridget? ... It's a gas ... did you ever think you would be sittin' in the same pub as Caroline Giovanni ... hey luk she is eyeing you up ... or is it me ... *(moves across the stage and realises she is still watching Jake.)* No, fuck, it's you . . .

JAKE *(shouts)*   No, I have a pint on order, thanks ... yeah it's great ... that was a lovely scene today ... very moving.

CHARLIE   Lying bastard.

JAKE   Yeah sure, come on over ... *(To Charlie)* Jesus, I am made man, she wants to join me.

CHARLIE   Jesus, I can feel my tongue tying itself in a knot ... I'm away over to the riggers ... I smell a waft of whacki backi comin' from that corner ...

JAKE   Ah no man, don't leave me on my own.

CHARLIE   Big lad like you scared of a woman.

JAKE   She's not just a woman, she is Caroline Giovanni.

CHARLIE   Here she comes, I'm off ... *(stops ... takes the script from his pocket.)* Just leave that sitting there ... okay ... don't be pushy just leave it where she can see it.

CAROLINE   You are in the movie then?

JAKE   Yeah ... Jake Quinn ... I'm just one of the crowd.

CAROLINE   I haven't seen you around.

JAKE   I was in that scene the day, you know when you
talk to the peasants about asking your father to give the land back.

CAROLINE   I didn't notice anyone I was so uptight about my
accent ... was it alright?

JAKE   You would think you were born here.

CAROLINE   Are you local?

JAKE   Down the road.

CAROLINE   Your countryside is so beautiful.

JAKE   Yeah, you appreciate it more when you have been
away ... I was in the States for a couple of years.

CAROLINE *(not really interested)* Yeah, what part?

JAKE   New York ... I travelled around as well, I went ...

CAROLINE   You are enjoying the movie.

JAKE   Yeah it's ... well different ... I would like to get
into movies proper like.

CAROLINE   You have a great face ... great eyes ... the camera
would love you.

JAKE   It certainly loves you ... your last movie was
brilliant ...

CAROLINE   This place is a bit crowded, would you like to
come back to the hotel for a drink.

JAKE   I don't think I would be allowed.

CAROLINE   Who would stop you?

JAKE   Well we were warned not to bother you.

CAROLINE   No you were warned not to bother me unless I
choose to be bothered and tonight I want you to come for a drink ...
(calls) Jock, will you go get the car, I want to go back to the hotel ... *(To
Jake)* Would you like to travel with us.

JAKE   Yeah sure ... *(looks up)* Ah well done Bridget ...
egg and onion.

CAROLINE   See you at the front door then.

JAKE   I think you should have your sandwich first.

CAROLINE   God no, I never eat after six o'clock.

JAKE   Could you pretend and take it with you?

CAROLINE   Why?

JAKE   Because this is a small town and I will get the
blame if you don't. *(Caroline moves away.)* ... would you like this?

CHARLIE *(delighted)*   She gave me a sandwich.

JAKE   She is driving me to the hotel for a drink ... I am
going with her in the car.

CHARLIE   Jesus, man, you're made ... did she notice the script?

JAKE	What did I tell you Charlie, it's who you know in this business.
CHARLIE	Tell her there could be a big part in it for her ... brilliant death scene ...
JAKE	Sorry Charlie, every man for himself.
CHARLIE	Take it with you, just in case.
JAKE	Aye, all right. See ya.

Dave, a Cockney, approaches Charlie.

DAVE	Hey Charlie, fancy a line?
CHARLIE	What?
DAVE	Fancy a line?
CHARLIE	Well I have never acted before but I'll give it a go. What do I have to say?
DAVE	Coke.
CHARLIE	COKE!!
DAVE	Jesus mate, want a loud hailer?
CHARLIE	Sorry ... you got coke?
DAVE	Yeah.
CHARLIE	Happy days ... fuck, I love the movies.

Next morning ... interior ... changing room ... Charlie is rushing about getting ready, hyper still from the coke the night before ... Jake enters relaxed ... whistling to himself.

Charlie and Jake change into costume.

CHARLIE	What happened, man?
JAKE	I think she was trying to ... you know ... seduce me.
CHARLIE	You ... Jesus she could have any man in the whole country ... the world, for Christ sake ... or maybe she wanted a bit of rough ... I know what it is ... in the movie she bonks a peasant ... in real life she bonks Kurt Steiner who is pretending he is Rory the peasant ... but if it were real real life she would be bonking somebody like you, a nobody ... well did you?
JAKE	I was surrounded by minders ... pretending they weren't listening. But them boys have eyes and ears in their arse.
CHARLIE	And what did you say to her?
JAKE	I told her I wrote poetry ... thought that would appeal to her ... you know the handsome heady Irish poet.
CHARLIE	You write poems?

JAKE   No ... but I had to think of something that would make me interesting, specially to somebody like her ... talent is sexy if you have eff all else.

Flashback ... romantic music ... Caroline's bedroom.

CAROLINE   Poetry ... that's fascinating.
JAKE   Yeah.
CAROLINE   Are you published?
JAKE   No ... well I don't believe in that.
CAROLINE   Really.
JAKE   That cheapens your poetry ... makes it too accessible ... then people interpret it and get it wrong.
CAROLINE   Would you recite one of your poems for me?

Present.

JAKE   So I picked one of Seamus Heaney's.
CHARLIE   Brilliant ... and I bet ye she was none the wiser.
JAKE   None.
CHARLIE   Must try that.

Flashback.

JAKE   Who blowing up these sparks
For their meagre heat, have missed
The once-in-a-lifetime portent of the comet's pulsing rose.
CAROLINE   There is no 'of' in the last line.
JAKE   Sorry.
CAROLINE   The once-in-a-lifetime portent, The comet's pulsing rose, there is no 'of' ... Seamus Heaney.
JAKE *(embarrassed)*   Yeah.
CAROLINE   You underestimate me, Jake ... I'm not just here to exploit the beauty of the land, I love it ... I know the history and the poets.
JAKE   It always works on Irish girls ...
CAROLINE   Maybe you should try a more obscure poet.

Present.

CHARLIE   Did you, you know ... up in her room?
JAKE   Give her one? She is sort of untouchable ... I mean she is Caroline Giovanni ... so I just left, but I have been invited into her Winnebago for coffee.
CHARLIE   You be careful.

JAKE	What you mean, careful?
CHARLIE	Well you don't want to be used like.
JAKE	She could use me any day.
CHARLIE	Then the press get hold of it. You know ... Extra

Gives Movie Star One in a Caravan ... know, like your man Hugh Grant and the prostitute.

JAKE   Made her famous didn't it ... and it's not a caravan, it's a Winnebago.

CHARLIE   Oh excuse me ... anyway, you go to the caravan and I will sneak up to the window with a Polaroid ... Front page of *The Sun* ... we could be fartin' through silk.

JAKE   No ... the mother would kill me.

CHARLIE   Mine too ... you know being brought up properly is a shaggin' handicap.

JAKE   Not knowing what you are going to do for the rest of your life is a bigger one.

CHARLIE   Come on man, we are on a movie ... guys would give their left testicle to be where we are ... forty quid a day, rubbing shoulders with stars.

JAKE   And then what, when it's over, then what?

CHARLIE   Don't even think about it, we have three weeks left ... tell you what, the riggers are boys to hang out with ... comin' down with coke ... Jesus, that stuff is magic, I was out of my head last night ... great job that ... good money, all the coke you can sniff ... what a life ... did she get a wee chance to have a wee butchers at my script?

Jake brings it out of his pocket ... obviously had forgotten.

JAKE   Sorry Charlie, just didn't find the right moment.

CHARLIE *(disappointed)* Aye ... these things have to be timed right ... it's all in the timing ... thanks anyway.

AISLING   Quiet everyone ... settle ... as soon as you get dressed, please make your way to the minibus immediately where Costume can check you.

CHARLIE *(eager to please)* Right, dead on, Aisling ... no problem ... we are ready ... I will gee up the rest for you ... and if you have a wee minute maybe you could have a wee skiff over this ... I would love you to be involved in it . . .

AISLING *(impatiently)* What?

CHARLIE   My film.

AISLING   Post it to the Production Office ... come on ... get a move on.

JAKE	You are pissin' against the wind, Charlie.
CHARLIE	No ... just not quite getting the right moment.

On the bus.

CHARLIE	I haven't dug turf since I was a wee buck.
JAKE *(sarcastically)*	Yeah it will be a nice romantic rural Irish scene.
CHARLIE	Ack I think it is ... all us diggin' away at the turf ...

Maeve comin' by on her horse and clockin' Rory and him clockin' her and thinkin' ... wow, I'd love to give her one ... and all the time the fiddles playing in the background ... I love the movies. Unreal man.

Bus stops.

SIMON	Is there a Jake Quinn here?
JAKE	Yeah.

SIMON *(on walkie-talkie to Aisling)* Aisling. Clem's not happy with the cows. The cows. He says they're not Irish enough. I don't know. Black fluffy ones, I suppose. Simon, 1st A.D. Quick word.

JAKE	Sure.
SIMON	Caroline Giovanni wants you to have coffee with

her ... The director has said you can have ten minutes ... then you will excuse yourself and leave.

JAKE	What if she doesn't want me to leave?
SIMON	Look mate, I am telling you, you have ten

minutes, and if you are not out in ten minutes I will come and get you.

CHARLIE *(to Jake)*   Jesus, ten minutes. Ten minutes ... sure that's more than any of the rest of us would get in a lifetime.

JAKE	Jesus, here's the heavy.

JOCK *(big Scottish heavy)* You Jake?

JAKE	Aye if you're Tarzan.
JOCK *(not amused)*	The name is Jock Campbell ... Ms Giovanni's

security ... You might have seen me last night in the hotel.

JAKE	No can't say I did.
JOCK	You will have ten minutes ... I will be outside the

door and when you hear me give two raps you will come out ... I mean ten minutes and not a second more. Wait here!

JAKE	Hold on, I didn't ask for this.
CHARLIE	Jesus, a brick shithouse on legs, you boyo.
JAKE	Suddenly I am being treated like I'm a potential

attacker ...

CHARLIE   Now see it from their point of view ... you are a nobody ... that is a potential security risk, you are an Irish nobody, that is a definite security risk, you are from the arse hole of nowhere in Ireland and you could be I.R.A., major mega security risk.

JAKE   Out to kidnap her.

CHARLIE   Got it in one.

JOCK   Mr Quinn. We have you listed as Ninth Avenue, New York.

JAKE   I am not long back, I haven't changed it yet ... you see I live here with my mother.

JOCK   When did you arrive back?

JAKE   Couple of weeks ago.

JOCK   And why did you leave America?

JAKE   I was homesick.

JOCK   And what is your mother's address?

JAKE   Listen mate, do me a favour will you ... go and tell Miss Giovanni, thank you but no thank you ... tell her I don't like coffee and I hope she is not too offended.

JOCK   You want me to tell her that? You're lucky to get a second chance, Mr Seamus Heaney.

CHARLIE   Jesus ... who do these people think they effen'well are?

JAKE   Me and my fekking poetry.

CHARLIE   What do you mean?

JAKE   I lied ... she knew it was Heaney.

CHARLIE   If I had bin you I would have lied to me too ... well nobody wants to admit to being a dickhead.

SIMON   Jake, could I have a quiet word?

JAKE   What Simon ... alright.

SIMON   I am going to get into terrible trouble if you don't keep that appointment ... the security check is necessary ... Ms Giovanni is worth at least six million and if anything were to happen to her . . .

JAKE   Fine, I understand that, just tell her I would not like to put her at risk.

SIMON   Jake ... it is very important for us to keep the stars happy, she simply requested that she would like you to join her ... and if you are clean then you should not worry about the security check.

JAKE   I had a parking fine in 1987, I think I would be a high risk ... and what is more I object to you lot checkin' me out, this is an infringement of my privacy.

SIMON   Well if you must go chatting up important people that's the price you pay.

JAKE   Fuck it, she chatted me up.

SIMON Look mate, don't go thinking you're anything special. Miss Giovanni has a habit of going ethnic. Helps her get into the part. I am giving you a quiet word of warning ... Ms Giovanni does not like to be snubbed, particularly by an extra, and it might be her request that you be removed from the set, so for your own good ...

JAKE That's it, Charlie, I am not going ... no way, they can sack me if they like.

CHARLIE Don't worry, just go and pass yourself ... let her do all the talking.

JAKE Look at all the extras, not one of them has tuk their eyes off me. Just watching and waiting.

CHARLIE Just jealous. Forty pound a day mate, forty pound a day and another three weeks and you never know, she could be your key into the movies.

JOCK Right, are you coming? You have ten minutes.

CHARLIE Good luck, Jake ... *(looks round)* What are youse all lookin' at, he is only away to give her one, two consenting adults aren't they ... *(To Caterer)* I'll take Jake Quinn's baked Alaska ... because he is having coffee with Caroline ... yeah, well me and him and Caroline is sort of friends now ... yes fresh cream on both would be lovely ... no thanks, two helpings is enough ...

Caroline is discovered in a yoga position centre stage, appropriate music playing.

CAROLINE Hi, how are you?

JAKE Fine.

CAROLINE Coffee?

JAKE Yes, please.

CAROLINE Sugar?

JAKE Two please.

CAROLINE Cream?

JAKE Yes please.

JAKE I am only allowed ten minutes.

CAROLINE We have all the time in the world. Your accent is so beautiful ... do you mind if you could read my lines and I put a tape on.

JAKE I thought you had one of them professional accent people.

CAROLINE I have but there is nothing like the real thing ... and besides you're far better looking ...

JAKE Am ... how would I go about gettin' into the

movies, what is the first step?

CAROLINE *(mimics his accent)* How would I go about getting into the movies ... that's just so beautiful ... how do I sound?

JAKE   Sounds great.

CAROLINE   Let's start on page seven.

JAKE   How did you get started?

CAROLINE   You don't want to hear about that. This first speech.

JAKE   I mean, should I have an agent or something.

CAROLINE *(angry)*   You don't want to get into the movies, it's shit, real shit ... now could you just read this for me?

JAKE   Rory, will your people ever accept me ...

CAROLINE   Don't mumble ... I need you to articulate ... again ...

JAKE   But Maeve is one of the landed gentry, she wouldn't talk like us anyway.

CAROLINE *(annoyed)* Excuse me?

JAKE   She'd have been educated in England. She'd talk different like.

CAROLINE   No, but she wants to fit in. She always has.

JAKE   Ah yeah, but she wouldn't have mixed with the locals until she started going out with Rory. You wouldn't pick up an accent that quickly.

CAROLINE   Look, I don't have time to sit here with you and discuss what my character would and would not do. Can we just read the script?

JAKE   No ... I think I had better be going.

CAROLINE   Your time isn't up yet.

JAKE   I'm sorry. I think it is.

Jake makes to leave ... Caroline shouts before he can get out.

CAROLINE   Jock ... I'm finished with Mr Quinn. (*Caroline attempts to say the words.*) Rory, will your people ever accept ... no ... shit ... Rory ... Rory ... fuck. *(screams)* Jock, get John in here now.

JAKE *(to Charlie)*   I feel like shit man, you know, being used like that.

CHARLIE   So you were just a sex object with an accent. I did that to a girl once ... met her on a ferry, French she was ...

JAKE   She said the movies are shit.

CHARLIE   She gets six mill' a picture and she thinks it shit, I am gettin' forty smackaronies and I think it's class.

AISLING   Quiet ... settle ... when Maeve approaches on the horse, everyone stops digging and looks at her ...

CHARLIE *(excited)*   Oh good, Caroline Giovanni is in our scene.

AISLING   We won't have Maeve in the scene, so the top of
my hand will be your eye line ... so when the camera rolls dig until I
raise my hand and my hand will be Maeve approaching on the horse ...
then you will all look up and stare at her ... when I drop my hand you
will look to the left and see Rory approaching Maeve on the horse.

CHARLIE   Oh brilliant, Kurt Steiner is gonna be in it.

AISLING   ... Now Rory won't be in the scene.

CHARLIE *(quietly)*   Fuck sake, is anybody working round here, only
us?

AISLING   So when you look to the left, Simon's hand will be
Rory approaching Maeve on the horse. All right, everyone OK?

CHARLIE   So it's us lookin' dispossessed at her hand,
pretending it's Maeve on a horse lookin' sorry for us ... I'm gonna miss
all this.

JAKE   What will you do?

CHARLIE *(brings his script out)* Maybe somebody will read this and say ...
Jesus, this is brilliant ... and I tell ye man ... I will be made ...

JAKE   Grow up, Charlie.

CHARLIE   And what, just keep touring round Ireland
waiting for movies?

JAKE   Even that's dying out ... they have used up most
of the forty shades of green by now.

SIMON   Now remember ... it's dig ... Hands over here ...
stop ... my hands over there ... turn over, speed, make it ... ready Clem
... and action.

*Music. They dig ... stop ... look up ... moving their heads as if watching
galloping horses and then stop ... then look the other way doing the same
action ... Jake starts to laugh ... then can't control himself.*

SIMON   Cut ... yes and what is so funny, mate?

JAKE   Sorry ... it's just hard ... you know her hand being
Maeve on a horse and your hand being Rory and ... *(laughs)* Sorry.

SIMON   Time is fucking money here, mate.

JAKE   Wasn't just me, everybody laughed.

SIMON   Right ... quiet, we are going to go for this again ...
this time with a bit of feeling. *(under his breath)* Bloody extras.

*They repeat the action as before ... Jake and Charlie just about control the
laughter.*

SIMON   And cut ... stay in position until we check the gate.

CHARLIE   Hey Jake ... if you were a movie star, I could be
your minder ... personal manager, line up the women, try them out first
so you won't be disappointed, know like the Queen has somebody to
taste her dinner.

JAKE   What is the commotion over there?

CHARLIE   Where?

JAKE   Fin looks like he's in a terrible state ... that's his
Da with him ... must be trouble ... Fin ... what's the trouble?

FIN   M' Da has brought terrible news, Jake ... Sean
Harkin ... drowned himself this morning. Da says Danny Mackin was up
in his top field and saw Sean walk into the water ... he didn't know if he
was coddin' or what for he had all his clothes on. Danny shouted at him
and said he saw Sean comin' back out ... Danny didn't know what to
make of it ... then he saw him walk into the water again and never rise
out of it ... Danny was too far away to do anything but raise the guards
... when the divers found him ... his pockets were full of stones ... he
came out of the water to fill his pockets full of stones.

SIMON   And the gate is clear. Let's move on.

ACT TWO

*Jake enters ... he is solemn ... he stands for a second or two before Charlie
enters ... Charlie enters reading his script ... He sees Jake, he walks up to
him and touches his arm as if to say he understands.*

AISLING   Quiet everyone ... settle ... On 'Action' I want you
all to cheer Rory as he emerges from the Big House ... this is very
important ... It is the final scene where Rory is now the owner of the Big
House ... because he has married Maeve and you know he is going to
hand back the land to the people. Big smiling faces and real joy ...
remember it's the big Happy Ending. Over to you, Simon. Turn over.

SIMON   Cheers Aisling, Turn over, Speed, mark it and
ACTION.

AISLING   Action.

Music ... they run forward ... stop and make weak attempts at the cheer.

SIMON   Cut ... Right everybody, we are going to go for
that take yet again. So ... Rory has just married Maeve, you know now
that he has inherited the land ... come on for Christ sake, show a bit
more jubilation ... You see Rory coming out of the big house, he's now

the owner of the big house. You all see him and cheer. *(They cheer.)* Aisling, let's show them what they're doing. PLAYBACK!

The music is played back ... Aisling and Simon demonstrate how it should be done.

SIMON Come on, if we don't get this we will have cloud cover. Turnover, speed, mark it and ACTION. Don't. *(To Aisling, who is about to say 'Action'. They cheer again, weakly.)* Cut, Jesus!

CHARLIE Hard work this morning. C'mon man, snap out of it.

JAKE Are you alright, Fin?

Fin is discovered downstage right.

FIN Sean always talked about getting out. He hated this place. He used to say to me, you and me, Fin, we'll escape. He always used that word – escape. He wanted to go to America. He wanted to be someone. You know that last film was made here, we were only kids, we all got carried away. Sean used to sit watching them day after day.

SEAN *(twelve years old)* Be brilliant to be in that film, wouldn't it, Fin?

FIN *(twelve years old)* You make loads of money.

SEAN Will we ask can we be in it ... ?

FIN We would have to dress up in them stupid clothes, I wouldn't be seen dead.

SEAN But maybe they would spot us and ... you know take us off to America to make our own film ... you know like Macaulay what's his name.

FIN My Da wouldn't let me go.

SEAN To be a millionaire?

FIN No, sure I have to take over the shop.

SEAN You would rather be a butcher than a millionaire?

FIN Well no, but my Da ...

SEAN Cuttin' up dead meat when you could be a superstar.

FIN I'll think about it ... I would have to ask my Da first.

SEAN I don't, my Da says us boys has to find something to do 'cos well there will be no need for too many farmers ... hey, where will you get meat if there will be no cows soon?

FIN No cows ... don't talk daft ... where will they all go?

SEAN I don't know, America ... all them trucks and

caravans and people, the town is going to be dead soon, we have to get into that film.

FIN   My Da won't let me ... he says the people's heads is gettin' carried away.

SEAN   Your Da is talking bollicks ... they are paying thirty quid a day ... I am going to save mine for America.

Present.

JAKE   Maybe he looked at me and realised there was no American Dream.

CHARLIE   Come on, some guys make it ... yer man that owns the hotel, didn't he leave with fifty dollars, then comes back and buys it inside two years.

JAKE   Yeah for every one of him there is fifty who come back without an arse in their trousers.

Clem, the Director.

CLEM   Hi I'm Clem Curtis, the Director ... we are goin' to have to go for another take on this ... this scene is very important ... this is the final scene in the movie, so let me explain ... I know we are shooting out of sequence and I am aware that not many of you know the story. Hello, hello. *(To Jake, who's not concentrating)* ... So I want you to imagine that when Rory walks out of that house he is about to answer all your hopes and dreams, whatever they are ... Rory has the answer, so that is what we want to see on your faces ... we will be doing some close ups, so we want to see real fucking ecstasy here.

JAKE   Real fucking ecstasy? Young Sean Harkin has killed himself yesterday because of real fucking ecstasy.

CLEM   Take it easy.

JAKE   Sorry ... it's just ... I'm sure you understand that we are finding it hard to jump for joy.

CLEM   Yes, we are aware of that and we are very sorry but we must get this shot right ... and I am sorry for the unfortunate use of the word ... so if you could give me some joyful animations.

SIMON   Too late, Clem, those clouds are about to hit in five seconds. I think they are here for the rest of the morning ... shall I break the extras for an hour and go for an interior ... Aisling ... break the extras.

AISLING   Okay everybody, we will pick this shot up again in an hour, so please no one leave the set ... At the end of the day I want everyone to go now to Costume. It's the big celebration tomorrow in the grounds of the Big House ... and you will have new costumes so please see Wardrobe before you leave.

CHARLIE   Jesus, is it not the funeral the morra, Jake?

JAKE   They will have to work round us ... the whole town will be there.

CHARLIE   Even so, they should stop anyway, mark of respect.

JAKE   It's the least they could do.

CLEM   Right folks, we are in total sympathy with you all and we have sent condolences to the family. *(Aside)* Have we sent condolences? ... But I am sure you appreciate we have been held up quite a bit with the weather. I am sorry it will be impossible to let you all free for the funeral tomorrow ... we have a long day with most of you in shot from early morning . . .

MICKEY   We have to pay our last respects ... he was related to most of us.

CLEM   Tomorrow is a big day for us ... we have a marquee being transported, truck loads of fresh flowers shipped over from Holland, three catering companies for the wedding feast ... we must finish by dusk tomorrow.

MICKEY   You will have to stop for the funeral ... we will all be there.

CHARLIE *(to Jake)*   Excuse me interrupting you, Clem, but why don't you just go ahead and do the wedding, only most of the guests leave to go to a funeral in the town. It's only a story ... this is the movies, can't you do what you want?

CLEM   We are behind schedule, if we don't do the wedding tomorrow and get finished, we are fucked.

JAKE   That's life.

CLEM   Do you people realise that each day we film, it costs at least a quarter of a million dollars?

MICKEY   Then how come we only get forty pound a day?

CLEM   Jesus.

JAKE   Well said, Mickey.

SIMON   Clem, let me deal with it.

CLEM   They are all yours, Simon ... just don't come back with a 'No' or the producers are goin' to have my balls.

SIMON   Listen, guys, we are in total sympathy with you ... but if we cut filming by two hours we would be in real crisis ... we need that for weather cover. It would be a disaster if we didn't wrap up that scene tomorrow ... We would have to go into another hire situation for the marquees ... the producers won't cover us if we run over ... I am prepared to pay all of you an extra twenty quid.

MICKEY   How much did he say, Jake?

JAKE   Not enough, Mickey.

SIMON   ... Guys ... seriously ... listen ... Push comes to shove, we could sack all of you. Remember that.

MICKEY   He can't sack us, we are in the can.

CHARLIE   What's that, Mickey?

MICKEY   We're on tape ... in the camera ... are you thick ... it will luk bloody daft in the last scene if the whole lot of us luked like a whole load of other ones, wouldn't it? We're in the can, in the camera, on tape – are you thick? ... The producer may be after his balls, but it's us that has them.

CHARLIE   Jake, where are you going ... we are not allowed to leave the set.

JAKE   We have an hour, I have to go somewhere.

Classroom bell.

JAKE   Brother Gerard ... Hello, Jake Quinn.

BROTHER GERARD   Jake Quinn, sure I remember you well ... how was America?

JAKE   Fine ... Brother I want to talk to you about young Sean Harkin.

BROTHER GERARD   A terrible tragedy, terrible for the whole family. He was a grand youngin. I remember his first year.

Flashback.

BROTHER GERARD   Cunas, cunas. Sean Harkin come up to the front of the class please. Now Sean here is going to read out his essay on cows ... come on Sean.

SEAN *(eight years old)* Cows are great big useful beasts. They are more useful than humans. They are more useful because you can get meat from them, then you can get milk and butter and they even make good school bags. Cows are the business because many people live off cows and they give you no bother as long as you feed them and milk them. A cow is even useful when it goes to the toilet because we need the manure to fertilise the land. If I were a cow I would feel very useful. I would rather be a dairy cow so that I didn't have to be killed. When I grow up I am going to have the best herd in Kerry.

Present.

BROTHER GERARD   Muy hu agus sigi sios. He was a nice child from a good family, then he just got carried away. The father sold off a lot of the land to make ends meet and the kid's hopes went with it. And how are you, Jake – what has brought you back from America?

JAKE   Homesick, Brother ... am Sean, was he a kid that got depressed or anything?

BROTHER GERARD   Not a bit of him ... you couldn't cut him with a bread knife ... he lived in another world ... a world he lived out in his head ... you know imagination can be a damned curse in this country.

JAKE   What did he talk about, what did he want?

BROTHER GERARD   Tell you the truth, he was as normal as the rest when it came to that ... they wanted to be rock stars, film stars, footballers ... if one of them had said a teacher or a dentist or something I would have dropped dead with the shock ... problem with Sean was, he was convinced he could be all the things he wanted ... and at times thought he was.

School Bell.

JAKE   Thanks Brother Gerard ... thanks.

CHARLIE   Hurry up, Jake, earache was lukin' ye, I said you were at the jacks.

JAKE   Thanks Charlie, where was I?

CHARLIE   You were standin' here.

SIMON   Aisling, change of plan. Light's perfect for the eviction scene.

AISLING   Great, Simon. The natives are a bit restless, I think we should go for it quickly.

SIMON *(speaks into his walkie-talkie)* Good girl. Right ... fine Clem ... I'll tell them ... Quiet ... Ms Giovanni would like to talk to you all for a moment, so don't leave your positions until she comes.

JAKE   Do we get on our knees.

CHARLIE   Give it a rest.

CAROLINE   Look, I am really sorry about what has happened ... I know you are a small neighbourhood and everyone is greatly affected by it ... it's such a terrible tragedy ... I just want you all to know that I appreciate you all being here and carrying on under such sad circumstances ... thank you ... and well ... just thank you.

Charlie claps and encourages others.

CHARLIE   Now that was very nice of her, she didn't have to do that.

JAKE   Know what gets me Charlie ... these people think
that it has nothing to do with them.

CHARLIE   It hasn't.

JAKE   Of course it has, terrible tragedy, I'll tell you
what's a terrible tragedy, filling young Sean's head with dreams.

CHARLIE   No different from me, that kid ... like all of us ...
like you, don't *we* dream, do you not fantasise about being the cock of
the walk, the boy in the big picture ... like, why couldn't it happen to us
if it happens to other people ... eh? Do you never get carried away into
that other world ... we are no different.

JAKE   Except that we are still alive.

AISLING   Quiet everyone, settle ... when you are ready we
will do the eviction scene ... that is, Rory and his family being evicted ...
The bailiffs gallop on, they dismount, go into the house. They eject the
furniture first and then the people ... No no. It is a silent scene ... no
angry abuse ... you are defeated men ... so watch in silence.

JAKE *(to Charlie)*   Aye dead on ... did you ever, as if all of us would
stand by and watch a whole family being evicted without opening our
mouths ... even if it was just ... go on you rotten bastards, just
something. Defeated broken men ... Oh that's no problem ... Typecast.

CHARLIE *(to Jake)*   Not yet ... *(brings the script out of his pocket)* If
only I could get one person to read this. You know they tell the rest ...
and it snowballs. That's how it happened.

JAKE   Charlie, you know as well as I do if that script
ever gets into one of their hands it will hit the bottom of a waste basket
and never see the light of day again.

CHARLIE   Look, I don't need this kind of negative shit, do
ya hear.

JAKE   Then get real ... Charlie ...

CHARLIE   Excuse me ... this is real ...

JAKE   And what if they say you have written a load a
bollicks and you'll never make nothing writing shit like that ... then
what?

CHARLIE   I won't believe them.

JAKE   You will, Charlie, and you know it.

SIMON   OK. We're going to go for this now. Remember
you're defeated, broken men. Turnover, speed, mark it, and ACTION.
OK Clem.

They enact eviction as detailed by Aisling.

SIMON   Lovely ... and we will check the gate ... if the gate is clear that is a wrap ... do you hear ... quiet ... that is a wrap for the night ... check your calls for the morning ... goodnight and pray for sun tomorrow or we are all in big trouble.

They take their 'extra' clothes off.

MICKEY   That Simon fella's off his head, rain hail snow, we still get our forty quid.

CHARLIE   What about the funeral? Are they stopping to let us go to the funeral?

MICKEY   No choice, we put our futs down ... power to the people, eh Jake ... they say they will get it all done only if we have sunshine for eight hours ... I puts my hand up like this to the wind, you see? ... and then I gets down on the ground and I listens to the earth and then I tuk my hat off and threw it up to see what way it would land and it landed the right way up, so I says ... it will be a scorcher, you won't see a cloud next or near the place ... and that convinced him.

CHARLIE   That's amazing.

MICKEY   A pity it's a load of bollicks ... here's the forty quid man comin', now that is what I call a ray of sunshine, Dermot.

They change into clothes.

JAKE   See you, Mickey. See you later. Charlie, I will take you to Sean's wake the night.

CHARLIE   But I never knew him.

JAKE   Won't matter ... you're with me ... hey, I'm sorry for earlier.

CHARLIE   It's alright ... I understand ...

JAKE   I shouldn't get on to you ... at least you're trying to do somethin' with your script ... Mickey has watched his whole way of life fall apart around him ... and now all it's worth is a backdrop for an American movie ... he depends on their forty quid a day and then he lives in hope for the next one ... he's some boy, he never lets it get to him.

Lighting change.

JAKE   Mr Harkin ... sorry for your trouble ... Charlie Conlon, he's on the film.

MR HARKIN   Hello Charlie ...

JAKE   Terrible tragedy, Mr Harkin.

MR HARKIN   Aye ... go on in there, Jake. I'll see you after the milkin' ... rain hail or death, the cows haft to be milked ...

JAKE   Sure, I'll do that for you.

MR HARKIN   No, you're all right, Jake, all Sean ever knew as a young one was the land ... same as you, Jake, aah he looked up to you ... I didn't know what to say to him when the land had let him down ... anyway, go on into the house, there is a feed and a bit of music ... I can give Sean nothin' more now but a dacent wake ... I will see you after milkin'.

The Wake. Charlie and Jake as if in a room full of people ...
Traditional music.

CHARLIE   Sorry for your trouble. I'm Charlie Conlon – a friend of Jake's.

JAKE   How's it goin' Malachy? ... alright Mary? How ya, Fin?

CHARLIE   How are you doin' ... hello ... it's like being on the set ... the same people.

JAKE   Hello Paddy ... Aye it's tough being in the movies.

CHARLIE   Great music.

JAKE   The family are all traditional players.

MICKEY   He is gettin' a great send off ... some of the best players in Ireland.

JAKE   Do you not play yourself then, Mickey?

MICKEY   I will get a few more gargles in me and I will see if the oul squeeze box will loosen up.

JAKE   How's it goin', Fin? ...

Takes Fin aside.

FIN   Jake, everything he wanted was somewhere else ... he hated this town. He said it let him down ... everybody let him down ... but sure that couldn't be helped ... that's the way it was and nobody's fault ... you know some of us just accepted that life wasn't great, but he wouldn't ... he stopped going out, he just got his gear and stayed in his room with his movies ... virtual reality. That kept him going, drugs and movies.

JAKE   What was it about that day? Why was it different from any other?

FIN   He had tried to get on the movie the day before but he was out of his head ... Then, that night in the pub ... they were all there ... all arse-lickin' the Yanks, it seemed he was right in the middle of the world he fantasised about ... you know, the beautiful American star, the movies. He knew the crew had coke ... they were all laughin' and joking and he just watched them and then he tried to score. He saw your woman talking to you and then he went up to her ...

Flashback.
Sean staggers over to Caroline.

SEAN   Caroline ... you are Caroline Giovanni.
CAROLINE *(panics)*   Go away.
SEAN   I only want to say hello, I am Sean Harkin.
CAROLINE   Get away from me.
SEAN   I won't touch you, I just want to look at you.
CAROLINE   Jock ... Jock ... I am being pestered, get rid of him.
JOCK *(grabs him)*   Right you, out, if I see you back in here I will break your two fuking legs.

Present.

FIN   He was put out on the street, out of the pub in his own town ... he sat outside on the street, I went with him.
JAKE   And then he watched me go off with her, didn't he?
FIN   Yeah.
JAKE   And what did he say?
FIN   Nothing.
JAKE   What did he say ... tell me?
FIN   I said he didn't say anything.
JAKE   He must have said something.
FIN   Waster ... fukin' waster, Fin ... what is she doing with a waster like Jake Quinn ... that's what he said.
JAKE   Jesus, Charlie.
CHARLIE   It's not your fault ... not one person is to blame.
JAKE   ... I have to get out of here ...

Simon is about to have a nervous breakdown . . .

SIMON *(on walkie-talkie)* I don't fuckin' believe this ... two truck loads of flowers and we have to scrap them ... can he not take shaggin' pills like anybody else ... Jesus ... right ... right ... Aisling ... Aisling.
AISLING   Aisling here, Simon.
SIMON   Aisling, we are going for an exterior ... Kurt has hay fever and wants the flowers scrapped from the marquee ... Jesus ... two effing trucks of effing flowers.

AISLING   Oh no ... can we send them back?

SIMON   Yeah, they'll be dead by the time they hit Holland. This is a nightmare, it took four hours to put them in for that wanker to tell us he had shaggin' hay fever. TURN THAT MUSIC OFF ... set up for the exterior street dance.

AISLING   Copy that, Simon.

JAKE   Hey fella, if you have flowers now they won't go to waste, young Sean Harkin's funeral today.

SIMON   It's not up to me ... and I can tell you by the time they get through to America and get a producer to ask another producer to ask the executive producer, the young fella will be dead and buried a week and we will have a shit load of dead flowers to dump ... Jesus, I am crackin' up.

CAROLINE   Excuse me, Simon ... Jake that is very touching and of course the flowers will be delivered to the Chapel ... Simon, see to it immediately. Whatever the cost, I will attend to it.

JAKE *(sourly)*   Thanks.

CAROLINE   I am really sorry, it must be so hard for you.

JAKE   Yes it is ... very hard ... and more so when I think of the way I treated him, the way you and everybody else treated him like he was a piece of muck on their boots.

CAROLINE   Excuse me? ... I didn't even know him.

JAKE   No, but you had him thrown out of the pub, in his own town in front of his own people, think about that for humiliation ... think about what that did to his self-esteem.

CAROLINE   I don't know what you're talking about.

JAKE   Course you don't, you come here and use us, use the place and then clear off and think about nothing you leave behind.

CAROLINE   Listen here, I work hard in this industry, I have worked for everything I have ever done, I have used nobody.

JAKE   Yeah, well maybe this industry that you work so hard for might be one of the things that drove that kid to do what he did.

CAROLINE   Don't be ridiculous.

JAKE   You're right, I am being called now to dance up and down the street for the big happy ending. Yes, I feel ridiculous.

He walks away ... Caroline stands a moment ... then leaves.
Music. Charlie and Jake dance as if with other people.

SIMON   Cut ... beautiful ... the Irish know one thing, it's how to dance.

CHARLIE   You would think he wasn't Irish.

JAKE   He just wishes he wasn't.

SIMON   Yeah mate, you're right, because every time you
fuck up I get it in the ear from these people ... ever hear the phrase ...
Irish, what do you expect? ... Well unfortunately for me they tend to
include the whole nation ... *(to his walkie-talkie)* Aisling, break the
extras for the funeral ... they have an hour and a half ... tell them
anybody that comes back smelling of alcohol will be put off the set.

MICKEY   Holy mother a Jasis, a funeral without a drink ...
never heard of it happening in my life and I have bin to more funerals
than the undertaker himself ... a dry funeral in Kerry, what is happening
to the world?

*Jake and Charlie stand face front as if in the Chapel. Charlie is sneezing.
Organ music.*

CHARLIE   Bloody flowers ... I suppose it doesn't matter
about my hayfever does it ...

JAKE   How can she do that ... she let them walk her up
to the front pew ... she didn't even know him ... she had him thrown out
of the pub like a piece of dirt ... bitch.

CHARLIE   She paid for the flowers, that's why ... Anyway it's
nice for the family ... come on, settle yourself, don't blame her ... she
didn't know the kid was going to kill himself.

JAKE   ... I am so fucking ...

CHARLIE   Stop it.

JAKE   Just don't know what to do ... it's not with her,
not with anybody on the film. It's . . .

CHARLIE *(sneezes)*   Do you mind, but I am moving to another pew ...
friggin' flowers . . .

Charlie moves away. Caroline being interviewed.

INTERVIEWER   Ms Giovanni, has this tragedy affected the filming
of *Quiet Valley?*

CAROLINE   As you can see most of the cast and crew are here
to pay our last respects ... so yes it has, but the people are so strong and
resilient and have elected to continue filming this afternoon.

INTERVIEWER   Miss Giovanni. Did you know Sean Harkin ...?

CAROLINE   I didn't but from what I hear he was a well-loved
son and friend ... we are all very shocked by the events. I just want to
get my car, please.

INTERVIEWER   I believe he wanted to be an extra on the movie.

CAROLINE   I wouldn't know about that ... *(walks away)*
Jock, I'm ready.

Interviewer goes after her.

INTERVIEWER   And what do you think of Ireland?
CAROLINE   Oh it is so magical ... the country is so dramatic.
INTERVIEWER   And when can we expect to see *The Quiet Valley*?
CAROLINE   Next year I would imagine.
INTERVIEWER   Well the whole country will be looking forward to
it and thank you, Ms Giovanni ... *(turns front)* Kevin Doherty for RTE
in County Kerry.

Marquee music.

SIMON   That's fine for level, thanks. Could we have
everyone in the marquees, we have set up and we want to get the
interiors done ... it will be long and slow, so be prepared.
CHARLIE   Be prepared that's me, Simon. Dib dib, I was in
the Brownies.
JAKE   What is it with you, Charlie eh ... every time I say
something that might need a bit of serious head stuff, you walk away.
CHARLIE   What are you on about?
JAKE   In the chapel ... you walked away from me.
CHARLIE   Hayfever.
JAKE   No that's just another excuse not to take on the
real world ... you change the subject, tell a stupid joke ... what is going
on behind that bloody annoying cheerful chappie eh ... you can't be Mr
Clown all the time.
CHARLIE   What ... who says I can't ... oh you want me to be
like Matt Talbot, batin' myself up, that would suit you, would it?
JAKE   No ... just want to know what makes you tick.
CHARLIE   None of your business.
JAKE   You have nothing in your life, you are going
nowhere and why is it doing my head in and not yours ... what is going
on, I need to know?
CHARLIE   Who says I am going nowhere ... I have done
somethin' ... I have my script ... I have something.
JAKE   Read your script ... it is the biggest load of oul
bollicks I have ever read in my life.
CHARLIE *(sits on the ground)* Bastard ... why are you hurting me? I
never do that to you ... why are you doing this?
JAKE   Charlie, it's every bad film you have ever seen,
no story, cardboard people ... I suppose it's based on real life experience
... is the Hero you, the one that goes in search of the baddies and blows
them away ... like Sean? Wake up, for Christ sake.

CHARLIE   And what, be like you, walkin' around hatin'
everything, everybody, lookin' for reasons to blame the world.

JAKE   I don't need to look for reasons, I look round me
and so should you.

CHARLIE   Sean again, is it? You are trying to use that kid to
try to justify your own miserable existence ... you want it to be your
fault, you want to be able to say that kid died because of me ... no,
believe me, you're not that fucking important.

JAKE   I could have gave him hope.

CHARLIE   You couldn't have give him nothing.

JAKE   I could!

CHARLIE   No you couldn't. It was too late.

JAKE   It wasn't.

CHARLIE   It was ... I know, I was where Sean was, I woke
up one morning and looked around me and I saw nothing ... a big black
hole of nothin' ... and I wanted to jump into that big black hole as far
down it as I could get, so I wouldn't have to wake up another morning
... and when I woke up in the hospital, you know what I thought, my
first thought ... Charlie, you are a pathetic bastard, you couldn't even do
that right.

JAKE   Charlie ... sorry ... sorry mate.

CHARLIE   It's alright, it's just the day that's in it, the kid
being buried, people are just over-emotional ... ignore me . . .

JAKE   Charlie, sorry what I said about the film ... I'll
read it again.

CHARLIE   Nah, you are probably right ... deep down I knew
it was bollicks ...

AISLING   Alright you two – into the marquee at once, less
of the chit-chat ... the tables have been laid out as a banquet ... I want
no one touching the food until we have a take . . .

SIMON   Aisling, Aisling, get that drunken old bollicks off
the set now. Clem is about to throw a wobbler ... I said now ... he has
just knocked over a trestle table full of drinks ... move him ... *(on
walkie-talkie)* Get me security. Why not? It's OK, I'll take care of it
myself – OK you, you had your fun, now move.

MICKEY *(drunk)*   They can't sack me I am in the can, Jake ... they
can't sack me, the last laugh is on me, Mickey Riordain ...
(sings) When all beside a vigil keep, the West asleep
The West asleep Alas and well my Aisling weep
When Connaught lies in slumber deep
There lakes and plain smile fair and free
Mid Rocks their guardian chivalry.

SIMON   For Christ sake … *(To Mickey)* Right you, you
were warned … move it.

MICKEY   You can't sack me, I am in the can.

SIMON   There are three hundred and fifty of you in the
can … nobody is even going to notice, now move it and don't come back.

MICKEY   You can't sack me … I am the only surviving extra
on *The Quiet Man*, you can't sack me.

SIMON   Move or we will call the police.

MICKEY   You see this ground you are standing on, ya
jumped up gobshite, this belonged to my grandfather, and you are
telling me, a Riordan, to get off my land … what is happening to the
world, Jake, what is happening to the shaggin' world?

SIMON   Aisling, call the guards will you, there is going to
be trouble. This oul bollicks won't leave.

MICKEY   No … there's no need, yous had young Sean
Harkin put out onto the street in his own town and you are not going to
do that to me.

JAKE   Don't go, Mickey stay … you never let nothing
beat ya Mickey, stay.

MICKEY   I will go of my own free will … in fact I resign.
Sing oh, let man learn liberty
From crashing wind and lashing sea.

Straightens himself … holds his head up.

CHARLIE   Jake … let him go, don't start. I can't take no
more of this … I am going into this marquee now, I am doing what is
asked of, I'm keeping my head down and that's that so don't fucking
start because I don't want to hear no more.

JAKE   Charlie, wait.

CHARLIE   I said knock it on the head.

JAKE   No listen, remember what you said earlier when
the Director wasn't going to stop for the funeral, you said, sure, stick it
in the film, this is the movies, you can do what you want … You are
right, Charlie, it's only a story … if it was a story about a film being
made and a young lad commits suicide … in other words, the stars
become the extras and the extras become the stars … so it becomes
Sean's story, and Mickey and all the people of this town.

CHARLIE   Yes and …

JAKE   Why couldn't it be done, don't we have the right
to tell our story, the way we want it?

CHARLIE   We could tell it 'til the cows come home but
would that …

JAKE *(excited)*   Yes cows ... that's it ... that's where it starts ... Brilliant, Charlie ... the cows are where it starts and finishes ... as he walked into the water to die the last thing he would have seen were the cows, the cows that should have been his future in the field looking at him ... what do you say, Charlie ...?

CHARLIE   What, you mean we do this movie?

JAKE   Why not, eh, we have just witnessed it all, haven't we ... you have been where Sean was, you could get into his head better than anybody ... you can write a script.

CHARLIE   A script ... you told me it was a load o' bollicks.

JAKE   Yeah, the story was, but you did it ... you sat down and did it.

CHARLIE   Who is gonna listen to the likes of us?

JAKE   Well you must have thought somebody was gonna read your script. Otherwise why were you shuvin' it up everybody's nose?

CHARLIE   I knew they wouldn't ... isn't that pathetic ... I knew nobody would read it.

JAKE   You are full of shit, man.

CHARLIE   You say that to me again and I will swing for you ... Mister hate-the-world ... I can't take any more knocks ... do you hear ... no more.

JAKE   Sorry Charlie, sorry, alright I understand ... I do ... Charlie it's just ... how do I put this ... Charlie, you and me are fucked, we have nothing, and we are going nowhere, but for the first time in my life I feel I can do something ... they can only knock us if we don't believe in ourselves ... and I believe this could work, Charlie, I do ... Please give it a go, we have nothing to lose, no money, no reputation, no assets.

CHARLIE *(indignant)* I have a tent.

JAKE   That's it. Canvas Productions.

CHARLIE   What?

JAKE   Thanks Charlie.

CHARLIE   Hey stall the ball there, I never ...

JAKE   We have the story, we go to one of these people here and say, tell us where to go from here ... they all started somewhere.

CHARLIE   They're all too busy clawing their way up to the top to stop and listen to us.

JAKE   Tomorrow at breakfast we get yer man Clem the director ... he sits over on his own and has his breakfast ...

CHARLIE   Well, what do we say to him?

JAKE	Tonight we plan out our strategy in our
Production Office.	
CHARLIE	Wha?
JAKE	In the tent ... Canvas Productions ... float it on
the Stock Market.	
CHARLIE	Yeah and if it rains we will be floatin' with it.

Clem is munching his breakfast and thinking.

JAKE   So the last image you see is Sean, going into the
water and the cows watching him ... the cows that should have been his
future, watching him as he drowns.

JAKE   Well Clem, what do you think?

CLEM   It's just not sexy enough.

JAKE   What ... what do ya mean?

CLEM   What if the Kid was pursued by Drug Pushers.

JAKE   But he wasn't.

CLEM   Movies aren't real life ... excuse me for a second
... *(He speaks into his walkie-talkie.)* Aisling, sweetheart, could you
bring me some more coffee ... no sugar, watching the figure ... you're a
gem ... *(To Jake)* Where was I ...? Oh yes ... you are going to need a love
interest.

JAKE   He loved the land ... his cows.

CLEM *(winces)*   Oh I've got a good idea, what if Fin was a girl ...
the girlfriend who tried to keep him straight.

CHARLIE   But Fin was his mate, he was all Sean had, he
couldn't keep a relationship with a girl.

CLEM   Well I am only trying to tell you, you won't move
it unless you are aware of these elements ... thank you Aisling, you are
an angel ... are we set up for the first shot?

AISLING   Almost there, Clem.

CLEM   Good, give me a shout I won't be long ... look
boys, why don't you take it to the Irish Film Board?

JAKE   But this could happen to any kid, any rural kid.

CLEM   Sure, but it's not commercial enough. How many
people want to see a film about a suicide? People want happy endings.
Life is tough enough. People don't go to the movies to get depressed.

CHARLIE   How can you have a happy ending about a kid
who drowns himself?

CLEM   He doesn't.

JAKE   But he did.

CLEM   No ... the farmer who sees him walk into the
water actually saves him ... just in time.

JAKE	And then what?
CLEM	Well ... that's the end.
AISLING	We're ready for you now, Clem.
CLEM	Super ... must go ... oh by the way do you have a title for it?
JAKE	Yeah ... *Stones in His Pockets.*
CLEM	What do you think of that, Aisling, as a title for a movie?
AISLING	Doesn't say much ... not very catchy ... a bit non-descript.
CLEM	This girl is learning well ... right Aisling, let's move.
CHARLIE	First knock back ... and Canvas Productions was only launched last night ... that must be a record.
JAKE	Do you think they are right?
CHARLIE	No ... No ... Jake ... I don't.
JAKE	Jesus ... neither do I ... God. All the time he was talking I kept saying to myself you are wrong ... Charlie, for the first time in my life I believed me.
CHARLIE	I'm so used to believing everything I do is bound to be no good.
JAKE	Not this time, Charlie.
CHARLIE	No ... not this time.
JAKE	So you have the opening scene of the film, people comin' onto the land to ask Mr Harkin can they shoot over the landscape ... but we see it from the kids' point of view and him a wee buck.
CHARLIE	So all you see is cows, every inch of screen, cows ... cows, just cows and in the middle of it all these trendy designer trainers.
JAKE	Like Aisling's?
CHARLIE	Exactly, sinkin' into a a big mound of steaming cow clap ... this is the first thing this child sees, the first intrusion into his world.
JAKE	Yeah ... Cows ... big slabbery dribblin' cows.

Jake and Charlie ... animated.

JAKE	Udders, tails, arses, in your face.
CHARLIE	Fartin', atin', dungin' ... mooin'.
JAKE	Big dirty fat brutes ... lukin' at ye ... wide shots.

CHARLIE	Yes, mid-shots.
JAKE	Yes. Close ups.
BOTH	Yes.

Blackout.

The End.

<u>Marie Jones</u> (1951-)

An actress and playwright based in Belfast. Born into a working class Protestant family, Jones left school at 15 and worked as an actress for several years before turning her hand to writing.

She co-founded Charabanc Theatre Company, an all-women touring group which was set up to address the lack of roles for women, and began writing as part of the group, contributing to plays like *Lay Up Your Ends* (1983), based on a 1911 strike by mill girls, *Oul Delf and False Teeth* (1984), on women's post-World War II hopes for a better life, *Gold in the Streets* (1986), and *Somewhere over the Balcony,* on life in the notorious Divis flats (1987). She remained with Charabanc until 1990 when she left and in 1991 co-founded DubbelJoint Theatre group.

She has also written extensively for Replay Theatre Company including *Under Napoleon's Nose* (1988) as well as *Stones in His Pockets*. Other plays in a prolific career include *The Hamster Wheel* (1990); *A Night in November* (1994) and the highly successful *Women on the Verge of HRT* (1996) as well as community plays like *Weddin's, Wee'ins and Wakes* and the musical, *The Chosen Room* (2008).

She has written extensively for radio and TV including: *Tribes* (1990); *Fighting the Shadows* (1992); *Wingnut and the Sprog* (1994); and the adaptation of her play, *The Hamster Wheel* (1991).

Stones in his Pockets received an Olivier Award and an Evening Standard Award for Best New Comedy in 2001. Marie Jones has received the John Hewitt Award for her outstanding contribution to the cultural debate in Northern Ireland, a Special Judges Award at the Belfast Arts Awards in 2000 and an OBE in 2002.

Sources and Additional Reading

Aston, Elaine, *Caryl Churchill*. London: Northcote House, 1997

Avery, Emmett (later vols. ed. Arthur H. Scouten, Charles Beecher Hogan and George Winchester Stone Jr,) *The London Stage 1660-1800*, vols 2-5. Carbondale: Southern Illinois University Press, 1960-1968

Baillie, Joanna, *Plays on the Passions* (1799-1802). Reissue New York: Garland, 1977

Baker, Elizabeth, *Chains* in Fitzsimmons and Gardner

Carhart, Margaret S., *The Life and Work of Joanna Baillie*. New Haven, Conn: Yale Studies in English, 1923

Cerasano, Susan and Marian Wynne Davies eds., *Renaissance Drama Texts by Women*. London: Routledge, 1995

Cousins, Geraldine, *Churchill the Playwright*. London: Methuen, 1989

Cotton, Nancy, *Women Playwrights in England c1363-1750*. Lewisburg: Bucknell University Press, 1980

Croft, Susan, *Re-writing the record: women's history as playwrights*. Ph.D thesis Norwich: University of East Anglia, 2007

Croft, Susan, ... *She Also Wrote Plays: an International Guide to Women Playwrights from the 10th to the 21st Century*. Faber and Faber 2001

Croft, Susan, ed., *Votes For Women and other plays*. London: Aurora Metro, 2009

Dronke, Peter, *Women Writers of the Middle Ages*. Cambridge: Cambridge University Press, 1984

Fitzsimmons, Linda and Viv Gardner eds., *New Woman Plays*. London: Methuen, 1991

Gainor, J.Ellen ed., *The Norton Anthology of Drama*. New York: W.W. Norton and Co., 2009

Goodman, Emma, *The Social Significance of Modern Drama.* (1914). Reissue New York: Applause, 1987

Goreau, Angeline, *Reconstructing Aphra: a Social Biography of Aphra Behn*. Oxford University Press, 1980

Griffiths, Trevor and Margaret Llewellyn Jones eds., *British and Irish Women Dramatists Since 1958*. London: Open University Press, 1992

Haight, Anne Lyon, *Hroswitha of Gandersheim; her life, times, and works, and a comprehensive bibliography.* New York, Hroswitha Club, 1965

Hrotswitha, *The Plays of Roswitha.* Translated by Christopher St. John. London: Chatto & Windus / New York, Benjamin Blom, 1923; reissue 1966

Hutner, Heidi ed., *Rereading Aphra Behn: History, Theory and Criticism.* Charlottesville: Virginia UP, 1993

Kelly, Katherine ed., *Modern Drama by Women: an International Anthology.* London: Routledge, 1996

Komporaly, Josefina, *Staging Motherhood: British Women Playwrights, 1956 to the Present.* Basingstoke: Palgrave Macmillan, 2006

Kritzer, Amelia Howe, *The Plays of Caryl Churchill.* Basingstoke: Macmillan, 1991

Moore, Honor ed., *The New Women's Theatre.* New York, Vintage, 1977

Morgan, Fidelis ed., *The Female Wits: Women Playwrights of the Restoration.* London: Virago, 1981

Pollock, Rhoda-Gale ed., *A Sampler of Women Playwrights.* New York & Frankfurt-am-Main: Peter Lang, 1990

Stowell, Sheila, *A Stage of their Own: Feminist Playwrights in the Suffrage Era.* Manchester: Manchester University Press, 1991

Sullivan, Victoria and James Hatch eds., *Plays By and About Women.* New York: Vintage, 1974

Todd, Janet, *The Critical Fortunes of Aphra Behn.* Columbia, S.C: Camden House, 1998

Tynan, Ken, *Curtains: Selections from the Drama Criticism and Related Writings.* London: Longman's, 1961

Michelene Wandor ed., *Plays by Women* vols 1-4. London: Methuen, 1982-1985

Wolfe, Heather, *The Literary Career and Legacy of Elizabeth Cary, 1613-1680.* Basingstoke: Palgrave Macmillan, 2007